CALVIN

A Biography

CALVIN

A Biography

Bernard Cottret

Translated by
M. Wallace McDonald

WILLIAM B. EERDMANS PUBLISHING COMPANY
GRAND RAPIDS, MICHIGAN / CAMBRIDGE, U.K.

T&T CLARK
EDINBURGH

Published with the aid of the French Ministry of Culture, Centre National du Livre

First published 1995 in French under the title *Calvin: Biographie*
© 1995 Éditions Jean-Claude Lattès.
English translation © 2000 Wm. B. Eerdmans Publishing Co.

This edition published jointly 2000
in the United States of America by
Wm. B. Eerdmans Publishing Co.
255 Jefferson Ave. S.E., Grand Rapids, Michigan 49503
www.eerdmans.com
and in the U.K. by
T&T Clark Ltd
59 George Street
Edinburgh EH2 2LQ
Scotland
www.tandtclark.co.uk

Published in collaboration with the
H. H. Meeter Center for Calvin Studies
at Calvin College, Grand Rapids, Michigan

Printed in the United States of America

05 04 03 02 01 00   7 6 5 4 3 2 1

Library of Congress Cataloging-in-Publication Data

Cottret, Bernard.
[Calvin. English]
Calvin: A biography / Bernard Cottret.
p.   cm.
Included bibliographical references and index.
ISBN 0-8028-4289-5 (hardcover: alk. paper)
1. Calvin, Jean, 1509-1564.
2. Reformation — Switzerland — Geneva — Biography.
3. Reformed Church — Switzerland — Geneva — Clergy — Biography.
4. Geneva (Switzerland) — Biography.
5. Geneva (Switzerland) — Church history — 16th century.
I. Title.

BX9418.C5913   2000
284 .2 092 — dc21
[B]   00-037142

British Library Cataloguing-in-Publication Data

A catalogue record for this book is available from the British Library

ISBN 0 567 08757 3

In memory of Clarisse

Contents

PART III: BELIEFS

John Calvin,
an Unfinished Portrait

I took up the life of John Calvin a few years ago out of wonder and exasperation. I then had — and may still have — mixed feelings about the bigotry of some of my fellow Christians, still retaining some heartfelt consideration, and even admiration, for the diversity of churches, their combined sense of ritual and the multiple expressions of their (common?) faith. As a committed Frenchman, with a sense of European solidarity, I felt it was my duty to reaffirm the dangers of amnesia against the risks of benevolent oblivion and to recall the blood, sweat, and tears that had also marked the Renaissance — as well as the Reformation. I was particularly pleased to welcome the German edition of my book in 1998. I am now very grateful that *Calvin* can reach an American audience and be made available to the English-speaking world, where Calvin's seminal influence can still be felt today, from the United Kingdom to the Republic of Ireland, South Africa, the United States, and the Commonwealth.

Sixteenth-century Europe was marked by the sudden collapse of ancient Western Christendom and the slow emergence of modern Europe out of its ashes.[1] While the south of Europe is still predominantly Catholic in its culture, the north is likewise mostly Protestant. As usual, France occupies an intermediate position, but it is nonetheless more Catholic than one thinks. A taste for relics, ossuaries, and patriotic bones has haunted the Republic, from the Panthéon

---

1. B. Cottret and Monique Cottret, "De la chrétienté à l'Europe," in *Histoire du christianisme, 1620-1750,* ed. M. Venard (Paris: Desclée, 1997), pp. 157ff.

in Paris — where so many great Frenchmen rest in peace — to the endless battlefields of Verdun. We could also turn to the grand lay ceremonies that still treat politicians as high priests.[2]

From the sixteenth century onward, the high tide of religious commitment coincided with a process of secularization. The Protestant ethic, and to a lesser degree its Catholic counterpart, was characterized by a common determination to eradicate superstititon and idolatry. It is nonetheless true that for Protestant Reformers, superstition and idolatry were equated with "Popish" doctrines and infamous practices, which smacked of paganism and outlandish barbarity.

The aim of my book was simply to recover the truth, or rather to reclaim the intelligibility of a man in his time. This re-creation is therefore primarily an interpretation. This is a historian's Calvin, the work of a university professor who is neither a theologian nor an ordained minister — though he has occasionally preached in his parish; it is therefore a layman's Calvin, in the narrow meaning of the term, without the glossy embellishments of forced sanctity or false devotion.

The "real" Calvin deserves more than the idolatry of the crowd. Unlike some modern televangelists, he eludes the camera; he was discreet, secret, shy. In short, he was the absolute opposite of a movie star, a true man in every sense of the word, as well as one of the greatest writers of the French language. Writer, thinker, preacher, city administrator — it is under all these heads that we will consider what was above all a destiny, a calling, a vocation.

Strength and Weakness

It is true that I do not speak of myself willingly; since nevertheless I cannot be entirely silent, I will speak of myself as modestly as I can.

JOHN CALVIN, 1539-40[3]

2. The work of Maurice Agulhon shows it clearly; the culture and symbolism of French politics are unknowingly entangled in secular forms fashioned by the church. We recall as evidence the political "religiosity" stressed by Agulhon in his *Marianne into Battle* (New York: Cambridge University Press, 1981). The same author also speaks of the "republican church." One could multiply examples from the remarkable works of Agulhon. The historian's Protestant origins have undoubtedly, by distancing him from it, aided him in understanding the legacy of Catholicism for French political traditions.

3. J. Calvin, *Lettre à Sadolet* (1540 for the French version), in *La vraie piété*, ed. I. Backus and C. Chimelli (Geneva: Labor et Fides, 1986), p. 85.

"Modesty, softness, and mildness";[4] such was Calvin in his own judgment. This brief self-portrait will surprise posterity, quick as it is to detect in Calvin a man of action, even a zealot. Calvin adds elsewhere: "I acknowledge myself to be timid, soft, and cowardly by nature."[5] He repeated the same idea on the eve of his death, calling himself "timid" and "fearful" before an astounded group of pastors, who knew by experience that the old fellow could raise up storms.[6] These various adjectives, gleaned from the intricacies of a discerning work otherwise reserved about their author, strongly underline the vigor of a character that owed all its energy to God alone.

The portraits of Calvin likewise leave an indefinable impression of moral strength and physical weakness: the grave, studious forehead so often throbbing with migraine; a burning gaze; sweetness stamped with severity; smooth cheeks contrasting with a carefully tapered beard, rounded off above the neck. Thus the young Calvin appears to us in the portrait in the Bibliothèque d'histoire de la Réformation in Geneva. A nervous man as well as a thinker, his head covered by a cap of elegant simplicity. The intensity of this clear gaze is also found in the later work in the museum of art and history in Berlin; the refined face, the diaphanous skin, and the circled eyes indicate long vigils. He hardly had a body. Sleeping little, eating similarly, prey to violent headaches, Calvin did not hesitate to dictate certain of his works while lying in bed at the end of a life of austere labor.[7] The clarity of his style and the transparency of his thought found their origin in this asceticism, crowned by a proverbial chastity. Fasting was neither mortification nor weakness for Calvin; instead, it was the result of a disgust for food, or rather a way of protecting his sickly body.[8] He was a meditator certainly, but nevertheless not a contemplative; a dreamer, and also an often inflexible man of action, sometimes even frantically so, from fear of yielding to weakness, to the secret "softness" and "mildness" that his adversaries hardly suspected. His slender, almost elegant body housed a will of iron; he was an intellectual, a writer, a craftsman in language and thought, immersed in a project

---

4. Calvin, *Lettre à Sadolet*, p. 83.

5. J. Calvin, *In librum psalmorum commentarius* (1557), preface, *Opera Calvini* (hereafter cited as *OC*) 31, col. 26.

6. On April 20, 1564; reported by T. Beza, *L'histoire de la vie et mort de Calvin* (1565), *OC* 21, col. 43.

7. This image of Calvin dictating certain of his works from his bed is confirmed by Beza, p. 35.

8. In the seventeenth century people still recalled this "great faster, even in his youth," who had no other aim in his privations but to watch over "his health and control the waves of migraine that afflicted him constantly," or to preserve the clarity of his mind "in order to write, study, and improve his memory." F. de Raemond, *L'histoire de la naissance de l'hérésie* (1605; Rouen: P. de La Motte, 1629), bk. 7, p. 885.

of reform that involved both church and city. He was a churchman more than a statesman, but a churchman as one is a statesman.

His costume hardly varies as we approach his different portraits: the gown of an academic or a pastor, the cap of a scholar. "His dress was low in price, to cover and not to adorn his body," we are told.[9] Calvin was a man of continuity, or even permanence, through the seasons of existence. The sobriety of his attire accorded with his ideal of proper "mediocrity," that Latin *mediocritas* that means avoidance of both splendor and poverty. The years hardly touched him; at most they accentuated the shadow he carried of age and of death. The anonymous French work of the seventeenth century that used to be preserved in the Bibliothèque du protestantisme in Paris follows the usual pattern; the artist was content in this portrait with presenting Calvin with a Bible in his hand, in a study surrounded by books. This rather conventional Calvin is found throughout an iconography otherwise poorly furnished in comparison with the importance of its subject. Protestantism distrusted pious images, and at most one could cite the seventeenth-century Dutch etching preserved in the Rijksmuseum in Amsterdam. Calvin and Luther are seated side by side, surrounded by Wycliffe, John Hus, Bucer, and various others. The candle on the table naturally represents the restored light of the Word of God, from which the pope and other creatures of the shadow turn away, defeated, after trying without success to blow out the divine flame.

A hieratic character is emphasized in the Memorial to the Reformation erected in Geneva in 1916.[10] Guillaume Farel, John Calvin, Theodore Beza, and John Knox occupy the central panel together. Little distinguishes these four bearded stone figures from each other: the same cap, the same pastoral robe, the same Bible in the hand. Precedence among the principals is absent; the Genevan monument associates preeminence with equality. An emblematic personage of the Reformation, Calvin appears only among his peers.

But the most moving of all these portraits is without dispute a rapid pen-and-ink sketch, taken by a student, Jacques Bourgoin of Nevers, in the latter years of the Reformer's life. An air of exhaustion has seized the preacher, afflicted as he is with a thousand torments; kidney stones, gout, hemorrhoids, and respiratory difficulties assail this frugal and disciplined man, who for a long time has made it a rule to take only one meal a day. The traits of the Reformer can be identified without hesitation despite the clumsiness of the design. A slight stoop emphasizes the organic continuity of the beard and the clothing. Two other faces of Calvin in the same document permit us to observe again the burning gaze we recognize.

9. Papirius Masson, *Elogia*, 2 vols. (Paris, 1638), *OC* 21, cols. 11-12.
10. The first stone was laid in 1909 on the 400th anniversary of John Calvin's birth.

The portrait of Calvin's character is one of the most difficult to present. The historian Lucien Febvre attempted it in 1949, but he entitled his lecture merely "A Sketch of John Calvin." He ended with this beautiful commentary: "Calvin was able to have himself buried in such anonymity that no one has ever been able to discover the place of his burial. He followed in this the law of Geneva: no individual tombs, no epitaphs, not even any crosses. Neither ministers praying over the grave, nor liturgy in the church, nor ringing of bells, nor funeral prayers. Nothing. True to the common law, Calvin did not build himself a tomb of dead stones. He constructed it from living stones."[11]

Neither Dictator nor Fundamentalist

Enigmatic, indeed disquieting, Calvin has acquired in this century a totalitarian reputation which the Austrian Stefan Zweig echoed in the 1930s. A tyrannical dictator without scruple, Calvin held Geneva, his adopted country, with a hand of iron. As for the *Institutes of the Christian Religion* itself, it was to the Protestant Reformation what the Napoleonic Code was to the Revolution.[12] Tongue in cheek, a recent biographer compares Calvin in many respects with Lenin. In fact, seized by the same secular passion, the author also attempts a parallel more daring than profound between Jesus of Nazareth and Karl Marx, both of whom had a certain influence on universal history.[13]

Calvinism, not surprisingly, has its *leyenda negra,* its black legend, which goes back to the sixteenth century. We will encounter it repeatedly on our path. In the 1960s some charitable souls still strove to assure us that, "neither angel, nor beast," Calvin was truly a man — and that on occasion he could even reveal himself as a friend.[14]

Two recent works have considerably enriched our perspective. The figure of Calvin has been restored to its context of Renaissance rhetoric. As Olivier

11. "Crayon de Jean Calvin." L. Febvre, *Au coeur religieux du xvie siècle* (Paris: SEVPEN, 1968), p. 267.

12. S. Zweig, *Triumph und Tragik des Erasmus von Rotterdam* (1934) and *Castellio gegen Calvin* (1936); English version, *Erasmus and Right to Heresy* (London: Souvenir Press, 1979), p. 191. Zweig found a supporter in a pastor of the Cathedral of Saint-Pierre in Geneva, the author of a vitriolic attack on the illustrious Reformer, *Jean Calvin et sa dictature* (Geneva: P. E. Grivet, 1948).

13. A. E. McGrath, *A Life of John Calvin* (Oxford: Blackwell, 1990), pp. xi-xii, 204. The author says (p. 14) that Calvin and Lenin "both were possessed of a remarkable degree of theoretical vision and organizing genius."

14. D. Hourticq, *Calvin, mon ami* (Geneva: Labor et Fides, 1963); R. Stauffer, *L'humanité de Calvin* (Neuchâtel: Delachaux & Niestlé, 1964). Also, A. Perrot, *Le visage humain de Calvin* (Geneva: Labor et Fides, 1986).

Millet has shown, Calvin, "rhetor and orator," is all the closer to his reader or his hearer because he pays attention to the composition of the sacred text. "God speaks" — Calvin's thought proceeds from this primary aspect of revelation.[15]

In the United States, W. J. Bouwsma has without doubt attempted the most audacious synthesis of the man Calvin in distinguishing in him two faces, or rather two individuals. One Calvin, a "conservative," detesting "discord" and trying to establish "order," "intelligibility," and "certainty"; another Calvin, a "humanist," open, attached to "paradox" and "mystery." In this psychological view, this new Calvin, or rather these Calvins, stand at the intersection of Thomas Aquinas with Montaigne.[16] In opting for a Calvin "in movement," our project therefore distinguishes itself in an essential respect from a representation that assumes the "relatively static" character of its subject.[17] We have greatly benefited, in recent years, from the cross-examination of Calvin's theological personality by Luther specialists. And among them, Heiko Oberman has raised the important issue of the link between the public Calvin and the private man, who, unlike the German Reformer, is extremely reluctant to voice his feelings and emotions.[18] David Steinmetz has likewise stressed the striking contrast between the "colorful personalities" of Martin Luther, or for that matter, Teresa of Avila, and the bookish, secretive Reformer of Geneva — even though Steinmetz admits that "there is no Protestant leader in the sixteenth century, with the obvious exception of Martin Luther, who left a more profound mark on Western culture than he did. For more than four hundred years Calvin has influenced the way successive generations of Europeans and American have thought about religion, structured their political institutions, looked at paintings, written poetry and music, theorized about economic relations, or struggled to uncover the laws which govern the physical universe."[19] Professor Steinmetz's fine study was published in the same year as the first French edition of my book, and we have shared a similar contextual approach. Calvin was not simply the author of the *Institutes of the Christian Religion*, that lasting Reformed monument. Neither was he a pure soul, but I have endeavored to give him back a body and a sense of belonging.

My good friend Pierre Chaunu, certainly one of our best Reformation

15. O. Millet, *Calvin et la dynamique de la Parole. Essai de rhétorique réformée* (Paris: H. Champion, 1992), p. 873.

16. W. J. Bouwsma, *John Calvin: A Sixteenth-Century Portrait* (New York: Oxford University Press, 1988), pp. 230-31.

17. Bouwsma, p. 4.

18. H. Oberman, "*Initia Calvini*," *Calvinus Sacrae Scripturae Professor* (Grand Rapids: Eerdmans, 1994), p. 114.

19. D. C. Steinmetz, *Calvin in Context* (New York: Oxford University Press, 1995), p. 3.

historians, once said to me after a radio program: "Do you fancy yourself having a glass of beer with Calvin now?" "Of course, not," came the answer. "But you can imagine the scene with Luther . . . ," he went on.

Indeed, Calvin was not the sort of man you could take out for a drink — even though the "pursuit of happiness" was not totally alien to him.[20] While there is so much to learn from Luther's *Tischreden*, the very idea of "table talk" would have been repugnant to Calvin.

Luther and Calvin? Two temperaments, to be sure. But also two distinct traditions. The comparison remains captivating to this day.[21] In the most dramatic moments, it hinges on the question of substance, as in the controversies surrounding the eucharist, or on the relationship between God and man. Calvin's understanding of mystery is closely fashioned by his philosophy of language, with its sharp dissociation between words and things.[22]

A portrait is stiff and frozen; in its very perfection it shows the transience of the features and the truth of the soul. Calvin can never be entirely "enclosed" — to take up a figure frequently employed by the author of the *Institutes*. Like Montaigne, Calvin deserves a portrait in motion.[23]

20. See M. Engammare's fascinating study of the concept of 'pleasure' and related notions in his "Irdiche Freude bei Calvin," *Calvinus Sicerioris Religionis Vindex*, ed. W. H. Neuser and B. G. Armstrong, Sixteenth-Century Essays and Studies, vol. 36 (1997), pp. 189-208.

21. This will be the subject of my forthcoming study of the Reformation from Luther to John Wesley and the Great Awakening.

22. "Pour une sémiotique de la Réforme. *Le Consensus Tigurinus* de Calvin," *Annales ESC* 39 (1984): 265-85.

23. J. Starobinski, *Montaigne en mouvement* (Paris: NRF, 1982).

PART I

YOUTH OF A REFORMER

CHAPTER 1

The Heavens at a Birth: July 10, 1509

Although the stars do not speak, even in being silent they cry out.

JOHN CALVIN[1]

July 10, 1509: "The disposition of the stars in this figure shows that this person should be endowed with good qualities, but that they should be accompanied by several evil characteristics."

F. DE RAEMOND, 1605[2]

Calvin's life was more secular than it seems. The Reformer never aroused the slightest personality cult among his entourage. Theodore Beza, who succeeded him in Geneva, described him with admiration certainly, but without excessive adulation, never sacrificing to the golden legend. As a friend of the dead man, he did not hesitate to celebrate his eminent role as the "champion" of God or to blacken his adversaries. For Beza Calvin was indeed the scourge of all heresies: "There will be found no heresy ancient or revived, or newly founded in our time, which he did not destroy down to its foundations."[3] But his zeal was tempered by the recognition of the faults of the departed. "I do not want to make a

1. *Opera Calvini*, ed. G. Baum, 58 vols. (Brunswick: Braunschweig, 1863-1900) (hereafter cited as *OC*) 33, col. 570, forty-sixth sermon on Job.
2. F. de Raemond, *L'histoire de la naissance de l'hérésie* (1605; Rouen: P. de La Motte, 1629), bk. 7, p. 880.
3. T. Beza, *L'histoire de la vie et mort de Calvin* (1565), *OC* 21, col. 25.

man into an angel," he confides in his *Life of Calvin,* which appeared some months after the Reformer's passing. Yes, Calvin was hot tempered and obstinate, "gloomy and difficult."[4] Beza describes the great man's birth with a careful sobriety: "He was born in Noyon, an ancient and famous town of Picardy, in 1509, on July 10, of a respectable family of middle rank. His father was named Girard Calvin, a man of good understanding and judgment, and therefore in great demand in the houses of the neighboring nobility."[5]

This is an "emblematic" sentence, "similar to those which open all biographies."[6] In the second version of Calvin's life, completed by Nicolas Colladon, the subject is treated laconically: "Let us be satisfied that, God wanting to be served by him at a certain time, He brought him into the world on the stated day."[7] He clearly wanted to avoid interpreting Calvin's admittedly unique destiny in terms of the stars: "I will therefore commence with his birth, which was on the tenth day of July of the year 1509 — which I note, not in order to search out in his horoscope the causes of the events of his life, much less the excellent virtues found in him, but simply from regard for history. And indeed, considering that he himself had such a horror of the abuses of judicial astrology . . . it would be doing him wrong to give rein to such speculations regarding his character."[8]

Thus is "judicial astrology" rejected, which in our day is called simply astrology, those predictions which claim to use the position of the stars to forecast the future. The future, according to Calvin, depended only on man himself, or at least on man listening to God. His first admiring biographers likewise found

---

4. Beza, p. 39.

5. Beza, p. 29.

6. D. Ménager, "Théodore de Bèze, biographe de Calvin," *Bibliothèque d'Humanisme et Renaissance* 45 (1983): 239.

7. *OC* 21, col. 53. T. Beza, *Vie de Calvin.* This life of Calvin exists in three different redactions:

    1. The first version, dated August 19, 1564, appeared shortly after the Reformer's death, in connection with his commentary on the book of Joshua: *Commentaires de M. Iehan Calvin, sur le livre de Josué. Avec une preface de Theodore de Besze, contenant en brief l'histoire de la vie et mort d'iceluy . . .* (Geneva: François Perrin, 1564). Various editions, including one in Latin.

    2. A second version, enlarged by Nicolas Colladon: *Commentaires de M. Iehan Calvin sur le livre de Iosué . . .* (Geneva: F. Perrin, 1565), in numerous editions.

    3. In 1575, a new version by T. Beza, published with Calvin's correspondence: *Ioannis Calvini Vita.*

See also J.-R. Armogathe, "Les vies de Calvin aux xvie et xviie siècles," in *Historiographie de la Réforme,* ed. P. Joutard (Neuchâtel: Delachaux & Niestlé, 1977), pp. 45-59; Ménager, pp. 231-55.

8. *OC* 21, col. 53.

themselves confronted with a particularly arduous task: while maintaining the exceptional, indeed providential character of Calvin's life, they had to reject the techniques used in the cult of saints or the legends of secular heroes. The biography of Calvin revived an ancient genre, the lives of illustrious men.[9] It was located at the necessarily difficult intersection between the biography of a saint and the celebration of a great man. A great man, moreover, is not a lay saint; his private virtues are less significant than his collective importance. From this perspective Calvin's precise influence is difficult to disentangle with accuracy; apart from the impact of his theological work, which is absolutely undeniable, his effect on the society of his time, and in particular on Geneva, is the subject of constant reevaluation.[10] Did these biographers manage in the end to avoid the snare of hagiography? Already in 1567, in a new edition, some accompanying words stated that Calvin's life was that of "a great servant of God," and added that it concerned "a holy man whom Our Lord has received into his glory." The description already smells of the incense of canonization — all the more because of pious mention of the "falsity of all that the Devil has vomited through his henchmen against the memory" of Calvin.[11] Neither Calvin nor Beza was responsible for these excesses; the refusal of a tomb that can be visited sufficiently marks the Calvinist determination to nip in the bud any temptation to create a cult of saints. No, Calvin fortunately smelled the sulfur too plainly to lend himself to the use of the reliquary.

From the side of his adversaries, Jérôme Bolsec insisted on Calvin's Picard origins, calling him "John Calvin of Noyon, a man among all others who were ever in the world ambitious, presumptuous, arrogant, cruel, malicious, vengeful, and above all ignorant."[12] But regarding the birth itself, he remained reticent: "Of his birth in the town of Noyon, in Picardy, in the year 1509, I will say nothing more." Bolsec preferred to enlarge on two subjects: John's father, Girard Cauvin, who had been "a most execrable blasphemer of God," and his son, the well-known Reformer, who had been "surprised in or convicted of the sin of sodomy" and branded with a hot iron, in lieu of being burned at the stake as he seemingly deserved.[13] The highly polemical, indeed frankly hateful text of Bolsec contents itself with inverting the traditional saints' lives: "Bolsec says

9. In 1559 Jacques Amyot opportunely published his translation of Plutarch's *Lives of Illustrious Men*, which enjoyed a considerable success.

10. E. W. Monter, *Studies in Genevan Government* (Geneva: Droz, 1964), p. 118: "An explanation of Genevan government and politics in terms of Calvin's personality . . . provides a wrong answer to a badly-put question."

11. *OC* 21, cols. 11-12.

12. J. Bolsec, *Histoire de la vie, moeurs, actes, doctrine, constance et mort de Jean Calvin, jadis ministre de Genève. Recueilly par M. Hierosme Hermes Bolsec, Docteur Médecin à Lyon* (1577), *Archives curieuses*, ed. L. Climber (Paris: Beauvais, 1835), series 1, vol. 5, p. 305.

13. Bolsec, p. 312.

nothing about Calvin's horoscope, but there are found in him the three pivotal themes of the entire controversy: Calvin's debauched youth and judicial branding, the botched resurrection, and the death 'while invoking the devils'; these three facts constitute in essentials . . . the reversed pattern of a saint's life."[14]

Astrology, on the other hand, later provided a magistrate of Bordeaux, Florimond de Raemond, with weighty arguments when he attempted at the beginning of the seventeenth century to explain the "birth of heresy": "This man, who was the author of so many evils, was born at Noyon in Picardy on July 10, 1509, an unfortunate day, being the birthday of our prolonged miseries."

Raemond thus described the ill-omened Calvin's map of the sky: "First, Saturn in the house of the Virgin shows that he would be a man of eminent learning, but learning badly based. . . . Mercury, in the house of the sun, promised him a strong memory, and the ability to put things down well in writing . . . since although Mercury was combust, this would not prevent him from having this good quality, which was also promised him by the heart of the Lion, located due south, the heart being the seat of understanding and prudence. . . ."[15]

These excellent qualities were unfortunately squandered. If in fact his co-religionaries saw in him, according to Raemond, a "second Saint Paul," the "Scorpion in the ascendant" decided that he could not "hold rank and station in the true church."[16] It was a pity. The saint and the heretic maintain a state of kinship in Raemond's work; the defender of Satan and the friend of God, good and evil approach and recede from each other in a complementary relationship within the secret network of convergences traced by the stars. It is written in the heavens.

Raemond clearly feared that evil thoughts would be imputed to him in turn. Astrology cannot substitute for Providence: "I am not however one of those who wish curiously to subject our destinies, our fortunes, and our birth to celestial influences, knowing well that the church, our mistress and conductress, reproves and condemns these opinions."[17]

God is the competitor of the stars. The God of Calvin, more than any other, broke with the pretensions of "judicial astrology." In 1549 the Reformer explained: "There has been for a long time a foolish desire to judge everything that may happen to men by the stars, and to inquire there and take counsel concerning what one should do."[18]

14. Armogathe, p. 46.
15. Raemond, bk. 7. Florimond de Raemond (†1603) had at one time been converted to Calvinism. His history had a considerable influence, noted by B. Dompnier, *Le venin de l'hérésie* (Paris: Le Centurion, 1985), pp. 34ff.
16. Raemond, p. 881.
17. Raemond, p. 881.
18. J. Calvin, *Avertissement contre l'astrologie qu'on appelle judiciaire* (1549), *OC* 7, col. 515.

This rejection shows its importance when compared to the tremendous "astrological anxiety" that marked the sixteenth century.[19] No golden legend existed for the life of Calvin. The destiny of the Reformer took on none of the traits of the marvelous proper to the lives of saints.[20] It entailed nothing miraculous — just the intimate sense of a calling which came to assume a sacred character. In the end Calvinist hagiography remained limited. Thus the pastor Charles Drelincourt, in the seventeenth century, despite the admiration, indeed the veneration that the personality of Calvin inspired in him, concluded his study in measured terms by calling the Reformer "A great man, whom God inspired extraordinarily for the illustration of his truth."[21]

Calvin's vocation was certainly "extraordinary" — under the theologian's pen the word carries a very strong sense. The "extraordinary" providence of God, without being equivalent to a miracle, which is accorded, often and no doubt wrongly, a spectacular quality, perceptibly approaches it. The "extraordinary" character of a vocation or an event — this is a miracle without prodigy or spectacle, the direct intervention of God in the course of history.

Calvin's vocation, his intimate sense of a mission which surpassed in importance the common destiny of men, was therefore not accompanied by any visible stigma. The outcome of this evolution is clearly found in the work of François Guizot in the nineteenth century. The former Protestant minister of Louis-Philippe had a plan at the end of his life for an illuminating tetralogy. Besides Calvin, his *Lives of Four Great French Christians* in the beginning would have included Saint Louis, Duplessis-Mornay, and Vincent de Paul. Guizot's Calvin apparently lacked warmth; he aroused "admiration" more than "sympathy."[22] Could the laicization of his personality be better demonstrated?

19. D. Crouzet, *Les guerriers de Dieu. La violence au temps des troubles de religion, vers 1525-vers 1610*, 2 vols. (Seyssel: Champ Vallon, 1990), 1:131.

20. On sainthood in the Catholicism of Calvin's time, see Christian Renoux, "Une source de l'histoire de la mystique moderne revisitée: les procès de canonisation," *Mélanges de l'École Française de Rome* 105 (1993): 177-217, as well as his "Sainteté et mystique féminines à l'âge baroque," an uncompleted *thèse* at Paris I under the direction of J. Jacquart.

21. C. Drelincourt, *Défense de Calvin* (Geneva: J. Aut, S. de Tournes, 1657), dedicatory letter, unpaginated.

22. F. Guizot, *La vie de quatre grands chrétiens français* (Paris: Hachette, 1875), p. 376.

Noyon, Provincial Homeland

John Calvin's attachment to his native town of Noyon appears undeniable; the mature man reserved for it the name of "homeland," *patria* in his Latin correspondence. In November 1552, learning of the destruction of his town by the Spaniards, he let his bitterness appear: "I have outlived my country, something I could never have believed. The town where I was born has been entirely destroyed by fire."[23] Some years later, learning of the sack of Saint-Quentin, he unburdened himself similarly in a letter to Melanchthon: "Hardly a day's march separates this town from Noyon. . . . If the news that is spread is correct, this will be the second time that I will outlive my country" (September 1557).[24]

Calvin, who was saddened on hearing in his Genevan refuge of the ravages falling on his Picard homeland, was not at all a rootless man. The cosmopolitanism of his thought and the international character of his enterprise harked back in him to a French passion: the taste for universality, that utopia of clarity and transparency that found in his language its point of attachment. Down to the end Calvin remained a man of a native soil, and of a childhood — of which we know practically nothing because of his reticence. The religious troubles, the Protestant desacralization of places, and finally the instinctive resistance this secretive character felt to writing about himself partly explain this aloofness. It was not until 1888 that anyone devoted a book to the Reformer's youth.[25] This gospel of youth, despite patches of shadow and certain inaccuracies, depended on documentation that has in part disappeared, destroyed by the ravages of the First World War.

The nineteenth century returned his psychological depth to Calvin by invoking anew, under cover of historical accuracy, a disavowed spirit of locale. In 1897 an article, at once modest and erudite, was published in the *Bulletin de l'Société l'Histoire du Protestantisme Français* entitled "The House Where Calvin Was Born, in Noyon." It undertook to show that a "portion of the house where he saw the light survives." From then on it was permissible to meditate: "Thanks to this one can contemplate at least a few points in the family horizon to which the eyes of the child John Calvin were accustomed, and climb the same steps that he must often have climbed and descended."[26]

The house where Calvin was born, restored in the twentieth century after

---

23. *OC* 14, col. 412, letter to Blaurer, November 19, 1552.

24. *OC* 16, col. 604, letter to Melanchthon, September 9, 1557.

25. A. Lefranc, *La jeunesse de Calvin* (Paris: Fischbacher, 1888).

26. N. Weiss, "La maison où est né Calvin, à Noyon," *Bulletin de la Société de l'Histoire du Protestantisme Français* 46 (1897): 374.

the terrible suffering of the Great War,[27] enables us to realize the Reformer's attachment to his town. The family home was located in the parish of Sainte-Godeberte. It was by the grain market, between the Rue des Porcelets and the Rue Fromentière. The grain market was, along with the cathedral, one of the nerve centers of the episcopal city, divided between its ecclesiastical vocation and its bourgeois aspirations. The important agricultural market of Noyon provided an outlet for the villages of the Santerre through the Oise Valley. But Noyon, episcopal seat of the Vermandois, also played a significant administrative role in the secular world. "Merchants were numerous in Noyon, more or less powerful according to the guild to which they belonged. Outstanding in importance were the grain merchants who ruled over the wheat market and the merchants of wool and linen. A notable position was also held by the tanners and tawers[28] established on the banks of the Verse and the Versette."[29] Young Jean Cauvin was baptized on July 10 at Sainte-Godeberte. His godfather, Jean des Vatines, was a canon of the cathedral.

The name "Calvin" is a later corruption of "Cauvin," derived from the Latin "Calvinus." The Cauvin family was of modest origin, a family of Picard watermen and artisans, for whom the windings of the Oise formed the entire horizon. The family's anchorage had been the village of Pont-l'Évêque, near Noyon. The grandfather of our Calvin practiced the trade of cooper there, in the waning of the Middle Ages. This honest craftsman had several sons. One, Richard, became established as a locksmith in the Auxerrois quarter in Paris. He must have founded a family there, since Jacques Cauvin, a cousin of our Calvin, practiced the same trade in the Rue du Renard. Another son, Girard, father of John Calvin, was established in his own right in Noyon in 1481. Rising one by one through all the degrees of provincial respectability, he achieved the bourgeoisie of the town in 1497.

The rise of the family was directly linked to the protection of a powerful ecclesiastical lord, Charles d'Hangest, bishop of Noyon from 1501 on, following the recommendation of Louis XII.[30] In 1525, when he had only three more

---

27. The part of the house called "Calvin's room" could still be visited in 1917. It was destroyed in 1918, during the battles that marked the second occupation of the city. A. Baudoux and R. Régnier, *Une grande page de notre histoire locale. Noyon pendant la première guerre mondiale* (Chauny: A. Baticle, 1962). The first stone of the present John Calvin museum was laid on July 10, 1927. Dedicated three years later, the monument suffered again in the war of 1939-45. Restored, it was again dedicated on July 17, 1955.

28. Tawers: workmen who prepared skins and bleached them.

29. G. Braillon, *Un cas de promotion sociale sous l'ancien régime. Les bourgeois gentilshommes de Noyon* (Noyon: Société archéologique, historique et scientifique, 1985), p. 3.

30. Charles d'Hangest was born in 1461. His father, Jean d'Hangest, seigneur de Genlis, had been a royal councillor and *bailli* of Evreux in 1477. See M. Reulos, "Les at-

years to live, Charles d'Hangest ceded his office to his nephew, Jean d'Hangest. Lacking sons, why not transmit his bishopric to a nephew? Girard Cauvin, apostolic notary, figures among the drafters of this document.

What do we know of Girard Cauvin that is not already confused with old wives' tales or with legend? Jacques Desmay, vicar-general of Rouen, came to Noyon to preach during Lent in 1614. During his stay he assembled the material for *Remarks on the Life of John Calvin Drawn from the Registers of Noyon, His Birthplace* (1621). Therein he deplored the libertinism of Calvin's father, "a sly man, of a sharp and crafty nature, skilled in chicanery, but a great rascal." The elder Calvin was led by his artful place-seeking "to neglect his domestic affairs and to manage poorly the fortune his skill advanced him to, being much employed by Messire Charles d'Hangest and Messire Jean d'Hangest, uncle and nephew, bishops of Noyon."[31] Still another belated portrait of Girard Cauvin has been preserved. Jacques Le Vasseur, at the beginning of the seventeenth century, celebrated in the man an "ardent spirit, among the most skilled in the finest practice and algebra of the law." But more specifically: "He inserted himself everywhere and intrigued actively in affairs, for which he was sought out and with which he was finally entrusted, everyone wanting to be served by a man so skilled in such fencing, who lacked neither diligence nor invention. He therefore became apostolic notary, procurator fiscal of the county, scribe in the church court, secretary of the bishop, and prosecutor of the chapter. . . . In short, he embraced so much that he burdened himself for the rest of his life."[32]

One embraces so as to hold better. But he who embraces too much burdens himself in his turn. What true credit should be given to these belated testimonies, bordering on proverbs, where stereotypes of men of law, wily and dishonest, overshadow the elements of proof?

Girard Cauvin certainly showed the exterior signs of success and of an honest bourgeois competence, rendered still more evident by the modesty of his origins. He had married as his first wife Jeanne Le Franc, the daughter of a former innkeeper of Cambrai, made wealthy in business. Pretty and devout, Calvin's mother undoubtedly habituated her son early to those pious exercises that later incurred the sarcasms of his *Treatise on Relics*. She died in 1515, leaving behind her an orphan still of a tender age.

---

taches de Calvin dans la région de Noyon," *Bulletin de la Société de l'Histoire du Protestantisme Français* (1964): 193-200.

31. J. Desmay, *Remarques sur la vie de Jean Calvin tirées des registres de Noyon, lieu de sa naissance* (1621). Reported by É. Doumergue, *Jean Calvin. Les hommes et les choses de son temps,* 7 vols. (Lausanne: G. Bridel, 1899-1917), 1:20. An incomplete edition of this extremely rare text exists: *Archives curieuses,* p. 2.

32. J. Le Vasseur, *Annales de l'Église de Noyon,* 3 vols. (Paris, 1633), pp. 1151-55.

It was therefore in a respectable bourgeois provincial milieu that Calvin saw the light of day. His father Girard had mounted one by one all the steps of respectability; a simple town clerk, then recognized by the episcopal court, he had been an *agent fiscal,* episcopal secretary, and finally procurator of the cathedral chapter. He lived a laborious life and embarked upon a judicial career, in the service of the clergy — who finally condemned him and turned against him. Girard died in 1531 in a state of excommunication as a result of his quarrels with the chapter. It was a struggle even to have him rest in consecrated ground. As for Charles, Calvin's older brother who took holy orders, he departed in his turn five years later, refusing the sacraments of the church that had tormented the last moments of their father's life. Little enough is known, however, about Calvin's two other brothers, Antoine and François. François undoubtedly died at an early age; Antoine was to go to Geneva, where his wife's levity earned him the reputation of a cuckold. To these four sons must be added two daughters, issue of a second marriage. Marie later rejoined her brother in Geneva, but hardly even the name of the second is known.

Linked to the church by its financial ties, the Cauvin family certainly could, according to Émile Doumergue's formula, "be clerical in its appearance and its functions" while revealing itself to be "extremely anti-clerical in its acts and its spirit."[33] In the spring of 1521 the young Calvin received his first ecclesiastical benefice, part of the revenue of La Gésine, the name of one of the altars of the cathedral; he received several barrels of wheat per year. This picturesque name, La Gésine, commemorated the nativity, or more precisely the confinement of Our Lady. In 1527 there was added the cure of Saint-Martin de Martheville, eight leagues from Noyon, finally exchanged two years later for that of Pont-l'Évêque. In 1529 La Gésine descended to Antoine, John's younger brother, but in 1531 Calvin recovered this benefice. Tiring of simony and nepotism, Calvin officially renounced his church revenues in 1534.[34]

The year of his first ecclesiastical benefice, 1521, apparently corresponds to a cutting of ties. Calvin was barely twelve years old. According to a recent hypothesis, the year of grace 1521 may have marked his departure for Paris and the Collège de la Marche.[35] The date ordinarily accepted is 1523. Whether it was 1521 or 1523 matters little (see app. 1 below). Calvin was provided with ecclesiastical benefices as he was preparing to undertake his active studies in Paris; moreover, he profited from the aristocratic protection of the family of

33. Doumergue, 1:22.

34. It appears that Calvin did not benefit from the revenues of La Gésine from 1529 to 1531 "for unknown reasons," as noted by F. Wendel (1905-72), *Calvin, sources et évolution de sa pensée religieuse* (1950; Geneva: Labor et Fides, 1985), p. 4.

35. T. H. L. Parker, *John Calvin: A Biography* (London: J. M. Dent & Sons, 1975), app. 1, pp. 156-61.

Hangest. The young man must have followed the Monmor children, the companions of his childhood studies — Joachim, seigneur de Moyencourt, and Yves, seigneur d'Ivoys — to Paris.[36] It is undoubtedly necessary to add a third Hangest, Claude, the future dedicatory of the commentary on Seneca's *De clementia*.[37] Louis d'Hangest, seigneur de Monmor and former grand equerry of Anne de Bretagne, was none other than the bishop of Noyon's brother. Did this noble protection weigh on the personality of the young Calvin? One may think that he owed to it in part his humanist formation, and also his haughty character, more inclined to voluntary friendships than to cronyism.

The succession to Charles d'Hangest in the bishopric of Noyon was not without conflicts. His nephew Jean d'Hangest, despite the recriminations of the chapter, insisted on sporting a superb beard. Confronted with the hostility of the canons, the good bishop ended by departing for Rome, where he accumulated debts. But this effervescent pilosity barely impeded the unleashing of smothered passions against the heretics. On January 16, 1534, Bishop d'Hangest addressed the chapter:

> To the deans and chapter:
> Because I am informed that these vicious unfortunates multiply more and more and that the scandal grows bigger and more terrible and moreover very close to us, and because the king admonishes us to do what is required by our position, I ask you to hold a procession next Thursday more honorable, if possible, than those preceding, and for my part I engage myself to be found there on the said day doing my duty, with the aid of the Creator, and may He hold you in his holy protection.[38]

College Life: From La Marche to Montaigu

The good child loves the school,
Virtue and God, and his Word;
To the vicious all is displeasing
That is pleasing to God.

MATURIN CORDIER[39]

36. Calvin himself mentioned in the course of his correspondence his very close acquaintance with the Monmors; letter to Monsieur De Falais, September 10, 1547.

37. Wendel, p. 4. Joachim, Yves, and Claude were the sons of Louis d'Hangest, seigneur de Monmor, and of his wife Marie du Fay d'Athies.

38. Lefranc, p. 200.

39. See J.-C. Margolin, "Catéchisme et instruction religieuse à travers quelques colloques scolaires du xvie siècle," in *Aux origines du catéchisme en France* (Paris: Desclée,

What did the young Calvin we left in Paris at the beginning of the 1520s become? To tell the truth, we know very little about this young provincial, who must have acquired some rudiments of Latin at the Collège des Capettes in Noyon. This was located on the road to Pont-l'Évêque, facing the Church of Saint-Maurice. The picturesque name "Capettes" derived from the short cape *(cappa)* worn by the scholars.

Paris at that time contained numerous colleges, venerable rivals: the Collège d'Harcourt, the future Lycée Saint-Louis, had been founded in 1280; the Collège du Cardinal Lemoine, the Collège de Navarre, and those of Montaigu, Du Plessis-Sorbonne, and Lisieux all dated from the fourteenth century.[40] Founded about 1200, the University of Paris was the oldest in the country (see app. 2).

On his arrival in Paris, the young Calvin probably lived with his uncle Richard, the locksmith, near Saint-Germain-l'Auxerrois. He must have received some private lessons from a preparatory master whom he later denounced for incompetence.[41] At the Collège de la Marche he was the "auditor" of Maturin Cordier, an eminent Latinist, one of the best teachers of his time. Cordier was convinced, with that ignorance that afflicts the most enlightened educators, that young boys should already express themselves in Latin when talking with their mothers. At the Collège de la Marche Calvin completed the required courses in grammar before being able to study theology or law. Cordier had the sententious character associated in all ages with pedagogical repetitiousness and didactic success. Born about 1479-80, this Norman had a jaundiced view of the Parisian colleges, where he presided from 1514 to 1530. Ultimately attracted to the Protestant reform, this excellent man taught the young strong and simple mottoes marked with the seal of common sense and untouched by the notions of later psychology. He was to pass away in 1564 at the age of eighty-five, after having taught his last courses at the Academy of Geneva. The good master presented in his *Mirror for Young People* certain sound principles, in which physical well-being balanced moral rectitude:

> The good child gladly hears
> Talk about God, because he believes in him;

1988), p. 135, for this quotation and those following. [Translator: Throughout this volume, in translating poetry I have followed the convention of preserving the verse form, although I have not tried to render it into English verse.]

40. Since the medieval period, higher education had emphasized two complementary exercises: the *expositio*, or master's lecture, delivered by a *régent* or professor, and the *disputatio*, which required the participation of the students.

41. *OC* 13, col. 525, letter to M. Cordier, March 13, 1550.

The naughty child does not want to hear
Words about God or to learn anything of him.

The logical result of which is:

The good child tries to live
According to Jesus and to follow him;
The naughty child follows Antichrist
And makes war on Jesus Christ.

One could also cite other passages in this *Mirror for Young People,* in which Cordier summed up his philosophy in 1559, at the end of his life:

The good child in listening
Is diligent, without chattering;
The naughty child has no desire
Except for babbling and badinage.[42]

Of a formidable effectiveness, these doggerel verses give a black-and-white picture of the world; good children and bad, workers and parasites, finally the pious and impious throw themselves into a battle without mercy. But behind this systematic and laborious character was hidden a remarkable expert in questions of translation. In 1530 he published a manual which showed an unambiguous desire to promote a classical Latin without obscurity or periphrases. *De corrupti sermonis emendatione* comprises a list of 1,800 faulty expressions used by pupils, with their corrections, arranged in fifty-eight alphabetical chapters and three supplements.

Cordier's method was original. It has not lost its interest for the teaching of living languages today. To lead the student to grammatical correctness the professor begins with his errors, and not the inverse. In other words, he concerns himself with taking account of the difficulties encountered by the child and examining their causes before promoting canons of good usage. A collection of foolish errors is a serious matter: "As a good humanist, Cordier strove against that direct transcription of vernacular terms and expressions into Latin which disfigured the good Latinity of his young students with so many Gallicisms. But for this purpose he concentrated in his *De corrupti sermonis emendatione* on these same Gallicisms, familiar phrases and proverbial expres-

---

42. From Cordier, *Miroir de la jeunesse.* J.-C. Margolin, "La civilité puérile selon Érasme et Maturin Cordier," in *Ragione e civilitas* (Milan: Franco Angeli, 1986), p. 34. "Maturin" was the correct sixteenth-century spelling, not "Mathurin."

sions found in the current speech, for which he gives the bad Latin translation (often pithy) current among young people, then the corresponding translation in good Latin."[43]

This certainly sets forth a "method" of teaching, provided the term is not given too restricted a meaning. Cordier abominated the received pedagogical methods; he placed the gospel at the center of his practice and criticized the brutality used in the schools: "The sages never approved this unnatural custom of bringing children only with strokes of the rod and with punishments to observe correct language." Moreover, his pedagogy derives here from his theology. The master cannot substitute himself for God; he can encourage the student to learn by his example, but he cannot substitute for him. Thus blows and bad treatment derive from an erroneous conception of one's relation to God: "It is your business only to plant or irrigate; God will make the plant grow." Or again: "See to it that your light shines in the eyes of all your pupils; then they will not only apply themselves to imitating you, they will admire you."[44]

If we have discussed at such length the character of Maturin Cordier, it is because for Calvin he would remain the model of the ideal master. Calvin would always demonstrate his gratitude to Cordier. In March 1545 he wanted to invite him to Geneva. In February 1550 he dedicated his commentary on the First Epistle to the Thessalonians to his former professor, who had become the principal of the College of Lausanne: "It is with good reason that you also have a place in my labors, since having first begun the process of study under your conduct and skill, I have advanced at least to this point of being able in some degree to benefit the church of God."[45]

---

43. O. Millet, *Calvin et la dynamique de la Parole. Essai de rhétorique réformée* (Paris: H. Champion, 1992), pp. 775-76. This linguistic purism was not restricted to the Latin of the colleges; it extended to the Latin of the church, from which Cordier wished to banish the words *ecclesia* and *missa* and replace them with *templum* and *sacra*. His Ciceronianism also extended to dress, where the good man wished to revive the word *toga* for the "upper robe worn by men." With similar logic, *tunica manicata* would mean "jacket," and *subucula* a "shirt of cloth worn under the doublet." J. Le Coultre, *Maturin Cordier et les origines de la pédagogie protestante dans les pays de langue française (1530-1564)* (Neuchâtel, 1926), p. 47. Our pedagogue made use of byroads: "It is a sort of dictionary of common usages, and the remarkable point is that it gives first the expression in common Latin, that is the Latin spoken as a living international language by the students of the Middle Ages, modified, clarified and simplified by practical needs, then the French translation, and finally the expression in classical Latin." G. Snyders, *La pédagogie en France aux xviie et xviiie siècles* (Paris: PUF, 1965), p. 21.

44. Cited by P. Mesnard, "Maturin Cordier (1479-1564)," *Foi, Éducation* (April-June 1959): 92-93.

45. *OC* 21, col. 349; J. Calvin, *Commentaires sur le Nouveau Testament*, 4 vols. (Paris: C. Meyrueis, 1855), 4:109 for this and the following quotations.

Calvin remembered his modest beginnings: "When my father sent me as a young boy to Paris, having only some small beginnings in the Latin language, God wished me to have you for a short time as my preceptor, so that by you I might be so directed to the true road and right manner of learning that I could profit somewhat from it afterwards."

Even more precious because it derives from Calvin, who was little inclined to autobiographical confession, this testimony contains interesting reflections on the methods of Cordier, as contrasted with the more widely accepted pedagogy of his time: "Since, when you had taken the first class and taught there with great honor; nevertheless, because you saw that the children formed by the other masters through ambition and boasting were not grounded in good understanding and grasped nothing firmly, but could only make an appearance with gusts of words, so that you had to start over and form them anew; being disgusted with such a burden, that year you descended to the fourth class."

Seeing that the students of the first class were not properly grounded, Cordier therefore asked to teach the students of the fourth. And it was thus that he made on the young Calvin — who was still called only Jean Cauvin — a permanent impression. Apparently this teaching lasted less than a year, since Calvin had the misfortune to be pushed against his will into the third class. "It was for me a singular favor of God to encounter such a beginning of instruction. And although it was not permitted me to enjoy it for long, since a thoughtless man, without judgment, who disposed of our studies at his own will, or rather according to his foolish whims, made us immediately move higher, nevertheless the instruction and skill you had given me served me so well afterwards that in truth I confess and recognize that such profit and advancement as followed was due to you."

The Collège de Montaigu had acquired a formidable reputation for harshness and severity. A Latin proverb stressed, among other characteristic traits, the teeth of its pupils sharpened by hunger and the fineness of their minds enlivened by bad treatment.[46] Evidently its culture hardly encouraged gastronomy. But would Calvin have thought of complaining? Admitted as a philosophy student to the famous college, did the young Noyonnais not feel a secret resentment? However, his respectable provincial income permitted him to be a *camériste* (or paying guest) at the college, thus dodging some of the rigor of its discipline, which was felt more heavily by poor or penniless residents. The institution, which was located at the present site of the Library of Sainte-Geneviève, facing the Panthéon, had been reorganized forty years before by Jan

---

46. *Mons acutus, ingenium acutum, dentes acuti;* literally, "sharp peak [i.e., Montaigu], sharp intelligence, sharp teeth."

Standonck, one of those who introduced the spirituality of the Brothers of the Common Life to France.

A curious person this Jan Standonck (ca. 1450-1504), "a Catholic reformer before the Reformation," according to Augustin Renaudet's description. When Catholicism felt itself threatened, his posthumous influence proved considerable. He imported into France a little of the spirit of the Brothers of the Common Life, developed in Holland by Gerhard Groote at the end of the fourteenth century; that is, criticism of medieval scholasticism, idealization of poverty, mysticism. Even certain laymen were invited to partake of this evangelical ideal. Becoming principal of Montaigu, he "imprinted on his college its already pronounced character of a seminary of poor clerics."[47] In his *Colloquies* (1518-33), Erasmus left a description of the Collège de Montaigu, where he stayed in 1495. The author indulges himself in some untranslatable Latin wordplay concerning the "sharpness" of this "acid" college, where apparently the privations of the body were thought to awaken the pupils to the pure joys of the spirit: "I carried nothing away from there except a body poisoned with infected humors and a very great abundance of lice."[48] Then follows a full-length portrait of Jan Standonck:

> In this college there then reigned Jan Standonck, a man with no evil feelings, but entirely deprived of judgment. Indeed, in memory of his youth, which he spent in the most extreme poverty, he concerned himself with the poor, and this should be strongly approved. And if he had relieved the misery of young men enough to furnish them with what was necessary for hard study, but without permitting excessive abundance to disorder them, this would have merited praise. But that he attempted to achieve this by giving them a bed so hard, a diet so strict and so little abundant, vigils and labors so overpowering that in less than a year from beginning the experiment he had brought numerous young people, gifted by nature and highly promising, either to death, or blindness, or madness, or even sometimes to leprosy (I knew several of them personally), so that he clearly put every one of them in danger; who would not understand that this was cruelty to those around him?[49]

This rather somber picture permits the author of the *Praise of Folly* to recall, in a list that is familiar to him, the abuses of convents and monasteries,

---

47. A. Renaudet, "Jean Standonck, un réformateur catholique avant la Réforme," in *Humanisme et renaissance* (Geneva: Droz, 1958), p. 134.

48. Erasmus, *Oeuvres choisies*, ed. J. Chomarat (Paris: Librairie Générale Française, Le Livre de Poche Classique, 1991), p. 772.

49. Erasmus, pp. 772-73.

where, similarly, one does not "encounter, possibly, the desire to kill" even when "encountering homicide." And he proceeds to describe the "tortures" that assailed the students: hunger, and for the only drink, "pestilential" water from a well which he holds responsible for the illnesses that certain of his contemporaries still suffer from. Not to mention the lodgings: "certain rooms at ground level, with rotten plaster, pestiferous from the neighborhood of the latrines"; or the corporal punishments: "I leave aside the extraordinary torture with the rod, even of the innocent."[50] In short, under the "appearance of religion" lay only cruelty, corrupter of those of an "inexperienced and tender age."[51]

This criticism of the medieval colleges was not devoid of polemical intent against the monasteries. It was one of the commonplaces of a sixteenth century preoccupied to the extreme with pedagogical questions.[52]

From the other side, pitying the masters and not the students, George Buchanan (1506-82) presented a report no less afflicting. A partisan of the rod in pedagogy and of the liberty of peoples in politics, this Scottish humanist taught in France for several years in the middle of the century. The poor teachers, he sighs, were obliged to wear themselves out beating the children for their own good, and then condemned to hear them whimpering all day long. This moving account does not fail to describe the sad condition of the penitential staff: "While the professor tires himself out, these parasitic children sleep or think about their pleasures. One, who is absent, has paid one of his comrades to respond in his place; another has lost his stockings; another looks at his foot, which shows through the gaping upper of his shoe. This one pretends to be ill, that one writes to his parents. One must use the rod; the faces are grimed with tears; there are sobs for the rest of the day."[53]

Standonck had attracted the enmity of Louis XII and had been obliged to flee, with the "joyous heart" and the "serene face" of one "judged worthy of suf-

---

50. Erasmus, p. 774.

51. Erasmus, p. 775.

52. Similarly, Montaigne leaves us a comparable description of the Collège de Guyenne in Bordeaux at a later period: "But, among other things, the discipline in the majority of our colleges has always displeased me. It would perhaps have been less injurious to err on the side of indulgence. It is a virtual jail of captive youth. They are made debauched by punishing them for it beforehand. On arriving in their place of business you hear nothing but cries, tortured children, and masters drunk with rage. What a means of awakening an appetite for their lessons in these tender and timid souls, to guide them there with a frightful, bloated face, and hands armed with rods! An iniquitous and pernicious practice." Montaigne, *Essais*, I, 26, *Oeuvres complètes* (Paris: Le Seuil, 1967), p. 80. Montaigne himself had been taught at the Collège de Guyenne in Bordeaux.

53. Cited by J. Quicherat, *Histoire de Sainte-Barbe*, 3 vols. (Paris: Hachette, 1860-62), 1:163-64.

fering disgrace for the name of Jesus,"[54] leaving his college in the hands of his faithful friend Noël Bédier (or Béda). A strong man, called for his energy to rule the entire faculty of theology, this Bédier (†1537) still exercised a certain influence on Montaigu in Calvin's time. But he was better known for his role as a conservative theologian with his face set against the challenge of the Protestant Reformation. Condemned in June 1520 by the bull *Exsurge domine* and excommunicated the following year, Luther aroused the anger of many Frenchmen. Becoming syndic of the faculty of theology in the same period (fall of 1520), Bédier participated actively in the repression of the "heresy."

Another figure of the university microcosm enjoyed at this time a solid reputation, arduously earned by means of thrashing students. Directing the Collège de Montaigu from 1514 to 1528, the dreadful Pierre Tempête terrorized all the stunned little children. This frightful being appeared to be drawn from one of those stories with which one fills children's anguished imaginations to help them fall asleep. Sadly celebrated, Tempête ruled the institution with a hand of iron, meriting without doubt that tyrannical renown of which an echo is found in Rabelais.

Rabelais, always on the watch for an apt word, did not fail to stigmatize the impetuous Tempête, or tempest, under the name predestined for him by God. The author of the *Fourth Book* repeats the epigram that circulated at the time, *Horridas tempestas montem turbavit acutum,* which might be rendered as "A horrible tempest troubled Montaigu." And Rabelais described the corporal punishments administered by this "great beater of scholars" to the "poor little children."[55]

Calvin doubtless suffered little personally from the brutalities of the impetuous tempest; he was, it is said, an intelligent child and a diligent student. He must, however, have encountered the gibes of his comrades, who dubbed him, according to a spurious legend, "Accusativus" — a savage nickname, merging without pity the word for the accusative case with that for an accusation, transforming the good student into a "teacher's pet." The able student was suspected of being an informer, quick to denounce his young comrades when they had committed a fault. True or false, the nickname does not lack spite.[56] Despite everything, the Picard without doubt benefited from an excellent education at Montaigu. (One imagines the timid young man rather as a well-behaved child than as a boisterous good-for-nothing.) Several

---

54. Renaudet, p. 149.

55. Rabelais, *Oeuvres complètes,* ed. P. Jourda (Paris: Garnier, 1962), 2:105.

56. É. Doumergue, who reports the anecdote, sees in it a Catholic calumny of the Reformer. This is obviously possible, but do not all the world's sluggards have the same tendency to attack good students? See Doumergue, 1:74.

able men taught during this decade at Montaigu, although we cannot be sure that Calvin attended their courses. At this point we are reduced to shaky conjectures. In the Latin version of his *Life of Calvin,* Theodore Beza mentions a teacher from Spain who taught the young man grammar.[57] Is this enough to conclude that he was acquainted with Antonio Coronel, the famous dialectician? Likewise we may mention the presence at Montaigu of the Scot John Mair (1469-1550). It would be a rather piquant thing if Calvin had been the student of John Mair, who counted Ignatius Loyola among his students. The first Jesuit and the most famous of the Reformers would have followed the same course, with an interval of some years. (Ignatius Loyola, born in 1491, was Calvin's elder by eighteen years; he died in 1556, eight years before the Reformer.) Unfortunately, no proof exists that Calvin received instruction from the Scot. The latter had long resided in Paris before returning to his distant country in 1531. He counted among his numerous students John Knox, the future Scottish Reformer. But whether or not he was directly influenced, Calvin repeated in his writings a certain number of themes Mair contributed to popularizing: emphasis on faith, predestination, stressing of the Word, and above all the assimilation of logic and grammar.[58] These themes are too precise for one to deny the possibility of an influence by John Mair on John Calvin's thought, and too general for one to draw the least positive conclusion from them.

Calvin Will Not Be a Priest

A change occurred before Calvin attained his twentieth year. Although committed from the beginning to the priesthood, Calvin did not take up studies in theology, as originally intended, but undertook studies in law. He moreover followed his father's advice by directing his steps henceforth to Orléans and Bourges.[59] Was this due to some family conflict with the clergy of Noyon? This is likely, considering Girard Cauvin's difficulties with the chapter. Calvin's later testimony remains laconic: "Since I was a young child my father had destined me to theology, but later, having considered that the science of the law regularly enriches those who follow it, this hope made him suddenly change his intent.

---

57. *OC* 21, col. 121.

58. T. F. Torrance, "La philosophie et la théologie de Jean Mair ou Major, de Haddington," *Archives de Philosophie* 32 (1969): 531-47, and 33 (1970): 261-93.

59. This change of direction occurred in 1528, unless we follow the shorter chronology of T. H. L. Parker, who places it in 1525.

Thus this was the cause why I was withdrawn from the study of philosophy and put to learning the laws."[60]

"The science of law enriches" — this euphemism sufficed to justify a change of orientation that remains mysterious. Calvin took himself to Orléans, where he followed the course of Pierre de l'Estoile, then to Bourges, where the famous Alciati taught. But did God not have other designs for him? Did the Father's purpose not lie hidden behind his father's choices? "However I forced myself to faithfully employ myself in obedience to my father," continues Calvin, "God still by his secret providence finally made me turn the rein in another direction." And the Reformer concludes retrospectively, "Although I still did not entirely abandon other studies, I nevertheless pursued them more slackly." A passage still more astonishing in its silence than because it admits us to intimacy with Calvin, it in fact concerns a tale of conversion (see chap. 3); the author tries to recover the latent feeling that presided at this change of professional orientation. The apparent triviality of the choice, motivated by all appearances by mercantile desires, does not cover the whole field. Calvin was destined to the priesthood; he embraced the study of law; but finally God recalled him to theology. This strange detour is an ironic illustration of the reforming career; there was no need to be a priest to reveal oneself as a theologian. This affirmation is at the very center of Calvin's life; in its apparent candor, his account reveals the profundity of a vocation.

But Calvin the theologian would be to the end Calvin the jurist. His thought remained permeated with the rigor, the geometry, the fascination, and the memory of the law.[61] A veritable revolution took place at the beginning of the sixteenth century: the rhetoric of Cicero supplanted medieval philosophy, buttressed by its syllogisms. Calvin initiated himself into humanist philology in connection with the study of juridical texts. A "new exegesis in the field of Roman law" was being established; it was based on the establishment of the text, its linguistic interpretation, and the knowledge of the institutions and the facts of civilization.[62] It must be said that Calvin, the student, benefited from the teaching of the greatest masters. He was also linked in friendship with various fellow students: François de Connan, François Daniel, and finally Nicolas Duchemin.

In Orléans he followed avidly the course of Pierre de l'Estoile, without doubt one of the greatest French specialists of his time. He was a conscientious churchman, respectful of tradition, and in 1528 he participated in the Council

60. OC 31, col. 22, Commentaire des psaumes (1577), preface.
61. J. Carbonnier, "Le calvinisme entre la fascination et la nostalgie de la loi," Études Théologiques et Religieuses 64 (1990): 507-17.
62. Millet, p. 39.

of Sens. Convoked at the Church of the Grands-Augustins in Paris, this assembly united the three bishoprics of Paris, Meaux, and Orléans in an agreement to fight it out with their local Lutherans, under the leadership of Cardinal Du Prat. No matter. Calvin, still little involved in this, greeted in L'Estoile one of his foremost teachers. His devotion to learning was intense. One may easily imagine the student, hunched over his books to a late hour. One may no less imagine Calvin the next morning, still lying in bed to run over again the lectures which he strove interminably to engrave on his memory.[63]

The Frenchman L'Estoile permanently impressed the Noyonnais during his stay in Orléans. Much more complex were the relations Calvin had in Bourges with the famous Italian Alciati. In company with Nicolas Duchemin, a dozen years his junior, and his fellow student François Daniel, Calvin took the road to Bourges in 1529, drawn by the reputation of the new law professor. Andrea Alciati (1492-1550) was a native of the Milan district. Established in Avignon in 1518, this jurist was summoned ten years later by Francis I to the academy of Bourges. Big, fat, and heavy, endowed with a large appetite, this man, who was called venal, must have also possessed a clear sense of his own value. His arrival at Bourges in April 1529 was followed after a few months by a students' strike. Well versed in classical Latin, the professor nevertheless rejected that restored language into which the French plunged with delight: he detected in it the affectations of a borrowed Ciceronianism. He did not lack wit, though, and he encouraged the recourse to literature for the understanding of the law. Energetically opposed, he did not fail to justify himself: "There are people who reproach me for the excessive conciseness of my style and demand abundance. I answer them that I strive deliberately for the former; indeed, I regularly laugh at those who write otherwise. . . . With the sole exception of Cicero, in whose work one commends the ideas as well as the expression, it seems to me that all the authors would have been better advised to strive for conciseness."[64]

Here again we are reduced to proposing hypotheses. It is tempting to think that Calvin, the friend of brevity, did not remain deaf to this type of argument. To all appearances he should have learned from the humanist Guillaume Budé his sense of erudition and from Alciati his unembellished style. It would be arbitrary to compare the law further with literature. On the other hand, a revival of legal studies coincided at this period with the development of humanist studies. Losing in part its technical character, the law, in the sixteenth century, became a "branch of the *studia humanitatis*."[65] The connection with literature,

63. Doumergue, 1:130, in his description of Calvin is probably accurate.
64. Millet, p. 53.
65. M. Ducos, "Les juristes," in *Prosateurs latins en France au xvie siècle*, 2 vols. (Paris: PUPS, 1987-88), 1:670ff.

the passion for grammar, and the interest in philology and history are traits of Alciati's teaching that may have influenced Calvin's later choices. Otherwise Calvin revealed mixed feelings about the Italian. He especially resented his disdain for France and for Pierre de l'Estoile, his former master. In March 1531 Calvin was in Paris, where he supervised the printing of his friend Nicolas Duchemin's *Antapologia*. This fellow student undertook the public defense of their good master L'Estoile, savagely attacked by Alciati in an anonymous *Apologia* which emphasized the laborious character of French education. Out of fidelity to his professor, and undoubtedly also out of national solidarity, Calvin unhesitatingly associated his name with this university polemic by writing a preface to the work. L'Estoile, he says in substance, has better things to do than respond to insignificant attacks.[66] This "respectful and fervent attachment" to L'Estoile shows plainly that the Calvin of 1531 had not yet embraced the principles of the Reformation.[67]

If Calvin the theologian preserved the soul of a lawyer while speaking of God and man, this is precisely because in the sixteenth century the law had seized a position in the humanist pantheon alongside grammar. Also at Bourges, the German Hellenist Melchior Wolmar (born in 1496) transmitted to him his passion for Greek letters. It is more difficult, however, to attribute to him a precise spiritual role, despite his Lutheran ideas. Calvin without doubt remained for the time being a young humanist, not at all attached as yet to the Reformation. It is indeed possible that he delivered his first sermons at Lignières, in the region of Bourges, but this would not have been anything unusual for a tonsured young man, the titulary of an ecclesiastical benefice. In any case, it implied no adherence to Lutheran ideas.[68] Calvin would, however, dedicate his commentary on Saint Paul's Second Epistle to the Corinthians to his old master Wolmar:

> I remember with what affection you maintained and reinforced the beginnings of my long friendship with you; how you were ready frankly to employ yourself and your power for me when you thought the occasion presented itself for showing your love for me; how you offered your influence to advance me, if the vocation to which I was then attached had not prevented me from accepting it. But there is nothing I have found as pleasant as the remembrance of that first time, when, being sent by my father to learn the civil law, I

---

66. N. Duchemin, *Antapologia adversus Aurelii Albucii defensionem* (Paris: G. Morr, 1531). This preface was Calvin's first published work (*OC* 10, col. 785).

67. A. Ganoczy, *Le jeune Calvin. Genèse et évolution de sa vocation réformatrice* (Wiesbaden: F. Steiner, 1966), p. 47. See also Q. Breen, *John Calvin: A Study in French Humanism* (Grand Rapids: Eerdmans, 1931), pp. 52-60.

68. Ganoczy, p. 54.

combined, having you for conductor and master, with the study of law that of Greek letters, which you were then teaching with great praise.[69]

Wolmar had been providentially placed by God in Calvin's road. He owed to him, not his spiritual conversion, but the love for Greek letters that would later serve his plans of reform. Calvin's fortune, however, was deflected by the difficulties of every sort that assailed his father. In the spring of 1531 the young man was in Noyon when his father fell gravely ill. Girard Cauvin passed away in a state of excommunication on May 26 at the age of seventy-seven.

Could Calvin still work for this church? In default of taking up the priesthood, could he think of following his father's course, putting his talents as a lawyer at the service of the clergy? This is unlikely. Certainly no knowledge seeps through to us of the silent pain, indeed the revolt of Calvin. One of the rare testimonies to his spiritual life appears in a letter of June 23 addressed to François Daniel. He had paid a visit to his friend's young sister while she was preparing to pronounce her vows in a nunnery. He did not discourage her from her religious commitment, but simply warned her not to trust her own strength.[70] Is this a veiled commentary on the conventual life and monastic commitments? Hardly. In any case, Calvin seems hardly more critical than many of his contemporary humanists, quick to repeat Erasmus's aphorism *Monachatus non est pietas* ("Monkhood is not the same as piety"). Still, in December someone proposed to obtain for the young man a post as judge in an officiality in Picardy.[71] Who knows? Calvin might have become one of those conservative church judges, thinking between two tedious ecclesiastical cases about increasing his provincial patrimony. But this would have been a great pity.

69. Calvin, *Commentaires sur le Nouveau Testament,* 3:517, preface to the *Commentaire de la seconde Épître aux Corinthiens,* dedicated to Melchior Wolmar, dated August 1, 1540.

70. *OC* 10, 2, col. 10. This same letter is sometimes dated two years later, in 1533.

71. *OC* 10, 2, col. 11, letter of F. Daniel, December 27, 1531. François Daniel had been Calvin's fellow student in Orléans.

CHAPTER 2

Dwarfs Perched
on the Shoulders of Giants

We are dwarfs perched on the shoulders of giants. Thus we see more things than they did and farther than they did, not because our sight is sharper or our height greater, but because they lift us into the sky and raise us up by means of their gigantic stature.

BERNARD OF CHARTRES, TWELFTH CENTURY

Was Calvin a child of the Middle Ages? His early childhood, at any rate, was in a universe still medieval. Scattered thinly through the works of his adult years, various autobiographical fragments show that Calvin, in that twilight zone of infancy, indeed participated in religious practices that he would later judge idolatrous. To reform is first to reform oneself. Among many sharp remarks about the miraculously preserved holy foreskins and drops of milk of the Virgin Mary, the mature Calvin allows this avowal to seep through: "Saint Anne, mother of the Virgin Mary, has one of her bodies at Apt in Provence, the other at Notre-Dame-de-l'Ile, in Lyon. Besides this she has one head at Trier, another at Düren in Jülich, and another in Thuringia in a town named for her. I omit those fragments which are found in more than a hundred places; and among others I remember that I kissed one part at the Abbey of Ourscamp near Noyon, where there was a great feast in its honor."[1]

1. J. Calvin, *Traité des reliques* (1543), in *La vraie piété*, ed. I. Backus and C. Chimelli (Geneva: Labor et Fides, 1986), p. 193. The Abbey of Ourscamp, of the order of Clairvaux,

But the young Calvin was shaped by childhood piety and feminine devotion, over which hangs the shadow of a mother lost too early. Elsewhere, again, Calvin acknowledges having been immersed in the "deep quagmire" of error, before his "conversion" — to which we will return. The young Calvin, like many of his contemporaries, must have sacrificed at first to the "superstitions of the papacy."[2]

That Calvin broke with the Middle Ages appears clear. But this does not imply that the Middle Ages broke with him. We must do away, as Lucien Febvre has already exhorted us, with the idea of a "Middle Ages that was infantile, stagnant, anonymous and, so to speak, all black and white,"[3] which gave way, compelled by the spirit of history, to the first glow of the Renaissance. No, Calvin was the restless heir of that singular medieval autumn which pursued him, and which he rejected with all the more energy because he belonged to a past too close to be entirely overthrown.

How can we say something new with old words? How should we define this period, the "humanist" or "Renaissance" sixteenth century? Neither "Renaissance," nor "humanism," nor even "Reform" or "Reformation" is entirely satisfactory, at least if it is given an exclusive meaning. The singular term "Renaissance," in its restricted sense, risks offending the feelings of the medievalists, who will not fail to remark that the theme of rebirth itself is very old. Disputed by some,[4] the term "Carolingian Renaissance" sufficiently demonstrates the wide use of a concept that is not applied exclusively to the sixteenth century, but can rightly be extrapolated to other periods. From the twelfth century on, one sees various intellectuals claiming the label of moderns, *moderni.*[5] "Humanism" incurs the same reproach; it is at the same time "a mirror and a snare."[6] Neither a concern with humanity nor a love for Greek and Latin texts was a creation of the sixteenth century. The adages "There is no authority other than the truth demonstrated by reason" and "This world was made for man" are not the work of a reborn sixteenth century, still less of the

---

dated back to the thirteenth century. É. Doumergue described its picturesque ruins in his work *Jean Calvin. Les hommes et les choses de son temps,* 7 vols. (Lausanne: G. Bridel, 1899-1917), 1:41-42.

2. J. Calvin, *Commentaire des Psaumes, Opera Calvini* (hereafter cited as *OC*) 31, col. 22, preface dated August 10, 1557.

3. L. Febvre, *Michelet et la Renaissance* (Paris: Flammarion, 1992), p. 14.

4. J. Le Goff, *Les intellectuels au Moyen Âge* (Paris: Le Seuil, 1972), p. 12.

5. Le Goff, pp. 14ff.

6. M.-M. de La Garanderie, *Christianisme et lettres profanes (1515-1535). Essai sur les mentalités des milieux intellectuels parisiens et sur la pensée de Guillaume Budé* (Lille: Atelier de reproduction des thèses, 1976), p. 3.

century of Enlightenment, burdened with progress. They go back to the Middle Ages, whose intellectual modernity has been forgotten.[7]

The third term of this semantic triad, "Reform," Catholic or Protestant, ergo the "Reformation" of the church, recalls the medieval ideal of *reformatio*. The term "reformed" is therefore not original with the Protestant churches; the earlier church used the concept in an essentially monastic sense. It meant reviving the spirit of the founders, "restoring the *ordo monasticus* in the splendor of its origin or of the 'golden age' of Cluny and of Saint Bernard."[8] The humanist reformers of the beginning of the sixteenth century remembered the *reformatio* of the thirteenth and fourteenth centuries and took it as their model. They were haunted by the grand theme of the "perfection of the church."[9] "At the beginning of the sixteenth century" there was a "meeting at the summit of clerics and laymen in a spirituality of monastic origin; those whom the breviary and the book of Hours, even membership in the same confraternity, had initiated into a common religious language were offered, to open their hearts, the same devout prayers and the same themes for meditation."[10]

The Council of Trent, which met from 1545 to 1563, condemned a certain number of abuses (accumulation of benefices, nepotism) and desired their "reformation." But here the term took on an essentially ecclesiastical meaning; it meant rationalizing and morally reforming the life of the clergy. The Protestant Reformation had a wider meaning: it implied that appeal to conversion and to Christian liberty that descended to all the faithful. On a monastic or at least clerical *reformatio*, Protestantism superimposed a lay Reformation.[11]

The sixteenth century, therefore, had a monopoly neither of humanism nor of the return to antiquity. Did it break with the past? Certainly. The Renaissance had an irreversible aspect; the nation-states in the political sphere and the religious Reformation shattered the universal norms of Latin Christendom. The vernacular languages — French, English, German — contested the reli-

---

7. La Garanderie, *Christianisme et lettres profanes (1515-1535)*, p. 59. The quotations are from Honorius of Autun.

8. J.-P. Massaut, *Josse Clichtove. L'humanisme et la réforme du clergé*, 2 vols. (Paris: Belles Lettres, 1968), 1:311.

9. N. Lemaitre, *Le Rouergue flamboyant. Clergé et paroisses du diocèse de Rodez (1417-1563)* (Paris: Le Cerf, 1988), pp. 65ff.

10. M. Venard, *Réforme protestante, Réforme catholique dans la province d'Avignon, xvie siècle* (Paris: Le Cerf, 1993), p. 245.

11. The tension between lay *reformatio* and monasticism preceded the Protestant Reformation. Humanism, or rather the humanists, as J.-P. Massaut notes, had varying relations with the monks. Humanism cannot be reduced to Erasmus. Humanism opposed to monasticism was countered at every step by another humanist current, represented by Clichtove, heir of the *devotio moderna* and of Gerson, who on the contrary exalted the monastic state. Massaut, pp. 438-39.

gious, juridical, and intellectual monopoly of Latin. At the end of this twentieth century, when Europe is reorganizing itself under our eyes, we have much to expect from the study of a reborn humanism.

This break from the past, however — dare we employ the often-debased word "progress" to speak of the sixteenth century? — can be maintained only on condition that we place it in a continuum. In his *General History of Protestantism,* Émile Léonard placed Luther in the lineage of Saint Bernard. Bernard of Clairvaux (1090-1153) thus was described as a "vigorous Reformer . . . , the only true predecessor of Luther."[12] The same remark has been made in Calvin's case.[13] And one can stress, more generally, how much the Reformers owed to a separation of knowledge from belief that found its origin in Duns Scotus (1266-1308) and above all in William of Ockham (1300?–1350?). Faith is not reducible to knowledge, and is above all not the same as knowledge. To them it was the ineffable and free gift of God. Would such a proposition, common to all the Reformers, have been imaginable without a previous crisis in the philosophy of knowledge? Was this irrationalism? Certainly not. But it entailed at least a limitation of the human capacity to see and understand the intentions of God. For Calvin, who already employed the metaphor, as later for Pascal, man was a "thinking reed."[14]

12. É. G. Léonard, *Histoire générale du protestantisme,* 3 vols. (Paris: PUF, 1961-64), 1:13.

13. A. N. S. Lane, "Calvin's Sources of Saint Bernard," *Archiv für Reformationsgeschichte* 67 (1976): 253-83. The author has minutely examined and weighed all the citations of Saint Bernard in Calvin's works. He concludes (p. 253) that "Bernard of Clairvaux was one of Calvin's favorite medieval writers," and points out that from 1539 to 1559 the different editions of the *Institution chrétienne* cited this author 41 times, mentioning all his major works. See also J. Boisset, "La Réforme et les Pères de l'Église: les références patristiques dans l'Institution de la religion chrétienne de J. Calvin," in *Migne et le renouveau des études patristiques. Actes du colloque de Saint-Flour (juillet 1975),* ed. A. Mandouze and J. Fouilheron (Paris: Beauchesne, 1985), p. 43. This author gives a count that differs, but still shows the importance of Saint Bernard, who is nevertheless far behind Saint Augustine: 204 references to Saint Augustine, 36 to Chrysostom, 29 to Ambrose, 24 to Jerome, 21 to Saint Bernard. Among the pagan authors, Plato comes first (18 mentions), ahead of Cicero (9) and Aristotle (8). Seneca comes far behind: 2 mentions. More recently, see C. Izard, "J. Calvin à l'écoute de saint Bernard," *Études Théologiques et Religieuses* 67 (1992): 19-41.

14. Calvin considered the metaphor too favorable to man in his *Institution de la religion chrétienne,* ed. J. Pannier, 4 vols. (Paris: Belles Lettres, 1961), I, chap. 2, "De la connaissance de l'homme," p. 96: "Although too much honor is still done to our capacities, in comparing them to a reed." The image seems to go back to antiquity.

Humanism: An Ambiguous Legacy

They had been greatly loved, the humanists; they were great ancestral figures. Without them, nothing that followed would have been possible. People were all the more vexed with Erasmus for his pride and, as Luther snorted, his "impiety." But was Erasmus, the grand diva of humanism, impious? Such foolishness was born of a vain polemic between the two men; "Du bist nicht fromm," exclaimed the former German monk, on reading the Dutchman. "You are not pious, Erasmus." The corridors of history still echo with this denunciation.

Like "Renaissance" and so many other terms we use today, the word "humanism" did not exist in the sixteenth century. It did not appear in its modern sense until 1877, to characterize the intellectuals of the Renaissance who were dedicated to restoring the ancient texts.[15] The humanists were devoted to the "humanities," those *"humaniores litterae"* that were recovering their interest in ancient languages and classical authors. "Humanism" preserves the semantic ambiguity and chronological imprecision of the term "Renaissance." What Renaissance? When did it occur? In one sense, one may trace humanism back to Petrarch and the Italian Trecento. The Renaissance, likewise, finds there one of its anchor points. Florence, Padua, Naples, Venice, Milan, Rome, not to mention Ferrara, Urbino, and Mantua — the entire Italian peninsula, in its infinite variety, must be evoked to give an account of an intellectual movement that transmitted to humanity the Mediterranean radiance of classical rhetoric and ancient politics.

To this solar radiance it is proper, however, to add the half-tints of northwestern Europe, of skies filled with water. It was in Flanders that the grand mystical aspiration of the *devotio moderna* was born; Ruysbroeck (1293-1381) and Gerhard Groote (1340-82) addressed themselves to a public of secular clerics and educated laymen, mindful of their interior lives and of salvation. One term sums up the piety of the time in its most exalted aspects: *imitatio*, imitation of Christ, imitation of Christ on the cross, carried to the point of delight in suffering. The picture evolved over time. The Christ of the Roman tympana was the judge of the last days, seated in majesty, but the Christ of the later Middle Ages drew nearer to man; he was incarnated in a crucified body, filled with pain. *Ecce homo*, "Behold the man!";[16] Pilate's phrase acquired an unaccustomed definition, becoming a virtual pictorial genre. Did not this bloody Christ, exposed to

15. The term *humanista*, however, dates from the end of the fifteenth century, referring to the specialists in literature and the "humanities."

16. John 19:5: "Then came Jesus forth, wearing the crown of thorns and the purple robe. And Pilate saith unto them, Behold the man!" The connections between the incarnation and this account have been noted by A. Boureau, *L'événement sans fin* (Paris: Belles Lettres, 1993).

view, testify at once to the abasement of God and the elevation of man? The obsession with death and with corpses, however, took its meaning only from hope. Ligier Richier, the sculptor of Lorraine who joined the Reform, undoubtedly offers us in the church of Saint-Étienne at Bar-le-Duc the most gripping illustration of this double mystery of death and resurrection. The work is late, from 1547, but it still belongs to the tradition of Nordic realism. A skeleton stands forward, its face gaunt, some shreds of muscles still attached to the bones. It turns its vacant gaze to the sky and offers its heart to God with a mute gesture.

But this imitation is also a spectacle, an exhibition, a mirror. Did not Christ offer to the faithful who contemplated and pitied him an inverse image of themselves, that of the innocent one sacrificed for their sins? Imitation becomes introspection, grief gives way to tenderness that emerges in the recollection of the fall of Jesus; the recitation of the rosary;[17] so many occasions offered to meditate on the five wounds of Christ, the seven words of Christ on the cross, the seven sorrows of the Virgin, not to mention the heart crowned with thorns, an adumbration of the Sacred Heart.[18] This deliberately sad piety, filled with pathos, also entered into the cult of the Virgin, which reinforced the Franciscan doctrine of her immaculate conception. "Sweet mistress of mercy," "mother of pity," "our advocate with God," Mary never ceased "to appease God's anger at the world." Her protective mantle gave birth to a proliferation of images, paralleling the popularity from 1350 to 1550 of the Pietà, the mother holding the body of her crucified son on her knees.[19] The Virgin who suffers is the one who protects; in her is an ambivalence that at once dilutes and strengthens the sad mystery of the cross.

The command to bear your cross was ancient; it went back to the Gospel and to the injunction to follow Christ step-by-step. It became a spiritual exercise in which Jesus, whose suffering and agony was recalled in the painted figure, suddenly became closer, more human. The ties produced by this identification made accessible the distant God whom one asked to be the confidant, almost the comrade, who would assist one at every turn. In return one dedi-

17. The rosary, from the sixteenth century on, assumed the recitation of three strings of beads, permitting meditation on the joyful mysteries, the sorrowful mysteries, and the glorious mysteries. Each recitation of the beads corresponded to one Credo, fifteen Paters, as many Gloria Patris, and 150 Aves. To find the total of the rosary, these were multiplied by three. The victory of Lepanto over the Turks in October 1571 was attributed to the rosary, as commemorated by the feast of Saint Rosaire beginning in 1573.

18. L. Febvre, *Au coeur religieux du xvie siècle* (Paris: SEVPEN, 1968), p. 29; P. Denis, *Le Christ étendard. L'Homme-Dieu au temps des réformes (1500-1565)* (Paris: Le Cerf, Jésus depuis Jésus, 1987), p. 44.

19. J. Delumeau, *Rassurer et protéger* (Paris: Fayard, 1989), pp. 261-89.

cated to him a carnal, exclusive passion which led the Englishwoman Margery Kempe to avoid entirely the caresses of her husband. When she set down her mystical experiences, about 1430, did not this Englishwoman display for Christ the exclusive compassion of a wife or a mother?[20]

The Imitation of Christ, attributed to Thomas à Kempis (†1471), is not an ordinary theological treatise. In it every Christian is invited to associate himself in an active dialogue with Jesus, the "well beloved," which leads to sainthood. Devotion to the cross takes a sense in which it is experienced by the believer, who is also called to associate himself with the sacrifice of Christ. Bear your cross, bear your cross in your turn, following the divine master: this is the strict ideal of this manual of practical holiness, which had a considerable success throughout Western Christendom. Under this ideal each Mass became a double oblation, an offering of the Son to the Father and an offering of the faithful to Jesus: "As I offered myself willingly to my Father for your sins, with arms extended on the cross and a naked body, reserving nothing and utterly immolating myself to appease God, so you should offer yourself to me every day in the sacrifice of the Mass, like a pure and holy Host, from the bottom of your heart and with all the strength of your soul."[21]

If the concept of the sacrifice of the Mass reappears in later Catholicism, the picture of salvation presented in the same text also anticipates predestination as it would later be theorized in Calvinism. "'It is I who should be praised in all my saints,' says Jesus, 'I who should be blessed above all and honored in every one of those whom I have thus elevated to glory and predestined, without any preceding merit on their part.'"

The combination of "antique culture, revealed and interpreted by Italy," with Nordic piety led to an unequaled deepening of Christianity.[22] The encounter of these two universes, the passion for antiquity and the devout life, emerged at the end of the fifteenth and the beginning of the sixteenth century in one man in particular, Erasmus of Rotterdam (1469?–1536). "More celebrated than understood,"[23] this man has not ceased to arouse passion; he is reproached for his taste for publicity, his careerist character, his ambition to endow Christianity with a new Saint Jerome.[24] That Desiderius Erasmus had an acute awareness of his own value goes without saying, and what was more natural than for him to take constant care to perfect his image? That a great man

20. *Le livre de Margery Kempe* (Paris: Le Cerf, 1989), preface by A. Vauchez, p. v.

21. *L'imitation de Jésus-Christ,* French translation by F. de Lamennais (Paris: Le Seuil, 1961), p. 225.

22. Venard, p. 249.

23. L. E. Halkin, *Érasme parmi nous* (Paris: Fayard, 1987), p. 9.

24. Lisa Jardine, *Erasmus, Man of Letters: The Construction of Charisma in Print* (Princeton: Princeton University Press, 1993), p. 4.

should play the role of a great man or a saint is in any case less objectionable than its opposite.

There is first the profile of Erasmus that Holbein left us in his magnificent portrait preserved in Basel: narrow lips, a sharp fold at the corner of the lips shadowing forth an impalpable smile, the eyes riveted to a pen that traces with care some words on paper. Despite this thoughtful immobility and the intense gaze that avoids our own, a curious impression of serenity rests on the face; one questions oneself about this enigmatic visage.

There also exists an Erasmus represented by a death's-head, angrily censored by the Spanish Inquisition. What a distance between the Erasmus who was offered a cardinal's hat in 1535 — which he refused, as others have the Legion of Honor — and the public enemy whose works were placed on the Index twenty years later! Between these two dates Western Christianity had been totally overturned; it had submitted to a confessional plurality that it still refused to admit, a plurality of which Calvin had been one of the most active creators. To be an Erasmian implied adherence to a project of internal reform of the church. But according to Calvin, this had ceased to be possible.

However, the rupture with humanism was not merely theological. It depended on other factors, admirably set forth recently by Robert Mandrou: What were these humanists, these reborn intellectuals who had ceased to be an order without exactly becoming a class?

> Difficult to place in our contemporary society, as the works of sociologists show, intellectuals are not easily classified even in the modern period. At the moment when the ecclesiastical institution broke up they ceased to pertain to an order, in the legal sense of the word, and thus escaped a relatively simple social definition. However, their activities and the needs of the trade they took up gave them a place apart in a world that traditionally located men and groups according to their activities, their birth, and the honors attached to these. When followed in their new careers and when seen frequently taking a commanding attitude, they give the impression of a sort of aristocracy.[25]

Erasmus and Luther were former clerics. Calvin, although no doubt tonsured at age twelve, never received ordination, let alone pastoral consecration.[26] Indeed, his characteristic principle was his total rejection of priesthood.

---

25. R. Mandrou, *Des humanistes aux hommes de science, xvie-xviie siècles* (Paris: Le Seuil, 1973), pp. 10-11.

26. His personal connections with clerical office were more accidental than deliberate: the ecclesiastical benefices of his childhood, and his university studies, which soon turned away from the priesthood.

Calvin was simply and entirely an intellectual, a man of knowledge rather than a holder of power. Or at least his power resided only in his knowledge and in the recognition his contemporaries accorded him.

But although changes largely overshadow continuities, Calvin remained, like so many other Reformers, a prodigal son of humanism. Christianity having split, would the republic of letters[27] succumb in turn? It was a curious solidarity, that of these intellectuals who passed from hyperbolic praise to denunciation as if to reassure themselves, wielding in turn the carrot of Christian love and the stick of anathema. Many of Calvin's friendships, and also of his enmities, are directly and astonishingly literary, connected with a thirst for communication and contact that curiously contradicts the apparent reserve of his personality. The tale of disappointed relationships fills pages and pages of correspondence. More and more supplanted, it is true, by recourse to national languages, the maintenance of Latin as a language of the elite aided this communication of spirits.

In his culture, in his origins, in his thought, Calvin was a humanist. He was a man of a generation whose heart beat in unison with the prodigious development of Greco-Latin philology. But this humanist legacy remained ambiguous; did not the admiration for antiquity lead to a Christianization of the ancients and a paganization of the Christians? From this standpoint "mythology furnished . . . the understanding of divine truth with tools, or more exactly with optical instruments. The theological enterprise therefore consisted in imposing on revealed principles a system of grand symbols drawn from the pagan stock and their literary and subconscious implications."[28] Thus, in a remarkable meditation on the saving cross, Guillaume Budé (1468-1540) came to compare Jesus with Hercules. The cross was "a sort of club of the celestial Hercules," triumphing over sin, itself assimilated to the "three terrible heads of Cerberus" and his "three mouths: lust, avarice and pride."[29]

---

27. The republic of letters, *republica letteraria;* the expression is attested in 1416 in a letter written in Florence by Leonardo Bruni. R. Morçay and A. Müller, *La Renaissance* (Paris: Del Duca, 1960), p. 21.

28. Marie-Madeleine de La Garanderie, "Le style de G. Budé et ses implications logiques et théologiques," in *L'Humanisme français au début de la Renaissance. Colloque international de Tours* (Paris: Vrin, 1973), p. 354.

29. Quoted from *De Transitu Hellenismi ad Christianismum* (1535), cited by M.-M. de La Garanderie, "Guillaume Budé," in *Prosateurs latins en France au xvie siècle*, 2 vols. (Paris: PUPS, 1987-88), 1:211.

The Renaissance

Except a man be born again,[30] *he cannot see the kingdom of God.*

JOHN 3:3

What then is the philosophy of Christ, which he himself calls a rebirth,
but the restoration of a nature created good?

ERASMUS, "EXHORTATION," *NEW TESTAMENT* (1516)[31]

Dead men are the best writers of our time. It is not rare even now to exhume from hidden drawers incomplete works or classes taught without result. Among these fortunate discoveries are the lectures of Lucien Febvre at the Collège de France between December 1942 and April 1943, which are like a great fountain of youth during the darkest hours of our history. There was indeed some reason, in those black years, for speaking of a "rebirth," or more precisely, remembering the title of the book which followed, for evoking *Michelet and the Renaissance.*[32]

The notions of the Middle Ages and the Renaissance define and exclude each other. One can say with Jean Delumeau that the terms "Middle Ages" and "Renaissance" are "united — and united in inexactness."[33] They are involved in the same sort of opinionated debate as the notions of "Revolution" and *"ancien régime"* for a later period. The Middle Ages assumes the Renaissance as the *ancien régime* does the Revolution. But is there not some risk in defining a period precisely by what it is not? Let us distrust these lapidary terms "Renaissance" and "Middle Ages," or at least keep in mind their relative and contingent character. What in fact was this *medium aevum,* this intermediary period, this period of latency or suspension which separated the peaks of antiquity from the glories of triumphant modernity? Almost in the manner of Victor Hugo, Febvre evokes the life in words, which "as soon as created fly with their own wings, pursue their fortune, recognize their destiny."[34] The question is, "When was the historical concept of the Renaissance born?"[35]

To a complex question there is a no less complex answer. Although

---

30. [Translator: It should be pointed out that the word *renaissance* in French means "rebirth." This should be borne in mind throughout this section.]

31. Erasmus, *Oeuvres choisies,* ed. J. Chomarat (Paris: Librairie Générale Française, Le Livre de Poche Classique, 1991), p. 455.

32. Febvre, *Michelet et la Renaissance.*

33. J. Delumeau, *La civilisation de la Renaissance* (Paris: Arthaud, 1967), p. 17.

34. Delumeau, *La civilisation de la Renaissance,* p. 25.

35. Delumeau, *La civilisation de la Renaissance,* pp. 31ff.

Michelet gave the word "Renaissance" its canonical character in the nineteenth century,[36] the metaphor preceded romanticism by several centuries. The idea of a Renaissance existed long before the sixteenth century. It was not the sixteenth century that created the Renaissance, but the Renaissance that created the sixteenth century. More recent works permit us to take the measure of the phenomenon: Petrarch (†1374) originated the division of time into three periods — the Roman Empire, the intermediate period, and the renewal.[37] The term *rinascità* is attested in Italian in 1550 in the work of the art historian Giorgio Vasari.[38] The sixteenth century was not content with exorcising the preceding centuries; "barbarity," "ignorance," "obscurity," like the adjectives "Gothic" and "dark," recurred inevitably to characterize the past age. The seventeenth century itself spoke of "entombed literature," as well as using the qualifications "rude," "coarse," or "rustic."

On the other hand, "Renaissance" gained ground. P. Richelet's *French Dictionary* (1680) spoke of a "renaissance of humane letters," and J. Joubert's French-Latin dictionary, in 1709, added "renaissance of humane letters and the fine arts." Across the Channel, Bolingbroke, in his philosophical works appearing in 1754, spoke of a "resurrection of letters."[39] But it was the nineteenth century that definitively fixed the term "Renaissance" in its present meaning. Besides Michelet, whose role was emphasized by Febvre, Jakob Burckhardt of Basel determined to reveal the principles of a Renaissance that found its highest expression in the Italy of the Quattrocento.[40] According to Burckhardt, this Italian fifteenth century was still permeated by an immemorial Italian aspiration that recalled the annals of ancient Rome. Burckhardt's Renaissance became a constant of European history. He defined under this head a first Carolingian Renaissance in the ninth century, even while stressing later centuries.

Renaissance, then, equals resurrection. The force of the metaphor grows from the soil of Christian culture. Erasmus is the proof. One must be reborn — born again — to enter the kingdom of God. Both antique and pagan, the Renaissance was spiritual. It was a first Age of Enlightenment, trusting in the capacities of reason. Were not the enlightened elite called to overcome the differences

36. The expression "the Renaissance" appeared in Michelet's course at the Collège de France about 1840, one century before the course taught by L. Febvre in the same place.

37. Jürgen Voss, *Das Mittelalter im Historischen Denken Frankreichs* (Munich: Wilhelm Fink, 1972), p. 24. See also the older work of Wallace K. Ferguson, *La Renaissance dans la pensée historique* (Paris: Payot, 1950).

38. P. Burke, introduction to Jacob Burckhardt, *The Civilization of the Renaissance in Italy* (Harmondsworth: Penguin, 1990), p. 11.

39. B. Cottret, *Bolingbroke. Exil et écriture au siècle des Lumières* (Paris: Klincksieck, 1992), 2:505-6.

40. *Die Kultur der Renaissance in Italien* (1860).

among men, or at least among Christians? In 1532 Rabelais allowed his enthusiasm to appear in this frequently cited passage of *Pantagruel:* "Today all disciplines are restored, the languages established: Greek, without which it is shameful for a person to call himself learned, Hebrew, Chaldean, Latin. . . . The world is full of learned people, of skilled teachers, of ample libraries, so that it is my view that neither in the time of Plato nor of Cicero nor of Papinian[41] were there such facilities for study as are seen today. . . . I see the brigands, the hangmen, the grooms today better taught than the doctors and preachers of my times."[42]

This famous statement of Gargantua to his son Pantagruel illustrates the spirit of the Renaissance. Undoubtedly it refers especially to the foundation by Francis I of the future Collège de France, where Greek and Hebrew were taught as a matter of course.[43] In particular, this passage contains a thousand notes of disdain for the still-recent times of darkness and unhappiness when the "Gothic calamity" had destroyed "all good literature."[44] On the other hand, God in his bounty had permitted a restoration of literature — although one may question whether it had reached the grooms. But no matter. The description recalls the wish formulated by Erasmus of seeing "the laborer, at the handle of his plow" singing "in his own tongue some verses of the mystical psalms" (*Paraphrase of Saint Matthew,* 1522).[45]

From Reform to Reformation

[The Reformation] was born everywhere of itself. Everywhere, in France, in Switzerland, it was native, a fruit of the soil and of differing circumstances that nevertheless yielded an identical fruit.

MICHELET[46]

41. Papinian (142-212), a Roman jurisconsult.
42. F. Rabelais, *Oeuvres complètes,* ed. P. Jourda, 2 vols. (Paris: Garnier, 1962), 1:259.
43. Such at least is the opinion of A. Lefranc, *Histoire du collège de France depuis ses origines jusqu'à la fin du premier Empire* (Paris: Hachette, 1893), p. 123.
44. "In fact, reference to antiquity for the men of the Renaissance was merely a ruse to express a certain number of discoveries and of protests against existing habits. They used the past to testify to their originality and their modernity, and they were caught in their own trap." J. Le Goff, comments in J. Huizinga, *L'automne du moyen âge* (Paris: Payot, 1977), p. xiv. [English title, *The Waning of the Middle Ages.*]
45. C. Longeon, ed., *Premiers combats pour la langue française* (Paris: Le Livre de Poche, 1989), p. 40. Erasmus's famous injunction is actually a paraphrase of John Chrysostom.
46. Michelet, *Histoire de France,* 12 vols. (Lausanne: Éditions Rencontre, 1965-66), 5:444.

Protestantism existed only by variation. That which for Bossuet became the very proof of its errors, the "variations of the Protestant churches," was the condition of its success. How to maintain the worship of the One in this diversity? Rather, how to maintain the worship of the One except in diversity? The Protestant Reformation is not explained by a history of ideas. It is not merely a history of transmission, of adoption, of movement through space. At least not entirely. Certainly, the Reformation was linked to the Book and to books. It claimed for itself the victory of printing. The book served as a new intermediary between man and God. It can be seen how the history of the book was a leaven for secularism, how its development, its reading, and the rising level of literacy displaced the ancient division between *oratores* and *laboratores,* those who prayed and those who worked. The book was also pluralist; it encouraged the formation of opinions, including public opinion. It created a new eagerness, a new thirst, a new need, a new desire. In its importance the revolution in media of the fifteenth and sixteenth centuries undoubtedly exceeded the impact produced by moving pictures, television, and satellite communication one after the other five centuries later.

The Protestant Reformation mastered printing; it laid claim unjustly to its exclusive use, indeed its authorship. Catholicism also employed the book. "Rome," a recent author notes maliciously, "was another Geneva."[47] The Protestant Reformation, however, remains identified with the Book and with books. The Englishman John Foxe pointed out in the sixteenth century: "We have great cause to give thanks to the high Providence of Almighty God for the excellent art of printing most happily of late found out and now commonly practiced everywhere, to the singular benefit of Christ's Church."[48]

Certain studies in their turn have insisted on the "anthropological significance of Protestantism," found in certain points: "the dominance of the written culture, the internalizing of a new rationality, the need for education as the double road to salvation and to success."[49] This is true, certainly, but does not this phenomenon extend far beyond the bounds of Protestantism? Or at least, is it not necessary to insist on the convergences that existed between the two Reformations, the Protestant and the Catholic? The development of education and of reading was not restricted to Protestantism. But it is true that the Protestant Reformation encouraged it greatly. The same argument applies to rationality.

47. Bruno Neveu, *L'Erreur et son juge* (Naples: Bibliopolis, 1993), p. 142.

48. Cited by B. Cottret, "Traducteurs et divulgateurs de la Réforme dans l'Angleterre henricienne, 1520-1535," *Revue d'Histoire Moderne et Contemporaine* 28 (1981): 466.

49. François Furet and Jacques Ozouf, *Lire et écrire* (Paris: Éditions de Minuit, 1977), p. 72.

The real mystery is elsewhere. How does one explain how the shattering of a common culture, that of medieval Christianity, was in turn accompanied by unity? In its diversity, in fact, the Protestant Reformation, or rather the Protestant Reformations, ended in common themes: rejection of purgatory, of the sacrifice of the Mass, and of the cult of saints; insistence on individual salvation; emphasis on grace and on faith; reading of the Bible. *Sola fide, sola gratia, sola Scriptura*. The Protestant Reformation, wherever encountered, is never either entirely the same or entirely different.

From Luther to Calvin

> In the year 1520 there appeared in the Duchy of Saxony in Germany a heretical doctor of theology of the Order of Saint Augustine named Martin Luther, who said many things against the power of the Pope and wrote lots of books, seeking to weaken it, and also against the ordinances and ceremonies of the church, saying that in many respects there were errors and abuses; and he wrote many books about this that were printed and published in all the cities of Germany and throughout the Kingdom of France.[50]

We live in a world of artless souls and of aseptic Christians; incense burns everywhere. Luther himself, who not long ago made Rome tremble, has acquired a reputation as a somewhat hotheaded monk, to whom some ecumenical Catholics would almost give a place in their devotions. The situation was entirely otherwise in the past. I have been told, for example, how in certain country districts of Europe it was the custom for farmers to call their pig Luther. This identification goes back to the sixteenth century. An anti-Lutheran prodigy occurred in northern Germany:

> In 1522, on the twelfth day of December, in the town of Freiberg it happened that a butcher on opening a dead cow found a monster in its belly, the picture of which was drawn and then shown publicly at that time through the town; which had the head of a large malformed man, with a large tonsure on the head, which tended toward white in color, and the rest of the body, in the shape of a cow, approached the shape of a pig, and the color of the skin was bay and dark, tending to red, with the tail of a pig, with a hood of doubled skin joining to the flesh of the neck. And it was kept for three days in the house of one Henry of Saxony; being dead, he afterwards had it dried; then

50. L. Lalanne, ed., *Journal d'un bourgeois de Paris sous le règne de François Ier* (Paris: Jules Renouard, 1854), p. 94.

he sent it to Frederick, Duke of Saxony, where it is now and can be seen any day.[51]

A monster, like a miracle, is a prodigy. But whereas the one reassures, the other never ceases to disturb. Both belong to a system of signs, beneficent or maleficent, from which mysterious correspondences can be read. "Renaissance men," one of the greatest specialists tells us, showed themselves "attentive to singularity, that is to that quality proper to each thing that is never either entirely the same or entirely different."[52]

Calvin belonged to the second generation of the Reformation. When he was born in 1509, Luther was about twenty-five.[53] Jean Cauvin was just emerging from childhood in 1517 when the Augustinian monk posted his Ninety-five Theses in Wittenberg. The German finally died in 1546, when the Frenchman still had eighteen years to live. They represented two generations, and also two temperaments: Luther, a man of overflowing charm and of driving fluency, sometimes to the point of harshness; Calvin, all cerebration, untiringly polishing his *Institutes* with the care of a lawyer. Thus, even in the seventeenth century, the Catholic Florimond de Raemond could not resist the temptation of facile comparison: "Their manners were as diverse as their opinions. Calvin was more regulated and composed than Luther, and showed from the beginning of his youth that he would not let himself be intoxicated by the pleasures of the flesh and the belly like Luther."[54] One might say in observing them that each already consciously adapted himself to a national image: Luther, the defender of German liberties, who addressed himself impetuously to the German nobility; Calvin, the pre-Cartesian *philosophe,* champion of the French language and of a classical analysis that was identified with clarity of enunciation. In 1914 the contrast between the two men unfortunately took on a sadly premonitory quality; Lutheranism became, for one of its historians, "as fundamentally German as Calvinism was French."[55]

The birth of the calf with a man's head assumed at the time a demonic character that immediately reflected on the person of Luther:

---

51. Lalanne, p. 95.

52. J. Céard, *La nature et les prodiges. L'insolite au xvie siècle en France* (Geneva: Droz, 1977), p. 487.

53. The date of Luther's birth is not known with certainty. The usual date given is 1483, at Eisleben, in Thuringia.

54. F. de Raemond, *L'histoire de la naissance de l'hérésie* (1605; Rouen: P. de La Motte, 1629), bk. 7, chap. 10, "Comparaison de Luther et de Calvin," p. 884.

55. L. Reynaud, *Histoire générale de l'influence française en Allemagne* (Paris: Hachette, 1914), p. 157. Cited by Febvre, *Au coeur religieux,* p. 5.

When Luther joined the house
Of the Augustinians in a human semblance
His face was without consumption,
Which he polluted through his arrogance,
As this monster shows its presence
To all men, difficult and strange,
Since he is thrown into the mire by vice.
Although knowing, wise and learned,
Saxons are harder than stones,
Who suppose this monster is in vain.
They will not give up or abandon their old sins,
Much as they feel the hand of the High Judge.[56]

Toward a Comparative History of the Reformations

"Protestantism: an unheralded birth" — we take this description from a recent author.[57] It is proper to distrust the trap of words, and in particular to avoid the identification of reform with Protestantism. The Reformation was above all an event: Luther's posting of his Ninety-five Theses on All Saints' Eve in 1517, the installation of Calvin in Geneva or in Strasbourg. Protestantism is a confession, or rather a body of confessions, connected by an undeniable kinship. That these confessions stem from this event seems indisputable; Protestantism should periodically renew itself by invoking the spirit of reform. Did not the Reformed church adopt the device, *Ecclesia reformata, semper reformanda?* This describes a reformed church, ideally called to reform itself without ceasing.

Protestantism and Reformation are therefore connected by a dialectical process. Historically, therefore, we must break this connection and question ourselves about the evidence we have taken as certain. Was Protestantism really the same thing as reform? Did reform inevitably require Protestantism?

The term "Protestant" certainly appeared early, in the opposition to Charles V in Germany in 1529. To protest was at the same time to affirm one's faith and contest the authority of the emperor. The term, however, imposed itself only with difficulty in France; although it occurred, the discourse of the classical period seems to have ignored it in practice, preferring usually to speak of "reformed religion" or "religion claiming to be reformed," of "Reformation,"

---

56. Lalanne, pp. 95-96. [Translator: This is doggerel verse in French.]

57. H. Bost, "Protestantisme: une naissance sans faire-part," *Études Théologiques et Religieuses* 67 (1992): 359-73. I have borrowed from this fine article part of its argument.

or of "Calvinism."[58] Its use by Bossuet also demonstrated the negative connotation of the term.[59]

The passage from Reform to Protestantism supposes therefore, if we may be permitted the neologism, a process of "confessionalization." This term exists in German. We propose, following Thierry Wanegffelen, to adopt it in French, distinguishing "confessional construction," which refers to the relations among the different confessions, from "confessionalization" proper, directed toward the faithful.[60]

Therefore we are now better able to take a general survey of Europe in the sixteenth century, onto which Calvin imposed his reflections and his actions. He was a contemporary of the Reformation, but he was located at the pivotal moment when the reforming event in its turn gave birth to a confession. Moreover, within the French-speaking area he would be the principal agent of this confessionalization. Calvinism did not proceed from Calvin's personal will or any wish of his to create a school or a movement of thought. No, the term, negative to begin with, was applied to that system which an intellectual of the first rank knew how to impose on still-confused tendencies. Reform in French countries became "despite Calvin, Calvinism."[61] Or again, "Calvin was not a meteor who suddenly invented Reformed Protestantism."[62] Within what space, then, and in what temporal context did he do his work?

A spiritual phenomenon, the Protestant Reformation did not proceed from the abuses of the church alone. It was not simply a rejection of the corruption that lies in wait for and seizes all human institutions. As Lucien Febvre de-

58. Bost, p. 363.

59. Bossuet, *Histoire des variations des Églises protestantes,* 2 vols. (1688; Paris: Garnier, n.d.).

60. T. Wanegffelen, "Les chrétiens face aux Églises dans l'Europe moderne," *Nouvelle Revue du Seizième Siècle* 11 (1993): 37-53. The author distinguishes two German terms usually rendered in French by the one word "confessionalization": *Konfessionsbildung* and *Konfessionalisierung*. The first term was invented in the 1960s by Ernst Walter Zeeden and refers to the "fragmentation" of Western Christianity of the Middle Ages into "confessions" (p. 39). The second, which appeared during the years 1970-80, describes "ecclesiastical norms" imposed "from above" on the faithful. Wanegffelen proposes to reserve "confessionalization" for the second term, while using "confessional construction" for the first case. I think it would also be possible to use "acculturation" to render *Konfessionalisierung*. Confessional construction itself reflects the medieval continuity within the rival contemporary churches.

61. Ferdinand Buisson, *Sébastien Castellion. Sa vie et son oeuvre (1515-1563)* (Paris: Hachette, 1892), 1:205.

62. O. Millet, "Les Églises réformées," in *Histoire du christianisme des origines à nos jours,* vol. 8, ed. J.-M. Mayeur, C. Piétri, André Vauchez, and M. Venard, 14 vols. (Paris: Desclée, 1992), p. 58.

clared in beautiful and bold pages, it is necessary to assign other causes to the Reformation "than the disorders of Epicurean canons or the temperamental excesses of the nuns of Poissy." In conclusion, what the clergy were reproached for was "not living badly, but believing badly."[63] Certainly, anticlericalism plays an incontestable role in Reformed thought. For the chaste Calvin it was invariably accompanied by the mention of sexual irregularities, the use of the term "vile whoremongers" for the clergy, or the recalling by indirect references of the filthy practices in the "cloisters, cells, and passages of monasteries," explaining that everyone knew what he was talking about.[64]

The first outbreak of the Protestant Reformation was indisputably German. On October 31, 1517, Brother Martin posted his Ninety-five Theses against indulgences. On January 3, 1521, the hotheaded Luther was declared anathema. He died in 1546, and less than ten years later, in September 1555, the Peace of Augsburg ratified the existence of rival Christian confessions in the Holy Roman Empire, Catholicism and Lutheran evangelism. In each state of the German mosaic, the subjects were supposed to submit to the religion of their prince or to emigrate.[65]

In Zürich Ulrich Zwingli also led a reform campaign, like Bucer in Strasbourg. England, for its part, displayed great originality; the Protestant Reformation extended over three centuries. In the 1530s the political rupture with Rome overshadowed all other considerations.

The case of France was radically distinct from the German or English one. The Peace of Augsburg ratified a segregation of Catholics and Protestants, who in theory were each confined to their respective states. In England the problem did not appear, since the religion of the king outweighed all other considerations — despite a Catholic revolt, harshly repressed, in the north of the country in 1536-37.[66] The French model led to a direct confrontation between Reformed Huguenots and papists, from which in the second half of the century the "wars of religion" were born.[67]

---

63. Febvre, *Au coeur religieux*, pp. 20-22.

64. J. Calvin, *Des scandales*, ed. O. Fatio (Geneva: Droz, 1984), p. 205.

65. This is the famous principle *cujus regio, ejus religio:* the religion of the prince is the religion of the state.

66. The revolt of Lincolnshire in October 1536 and especially the "Pilgrimage of Grace" during January-February 1537 in the northwest. See B. Cottret, E. Cruickshanks, and C. Giry-Deloison, *Histoire des îles britanniques, xvie-xviiie siècles* (Paris: Nathan, 1994), p. 48. Among the most stimulating reinterpretations of the Reformation across the Channel are R. Whiting, *The Blind Devotion of the People: Popular Religion and the English Reformation* (Cambridge: Cambridge University Press, 1989), and C. Haigh, *English Reformations: Religion, Politics, and Society under the Tudors* (Oxford: Clarendon Press, 1993).

67. Wanegffelen, "Les chrétiens face aux Églises," p. 46.

But along with this first wave of reform, called "magisterial," modern history recognizes the existence of a "radical Reformation," in which social aspirations were mixed with apocalyptic expectations.[68] Luther, Calvin, and more generally all adherents of the moderate Reformation avoided like the plague all these inspired tendencies, in which they saw the germs of social insubordination and of religious fanaticism; Calvin spoke of "fanciful" people.

Monsieur François — Who Is Entirely French

France will one day be named Francis [François];
Frenchmen [français] are diligent servants of their Francis;
Therefore this country of France to Francis
Was dedicated . . .

FRANÇOIS TISSARD, BEFORE 1507[69]

The Renaissance is incarnated for us in one monarch, Francis I, "François, roi des François," as people were pleased to phrase it in poetry. This play on words reappeared constantly. Even before the beginning of the reign an assembly of notables was held in 1506 at Le Plessis-lès-Tours. It concerned permission for the marriage of Francis, duke of Valois, with Claude of France, already promised to Charles of Austria, the future Charles V. In his speech of May 14, the canon Thomas Bricot addressed himself in these terms to Louis XII: "Your majesty, we have come here at your good pleasure to make a request of you for the general good of your kingdom, which is that your very humble subjects ask that it may please you to give Madame your only daughter in marriage to Monsieur Francis [François] here present, who is entirely French [français]." A few years later the humanist Guillaume Budé repeated the formula in a letter inviting Erasmus to Paris (February 5, 1517).[70]

---

68. G. H. Williams, *The Radical Reformation* (Kirksville, Mo., 1992).

69. Manuscript dedication of a Latin translation of Euripides, cited by A.-M. Lecoq, *François Ier imaginaire. Symbolique et politique à l'aube de la Renaissance française* (Paris: Macula, Art et histoire, 1987), p. 66. On royal symbolism see also F. Joukovsky, "Humain et Sacré dans la galerie de François Ier," *Nouvelle Revue du Seizième Siècle* 5 (1987): 5-23.

70. J. Garrisson, *Royaume, Renaissance et Réforme (1483-1559)* (Paris: Le Seuil, 1991), p. 68: "Rex hic est non modo Francus, quod ipsum per se amplium est, sed etiam Franciscus" [This king is not only a Frank, which is already important in itself, but also Francis (by name)]. The "only daughter" in this passage is Claude of France, sister of Renée, summoned to marry the future duke of Ferrara. It therefore does not mean the king's only daughter, but the only one of an age to marry.

Francis I succeeded Louis XII on Monday, January 1, 1515; his joyful coronation took place on the twenty-fifth, the feast of Saint Paul. Everything was providentially combined: the first day of the week, the first month of the year, the first day of the year, without counting the additional accident (but was it an accident?) that Francis was also the first of the name. The omens accumulated and converged; this reign would be that of unity. François, "king of the *françois*," was the chosen of God: "Along with the prerogative of bearing the first name of King, you were made king the first day of the year, the first day of the month, the first day of the week."[71]

In January 1515, then, Francis I came to power, "twenty years old . . . , king of the most beautiful kingdom in the world, as the Venetian ambassadors affirmed. Although the sovereign was still very young, the traits of his character already revealed themselves. The young prince brought up to be king understood himself as such, different from others, but he had, like many men of the Renaissance, a taste for luxury, for display, for glitter." And above all he showed himself "animated by the extraordinary joy in living proper to that gluttonous generation in which Rabelais accompanied Erasmus."[72]

Born in 1509, during the last years of the reign of Louis XII, "father of his people," young John Calvin was the contemporary of Francis I. And without doubt he hoped a Renaissance of letters would coincide with a Reformation of the church. Might the king of France not be the agent, designated by God, for this renewal? Francis I died in 1547, and the reign of his successor, Henry II, is generally depicted in more somber colors. The picture of a king is not a neutral thing; one always tries to give him the coloration of his period. Thus the comparison of Francis I and Henry II becomes in the hands of their historians that of two epochs: "There is much less in the second: less a prince of the Renaissance, less charismatic, less sensitive to arts and letters; on the other hand, more withdrawn, colder, more somber, perhaps because of a lack of tenderness in his infancy."[73]

But Francis appeared destined to a happy end: "The play on words on the very name of the king, Francis, that identified him personally with the kingdom . . . and which decked him with the virtues traditionally attributed to his subjects, 'frankness,' courage, added equivocation to misunderstanding. For this omen of the name could also be understood by naïve souls as a providential guarantee of the young king's attachment to those French customs that made the prince a 'good shepherd,' always acting according to the wishes and for the welfare of his people."[74]

71. Lecoq, p. 142. Speech by a representative of the University of Paris, March 1515.
72. Garrisson, p. 123.
73. Garrisson, p. 125.
74. M. Fumaroli, in preface to Lecoq, pp. 8-9.

The salamander prince, elect of God, or new Constantine — these are some of the epithets pointed out by Anne-Marie Lecoq which display the success of the young monarch. Should not such a king full of grace be compared to the "beloved" of the Song of Songs?[75] The "protégé of the archangels and the seraphim" was a Renaissance prince, protector of arts and letters, from whom all benefits were expected. What object could be more worthy of a king's attention than the reformation of the church?

The Concordat of Bologna endowed the king of France with extensive powers. This agreement, worked out with the papacy from December 1515 to August 1516, insistently emphasized the merits of the "most Christian" king and the privileged position of France, "oldest daughter of the church." Leo X granted Francis I the power to designate the holders of major benefices: bishoprics, abbacies, and priories. The text artfully deplored the fact that the elections of bishops, abbots, and priors, respectively by the chapters or by the assemblies of religious, had given rise to all sorts of abuses. As a precaution, the royal power would take away an undesirable temptation from the ecclesiastics, removing from them all occasion to sin through those incessant intrigues and trafficking in simoniacal influence that periodically disturbed the blessed and discreet souls of the men of the church. Monks and canons could henceforth devote themselves to holy prayer and study, leaving to the king the problem of filling vacant offices. The Holy See, on its part, affirmed its rights over the church of France at the expense of any conciliar authority. But was not this to ignore the Gallican liberties? The Faculty of Theology of Paris protested; the Parlement of Paris recoiled, and it did not register the concordat until compelled to do so in March 1518.

But important international obligations also weighed on the period. The country was constantly at war with the Hapsburgs, whether Charles V or his son Philip II. In 1521-26, then again in 1527-29, again in 1536-38, in 1542-44, and finally in 1551-59, Valois and Hapsburg collided, almost without respite.

The Protestant Reformation, a Revealer of Culture?

When one examines the grand theological themes of the Reformers, justification by faith, the role of the Word, the criticism of ecclesiastical abuses, one does not understand clearly the emotion aroused by "Protestantism" — if we may be permitted to use this overly-definite term. How could an internal religion and an ideal of doctrinal purity arouse entire populations, and provoke equally violent reactions in opposition? We agree with the analysis of a recent

75. Lecoq, *François Ier imaginaire*.

work: "[The religious polemics of the sixteenth century] concerned essential points of dogma: salvation, the place and significance of the sacraments, the legitimacy of pontifical power. . . . However, the debate about the veneration of saints always ultimately reemerged from behind the fundamental questions. . . . In the street, between Protestants and Catholics, the conflict very often arose over the cult of saints, as though on both sides it was felt to be the core of daily worship."[76]

And to continue: "It is also symptomatic that each Reformed advance was accompanied by an iconoclastic furor." Iconoclasm, the breaking of statues, interpreted as the destruction of idols, was a scandalous action that undeniably accompanied Protestant progress. It was not the work of the Reformers themselves. Calvin distrusted these savage manifestations: "God has never commanded the overthrow of idols, except to each one in his own house, and in public to those he has armed with authority."[77]

The problem was not only doctrinal. Protestantism provoked an anthropological rupture, it overthrew customs, it collided with profound convictions. And, in the first place, it collided with the link between the living and the dead, people's active intercession in favor of their dead, and in return the care the saints in heaven took of affairs here below. How can you accept, the Reformers were reproached, that "the souls of the living and the dead have nothing in common," that "they do not communicate at all with us and have forgotten all common affinity and society with us"?[78] Death, the essential moment of Christianization, had lent itself to a careful accounting, whose revenues were not negligible when Luther denounced the traffic in indulgences. This mercantile character and these abuses cannot by themselves explain the will to reform; the funeral practices of the end of the Middle Ages had an integrated character. One spoke "less of the moment of death than of the period of death," at the risk of uniting wake, funeral, and period of mourning, which antedated Christianity. "These ritual practices seemed to correspond to an idea of a passage to the hereafter that did not occur all at once but had its proper duration, and stages it was necessary to pass through."[79] Moreover, it could similarly be demonstrated that the choice of a sepulchre emphasized burial beside one's ancestors, making

---

76. J.-M. Sallmann, *Naples et les saints à l'âge baroque (1540-1750)* (Paris: PUF, 1994), p. 99.

77. *OC* 18, cols. 580-81, letter from Calvin to the church of Sauve, July 1561. See O. Christin, *Une révolution symbolique. L'iconoclasme huguenot et la reconstruction catholique* (Paris: Minuit, 1991), p. 117. Also S. Deyon and A. Lottin, *Les "casseurs" de l'été 1566. L'iconoclasme dans le Nord* (Paris: Hachette, 1981).

78. J. Sadoleto, *Épître* (1539), in Backus and Chimelli, p. 75.

79. J. Chiffoleau, "Pratiques funéraires et images de la mort à Marseille, en Avignon et dans le comtat venaissin (vers 1280-vers 1350)," *Cahiers de Fanjeaux* 11, p. 277.

lineage more important than marriage.[80] The invention of purgatory derived from the same fundamental need.[81]

Protestantism is a religion of discontinuity; between man and God it places only one mediator, Jesus Christ. Time itself, like space, became henceforth homogeneous, linear, reduced to fluidity, without those natural landmarks provided by a miraculous fountain or by the celebration of the feasts of saints. Pilgrimage was the established form of a piety that closely associated walking with remembrance. Why would Calvin basically condemn Catholicism? Because of its "paganism," the cult of saints, the sacrificial ritual of its eucharistic celebrations, but also its sensuality.

That which was feared, that which was dreaded, that which was abhorred was sacrilege, the impious deed that would excite the anger of God against men. "Orthodox anguish at the profanation of sacred space" and "the simultaneous collective violence of purification and of imploring the divine pardon" have been rightly emphasized.[82] The most elementary form of anti-Protestantism was nourished by this apprehension; it fell in with an old obsession that preceded the Reformation itself. But the presence of a rival Christian confession revived the stories of hosts that bled and of statues that moved. A silent disquiet, an ancestral fear centered on the consecrated species. Thus, in 1516:

> It happened in the town of Poitiers that a fool caused the precious blood of Our Lord to fall on the corporals (they being on the altar) while a priest sang the Mass; and this was after the consecration, when the said priest raised the chalice, and the wine consecrated was white; on which a beautiful miracle occurred, for as soon as it fell on the sacred corporals, it became red; and it was immediately collected with great diligence and reverence by the priests. And a reliquary was made for its adoration. And the malefactor was condemned to be enclosed between two walls without being killed, since he was insane, and he was told he would never leave there and would eat only bread and drink only water.[83]

The incident does not visibly assume any precise ideological outline. The poor wretch, author of the sacrilege, is described to us as a simple "fool," perfectly "insane," whom we would judge irresponsible today. The fear of heretics

80. Chiffoleau, pp. 280ff.

81. J. Le Goff, *L'invention du Purgatoire* (Paris: NRF, 1981).

82. D. Crouzet, *La nuit de la Saint-Barthélemy. Un rêve perdu de la Renaissance* (Paris: Fayard, 1994), p. 18.

83. Lalanne, p. 38.

became more defined during the 1520s. "Lutherans" were mentioned more and more, without the term having any precisely defined theological meaning. Francis I was detained as a prisoner by Charles V after the disaster of Pavia (February 1525), and at the instigation of Clement VII, who was disquieted by the proliferation of "blasphemies," or attacks on the veneration of saints, the opportunity was taken to increase the religious pressure on those believing wrongly (bull of May 17, 1525):

> Louise, mother of the king, etc. Since our Most Holy Father the Pope, desiring to extirpate, extinguish and abolish this miserable and damned sect and heresy of Luther and guard against and prevent its spread in this said kingdom, has appointed and deputed as commissioners certain of our very dear and well beloved counselors of the king, our said lord and son, in his Court of *Parlement* in Paris, and other good and notable personages, to inform themselves about, look into, and understand what is needed for the rebuking, correction, and punishment of those who have been or will be found stained and infected by this miserable sect. . . .
>
> We, for these reasons, who desire strongly and with all our heart such errors and heresies extinguished and abolished, knowing perfectly the goodwill that the king, our said lord and son, has in this matter, like a most Christian king, for the good and universal repose of all Christendom; wanting on our part above all things to set our hand to such a good, holy and salutary work so that it may have a clear and final effect, following the goodwill, desire, and wish of our said Holy Father and the will of the king, our said lord and son.[84]

There was a memorable session of parlement on December 31, 1527. In the name of the church of France, Cardinal Bourbon reminded the king of his filial sentiments toward His Holiness and the need to struggle against the "damnable and insupportable Lutheran sect." Francis I took the opportunity of calling his kingdom to witness the villainy of Charles V, who had kept him prisoner. No, Francis I did not intend to respect the clauses of the Treaty of Madrid extorted from him by force: renunciation of Italy, cession of Burgundy. And the king was reminded with pride, in the address of his loyal nobility, that he had been "born a gentleman" and not a "king."

Francis I did not have the temperament of a persecutor. He can be seen intervening for a long time, for example, to stop the proceedings against Louis de Berquin, finally burned in April 1529 while the king was away from

---

84. M. Isambert, ed., *Lettres patentes de la régente . . . relative aux poursuites à exercer contre les luthériens. Recueil des anciennes lois françaises* 12 (Paris: Belin-Leprieur, 1828), p. 231.

Paris.[85] The execution of this gentleman followed the first religious turning point of the reign, linked with the affair of the Rue des Rosiers.

An act of vandalism, perpetrated in the parish of Saint-Gervais, had incalculable consequences for Paris. During the night of Monday, June 1, the day after Pentecost, into Tuesday, June 2, 1528, an unknown person crept up to an image of Our Lady, on the wall of the house of Louis de Harlay, seigneur de Beaumont. The dwelling of this lawyer, a councillor of the city of Paris, was on the corner of the Rue des Rosiers and the Rue des Juifs. The scene took place exactly opposite a hidden door of the church of Petit-Saint-Antoine. The attackers struck numerous blows to the heads of the Madonna and child with a knife, decapitating them. The heads were then dashed to pieces on the stones, while the statue's canopy was dragged through the mud and trampled under foot. The identity of these "breakers of images" is not known.

The king, it is said, was so "enraged and upset" that he wept. For the next two days it was announced throughout the capital with loud blasts of a trumpet that a reward of a thousand gold ecus would be paid to whoever would provide information about the guilty person or persons. But this had no result, nor did the inquiry that followed.

The reaction of Francis I was in fact very sharp. A letter addressed from Fontainebleau to the Parisians, dated June 5, mentions the "scandalous event," which injured "God, our creator," his "glorious mother," and his saints.[86] But the following week processions began to be organized. On Tuesday, the ninth, the university organized its own expiatory procession:

> The rector . . . , accompanied by all the clergy of the university and the doctors, *licenciés*, bachelors, and masters of arts, and the students, with the masters of children under twelve, each with a lighted wax candle in his hands, all went in procession with great reverence to the churches of Saint-Gervais and of Sainte-Catherine du Val des Écoliers, as far as the place where the said image was, and the street was hung with cloth and a beautiful canopy hung above the image; also the four mendicant orders were there, from Saint-Martin-des-Champs and other churches, dressed in copes, singing with great honor and reverence, which was lovely to see.[87]

---

85. This case interested the young Romain Rolland, author of a learned article about it. "Le dernier procès de Louis de Berquin, 1527-1529," *Mélanges d'Archéologie et d'Histoire. École Française de Rome* 12 (1892): 314-25.

86. A. Tuetey, ed., *Registre des délibérations du bureau de la ville de Paris* (Paris: Imprimerie Nationale, 1886), 2:24.

87. Lalanne, p. 347.

But the main ceremonies were to coincide with Corpus Christi, beginning on June 11. The king was then seen to participate "very devoutly" in the solemn procession. This was intended to beg the forgiveness of the Most High and ask his blessing on the kingdom; the king thus lent himself willingly to an expiatory ritual that required him to carry "a torch of burning white wax, his head bare, in very great reverence." He was surrounded by clarions, trumpets, and oboes, which played beautifully. He was accompanied by a synod of representatives of the holy church and by his aristocratic entourage: "With him were the Cardinal of Lorraine and many prelates and great lords and all his gentlemen, each with a burning wax torch." These gentlemen cautiously advanced "to the place where the said image was, in very great honor and reverence." It was a beautiful and "devout" spectacle.[88]

It began again the next day:

Also, the next day, which was Friday, June 12, there were general processions of all the parish churches of Paris, in which were the four mendicant orders with all the clergy of the great church of Notre-Dame de Paris and of the Sainte-Chapelle du Palais, with banners, crosses and many holy relics, and they went to Sainte-Catherine du Val des Écoliers[89] in procession, very reverently, and in the said church were the king and all the nobility, lords and gentlemen, and the king heard Mass in the said church, and the said Mass having been heard, he went in procession, in good order, along with the processions mentioned above, his head being bare, carrying a candle of white wax in his hand, and many lords and all the gentlemen having candles in their hands; and there was the Bishop of Lisieux, the king's grand almoner, dressed in his pontifical robes, carrying a beautiful silver image which the king had had newly made, about two feet long, which was about the same length as the other and weighed, it was said, eight marks of silver.[90]

Friday, the day that recalled so strongly the passion of Christ and his blood shed for the redemption of men, marked the peak of the processions. The fault was not only expiated, it was repaired; a silver image, whose weight and magnificence amazed the onlookers, was carried in triumph. Jean Le Veneur, bishop of Lisieux, preceded the king:

88. Lalanne, p. 348.

89. This Augustinian priory was located until 1767 at the present corner of the Rue de Sévigné and the Rue Saint-Antoine.

90. Lalanne, p. 349.

Which bishop was before the king, and he carried the said image to the place and set it on the highest wooden step that had been made; then the king and he put it very humbly on the base where the other had been, bowing three times, the said bishop uttering beautiful prayers and praises to the glorious Virgin Mary and her image.

Then, this done, the trumpets, clarions, and oboes began to play very melodiously, and the king and the Cardinal of Lorraine presented their candles to the said image, and afterwards all the other lords and gentlemen of his court did the same; which candles were taken by the curé or vicar of the church of Saint-Gervais and carried away, and similarly the stone image of Our Lady was displayed in the parish church.[91]

The streets of the city were also richly adorned:

And it should be noted that the streets were very honorably draped, and over the said image was a large beautiful canopy of red silk, which had been provided from the house, but nevertheless [the king] sent his own of cloth of gold and silver to be hung under the other that was there, and he had his beautiful altar cloth of cloth of gold and embroidery hung on the wall to the right of the image, and it showed Saint Francis. And in the said procession were the court of *parlement*, the *prévôt* and *échevins* of the city, and the archers and crossbowmen.[92]

A few days later, on June 16, it was the Minims' turn to make their pilgrimage, followed on the seventeenth by the Hospital of the Quinze-Vingt.

As for the martyred statue, it was carried to Saint-Gervais, where it was said to have "often worked great miracles." In particular it seems to have served as a "sanctuary of respite," permitting children born dead to return to life long enough to receive baptism.[93] "It should be known that for several days after this, the said stone image, which was carried to the church of Saint-Gervais, often worked great miracles and restored two infants from death to life, and the people made many offerings and vows to it, and similarly to the silver image that was in the place where the stone one had been, at the corner of the aforesaid house."

Known as Notre-Dame de Souffrance, the statue continued to shape the

91. Lalanne, pp. 349-50. There is another description of this famous scene, accompanied by an excellent commentary, in T. Wanegffelen, *La France et les Français. xvi*[e]*-milieu xvii*[e] *siècles. La vie religieuse* (Gap: Ophrys, 1994), pp. 21-28.

92. Lalanne, p. 350.

93. Lalanne, p. 351. J. Gélis, *L'Arbre et le Fruit. La naissance dans l'Occident Moderne (xvi*[e]*-xix*[e] *siècle)* (Paris: Fayard, 1984); for "sanctuaries of respite," see pp. 509ff.

piety of the Parisians of the nineteenth century. An expiatory ritual was still celebrated at Saint-Gervais in that century on the Tuesday of Pentecost in memory of the attack in 1528. On the other hand, the silver image that once replaced it on the Rue des Rosiers was less fortunate; stolen in 1545, despite the grating that protected it, it was replaced by a wooden replica. Broken again by the heretics in 1551, it was finally carved in marble and ceremoniously offered by the bishop of Paris.

The affair of the Rue des Rosiers, although it caused a considerable stir, was not an isolated incident. Other accounts of the period mention similar events. "It was learned at the same time that in a village four or five leagues from Paris two men had been arrested who had broken another image of the Virgin at the request of a shepherd and who confessed that they had similarly broken to pieces several others, and that for every image that they broke they were given 100 sous."[94]

Rumors, fears, the disappearance of consensus are some effects of the Protestant phenomenon that dissolved the traditional social fabric. The Reformation, from four centuries' distance, acts as a powerful revealer of culture. It was not so much the idea of God that changed as the image of the world. The heavens and the earth became a great "deserted and neutral theater" from which Christian marvels were spontaneously excluded as idolatrous or magical.[95]

94. M. Félibien, *Histoire de la ville de Paris*, 5 vols. (Paris: Guillaume Desprez, 1725), 2:982.

95. A. Besançon, *L'image interdite. Une histoire intellectuelle de l'iconoclasme* (Paris: Fayard, 1994), p. 255.

CHAPTER 3

To Be Twenty-One in 1530

When men of spirit are born in our times . . . the ambition to become famous consumes them, and they become rivals in their haste to leave a name to posterity; they publish the fruits of their talents without reflection and without discretion.

CALVIN, *COMMENTARY ON SENECA*, 1532[1]

Calvin the reformer or Calvin the man of letters? Neither judge nor priest, Calvin seemed to center all his ambitions on the latter, at least until the need to choose became too strong. "The need to choose,"[2] which confronted his generation, applies perfectly to Calvin at the time of his entry into adult life. It explains his choices as an adult. What did it mean to be twenty-one in 1530? By a family decision Calvin had been led to renounce the priesthood forever; his studies in law had also interested him, but he nevertheless did not embark on a legal career. He dallied on his way, wandering into byroads; his sole, true passion in 1530 was the humanities. Calvin was eager to learn, to understand, to enrich his mind; Greek had opened infinite vistas to him, and he added to it the study of Hebrew. Would he then have been content with the basics, thanks to contact with François Vatable, if he had not renewed his studies later in Basel

---

1. F. L. Battles and A. M. Hugo, eds., *Calvin's Commentary on Seneca's "De Clementia"* (Leyden: Brill, 1969), preface, p. 4.

2. M. Venard, ed., *Le temps des confessions (1530–1620/30)*, in *Histoire du Christianisme des origines à nos jours*, vol. 8, ed. J.-M. Mayeur, C. Piétri, A. Vauchez, and M. Venard, 14 vols. (Paris: Desclée, 1992), introduction, p. 9.

and Strasbourg? We do not know exactly.[3] But it doesn't matter. Calvin was the man of a decade, of his decade, the 1530s, when he marched in step with his whole generation, avid for science, antiquity, and the restoration of literature.

Calvin moves, shifts, remains hard to grasp — like any twenty-year-old. The very transience of existence is a form of thought. At the death of his father in 1531 he returned to Bourges and Orléans, only to head once more to Paris. In October he settled in Chaillot, but in May 1532 he returned to Orléans for a year. His movements are hard to trace; he seems to have lived off lessons he gave on Seneca, particularly as a teacher at the Collège de Fortet in Paris. At the same time he followed the course of the Hellenist Pierre Danès, who taught in the precincts of the Collège de Cambrai, at the present site of the Collège de France. Above all, he labored on his first book, his commentary on Seneca's *De clementia*, which appeared in April 1532.

Troubles and Splendors of French Humanism

We presented philosophy to you as a poor wench who was to be married, and we begged you to give her a dowry. You promised us, with that natural and spontaneous bounty that is yours, that you would found a school, a nursery, so to speak, of savants, of renowned scholars.

GUILLAUME BUDÉ TO FRANCIS I, 1529[4]

Requested persistently by Guillaume Budé in the name of the "scientific community" of the age, did the foundation of the college of royal professors, ancestor of the Collège de France, mark a real turning point in Parisian intellectual life? In March 1530 the name "college," moreover, was deceptive, considering the modesty of its origins; the title "royal" was extended to certain scholars, without however granting them any particular buildings. The "royal professors" or "lecturers" quickly aroused the enmity of the Sorbonne, their rival. These scholars did not enjoy any premises of their own, and it was not until 1610 that the first stone of a building was laid.

In 1530 the college had only a few posts and was not an establishment. The courses were given in the different colleges by the royal lecturers, aided by assis-

---

3. F. Wendel, *Calvin, sources et évolution de sa pensée religieuse* (Geneva: Labor et Fides, 1985), pp. 11-12. See also A. Baumgartner, *Calvin hébraïsant et interprète de l'Ancien Testament* (Paris: Fischbacher, 1889), pp. 8 and 14ff.

4. G. Budé, *Commentarii linguae graecae* (1529), preface. Cited by A. Lefranc, *Histoire du collège de France depuis ses origines jusqu'à la fin du premier Empire* (Paris: Hachette, 1893), p. 103.

tants. Pierre Danès and J. Toussaint occupied chairs of Greek, and Hebrew was entrusted to François Vatable and Agathius Guidacerius and to Paul Paradis, who joined his first two colleagues in 1531; as for the teaching of Latin, it was provided from 1543 on by Barthélemy Latomus. Mathematics was entrusted to Oronce Fine. But Hebrew and Greek were the great innovations, allowing a true humanist program that would lead to a better knowledge of the sacred texts.

The old Sorbonne[5] took umbrage at this indirect attack on its theological monopoly; how long could one claim to teach ancient languages without admitting the repercussions this would have on sacred doctrine? Could the "Lutheran" heresy be contained? On April 30, 1530, the theological faculty condemned two propositions as untenable, with its eyes fixed on the "royal lecturers": "Holy Scripture cannot be well understood without Greek, Hebrew, and similar languages. . . . A preacher cannot explain the Epistles or the Gospel according to the truth without the said languages."[6]

The future Collège de France won the first set. The teaching of ancient languages, without the counterweight of dogma, disturbed the theologians. But their anathemas proved ineffective in the spring of 1530, and in January 1534 they began legal proceedings against the royal lecturers. How should this quarrel be interpreted? "The theologians did not find fault with the basic principle of teaching other ancient languages besides Latin. . . . They wanted to prohibit the lecturers from employing Greek or Hebrew texts from the Bible in their lectures."[7] The basis of the affair was the interpretation of Holy Scripture, which according to the Sorbonne belonged to the theologians and not the linguists. The royal judge rendered a Solomonic judgment: "The king . . . does not intend that such teaching of foreign literature should cause any damage . . . to the interpretation of holy Scripture received and approved by the universal church, which might occur if the interpreters of the Hebrew language wished to interpret the books of holy Scripture without being well grounded and instructed in the faculty of theology."[8]

The judge also insisted on the "mystical" sense of the text, which does not derive from mere grammar but from hermeneutics. It follows therefore that translation cannot be emancipated from the control of theology, which alone knows final purposes: "Which mystical sense and meaning cannot be understood and declared by anyone who wants to interpret holy letters unless he is

5. In a general sense, the custom of the Reformers was to use "the Sorbonne" to refer in a pejorative way to the faculty of theology.

6. Bibliotheque Nationale de France, Mss. Lat. 3381b, fol. 110. Cited by Lefranc, pp. 122-23.

7. J. K. Farge, *Le parti conservateur au xvi*ᵉ *siècle. Université et Parlement de Paris à l'époque de la Renaissance et de la Réforme* (Paris: Collège de France, 1992). Preface by M. Fumaroli, pp. 13-14.

8. Farge, p. 128.

educated in the faculty of theology. And if he has only knowledge of the Hebrew and Latin languages without the profound doctrines of theology, he might by his interpretation deviate from the translation made and received by the church, from which extraordinary injury might result."

The royal lecturers, however, did not admit defeat. Encouraged by royal moderation, in 1535 they organized "regular lectures on the Old and New Testaments." Should one therefore hail the "momentary victory of the humanists" in Paris at the beginning of the 1530s?[9] Possibly, but for how long?

Budé and his friends indeed knew how to promote their ideas with eloquence. The "alliance between the Crown and humanism," as Marc Fumaroli justly wrote,[10] preceded the true emergence of the Collège Royal.

Remembering 1530: French Evangelism

In 1530 Calvin's enthusiasm and vocation as a humanist still displayed no traits of the Reformer. They paralleled one of the most significant episodes in French culture, the foundation of the college of royal lecturers, the ancestor of the Collège de France. So much for the history of the period. But the biography of a man, the search for an individual "in his time," is inseparable from the larger picture. Religious and intellectual history, like political history, cannot do without the recounting and reconstruction of individual destinies.

Thus Calvin, even in his love for literature, was also formed by the views of his contemporaries. Possibly without his knowledge, his existence was influenced by the questions tirelessly posed by the men who surrounded him. Therefore we need to briefly reconstruct certain lives, to understand better the encounter that took place between humanism and salvation.

The religious Reformation, in its plurality, stemmed directly from a theology of salvation. By definition, salvation is individual in Christianity, or at least more individual than collective.[11] How does one describe, other than in a personal manner, the anguish of Martin Luther, this monk preoccupied with his salvation? "Only experience makes a theologian":[12] this 1531 aphorism of Luther's shows the importance of individual personal history in the project of

9. O. Millet, *Calvin et la dynamique de la Parole. Essai de rhétorique réformée* (Paris: H. Champion, 1992), p. 115.

10. Farge, p. 15.

11. For the importance of religious phenomena in the development of Western individualism, as compared with other societies, see Louis Dumont, *Essais sur l'individualisme. Une perspective anthropologique sur l'idéologie moderne* (Paris: Le Seuil, 1983), pp. 33ff.

12. "Sola experientia facit theologum." Cited by J. D. Causse, "Luther et l'angoisse de l'enfer," *Études Théologiques et Religieuses* 69 (1994): 516.

reform. Luther was not the founder of an empire, he was a monk in quest of salvation. His history "is in the first person singular."[13] Pierre Chaunu expressed it admirably, following Lucien Febvre: the Protestant split was not "centered on the church, but on salvation."[14]

It undoubtedly required some daring for Febvre to publish in 1928 a forthright book, which has already become a classic: *A Destiny: Martin Luther.*[15] The word was out: "destiny," that concept said to have been created by antiquity and revived by romanticism before being diluted by fortune-tellers, again had a meaning for serious history. Or rather, there was no history except that of men seen as individuals. Moreover, if we wish to reconstitute the intellectual atmosphere that surrounded Calvin's youth and development, again and again we find nothing but individuals. The picturesque here takes precedence over an ordered list; here, in living color, are Jean Vitrier, Briçonnet, Gérard Roussel, and Marguerite de Navarre, those exceptional personalities, true figureheads of a French evangelism from which Calvin would break free. Jean Vitrier was an independent, a precursor. Briçonnet and Marguerite de Navarre were two lodestones who acted as magnetic poles, attracting to themselves outstanding personalities, the Lefèvres, the Roussels, in search of enlightened protectors. All were interested in reform, certainly, but a "reformist" rather than "Reformed" reform, so to speak, a reform internal to the church that did not end in separation and would ward off a split. In short, Calvin's character will remain a mystery if one ignores all this evangelical movement, relatively hidden, that the young Noyonnais would end up challenging and accusing of being lukewarm.

Written around 1528, the *Farce of the Theologasters,*[16] attributed to Louis de Berquin, uses allegory to describe the religious situation of the time. The Text of the Bible and Faith are personified; they collide with the clergymen, Fratrez and Théologastres. Mercury, arrived from Germany, rejects the label of "Lutheran" applied to him: "No, not at all, I am a Christian."[17] Clément Marot exclaimed similarly in 1534:

> . . . I am not Lutherist,
> Or Zwinglian, still less Anabaptist;
> I belong to God through his son Jesus Christ.[18]

---

13. Causse, p. 517.

14. P. Chaunu, *Le temps des Réformes* (Paris: Fayard, 1975), p. 417.

15. L. Febvre, *Un destin: Martin Luther* (Paris: PUF, 1968), new edition with an afterword by Robert Mandrou.

16. *Farce des théologastres.*

17. F. Higman, *La diffusion de la Réforme en France* (Geneva: Labor et Fides, 1992), p. 40.

18. C. Marot, *L'adolescence clémentine,* ed. F. Lestringant (Paris: NRF, 1987), p. 127.

Jean Vitrier (ca. 1456–ca. 1500)

What claim to sanctity did this Franciscan of Saint-Omer have, who did not "walk barefoot," did not "sleep on the bare ground," and did not "live on bread and water"?[19] In place of uselessly mortifying himself and devoting himself to asceticism, Erasmus's Jean Vitrier truly listened to his neighbors. He was a clean, almost hygienic saint, who did not confuse the filth of the monasteries with spirituality, an open-air saint whom anyone could address without fear. A reader of Origen's words, to which he introduced Erasmus, this preacher taught a religion of the heart, sensitive to the motley crowd of laypeople, men and women, who pressed themselves on him: "Oh blessed Holy Spirit, usher and entrance to all graces and illuminations, open the door to me; let me have entrance and access to your divine presence and love. Lord, I cry to you."[20]

As a reformer, he criticized indulgences, which enabled the faithful to make lucrative investments in what could be believed to be a better world. All this ended in a fight with two good nuns who were enraged at the insinuations of the Franciscan who doubted their virtue. This suicidal attack, this indecent disorder of soutanes, ended in a broken tooth on the women's side and a damaged girdle on the masculine side — the rope girdle being, as it were, the emblem of virility in the dress of a Franciscan — as well as many scrapes and bruises on both sides. A Dominican bishop, Jean Levasseur, who was a doctor of theology, seized on the pretext of this preposterous war to restore, if not the peace of the church, at least that of the convents. Oh, extreme punishment! Poor Jean Vitrier saw himself condemned for his sins to relegation among the nuns of Courtrai. The exact date of his death is not known.

Lefèvre d'Étaples (ca. 1460-1536)

"Christ is the spirit of the whole Scriptures. And the Scriptures without Christ are only writing, and the letter that kills," exclaimed Lefèvre in 1524.[21] Unlike Erasmus, to whom he is readily compared, Jacques Lefèvre d'Étaples, called Fabri, enjoyed undiminished credit with the Reformers. In 1517 Luther praised his gifts as a theologian: "I fear that Erasmus does not exalt Christ sufficiently or sufficiently expand upon the grace of Christ, of which he is much more ignorant than Lefèvre d'Étaples; with him human things prevail

19. Erasmus, *Oeuvres choisies* (Paris: Le Livre de Poche, 1991), p. 1000.
20. André Godin, ed., *L'Homéliaire de Jean Vitrier* (Geneva: Droz, 1971), p. 87.
21. Cited by Guy Bedouelle, *Lefèvre d'Étaples et l'intelligence des Écritures* (Geneva: Droz, 1976), pp. 215-16.

over divine ones."[22] Like Calvin after him, and so many other evangelicals of his time, Lefèvre was a Picard. In 1492 he took his first decisive journey to Italy, where he encountered Barbaro, Ficino, and Pico della Mirandola. While Hermolao Barbaro was trying to restore the knowledge of Aristotle, Marsilio Ficino was a devoted disciple of Plato, but of a Plato more Christian than genuinely classical. As for Pico, he was the agent of a synthesis, that of the Hebrew, Chaldean, and Greco-Roman heritages. Ordained a priest at an unknown date, Lefèvre spent his whole life under the shadow of a monastic life that he never embraced.

The protection of Guillaume Briçonnet meant his needs were met while he edited mystical works and undertook a critical revision of the Vulgate, the Latin translation of the Bible that dated back to Saint Jerome. A violent polemic arose in 1517 when Lefèvre published his opinion that there were not just one but three different Mary Magdalenes in the Gospels.[23] Francis I stopped the prosecution of the scholar, who lived henceforth at Meaux with Briçonnet. In 1525, Francis I having been imprisoned by Charles V, the Sorbonne took advantage of the opportunity to condemn several propositions of Lefèvre's, and he fled to Strasbourg. The theologian lived out his days in Nérac with Marguerite de Navarre. Calvin made a brief visit to the scholar in the latter years of his life.[24] He is remembered especially for his work as a translator of the Bible into French.[25] But one should avoid "Protestantizing" to excess this evangelical, who was devoted to the Word of God and a critic of "superstitions," but was otherwise quite moderate. Let us, here as elsewhere, refrain from anachronism. Lefèvre was not a Protestant despite himself, even if he anticipated certain elements of the Reformation; his attachment to the immaculate conception of the Virgin Mary and his belief in purgatory sufficiently demonstrate this. "He will never be found attacking dogma or the liturgy," wrote a recent historian, "and there is no reason to doubt that Lefèvre did not truly consider these as mere human traditions but as affirmations founded on Scripture."[26] All in all, Lefèvre was "closer to the Reformers in his silences than in his words."[27] What reason, then, is there to annex him to either camp?

22. Bedouelle, p. 2.

23. Mary of Bethany, Mary of Magdala, and Mary the sinner.

24. P. E. Hughes, *Lefèvre, Pioneer of Ecclesiastical Renewal in France* (Grand Rapids: Eerdmans, 1984), p. 196.

25. *Traduction française du nouveau testament* (Paris, 1523). The translation was based on the Latin version of Saint Jerome, or Vulgate: *Bible* (Antwerp, 1530).

26. Bedouelle, p. 211.

27. Bedouelle, p. 235.

Guillaume Briçonnet (1472-1534)

Bishop of Lodève, then of Meaux, he surrounded himself with various scholars, including Lefèvre and Roussel. Most of these were representatives of a "Catholic Reformation" far removed from what was to become Protestantism.[28] Guillaume Farel in particular did not linger long in this reformist camp; the reformer of Neuchâtel, the future companion of Calvin, aimed at a much more radical restoration of Christianity than his colleagues here. The Meaux group met its most severe test in 1525, after the disaster of Pavia. Briçonnet and his colleagues were henceforth suspect, and various members of the group were forced into exile.

Briçonnet died eight years later, having admitted, "This world is a prison."[29] His correspondence with Marguerite d'Angoulême, the king's sister, displays a devout piety, deeply involved in mystical allegory. For example, his great letter of December 1521 makes a direct line between eucharistic devotion, the indissoluble union of the two natures of Christ, and the union of the faithful soul with its God: "As Saint Paul says, carnal and temporal marriage is only the shadow of spiritual marriage, which is the union of all faithful souls in a spiritual body of which Jesus Christ is the head."[30]

Marguerite de Navarre (1492-1549)

The sister of Francis I married first Charles d'Alençon and then Henri d'Albret, ruler of Navarre. She loved at the same time the king her brother, fine literature, and the philosophy of Christ.[31] Indeed, it seems that she mingled them in her affections. Francis I, God's anointed, was a symbol of Christ, indeed her own personal Christ, as Marguerite confides in her verses:

> Oh God, all good, examine his heart . . .
> Crown in him all great virtues,
> And through your Christ grant the requests
> That for mine, so humbly, I make.[32]

28. J. Viénot, *Histoire de la Réforme française*, 2 vols. (Paris: Fischbacher, 1926-34), vol. 1. See also the *thèse* of M. Veissière, *L'évêque Guillaume Briçonnet (1470-1534)* (Provins, Seine et Marne: Société d'Histoire et d'Archéologie, 1986).

29. G. Briçonnet and M. d'Angoulême, *Correspondance (1521-1524)*, 2 vols. (Geneva: Droz, 1975-79), 2:265.

30. Briçonnet and d'Angoulême, 1:83.

31. J.-L. Déjean, *Marguerite de Navarre* (Paris: Fayard, 1987).

32. Marguerite de Navarre, *Les marguerites de la Marguerite des Princesses*, ed. F. Frank, 4 vols. (Paris: Librairie des bibliophiles, 1873), 3:224.

Marguerite was constantly in contact with Guillaume Briçonnet, and incurred prosecution by a party of conservative clergy who objected to the appearance of her *Mirror of a Sinful Soul* in 1531.[33] The Sorbonne fired its thunderbolt in October 1533, condemning the anonymous work, recently reprinted. Francis I was angry; he loved his sister too much to permit anyone to treat her with disrespect.

Theodore Beza, Calvin's successor in Geneva, later reproached Marguerite for her moderation. She was also reproved for her editing of a collection of stories in the manner of Boccaccio, the *Heptameron,* published posthumously in competition with Boccaccio's *Decameron*. Henry IV's grandmother was indeed worth a Mass.

Gérard Roussel (†1550)

"Justification is because of faith. . . . We say with Saint Paul that faith justifies, because faith is like a hand that takes hold of and receives Jesus Christ, with his life and justice, and makes them ours. But God is the one who gives this hand, who puts Jesus Christ and his justice in this hand, who makes this hand able to take hold of and receive them. . . . This faith to which justification is due does not take hold of and receive only the life of Jesus, which is the observance of the law, but also seizes and receives and appropriates his death, which is satisfaction for the transgression of the law."

Thus did the bishop of Oloron express himself, protected by Marguerite de Navarre in his order for church visitations.[34] Justification by faith here accompanies a piety that remains Catholic. An emphasis on faith and on the unique sacrifice of Jesus Christ and a rejection of the merits and the invocation of saints are themes generally seen as Protestant but retained by Roussel. His case, as we shall see, was far from unique.

Born in Vaquerie, near Amiens, Gérard Roussel followed the path of his compatriot Lefèvre d'Étaples to Paris. In 1533, as in the two preceding years, he preached to the court during Lent. The faculty of theology was up in arms; its syndic, Noël Béda, was banished from Paris in May by the king. Calvin, however, later reproached Roussel for his lukewarmness or inconsistency. Certain historians have followed his lead, and hold that Roussel was a closet Calvinist,

---

33. M. de Navarre, *Miroir de l'âme pécheresse, auquel elle recognoist ses faultes et péchez, aussi ses grâces et bénéfices à elle faictz par Jésuschrist son époux . . .* (Alençon, Orne: Simon Dubois, 1531).

34. C.-G.-A. Schmidt, *Gérard Roussel, prédicateur de la reine Marguerite de Navarre* (Strasbourg: Schmidt & Grucker, 1845), p. 229.

preferring a cozy ecclesiastical career to the "true faith." This remains to be seen.

François Lambert, French "Lutheran" (1486-1530)

The term "Lutheran" requires analysis. François Lambert, because of "national" temperament, if one may say so, separated himself from the German Reformation. He is one of the links that make it possible to explain the birth of Calvinism. Born in Avignon, this Franciscan went to Wittenberg in January 1523, having already been in Bern and Zürich, and married soon afterward. Around 1520 he had published in Lyon a "book of piety modelled on the Marian rosary," *The Crown of Our Lord Jesus Christ.*[35] "The author here lists thirty-three mysteries of the life of Christ to be meditated on at the rate of one a day, in a very ritualistic context of preparatory prayers and concluding invocations. Is it necessary to underline Brother Lambert's Christocentrism, as opposed to the Marian devotion of the rosary? But our Franciscan did not conceal any of the privileges of 'Our Lady,' and sought her intercession as well as that of the angels and the saints. He also believed in the Immaculate Conception, and prayed for the Pope, 'Jesus' lieutenant on earth.'"[36]

This collection of meditations on Jesus Christ is based on the number thirty-three; thirty-three engrossing mysteries correspond to the thirty-three years of the life of Christ. Each spiritual exercise, similarly, is introduced by the recitation of thirty-three Paternosters, in the manner of the rosary. We are indeed again and still held by the logic of the *Imitation of Christ.*

Disappointed by Zwingli, Lambert planned to introduce Lutheranism into France, and he sought a protector; he solicited the parlement of Grenoble, the count of Savoy, the bishop of Lausanne, the government of Metz, and even Francis I, one after the other.

Wittenberg, Metz, then Strasbourg — where he was to be found in 1524 — held Lambert for a time, and he took a firm stand in favor of the marriage of priests. He wrote for Hesse a program of Reformed discipline, the first in history. But in January 1527 Luther wrote to Philip of Hesse to condemn this document as untimely and impractical for the time being. We quote from his letter this illuminating sentence: "My opinion is that one should proceed like Moses, who did not codify and promulgate the majority of his laws until they had been in force among the people for centuries. . . . For I know well, and I

---

35. *La couronne de Notre Seigneur Jésus-Christ.*

36. M. Venard, *Réforme protestante, Réforme catholique dans la province d'Avignon, xvie siècle* (Paris: Le Cerf, 1993), p. 136.

have found from experience, that if one enacts laws to be applied too early, this rarely gives good results; the people are not sufficiently prepared for them." Finally Luther give a decisive judgment: "Theory and practice are different things."[37] A cruel rejection for Luther's admirer! But to what degree was the difference between the two men national and cultural, or rather cultural because it was national?

Is Luther's moderation in face of the intellectual and juridical character of French culture not already the beginning of the difference between two Protestant confessions, Lutheran evangelism and systematic Calvinism?

Seneca's *De Clementia*, 1532

Every writer remembers vividly his first book. Calvin was no exception; all his energies appear to have been absorbed at the beginning of the 1530s by the appearance of Seneca's *De clementia*. This Roman philosopher of the first century of our era had written his treatise for the benefit of the young Nero, whose principal virtue, as everyone knows, was not clemency. Should one see here an oblique commentary on contemporary conditions? Was Francis I likewise summoned to exercise clemency toward his subjects involved in the Reform movement? During these years the king remained the strongest defender of religious moderation, but the provincial councils of the French church condemned the new ideas ruthlessly. Indeed, Louis de Berquin, previously safeguarded by the king's special protection, was burned in Paris in April 1529 in the absence of Francis I. However, nothing in Calvin's commentary confirms such a hypothesis about the author's purpose. That Calvin had espoused the humanist cause appears indisputable; in his culture, in his references, in his young ambition, he wished to equal, indeed surpass, his masters. But no evidence permits us to conclude that he was urging Francis I to moderation toward the "heretics."

Seneca's text is a "mirror for the prince," intended to moderate the temptations of power by hedging it with wisdom and right reason.[38] Calvin, however, points out in a note, citing the thirteenth chapter of the Epistle to the Romans, that Christianity for its part insists on obedience in subjects.[39] In

---

37. É. G. Léonard, *Histoire générale du protestantisme,* 3 vols. (Paris: PUF, 1961-64), 1:105.

38. See P. Grimal, *Sénèque* (Paris: Fayard, 1991), pp. 119ff., for a very fine analysis of *De clementia*. The importance of this work for medieval mirror-of-prince literature has been emphasized by Maria Bellincioni, *Potere ed etica in Seneca* (Brescia, Lombardy: Paideia, 1984), p. 9.

39. Battles and Hugo, p. 30.

short, all the indications agree; Calvin the humanist, the lover of fine language, made his literary debut without his work taking on any specific religious significance. Seneca had indeed permanently influenced Christian thought, in particular Lactantius and Saint Jerome. However, "There were profound differences between Stoicism and Christian thought; the former held that human reason could attain, by itself, to wisdom, while the latter insisted on the decisive role of divine 'grace.' Without this, nature was helpless, original sin having corrupted it so profoundly."[40]

These views reappeared in the mature Calvin, who was prompt to condemn blind confidence in the light of corrupted nature. But nothing of this occurred to the young author. In his first work of scholarship, Calvin aimed at a masterpiece. Full of fire, he set all his hopes on a critical edition of one of the major texts of antiquity. This man of twenty-two already frankly set himself up as a defender of French intelligence and a rival of Erasmus. Clearly, Calvin had not yet traveled his road to Damascus; without departing from Christianity, his personal philosophy remained that of the elite of his time. "The commentary on the *De Clementia* bears the imprint of Erasmian morality; it exalts, in the manner of the Stoics, a providence 'that eliminates chance and directs princes,' and contains some criticism of superstitions opposed to 'religion,' but certainly still does not possess the least evangelical character. Beza himself did not try to present it as such. He merely praised its moral gravity, so worthy of its young author."[41]

National affirmation has the highest place in this double pleading for Seneca and Budé, against Cicero and Erasmus. Calvin's homage is addressed in the first place to the French tradition, or at least to its humanists, judged superior to the Dutchman. The work is dedicated to Claude de Monmor, abbot of Saint-Éloi, Calvin's old comrade from Noyon. With the insolence of youth, Calvin lets fly some arrows at Erasmus, seeking to tarnish his fading reputation.[42] His defense of Seneca is unquestionably an attack on Erasmus. Had Erasmus not attempted twice, in 1515 and in 1529, to produce his own edition of Seneca?

If he insolently put Erasmus in the second rank, he returned the place of honor to Guillaume Budé, "finest ornament and pillar of literature."[43] Thanks to him France deserved the palm of knowledge. Calvin used almost the same terms in speaking of Seneca, "one of the true pillars of philosophy and of Roman eloquence."[44] Certainly, according to Calvin, Seneca came behind Cicero,

40. Grimal, *Sénèque*, p. 111.
41. A. Ganoczy, *Le jeune Calvin. Genèse et évolution de sa vocation réformatrice* (Wiesbaden: F. Steiner, 1966), p. 59.
42. Ganoczy, p. 6.
43. Ganoczy, p. 114.
44. Ganoczy, p. 12.

but behind this concession one feels a true passion for Stoic wisdom springing up.

Seneca presented an enigmatic face. Did not Stoic philosophy almost attain moral perfection? Did not the sublime character of Roman wisdom approach Christianity? "If one reads Seneca as a pagan author, he wrote in a Christian fashion; if one reads him as a Christian author, he wrote in a pagan fashion," Erasmus concluded, even if for years he attacked a style he judged grandiloquent and affected.[45] This ambivalence of Erasmus is at the heart of the Renaissance phenomenon.

"The dice are cast," Calvin exclaimed importantly on April 22, 1532. Would the book, published at the author's expense, gain the Picard the recognition he hoped for? He tried to draw the attention of the universities in Paris and Bourges to his work, and engaged Philippe du Laurier, a bookseller in Orléans, to distribute a hundred copies.[46] He confided to François Daniel at the same time that he did hope to recover his costs. He also asked about the reception of his book.[47] It was an impoverished and uncertain Calvin who awaited an unlikely success, before setting out for Orléans to obtain his degree of *licencié en droit,* his law degree. He would represent the "Picard nation" there among his fellow students. But we know practically nothing about the period from May 1532 to October 1533. In August 1533 we pick up his trail again in Noyon, where he attended a meeting of the chapter. Without any formal proof, one may suppose that Calvin made use of this second stay in Orléans to deepen his knowledge of the Bible and of the Fathers.

Conversion, during 1532-33

An enigma lies at the heart of Calvin's life. How did the young and brilliant humanist, author of a commentary on Seneca, become Calvin the Reformer? At the end of what invisible path did Calvin meet God? Why did he consecrate his existence to him? What is the meaning, finally, of his vocation? These are serious questions, questions without answers, questions which leave the beaten path of historical investigation. Whether Calvin actually encountered God, or whether this vocation had only a fictional or imaginary character, our approach remains the same. We can only collect evidence; in history faith is an unidentified object.

However, how can one write a religious history that ignores the transcendent, or that treats faith only as a system of symbols, neglecting the meaning at-

45. Millet, p. 59.
46. Battles and Hugo, p. 387.
47. *Opera Calvini* (hereafter cited as *OC*) 10, 2, cols. 19-20.

tached to them? Calvin speaks about faith, even about his own faith, but he often does so in a discreet manner, with extraordinary reticence. His conversion undoubtedly occurred during the years 1532-33. But this hypothesis, as we shall see, poses as many problems as it appears to resolve.

Moreover, Calvin's testimony on the matter is all from later years. A decade after the period we are currently dealing with, Calvin mentioned in the course of a sentence in his *Letter to Sadoleto* the career as a respectable scholar that appeared open to him. If he had only sought his own "profit," could he not have been content to "pursue his studies in some respectable and free condition"? In short, Calvin might have been satisfied with writing books about Seneca, or becoming a sort of second Budé. He would have thus obtained the "honors" and satisfactions he could have legitimately aspired to.[48] But God chose Calvin. He "illumined" him with the "light of his Spirit." His Word was a living "torch" that spoke to Calvin's "heart."[49]

God chose Calvin, Calvin did not choose God: this is the very formula of election. God mysteriously chooses certain beings. God chooses in the same way as he rejects, without reason, by the arbitrary action of his grace. The grandeur and the risks of this psychology may be discerned without difficulty. Does it not risk ending in fanaticism or madness? Is it God who chooses a man, not a man who chooses God, who invents and defines God? Calvin felt the objection; he anticipated it, he forestalled it, he resolved it: "All these things demonstrate not what we are, but what we have wished to be."[50] An element of *desire* enters into conversion.

Desire and apprehension. Calvin hesitated to take the step. His stumbling block was the doctrine of the Eucharist. The consecrated elements, the bread and the wine, were they only symbols, or must one recognize in them a spiritual presence of Christ, dead and resurrected? Irreconcilable positions divided the Reformers; Calvin feared their conflicts and turned aside at first from the Reformation. During the 1550s he remembered his hesitations and reconstructed them mentally. Calvin, in contrast with Zwingli, would never accept a purely symbolic interpretation of Holy Communion: "As I began to emerge a little from the shadows of the papacy, and having enjoyed a small taste of the pure doctrine, when I read in Luther that Oecolampadius and Zwingli left nothing of the sacraments but naked figures and symbols without reality, I confess that this turned me away from their books, so that for a long time I refrained from reading them."[51]

48. J. Calvin, *Lettre à Sadolet* (French version 1540), in *La vraie piété,* ed. I. Backus and C. Chimelli (Geneva: Labor et Fides, 1986), p. 85.

49. Calvin, *Lettre à Sadolet,* p. 110.

50. Calvin, *Lettre à Sadolet,* p. 87.

51. J. Calvin, *Secunda defensio . . . de sacramentis fidei, contra J. Wesphali calumnias* (1556), *OC* 9, col. 51. French translation in *Recueil des opuscules* (Geneva, 1566), p. 1503.

But his main discussion of his conversion comes still later. It is found in his 1557 preface to his *Commentary on the Psalms*. Let us read the text together. It contains an account of conversion inspired by the example of David:

> My condition, no doubt, is much inferior to his [David's], and it is unnecessary for me to stay to show this. But as he was taken from the sheepfold, and elevated to rank of supreme authority; so God, having taken me from my originally obscure and humble condition, has reckoned me worthy of being invested with the honourable office of a preacher and minister of the gospel. When I was as yet a very little boy, my father had destined me for the study of theology. But afterwards, when he considered that the legal profession commonly raised those who followed it to wealth, this prospect induced him suddenly to change his purpose. Thus it came to pass, that I was withdrawn from the study of philosophy, and was put to the study of law. To this pursuit I endeavoured faithfully to apply myself, in obedience to the will of my father; but God, by the secret guidance of his providence, at length gave a different direction to my course. And first, since I was too obstinately devoted to the superstitions of Popery to be easily extricated from so profound an abyss of mire, God by a sudden conversion subdued and brought my mind to a teachable frame, which was more hardened in such matters than might have been expected from one at my early period of life. Having thus received some taste and knowledge of true godliness, I was immediatly inflamed with so intense a desire to progress therein, that although I did not altogether leave off other studies, I yet pursued them with less ardour.
>
> I was quite surprised to find that before a year had elapsed, all who had any desire after purer doctrine were continually coming to me to learn, although I myself was as yet but a mere novice and tyro. Being of a disposition somewhat unpolished and bashful, which led me always to love the shade and retirement, I began to seek some secluded corner where I might be withdrawn from the public view; but so far from being able to accomplish the object of my desire, all my retreats were like public shools. In short, whilst my one great object was to live in seclusion without being known, God so led me about through different turnings and changes, that he never permitted me to rest in any place, until, in spite of my natural dispostion, he brought me forth to public notice. Leaving my native country, France, I in fact retired into Germany, expressly for the purpose of being able there to enjoy in some obscure corner the repose which I had always desired, and which had been so long denied me.[52]

---

52. J. Calvin, preface to *Commentary on the Book of Psalms*, trans. James Anderson, vol. 1 (Grand Rapids: Eerdmans, 1948), pp. xl-xli.

Calvin continues, developing the reference to King David: "As that holy king was harassed by the Philistines and other foreign enemies with continual wars, while he was much more grievously afflicted by the malice and wickedness of some perfidious men amongst his own people, so I can say as to myself, that I have been assailed on all sides, and have scarcely been able to enjoy repose for a single moment, but have always had to sustain some conflict either from enemies without or within the Church."[53]

The figure of King David continued to fascinate Calvin. In his preaching he presented him as a model for all believers: "David was indeed a man subject to the same passions that torment us and throw us to and fro, and there is no doubt that he was pestered by many temptations which could distract his spirit. But to deal with all occasions of weakness and have a certain guide he focused on what God showed him; he meditated on and considered that."[54]

This meditative David who fascinated Calvin so much was not the shepherd who confronted Goliath, nor the king in his splendor. Calvin's David was the psalmist, or at least the presumed author of the psalms, who sought out the face of the Lord. David, for Calvin, shone as much in his grandeur as in his humility. He thus presents the ideal type of the faithful soul who owes his elevation only to the choice of God.

The Interpretation of the Account of Conversion

This famous text is difficult to understand. Should it be seen as the account of a single event, or of a gradual development? Is Calvin speaking of himself personally or describing an experience common to every believer? Finally, how much is rhetoric and how much is living testimony? Should the historian then consider exactly when this conversion occurred?[55]

On the other hand, various studies have tended to minimize these biographical and chronological perspectives. Thus A. Ganoczy insisted on the belated character of this account, written by Calvin seven years before his death. Calvin, he argues, wrote it neither as a historian nor as a writer of memoirs but as a theologian, anxious to prove the infallible predestination of God and the supernatural origin of his vocation. In particular, the "sudden conversion" mentioned in the text takes on its true meaning in Latin. It must be understood as *conversio subita*, a conversion "suffered" (*subie* in French) by Calvin, and not an instantaneous conversion *(conversion subite)*: "Only at a mature age did Calvin describe

53. Calvin, preface to *Commentary on the Book of Psalms*, p. xliv.
54. *OC* 8, col. 425.
55. J. Delumeau, *Naissance et affirmation de la Réforme* (Paris: PUF, 1965); new edition, 1973, p. 113.

his own spiritual transformation as a 'conversion.' . . . He did not do this clearly except once, and still in a context of systematic theology. Thus it is clear to us that this *a posteriori* interpretation of a long-ago event was formulated according to the concept of 'conversion-penitence' developed from a long study of Scripture. The adjective *subita* was not introduced by a chronicler's care for precision, but by the desire of a theologian to emphasize the divine origin of the event."[56]

O. Millet, more recently, also insisted on the "typological rather than biographical perspective" of this account of conversion.[57] And the same author pointed out the equestrian element in the story of conversion: "God . . . finally made me turn the rein in another direction."[58]

These approaches are of great interest. A. Ganoczy is justified in noting that for Calvin the idea of conversion was subordinated to the idea of vocation. One should also not fail to emphasize the importance of the conversion of Saint Paul in the body of Christian literature. Every conversion is, in its way, a road to Damascus. But why did Calvin not cite the apostle Paul here? Why, moreover, contrary to the expectations of his readers, did he employ the figure of King David?

David, the shepherd who became a king, and Jonah, the prophet pursued by his vocation, are two images of the same call to conversion. Calvin did not become a king; one can hardly even call him a prophet. But exactly what significance did he attach to the royalty of David? In his writings biblical figures take on an aspect of recapitulation. The reference to David is spiritual, even existential, not historical; God lifts up those he has chosen. David, intended for the highest destiny but subjected by his Lord to every adversity, is the ideal type of the elect. God gave him the power he also accorded to Calvin and to all those he chooses irresistibly, not as a result of their merits, but because he disposes of his creatures at will. Why should we deny that Calvin's conversion took place and

56. Ganoczy, p. 302. There is an interesting critique of this thesis with a return to a biographical perspective, which we have largely followed in our own account, in D. Fischer, "Conversion de Calvin," *Études Théologiques et Religieuses* 58 (1983): 203-20.

57. Millet, p. 522.

58. Millet, p. 522. H. A. Oberman makes the same point: *Initia Calvini: The Matrix of Calvin's Reformation* (Amsterdam: Koninklijke Nederlandse Akademie van Wetenschappen [Noord-Hollandsche], 1991), p. 8. T. Wanegffelen remarks with justice in his review, "An equestrian metaphor; therefore no connection with the 'conversion' of Saint Paul." *Revue de la Bibliothèque Nationale* 45 (fall 1992): 71.

Could one properly attempt a typology of conversion? The Christian West seems to have been dominated by a double archetype: the sudden conversion, following a crisis (Saint Paul, Saint Augustine); and the diffuse or repetitive conversion, common in Puritan literature (Bunyan in seventeenth-century England). See A. H. Hawkins, *Archetypes of Conversion* (London and Toronto: Associated University Press, 1985), in particular pp. 92ff. The author was strongly inspired by the work of William James at the beginning of the twentieth century.

that it corresponded to a rupture with the old church? Yes, for Calvin his conversion indeed corresponded to an authentic "biographical identity crisis":[59] a young humanist, a lover of literature and destined for success, became a lover of Jesus Christ, eager to respond to a call. O. Millet addresses the fundamental question of Calvin's "Augustinian complex":

> Calvin, the reader of the *Confessions*, the correspondence, and the *Retractations* of Saint Augustine, in fact has nothing to tell us about his personal evolution. The humanist figure of the literary man, rediscovered in the West in Petrarch's reading of the *Confessions*, the fascination with the moral and religious personality of great authors as found in their texts, the idea, finally, that the individual biographies of these authors aid in the comprehension of their works, all this is indeed present in Calvin's prefaces and in the whole of the Reformer's work, but embedded in cultural and spiritual discourses, discoverable, but obliterated as soon as they rise to the surface of the discussion.[60]

Autobiographical testimony, however, is not devoid of all documentary value. The paper persona, who appears in the writings of maturity, is also an individual. *The Institutes of the Christian Religion,* a text which as a whole has no intimate character, nevertheless throws a light on the meaning of conversion for Calvin. Referring to Hebrew and Greek, the author rejects the distinction between "conversion" and "penitence."[61] It follows that conversion, like what is called penitence, is an ineffable gift of God. The Catholic practice of confession of sins has produced a useless feeling of guilt in sinners; the very idea of "contrition" has engendered "despair" in believers, provoking "torment of soul."[62] The Calvinist view of election, the intimate experience of conversion, and that predestination which is its dogmatic side, are the absolute opposites of a "pastoral theology of fear."[63]

59. G. Theissen, "Identité et expérience de l'angoisse dans le christianisme primitif," *Études Théologiques et Religieuses* 68 (1993): 168.

60. Millet, p. 553.

61. J. Calvin, *Institution de la religion chrétienne,* ed. J. Pannier, 4 vols. (Paris: Belles Lettres, 1961), II, chap. 5, "De pénitence," p. 175.

62. Calvin, *Institution,* II, p. 189. One sees clearly here what distinguished Calvinist predestination from Jansenist predestination, namely, that the latter valued contrition (or perfect contrition) as against the attrition (or imperfect contrition) of the Jesuits.

63. J. Delumeau, *La Peur en Occident* (Paris: Fayard, 1978), p. 27. A. Ganoczy wrote was only partly right when he wrote that in Calvinist *conversio* "the vivifying effectiveness of grace and the abandonment of man to faith . . . are predominant over mortification, contrition, and separation from the past" (p. 302). Certainly. It is all the more true because Calvin rejects this very notion of contrition, and still more, mortification, which has no meaning in good Calvinist theology.

CHAPTER 4

The Most Dreadful Popish Mass: 1533-34

> *For such an high priest [Jesus Christ] became us, who is holy, harmless, undefiled, separate from sinners, and made higher than the heavens; who needeth not daily, as those high priests, to offer up sacrifice, first for his own sins, and then for the people's: for this he did once, when he offered up himself.*
>
> HEBREWS 7:26-27

The whole history of Christianity is that of reading. The Bible is the book *par excellence,* the Book of books, but also a book containing other books, a multiple book. The Bible plays a fundamental role. But divergent readings, differing emphases, and the exclusive endorsement of certain passages produce often-contradictory results. Two books of the Bible played a special role in the reforms of the sixteenth century, the Epistle to the Romans and the Epistle to the Hebrews. Both attributed to Saint Paul, these two apostolic letters express different theologies. (Today scholars agree that the second of these texts is not by the same author.) Romans, meditated on at length by Luther, also gave French evangelism its special themes: justification by faith and the supremacy of grace over law. Rabelais's imaginary Abbey of Thélème is a representation of the chosen society of "free" men, educated and wellborn, who, freed from both want and constraint, can live under the reign of grace. "Do as thou wilt": this anarchical, libertarian advice found its inspiration in Saint Paul. The motto only applies to regenerated humanity, and Calvin never ceased to attack the "spiritual libertinism" that resulted from a too-liberal interpreta-

71

tion of the apostle. But whether justified or not by the texts, the tendency existed in the sixteenth century.

Hebrews, on the other hand, is entirely concerned with the somber mystery of metaphysical atonement. The unique sacrifice of Christ the redeemer became for the partisans of the Reformation the definitive argument against the Catholic Mass. How could the clergy dream of reenacting an expiation of sins that took place once for all time? The Mass, from this perspective, expressed an idolatry which must be forsaken without further delay. Separation succeeded participation.

The problem for the historian is not to endorse this or that interpretation of the Pauline epistles, a task that can be delegated to the theologian or the exegete. But we should note, referring again to Lucien Febvre, that an earlier French evangelism, more reformist than Reformed, took Romans as one of its preferred texts. On the other hand, the irreversible break of 1534 occurred over the question of the Mass, and was sustained among the Reformers by meditation on Hebrews:

> The Mass? Violent, intense, intrepid men dared to attack it at its roots. A sacrifice, they said, but of what? Certainly, Our Lord in truth gave his body, his soul, his blood, his life in satisfaction for us, poor sinners. But to claim to repeat this total sacrifice — would not this be by an execrable blasphemy to hold the sacrifice of Christ to be ineffective, insufficient, imperfect? What then are the Catholic priests, these "despicable high priests" with whom the earth is filled, what are they doing in their Mass and by their Mass, except to regard themselves as if they, the wretches, were "our redeemers," the substitutes for Jesus or his apostles?[1]

Did this thunderbolt fall from a clear sky? The king seemed to favor the humanists. Until December 1533 he kept Noël Bédier out of the capital. Francis I was scarcely a supporter of religious intransigence, especially when it targeted his own immediate entourage. Had not the hotheaded syndic of the faculty of theology criticized Gérard Roussel, the preacher of the queen of Navarre? Roussel had been entrusted with preaching the Lenten sermons in the Louvre. This should have alerted contentious spirits to the need for greater cau-

---

1. L. Febvre, "La messe et les placards," in *Au coeur religieux du xvie siècle* (Paris: SEVPEN, 1968), p. 168. The author points out accurately that the Epistle to the Hebrews, incorrectly attributed to Saint Paul, is rather distant theologically from the Epistle to the Romans. He draws the logical conclusion that the Placards departed from the great Pauline themes like justification by faith to which many humanists subscribed.

tion, but Bédier had hardly any; the bishop of Paris, Cardinal Jean du Bellay, and the king himself were exasperated.

Provocations resumed. In October the students of the Collège de Navarre put on a play full of veiled allusions to Marguerite de Navarre and Roussel. *The Mirror of a Sinful Soul,* reprinted without the author's name, had just been condemned by the theologians. The faculty of theology, improperly called the Sorbonne, rushed to judgment. Apparently written about 1527, the work was not unknown to the public.[2] Everyone knew its author's identity: Marguerite de Navarre, the king's sister. On the whole an irenic and conciliatory spirit, Marguerite succeeded Briçonnet as aristocratic protector of French evangelism. Her Château of Nérac henceforth provided political asylum and spiritual oasis offered until recently by Meaux. It was there that the poet Marot took refuge in December 1534, before having to flee to Ferrara.

Henry IV's grandmother combined pietism with ribaldry. Sacred and secular tendencies, later judged contradictory, were at least coexistent in her. Marguerite, one personality or two? "No, she did not have a split personality," answered Febvre, marveling over "the marriage of those perpetually vowed to separation, the Christian and the hedonist."[3] A Christian combined with a hedonist was in itself a complete feminine ideal.

In hindsight these tensions between conservatives and reformers appear limited the scope. The decisive break occurred a year later, almost to the day, in October 1534, over the question of the Mass.

The Speech of Nicolas Cop, November 1, 1533

A man is justified by faith without the deeds of the law.

SAINT PAUL, ROMANS 3:28

A metamorphosis occurred during the fall of 1533. Calvin the spectator became Calvin the actor. The aspiring humanist returned to Paris in the fall of 1533. In the last days of October he described to François Daniel, "a lawyer in Orléans," the atmosphere that existed in Paris and the scandal of the play against Marguerite de Navarre.[4] In his letter he mentioned a mysterious "M.G.," who may very well have been Maître Gérard, in other words Gérard

---

2. A first edition had been printed in Alençon in 1531.
3. L. Febvre, *Amour sacré, amour profane. Autour de l'Héptaméron* (Paris: NRF, 1971), p. 370.
4. *Opera Calvini* (hereafter cited as *OC*) 10, 2, cols. 27-30.

Roussel.[5] Judging by the tone of his letter, Calvin found himself fully committed to the moderate reformist party that numbered Marguerite and Roussel among its members. Its greatest deed was planned for November 1.

Nicolas Cop, the new rector of the university, was the son of Guillaume Cop, Francis I's physician. He was a humanist from Basel, close to Erasmus and Budé, and therefore favorable to reformist ideas. On November 1 the rector was required, according to custom, to give an address welcoming the new term of the university at the Church of the Cordeliers (not the Church of the Mathurins, as is sometimes said). The four faculties were represented: theology, law, medicine, and arts. Referring to the text for the day, the Sermon on the Mount, Cop transformed this conventional oration for All Saints' Day into a veritable manifesto of the new spirit.

Was Calvin not the author of this text? Would he not have contributed to its wording? Or at least have inspired certain passages? The question remains open. The attribution came late, after the death of Calvin. Theodore Beza, who certainly discovered a fragment of this text among his friend's papers, timidly arrived at this conclusion only in 1575.[6] Although Calvin may have participated in the work, this does not mean that he was its author. Various intriguing indications show clearly Calvin's involvement at Nicolas Cop's side. A fragment of this text in Calvin's own hand exists in Geneva, while the complete version, corrected by Cop, was henceforth located in Strasbourg.[7] What should be deduced from this?

The wish to make Calvin the author of this text at all costs smacks of fetishism. We do not see why Cop would not have been capable of writing the speech he delivered. On the other hand, that Calvin participated in its writing and that he even exercised a friendly influence over Cop appear more reasonable. But to go beyond these sensible conclusions is to confuse history with adulation of the dead, or perhaps to want to endow French Protestantism with a specific act of foundation, organized by an exceptional individual: Calvin, the new Luther, giv-

---

5. A. Ganoczy, *Le jeune Calvin. Genèse et évolution de sa vocation réformatrice* (Wiesbaden: F. Steiner, 1966), p. 64.

6. This is the interpretation proposed by K. Müller, who himself disagreed with this attribution, in his important article, "Calvins Bekehrung," in *Nachrichten von der Gesellschaft der Wissenschaften zu Göttingen* (1905), p. 231.

7. Two manuscript versions of this text exist at the present time: one, in Calvin's hand, is in Geneva, Bibliothèque publique et universitaire, Ms. fr. 145, fol. 85; the other, more complete, corrected by Cop, is in Strasbourg, archives Saint-Thomas, n° 174, *Varia ecclesiastica*, IX, ff. 334-337v. They have been published respectively in *OC* 9, cols. 873-75, and *OC* 10, 2, cols. 30-36. We have used the critical edition edited by J. Rott in *Regards contemporains sur Jean Calvin* (Paris: PUF, 1965), pp. 43-49. It is probable, moreover, that the two known manuscripts are themselves copies of an original draft of the text.

ing his compatriots a manifesto, as the German had produced his Ninety-five Theses in 1517. This approach belongs more to myth than to reality.[8]

The speech derived from the Erasmian perspective of the "philosophy of Christ." In this sermon Jesus Christ occupies a central position; he is the One who saves and teaches. The unique character of his ministry is clearly affirmed, but this does not prevent an invocation to the blessed Virgin Mary, his mother, introducing a recitation of the angelic salutation, "Ave, gratia plena." This Marian allusion, moreover, has been angrily crossed out in the manuscript version preserved in Strasbourg.

The Beatitudes follow, in the version in the Gospel of Matthew. "Blessed are the poor in spirit." But so many Christians are prisoners of gold and silver. The law is opposed to the gospel; only the grace of God matters, and not the merit of works. As for the sophists, they have forgotten faith, along with the love of God. "Blessed are they that mourn." But where, then, are those who rely on God, knowing that faith alone, and not works, justifies? This is the chief teaching of Luther, the reader of Saint Paul. And it was indeed by the light of Romans that Cop read the Beatitudes. Lefèvre, Briçonnet, and Marguerite de Navarre also believed in justification by faith alone, which had an extraordinary impact on the age. "Blessed are the peacemakers." Can one indeed be sure that the church does not rely more often on the sword than on the Word to defend its teaching? "Blessed are they which are persecuted." How far will this provocation go? In the charged atmosphere of the 1530s, to recall that the names "heretics," "seducers," and "impostors" might be applied to the authentic disciples of Christ was a delicate matter.

The Beatitudes and nothing but the Beatitudes; was the act of speaking on them revolutionary in itself?[9] How does one explain the provocative, indeed scandalous character of this speech to open the new university term? Salvation by faith *(sola fide)* and emphasis on grace *(sola gratia)* were "Lutheran" themes in one sense, but they were not rejected by the reforming humanists who were friends of Roussel and Marguerite. The explanation ends, despite everything, in

---

8. Rott, *Regards contemporains sur Calvin*, p. 29, however, inclines toward Calvin's authorship, while recognizing the ideological character of this quest for a Calvinist version of the "Wittenberg theses."

9. Cop's speech, examined with a magnifying glass, contained nothing heterodox for a Catholic theologian of the 1960s. Does the same apply thirty years later? We will be careful not to assert it. But A. Ganoczy, undoubtedly one of the foremost Catholic students of Calvin, affirmed without hesitation in 1966: "To the Catholic theologian of today there appears nothing formally heterodox in this address. The orator certainly cites entire passages from Luther, but these passages contain a doctrine substantially Catholic. . . . Neither *sola fide* nor *sola gratia* is in itself a Catholic principle, but they can, nevertheless, express an authentically Catholic doctrine" (Ganoczy, p. 70).

an impasse. Why did a commentary on the Beatitudes provoke such an uproar in the fall of 1533? Was it for purely theological reasons? If we concede to A. Ganoczy that it is erroneous to see in this address, according to a formula that in any case is anachronistic, "the first manifestation of French Protestant-ism," how do we then explain the prosecutions directed against Cop and the flight of Calvin?[10] While Cop went to Basel, Calvin barely had time to leave Paris. He stayed several days in Angoulême with his friend, the canon Louis du Tillet. In Paris his room in the Collège du Fortet was gone over with a fine-tooth comb, his papers confiscated, his correspondence seized.

What had happened? Why this sudden virulence? It was due to a series of convergent causes. The doctrine of salvation by faith and the very tone of the discourse were henceforth perceived as purely Lutheran. Moreover, Francis I had just married his second son, the future Henry II, to the pope's niece, Catherine de Medici. He was trying to keep in the good graces of the Holy Father, Clement VII, while still negotiating the following year with the German Lutheran princes through Guillaume du Bellay as intermediary.

The pope issued bulls; the king attended to his affairs. Already on August 30, 1533, Clement VII had begged the Most Christian King to put his words into action to extirpate "the Lutheran heresy and other sects infesting this king-dom." On November 10 he repeated his injunctions. The two men met in Mar-seille to "consult together about matters that concern the Christian religion," the struggle against the Turks abroad and the repression of heresy at home, "be-fore things fall into greater uproar than they have already." Such were the goals of this interview, in which France applauded a diplomatic victory over the em-peror.[11] That Francis I, and not his rival Charles V, should achieve Christian unity — this utopian ideal took shape in men's minds in the course of the year of grace 1533. Bédier returned triumphantly to Paris in December; the French "Lutherans" henceforward had everything to fear.

Calvin found refuge with du Tillet. The friendship between the two is un-doubtedly one of the most revealing indications of the atmosphere of the 1530s. The two men ended up on opposite sides; their roads diverged when du Tillet remained faithful to the religion of his fathers while Calvin became the famous Reformer acclaimed by posterity. A fascinating correspondence illus-trates this later conflict (see chap. 7).

In January 1534, then, Calvin was in Angoulême. The du Tillet family was celebrated for its erudition and its urbanity. Ennobled in the preceding century,

---

10. Ganoczy, p. 70. The condemned formula is found in the work of J. Rott, "Docu-ments strasbourgeois concernant Calvin," in *Regards contemporains sur Calvin*, p. 29.

11. Martin du Bellay and Guillaume du Bellay, *Mémoires*, ed. V. L. Bourrilly and F. Vindry, 4 vols. (Paris: Société de l'histoire de France, 1908-19), 2:197 and 230.

the du Tillets presented a marvelous example of social success. Élie, the father, held the office of vice president of the Chambre des Comptes in Paris. One of his sons was *valet de chambre* to the king, and two others were in the church. Louis was a canon of Angoulême, while Jean was called to the highest ecclesiastical offices, becoming in turn bishop of Saint-Brieuc, then of Meaux. Calvin took advantage of this visit to read, improve himself, and perfect his knowledge of the Holy Scriptures and the Fathers, thanks to the books furnished from the library. In his exile, placed in the hands of God, the scholar testified to his perfect happiness.[12] Florimond de Raemond recounts in striking terms the benefit of this stay in Angoulême for Calvin: "Angoulême was the forge where this new Vulcan shaped on the anvil the strange opinions he later published; it was there that he first wove, to surprise Christendom, the fabric of his *Institutes,* which one can call the Koran, or rather the Talmud of heresy."[13]

However, Calvin-Vulcan, contrary to his legend, had undoubtedly not yet entirely cut the umbilical cord connecting him to the official church. It seems, indeed, that he gave an occasional sermon or prayer. In April he went to Nérac, where he met Lefèvre d'Étaples, and then he returned to Noyon. There he solemnly renounced his ecclesiastical benefices (May 1534). It seems he then returned to Paris and to Orléans. It was apparently there that he wrote the preface of his second book — published, however, eight years later, in 1542.

The *Psychopannychia* (1534)[14]

For that which befalleth the sons of men befalleth beasts; even one thing befalleth them: as the one dieth, so dieth the other; yea, they have all one breath; so that a man hath no preeminence above a beast: for all is vanity.

ECCLESIASTES 3:19

Calvin's little treatise on "soul sleep" has not had the same literary good fortune as the other works of its author. It was undoubtedly written during the crucial period that followed Cop's speech. Indeed, it is likely that Calvin put together

---

12. *OC* 10, 2, cols. 37-38, letter to F. Daniel, January 1534(?).

13. F. de Raemond, *L'histoire de la naissance de l'hérésie* (1605; Rouen: P. de La Motte, 1629), bk. 7, pp. 883-84.

14. The *Psychopannychia* (about 1534) is found in *OC* 5, cols. 165-232. Another edition may be used as an introduction: W. Zimmerli, ed., *Psychopannychia* (Leipzig: A. Deichert, 1932). A French version is in P.-L. Jacob, ed., *Oeuvres françaises* (Paris: G. Gosselin, 1842), pp. 25-105, reproducing the edition of Geneva: *Psychopannychie* (1558).

part of his argument in Angoulême, in the house of his friend du Tillet. Calvin here appears to defend the doctrine of the immortality of the soul, and he criticizes the Anabaptists. It is at least as important to know how to choose one's enemies as one's friends; this is well known. Thus in these pages Calvin selected the Anabaptists as his adversaries, and not, as one would have expected, the "papists," defenders of Roman orthodoxy. The Anabaptists — actually those who rejected infant baptism — remained for Calvin until the end of his life the representatives of a radical reformation which he abhorred and whose sectarian tendencies he denounced.

On what grounds did Calvin condemn the Anabaptists in these pages? Not so much because of their avowed position on baptism as because of their supposed "mortalism." "Mortalism," which in fact contaminated a whole branch of radical thought, was the idea, simple in itself, that the dead sleep until the last judgment. Calvin dedicated his *Psychopannychia* to these adversaries, with the subtitle, "A treatise in which it is proved that souls are awake and live after they leave their bodies, against the error of certain ignorant people who think that they sleep until the last day." The author described the object of his work in these terms: "Although certain good people have long solicited me, indeed urgently pressed me to write something to curb the folly of those who stupidly and confusedly dispute today about the sleep or the death of souls, until now I have not been able to respond to their prayers and urgent requests, since I have a spirit so opposed to all contention and debate. And certainly I then had some reason to excuse myself, partly because I hoped that soon this nonsense, finding no adherents, would vanish, or would merely languish in obscurity among a mob of chatterers."[15]

In fact, Calvin deplored the spread of the movement. Mortalism was gaining ground. "In the beginning only a few prated in a confused way that the souls of the dead sleep, and did not make it understood just what they meant by this sleep."[16]

Calvin was touched to the quick by this doctrine. And behind the dogmatic position he adopted, one senses a real discomfort. Was it indeed to dissuade his contemporaries from following the Anabaptists that he undertook this polemic? Or may one not think that Calvin, still uncertain, settled accounts here with himself? If its urgency appeared so great to him, why did he wait so long to publish his treatise, and also to translate it into French? The text was not published in French until 1558. In this first polemical work Calvin served his apprenticeship; he invented a style, that biting and mocking tone of ridicule that would never leave him. He also discovered to his cost how difficult re-

15. Calvin, *Oeuvres françaises*, p. 25.
16. Calvin, *Oeuvres françaises*, p. 26.

course to Scripture, and to Scripture only, makes the use of arguments from authority. "They draw no fewer people to their error by their confused noise and babble . . . than if they had printed books that had spread through the world." And, on a more personal note, "I do not know how I could purge myself of treason against the truth of God if in such a great emergency I kept quiet and concealed my views."[17]

A second edition, dated from Basel in 1536, again takes up this idea, one of the constants of Calvin's thought. The Bible is a knotty, difficult text, whose interpretation demands extensive knowledge. If brought into contact with it unceremoniously, many minds are upset and seized with confusion. The Bible is too old a text in too new a world: "The Word of God is not new, but such as it has been since the beginning it is still, and ever shall be, and just as they blunder greatly who argue for the newness of the Word of God when it returns to the light after having been suppressed and buried by perverse usages and indifference, so they sin equally in another way who, like reeds, are moved by every wind, and, what is more, are shaken and bent by the smallest breath."[18]

A terrible indictment. The text that saves is also that which disturbs and condemns. Like strong drink, it intoxicates and goes to the heads of naive readers. Calvin always distrusted free investigation, spontaneous reading of the text, and its unregulated rearrangement. But was not this also because he had doubts about his own theological grounding? Rarely cited, this first theological text of Calvin's gives unimpeachable testimony to the Reformer's state of mind during the months that surrounded his conversion.

Despite what he claimed, Calvin did not in fact write for any reader. Calvin wrote mainly, at least, for himself; he presented himself with a certain number of warnings and tried to see clearly into himself and around himself. Above all, he expressed his final concerns about the Reform, that it might degenerate into Anabaptism. This is the paradoxical reason why this text of transition or separation does not examine the Roman Church, which he was leaving, but the Reformed churches, which he was considering.

Calvin was clumsily trying to understand. He collided with this central question of death. The existence of the soul was not in question; the debate was over its nature. Does it survive the body? Or does it perish with it? Is it an individual principle, or a sort of essence without consciousness? Calvin tried to put the opposing doctrines into words:

> Our conflict therefore is over the soul in man, which some indeed confess is something, but after a man is dead they think it sleeps until the day of judg-

17. Calvin, *Oeuvres françaises*, p. 26.
18. Calvin, *Oeuvres françaises*, p. 29.

ment, when it will awaken from its sleep without memory, without any intelligence or feeling whatever. Others do not concede that it is a substance at all, but say it is only an aspect of life, brought into action by the breath of the arteries or the lungs, and that since it cannot survive without a body it dies and perishes together with the body, until the man as a whole is resurrected. But as for us, we maintain that the soul is a substance and that it truly lives after the death of the body as something equipped with sense and intelligence, and we undertake to prove the one and the other by clear testimony from Scripture.[19]

Thus three positions are theoretically possible once the existence of the soul is admitted: the soul sleeps until the last judgment; the soul dies with the body and, like it, is resurrected at the end of time; or finally, the soul survives the body, from which it is separated at death. It is this last solution, individual survival before the resurrection, that Calvin favored.

Calvin encountered difficulties in justifying this rather conventional position by the Scriptures. He particularly distrusted Ecclesiastes, the book of the Bible in which there is clear mention of the breath that animates both men and beasts. Calvin believed, together with his culture, in the survival of the soul and in the axiomatic distinction between men and animals, which have no title to immortality. Although undoubtedly worthy, Calvin's point of view would have lacked originality had he not brought up in his demonstration the fundamental question of time. As he built up his arguments, Calvin became aware of a hidden problem. The issue was no longer so much the existence of the soul and of the body as the conception of time. What are yesterday and today? What do these terms mean? Do they have an absolute value? Calvin came to ask himself about the very notion of "beginning." "If there has only been yesterday, He who was not before the beginning of the Old Testament at some time began to exist. What becomes of Jesus, this eternal God, first-born of all creatures according to his humanity, and the Lamb sacrificed from the beginning of the world?"[20]

This is a complicated argument, meandering through verbal thickets. The assertions of this first treatise are more often only inverted questions. Calvin here expresses one of his constant obsessions: Where should Christ henceforth be placed? Where should he be put, in time and space? Where is he found then, this Lamb "slain from the foundation of the world"? The text to which Calvin implicitly refers is found in Revelation, undoubtedly the New Testament book he cites with the greatest hesitation.[21]

19. Calvin, *Oeuvres françaises*, pp. 32-33.
20. Calvin, *Oeuvres françaises*, p. 61.
21. Rev. 13:8. The debate on the interpretation of this passage is briefly treated in B. Cottret, *Le Christ des Lumières* (Paris: Le Cerf, 1990), pp. 147-49.

We must reverse our perspective. Calvin's first theological treatise interests us more in the questions it poses than in the answers it claims to give. The relations between the soul and the body, eternal life, the resurrection, and finally the role of Christ, the veritable keystone of the Calvinist theological edifice, are so many confusing realms of research that opened in front of this man of twenty-five, confronted with an internal crisis from which flowed one of the major currents of Protestantism.

What should one think about this intermediate period that separates the death of an individual from the last judgment? In what may be his finest book, Pierre Chaunu recapitulated in a magisterial fashion as a historian and as a believer the questions of Christians about death. They are at the very heart of Calvin's attitude. Certainly, a strange amnesia has struck us today. "A very strange accident happened to us yesterday; we forgot we had to die," Chaunu forcefully points out.[22] The situation in sixteenth-century Europe was entirely different. Calvin lived in a world where death, agony, and disease were constantly present and unceasingly appeared. But that did not dull his fear of death. Calvin, indeed, belonged to the category of the anguished.

Christian death had to confront a double heritage. "Primitive Christianity seems to have built its idea in a very simple manner; it preserved and superimposed two somewhat heterogeneous ideas, the shade and the resurrection." Thus, Chaunu continues, the immortality of the soul of the ancients, that "unhappy and pale survival of the shade," should be distinguished from the Christian resurrection. It follows that the perspective of early Christianity was entirely dominated in its first centuries by the expectation of an imminent resurrection.[23] But then came the age of "encumbering time."[24] The length of the wait overcame the expectation; the end of time receded. An intermediate phase was filled with light and with shadows, the souls of the departed. This was a time of waiting, a time of the church, a time of intercessory prayers for the departed — until the scandal of indulgences, denounced by Luther. Protestantism cut to the quick; it suppressed purgatory and Masses for the dead. It was predictable that Calvin in his turn would pose to himself the question of death and of time. If we believe in the hypothesis of a "conversion" for Calvin that can be clearly located in time during 1532-33, it was on the whole logical that this young man's view of death underwent new developments. Was the *Psychopannychia* a treatise against Anabaptists? No doubt. But still more was it a self-examination, following upon the Stoic

22. P. Chaunu, *La mort à Paris: xvi*ᵉ, *xvii*ᵉ, *et xviii*ᵉ *siècles*, rev. ed. (Paris: Fayard, 1984), p. 3.
23. Chaunu, pp. 83-84.
24. Chaunu, p. 86.

temptation represented by Seneca. What does one know, what can one know, about death, about one's own death? How can one reconcile Christianity and the wisdom of the ancients? How can one keep the Reform from ending up as a sect? Finally, where should one place the resurrected Christ? The book pursues a double purpose. Its avowed end is of course the refutation of Anabaptism, but this does not exhaust its latent meaning. According to a recent interpretation, Calvin was confusedly aware of the gulf that divided the immortality of the soul, defended by Plato, from the Christian resurrection.[25] These are questions that permeate this first polemical text, in which the answer never exhausts the meaning of a question.

1534: The Placards

I have been moved by good feeling to compose and reduce to writing certain true articles on the important abuses of the Mass, which articles I desire to be published and posted in all the public places of the earth.

A. MARCOURT, 1534[26]

We used to be in the best and finest of situations. We have just fallen, through the fault of the most inept, into a period of calamity and anguish.

JOHANN STURM TO MELANCHTHON, MARCH 1535[27]

The split between Reformers and conservatives was accomplished. At the moment when Calvin distanced himself from the Roman faith, an event provided the spark that ignited the blaze. Placards, posted in various parts of the kingdom, deliberately assailed the heart of the Catholic system, the Mass, the expression of a sacrality that separated priests from laymen in the regular reenactment of the sacrifice of the cross. Were the Placards of 1534 a turning point? It has long been believed so, but this must still be explained. The impudent temerity of these articles marked a sharp break, but the political position

25. H. A. Oberman, *Initia Calvini: The Matrix of Calvin's Reformation* (Amsterdam: Koninklijke Nederlandse Akademie van Wetenschappen [Noord-Hollandsche], 1991), p. 31.

26. A. Marcourt, *Petit traité . . . de la sainte eucharistie* (1534), in G. Berthoud, *Antoine Marcourt, Réformateur et Pamphlétaire, du Livre des Marchands aux placards de 1534* (Geneva: Droz, 1973), p. 158.

27. É. G. Léonard, *Histoire générale du protestantisme*, 3 vols. (Paris: PUF, 1961-64), 1:209.

of the "Lutherans" had been constantly deteriorating during the previous year. The meeting in Marseille between Pope Clement VII and Francis I in the fall of 1533 had given hope to the enemies of evangelism. On January 4, 1534, the procession of the university to the Cathedral of Notre-Dame was accompanied by a solemn sermon "to give thanks to God and the Virgin Mary and all the saints for the king's goodwill toward the Catholic faith."[28] Francis I promulgated an edict against any "concealers" of Lutherans, who might hide heretics. In return, he promised to give informers a fourth of any property seized.[29]

This does not diminish the highly symbolic importance of the Placards. Luther's Ninety-five Theses of October 31, 1517, had no exact equivalent in France, but a great public event, the Affair of the Placards in October 1534, rendered the situation in France irreversible. The scandal concerned the Mass. The excitement was all the greater because the relations between heaven and earth, indeed between the living and the dead, were affected. The scandal of the Placards revolved around their interpretation of the Epistle to the Hebrews, which emphasized Christ the mediator, Christ the sole priest, Christ who by his unique sacrifice rendered illusory the priesthood of men and transformed the clergy into parasites, babblers, and impostors. What need does one still have for priests and their intercessions, mused Marcourt, repeating mentally that Christ "offered himself up" "once and for all"?[30] Even more than Romans, Hebrews was the cornerstone of the French Reformation. In the space of one night an invisible frontier cut across the kingdom, henceforth separating French evangelism from the Protestant Reformation. Neither justification by faith, nor the role of the Word, nor the predominance of Scripture had constituted a clear line of demarcation between the two camps. But the Mass — behold the watershed that henceforth divided two confessions. Between October 17 and 18 "a dream dissolved," that of a unity henceforth lost.[31] The agitation was considerable:

> In the year 1534 . . . placards were posted by heretics against the holy sacrament of the altar and the honor of the saints. Which being learned by the court, it was announced by the sound of two trumpets and proclaimed in the *palais* from the marble table that if anyone could indicate the person or persons who had posted the said placards, revealing it with certainty, he would be given 100 écus by the court. On the other hand, those found concealing them would be burned. By which means, as God wished, the thing came to

28. J. Dupèbe, "Un document sur les persécutions de l'hiver 1533-1534 à Paris," *Bibliothèque de l'Humanisme et Renaissance* 48 (1986): 410.

29. M. Isambert, ed., *Recueil des anciennes lois françaises* (Paris: Belin-Leprieur, 1828), XII, p. 402.

30. Heb. 7:27.

31. J. Jacquart, *François Ier* (Paris: Fayard, 1981), p. 269.

light, so that soon afterwards several were taken and brought as prisoners to the Châtelet.

The following Thursday and Sunday general processions were held for this reason in which the *Corpus Domini* was carried, the streets being decorated.

There was a rumor that such placards had also been posted at the Château d'Amboise, where the king then was, and that the king had sent to the Court of *Parlement* and to the *lieutenant criminel* to have them enforce strict justice.

There was also a rumor that for this reason the king had raised the wages of the *lieutenant criminel* by 600 livres a year for life, besides and in addition to his regular wages.

And on the following Thursday and Sunday general processions were held in which the *Corpus Domini* was carried and the streets were decorated.[32]

The move was a response to provocation. In Paris, in Orléans, in Amboise, and even in Blois, on the door of the king's bedchamber, were affixed "True Articles on the Horrible, Great, and Important Abuses of the Papal Mass, Devised Directly Against the Lord's Supper of Jesus Christ."[33] The time for conciliation was past; from now on people were separated into two camps, their quarrel being principally over the Eucharist. Certainly the search for a compromise continued,[34] but in hindsight the rupture appears to have been irreversible. "The Mass is idolatry," said the author of the incriminated document; people were outraged by this sacrilegious statement. If we may be permitted a semi-anachronism in speaking of emerging realities, "Protestants" and "Catholics" had the same concern, despite their profound differences. Both sides wanted to fight against sacrilege. They showed the same mentality, but they interpreted sacrilege differently. For some the Mass was sacrilege, while for others it was blasphemous to claim this.

Who was responsible? Antoine Marcourt, another Picard, like Lefèvre d'Étaples and Calvin.[35] This pastor of Neuchâtel was aided by numerous accom-

---

32. J. Lalanne, ed., *Journal d'un bourgeois de Paris sous le règne de François Ier* (Paris: Jules Renouard, 1854), p. 441.

33. "Articles véritables sur les horribles, grands et importants abus de la messe papale, inventée directement contre la sainte Cène de Jésus-Christ."

34. On this subject see the entirely remarkable work of T. Wanegffelen, "Des Chrétiens entre Rome et Genève. Une histoire du choix religieux en France, vers 1520-vers 1610" (*thèse* at the University of Paris I [Panthéon-Sorbonne], November 12, 1994; typescript, 2 vols., 913 pp.).

35. Marcourt, however, was still more radical than Calvin in his theology, being influenced by Zwingli, the reformer of Zürich. For him the Lord's Supper is purely symbolic, while for Calvin there is a real presence, albeit spiritual, of Christ in the elements.

plices throughout the kingdom, enabling him to distribute in many places this poster, thirty-seven centimeters by twenty-five, printed in Gothic characters. The heart of the crime was the repudiation of the Mass. The Protestant Lord's Supper and the Catholic Eucharist are distinguished by several essential features that emerge clearly in this provocative text.[36] Therein the Mass was described as blasphemous. The unique sacrifice of Christ could not be repeated in any circumstances. Hence a very strong anticlerical attack is mounted against the "wretched high priests, who, as if they were our redeemers, put themselves in the place of Jesus Christ, or make themselves his companions."

According to Marcourt, the Mass is not merely blasphemous, its contents are also idolatrous. "In this unfortunate Mass almost the entire world has been provoked to public idolatry, when it was falsely given to understand that under the species of bread and wine Jesus Christ is corporeally, really, and in fact . . . contained and hidden." Christ is not physically present in the elements. He was resurrected, rose to heaven, and is seated on the right hand of the Father. Communion therefore assumes a commemorative value. "The fruit of the Lord's Supper of Jesus Christ is to make a public protestation of faith, and in immediate confidence of salvation to make a present memorial of the death and passion of Jesus Christ." The Mass, on the other hand, is an absurd proceeding, an indescribable farrago of "chimes, howling, singing, ceremonies, lights, incense, disguises, and other sorts of monkey business." As for the priests, they are wolves that feed on the tender flesh of the flocks. "Like brigands they kill, they burn, they destroy, they murder all those who contradict them."

The break with reformist humanism was henceforth complete. Guillaume Budé, the great Budé who had been one of the leading forces behind the future Collège de France, allowed his indignation to break out in a testamentary text, *The Movement from Hellenism to Christianity* (March 1535). Inspired by Saint John Chrysostom, this manifesto was an urgent plea for the retirement of the wise and for the spiritual fulfillment of the incarnate Word. Budé called for a peaceful colloquy in which the scholars of the Catholic and Reformed parties might meet. But he condemned without appeal the Protestant Reformation, which he considered populist, and affirmed his trust in tradition and the ecclesiastical hierarchy. At the heart of this denunciation was his indignation at "the abominable crime committed by madmen."[37] The

---

36. The exact text of these placards was long unknown. It was not rediscovered until 1943, in Bern, in the binding of a sixteenth-century book. We cite it here following the transcription given in Berthoud, pp. 287-89.

37. G. Budé, *De transitu Hellenismi ad Christianismum* (1535); *Le passage de l'hellénisme au christianisme,* ed. M.-M. de La Garanderie and D. F. Penham (Paris: Belles Lettres, 1993), p. 6.

author continues, describing in his preface, dedicated to the king, the expiatory measures that culminated in the procession of January 21, 1535:

> You not only wished that the affair be investigated with the greatest care and the greatest rigor, you also ordered that the sacrilegious plot that had been unveiled be punished, and you sent reliable messengers everywhere, supplied with orders. You also commanded, as is usual in such circumstances, that prayers and public supplications be decreed. Then, on the day assigned for these prayers, you came to this city, the capital and glory of the kingdom, the particular and legitimate seat of the empire I have spoken of; you ordered the suspension of business and the closing of shops as on holidays.
>
> Having enjoined each man to carry a torch, you, advancing from the royal palace to the nearest church, where all the prayers were to begin, accompanied by the most brilliant escort — a form of court service — you decided that a cortege of incredible length, the most impressive in the memory of man, should assemble and proceed in great pomp, in order to appease the anger of God and wash away the pollution of the monstrous crime by all the best expiatory rites one could legitimately imagine or draw from tradition.

The next section offers a fascinating insight on Catholic devotion to the Eucharist. To counter the blasphemy expressed against the elements, there was no other response possible except the display of the host. The Affair of the Placards called for a metaphysical reparation, culminating in the adoration of the Holy Sacrament:

> In the course of the solemn and devout procession of the most holy sacrament in which God is present, and while a very great number of torches illuminated everything almost to the point of obscuring the light of the sun, and a very long line of reliquaries came in front, according to custom, serving simultaneously as instruments and agents for prayers and supplications; you, less like a king than like a pious flag-bearer and choir-leader for the multitude of torch-bearers, you attracted all eyes both from below and from above. In fact you visibly dominated with your bare head the compact circle of great men of which you were the center, and the dignity of your royal visage surpassed, in standing out from it, a body of nearly a thousand distinguished men. A part of them, recognizable by their collars made of scallops,[38] surrounded and escorted under your eyes the canopy with six bearers of the sacrosanct expiatory victim, offering the spectacle of an admirable devotion.[39]

38. Collar of the Order of Saint Michael, founded in 1469.
39. Budé, *Le passage de l'hellénisme au christianisme*, pp. 6-8.

While Budé, in this eloquent account, insists that the Eucharist, the body of Christ, had in a way come to avenge a personal affront, another witness mentions the presence of relics, "that is, the head of Saint Philip and the picture of Saint Sebastian, the reliquary of Saint Marceau, a very large silver image of Our Lady, and other relics," carried by the Parisian clergy. The clergy of the Sainte-Chapelle joined the procession in turn, adding their fragment of the "true cross, the head of Saint Louis, and other relics." Also various Lutherans were burned to add to the fun. The burning of heretics was back in fashion.

Chancellor Duprat organized the repression. Born in 1463 at Issoire in Auvergne, dying on July 9, 1535, in Paris, this scion of the bourgeoisie pursued a church career after the death of his wife. Archbishop of Sens, a cardinal, and finally a papal legate, he presided over the 1528 Council of Sens that condemned the "Lutherans." The Affair of the Placards increased his influence even further:

> Duprat, faced by the movement contesting Catholicism and its institutions, went ahead of Francis I, who was known to be more hesitant or more tolerant, at least before the Affair of the Placards. This scandal precipitated the king into the conservative party, which, in fact, would best serve the interests of the monarchy. Duprat then found himself supplied with power to fight against those he considered as invaders of the royal prerogative. He had lists of suspects drawn up and ordered imprisonments and executions. In January 1535 he conducted a highly macabre procession through the Paris streets in which the king, the ambassadors, and the counselors of the *parlement* participated. Its program involved six stops for meditation; in these six halting places were six stages for the sovereign and, opposite them, six stakes for burning six persons condemned for their participation, real or supposed, in the Affair of the Placards.[40]

A vicious circle then began, a desperate sequence of hasty provocation and brutal repression. But to neglect the metaphysical import of this vicious circle would be to misunderstand its meaning; iconoclastic profanation was matched by compensatory reparation. More fundamentally, as in the affair of the Rue des Rosiers, a cycle of expiation and of substitution was taking place. The parallel between the scandal of 1528 — the decapitated Virgin — and the events of 1534 — the Placards — shows the similarity between iconoclasm and blasphemy. In both cases the later atonement had an imitative aspect: the statue was replaced, the contested Sacrament of the Altar was venerated. The Eucha-

40. J. Garrisson, *Royaume, Renaissance et Réforme (1483-1559)* (Paris: Le Seuil, 1991), p. 179.

rist, the body of Christ displayed in the monstrance, was the antidote used in 1534 to purify the kingdom, polluted in thought or action by those responsible for the Placards. The sacred things — the host, the relics — reoccupied the space from which they had been expelled by sacrilege, destruction, or blasphemy. Expiation and substitution — is this not the very definition of sacrifice? What is sacrifice if not substitution? What is substitution if not identification, in an analogical sense? The consequence was an obvious raising of the stakes; Catholicism reinforced the sacrificial meaning of its acts and of its message at the very moment when the Reformers denied it. We will find the outcome of this conflict in Calvin, in his rejection of the Catholic Eucharist and his entirely spiritual conception of the real presence.

In January 1535 Marcourt renewed his provocations by distributing his *Short Treatise on the Holy Eucharist*.[41] The repression kept pace with this new provocation; a list of heretics was drawn up, expiatory processions were repeated, and finally, burnings were held to dissuade objectors. Jérôme d'Hangest, a relative of Calvin's first protectors in Noyon, joined the war against the Reformers, those agents of darkness who obscured the light of the gospel. "You, wretched and brazen . . . , say, This is not your body, Jesus Christ, but is merely plain bread."[42]

The bread is bread; the proposition is one of absolute rationalism. But if one adds that the bread is bread as Christ is God, the equivalence is combined with a hidden meaning. The reforming proposition was located at a turning point, that of the disenchantment of the world and of religious faith. Never more plainly than in Calvin can that ambivalence of faith be discovered that secularizes words and things in its determination to give no worship to anything but God.

---

41. *Petit traité de la sainte eucharistie.*

42. J. d'Hangest, *Contre les ténébrions, lumière évangélique* (Paris: J. Petit, 1535), cited by F. Higman, *La diffusion de la Réforme en France* (Geneva: Labor et Fides, 1992), p. 76.

CHAPTER 5

The Lovers of
Jesus Christ: 1535-36

To all lovers of Jesus Christ and of his Gospel, greetings.

J. CALVIN, PREFACE TO OLIVÉTAN'S BIBLE, 1535[1]

The proposition that Calvin was converted to Protestantism has no meaning, for in the 1530s Protestantism was not a body of doctrine which one had merely to adhere to. This is not the case even today, and was even less so in that formative century. Calvin did not in fact employ the term "Protestant" in defining himself. To this risk of anachronism is added another, a lack of understanding of the mechanisms of religion. Religious faith, like political conviction, is a matter of commitment more than of certainty. Calvin was content to respond to a call; he became, to adopt the admirable formula he himself employed, a "lover of Jesus Christ."

What did "Christian" mean for the sixteenth century? We must avoid the trap of words, using them, of course, because otherwise history becomes impossible, but refusing to be tied down by them. Thus "Christian," "Catholic," "evangelical," "Lutheran," and even "Protestant" are so many ensnaring terms, which require the same watchfulness as "Renaissance" or "Reformation." This wearing out of words is a continual process.[2] Because everyone was a Christian

---

1. The text of this preface is available in I. Backus and C. Chimelli, eds., *La vraie piété* (Geneva: Labor et Fides, 1986), pp. 13-38. References are to this edition.

2. Thus even at the end of the sixteenth century the Spanish version of the *Institutes*

in the sixteenth century — some with more conviction, some with less, of course, but institutionally everyone belonged to the same church — how, then, do we define the difference? How do we give a "purer meaning to the words of the tribe"? Behind the word "Christian" stood the call to an authentic evangelical life. A Christian was a disciple of Jesus Christ, Lord and master. The relationship of the disciple to his Lord is made up of love, of confidence, of a fidelity that cannot exist without reciprocity. This is what marks the Calvinist conception of faith, a relationship between man and God in which God has the first initiative. And the believer in all this?

Calvin, a believer, was "a lover" of Jesus Christ. The simple name "Christian" in his writings takes on its true metaphysical dimensions; it indeed becomes a challenge to the church, the whole church. This strong lay coloring, this pride in being counted among the number of the elect, appears implicitly in the preface Calvin wrote a little later for his cousin Olivétan's Bible: "We are all called to this inheritance without distinction of persons; male or female, small or great, servant or lord, master or disciple, cleric or layman, Hebrew or Greek, Frenchman or Latin, none is rejected; anyone who will with assured trust receive what is sent to him, who will embrace what is presented to him, in short, who will recognize Jesus Christ as what he has been given by the Father."[3]

Faith, saving faith, faith that alone brings salvation, as Luther had just been teaching, is the common possession of all humanity. At least, all people are called, even if some are less strongly called than others, as the statement would be corrected by the doctrine of predestination. The Protestant Reformation destroyed the axiomatic distinction between the faith of the ignorant and the faith of the educated. Nevertheless, a treatise on devotion for the use of the laity in 1527 still recognized the impassable gulf that separated "simple people" who did not have "perfect knowledge of the Holy Gospel, like the clerics," from "those with wisdom and learning." Simple people were granted minimal knowledge, enough to permit them to recognize that they were sinners, to confess their sins, and to reach paradise without hindrance.[4] In short, salvation depended strictly on the church and on this minimal and implicit faith in the validity of its sacraments. In rejecting this mediation, or at least in minimizing it, the message of Reform was potentially egalitarian, not with regard to the social system of course, but spiritually. It rejected in advance this dichotomy between a popular religion and an educated religion. This message was manifestly aimed

---

defined Calvinist doctrine as "Catholic" and "apostolic." C. de Valera, ed., *Institucion de la religion christiana* (Ricardo del Campo, 1597), translator's preface. If Catholic means "universal," today every Christian church might claim this title.

3. Backus and Chimelli, p. 32.

4. Guillaume Petit, *Le viat de salut* (Troyes: J. Lecocq, 1527). Cited by F. Higman, *La diffusion de la Réforme en France* (Geneva: Labor et Fides, 1992), p. 57.

at the priests, the *Nomenklatura* of the church, accused of having appropriated to themselves a Word that was public property. Access to the Bible constituted a right, a claim, an expectation, reinforced by a cultural impatience, an appetite for reading, a yearning that found in the alpha and omega of the Bible reasons to know, to believe, and to hope. Calvin insisted in the same preface: "And will all we men and women who carry the name of Christians nevertheless permit them to take away from us, hide, and corrupt this Testament, which so justly belongs to us, without which we cannot pretend to any rights in the kingdom of God, without which we are ignorant of the great benefits and promises Jesus Christ has given to us, and of the glory and blessedness he has prepared for us?"

The World Book

The holy Scriptures,
The books of piety
Concerning salvation
Abound today
In many countries.

S. BRANT, *THE SHIP OF FOOLS* (1494)[5]

What was the Bible in the past? For men of the first modern period, from the end of the fifteenth to the eighteenth century at least, it was a sort of encyclopedia, a summary of knowledge of words and things, of the world and of themselves. What was asked of the Bible? Spiritual testimony certainly, just as today, but also a synthesis of the most ancient wisdom, an inventory of things visible and invisible. In short, this book about God spoke intensely to men and about men. The Protestant Reformation owed its success to the Book; it incorporated it, made it its own, and joined forces with it. The history of the supreme Book is identified with that of books in general, to such a point that they are hard to separate. Man, reader of the Book; man, the subject of the reborn book; and the bookish man within Protestantism still pursue us and obsess us at the same time. But how can we make distinctions between apologetics and commentary, myth and history?

What was the first printed book in human history? A Bible, of course, set up in 642 folios of forty-two lines each. Gutenberg's *Biblia latina* (ca. 1450–ca. 1455) had a run of probably 150 copies, on paper or, at greater cost, on parch-

---

5. S. Brant, *La Nef des Fous* (Strasbourg: Nuée Bleue, 1988), p. 3. The original, *Das Narren Schyff*, appeared in Basel in 1494. It was followed by a Latin version, *Stultefera Navis*, in 1497.

ment. Small in comparison with today's runs, it was considerable if one takes into account the slowness of manuscript preparation in those days, the silent and endless copying that was brusquely supplanted by the multiplying power of print. The invention of printing and the experiencing of the Bible were henceforth intimately linked in men's minds. The Bible had been printed, the whole Bible. But which Bible were people to read? How could the authenticity of the text be guaranteed at the moment of its proliferation? The Italian humanist Lorenzo Valla (1405-57) was aware that a revision of the Latin versions was necessary, in the name of both grammatical precision and semantic exactitude. Were not the most ancient texts of the New Testament in Greek?

This great project fell to the lot of Erasmus. In England, where he went during his youth, humanist studies benefited from the support of Thomas Linacre and William Grocyn, two Hellenizing scholars educated in Italy. In 1516 Erasmus published his *Novum Testamentum* in Basel, based on Oriental manuscripts.

The Hebrew Bible proved to depend on separate editions of the different books, emanating from Spain and Italy. A complete version emerged from the press in Soncino near Mantua at the end of the fifteenth century. Another was printed near Naples. Meanwhile the study of Hebrew developed among scholars. Johannes Reuchlin (1455-1522) in 1506 published his *De rudimentis hebraicis*, which gave a method for learning vocabulary, grammar, and writing. The author also suggested numerous corrections to the Latin Bible. A Christian, fascinated by the cabala like Pico della Mirandola before him, he drew his knowledge from a Jew he met in Rome, Obadiah Sforno. Around 1515 several Hebrew Bibles were published in Venice. The Augustinian Felice de Prato also produced a *Biblia hebraica rabbinica* that was published in the city of the Doges in 1517. Other editions followed.

The polyglot Bible sponsored by Cardinal Ximénez de Cisneros marked a consummation. It came from the trilingual University of Alcala in Spain and appeared in 1517, with various *conversos*, former Jews, participating in it. Hebrew, Greek, and Latin coexisted in the five volumes of this monument of erudition, along with a dictionary and a grammar. In September 1518 a trilingual college opened in Louvain.[6] Twelve years later came the Parisian project of the college of royal lecturers, the future Collège de France.

The restoration of the Scriptures in Hebrew and Greek and their publication were not the whole of the colossal work of erudition undertaken in the sixteenth century.[7] The Latin Bible itself was not uniform; various versions circu-

6. Latin was taught by Adrian Barlandus, Greek by Rutger Rescius, and Hebrew by a converted Jew, Matthieu Adrien.

7. The Greek version of the Bible, or Septuagint, which went back to antiquity, ex-

lated.[8] In 1509 Lefèvre d'Étaples published a psalter, the *Quincuplex Psalterium*, which took account of several Latin versions of the text.[9] Three years later, in 1512, his version of the Pauline epistles gave the official text along with an alternative translation in smaller type. The editor Robert Estienne (1503-59) began the division into chapters and verses always used today. His Bibles of 1528 and 1532 gave Latin variants that were closer to the Greek or Hebrew text. In 1551 Estienne published a Greco-Latin New Testament, introducing the present divisions.

The Europe of the Bible

The Hebrew Bible, the Greek Bible, and the Latin Bible were not the only ones to attract the attention of the people. The translation and printing of the text in the different European languages served to reinforce national identities that were being more and more asserted. Overthrowing accepted ideas, J. Delumeau has insisted on the importance of those editions of the Bible that *preceded* the Protestant Reformation.[10] It was not the Reformation that created a need to read Scripture, but the reading of Scripture that brought about, partially at least, the Reformation. From 1520 to 1530 the Bible was a frontier of expectation.

The figures speak for themselves: between 1466 and 1522 about twenty-two editions of the Bible were printed in High or Low German, from Strasbourg to Cologne to Lübeck to Augsburg. The publication of Luther's New Testament in 1522 therefore merely accentuated an existing editorial phenomenon, rather than creating it from scratch. The phenomenon was, moreover, European. The Bible appeared in Italian in 1471, in Dutch in 1477, in Spanish in 1478, in Catalan in 1492, not to mention Dutch and Czech editions before 1480.[11]

---

isted at first only in manuscript form. This shows the lack of interest that surrounded it. A Venetian edition appeared in 1518, and another in Strasbourg in 1526. Zwingli was one of the rare individuals who gave it serious consideration.

8. The Gutenberg Bible, for example, was derived from a Dominican revision of 1226, the *Parisiensis parvi;* others came from another revision of 1471, used in Basel and Lyon at the end of the fifteenth century, known under the name of *Fontibus ex graecis,* after the first words of its declaration to the reader. Several corrections of the Vulgate saw the light in the sixteenth century. In 1511 a new revised edition of the *Fontibus ex graecis* appeared in Venice. In 1546 the Council of Trent appealed for a definitive edition of the Vulgate. This proposal achieved its end in the version of 1592.

9. G. Bedouelle, *Le Quincuplex Psalterium de Lefèvre d'Étaples* (Geneva: Droz, 1979).

10. J. Delumeau, *Naissance et affirmation de la Réforme* (Paris: PUF, 1965); new edition, 1973, pp. 71-72.

11. For an evaluation of these see P. H. Vogel, *Europäische Bibeldrucke des 15. und 16. Jahrhunderts in den Volksprachen* (Baden-Baden: Heitz, 1962); Bibliothèque nationale, Dé-

The situation henceforward in France is better known.[12] Two types of works had coexisted since the end of the Middle Ages, "abridged" Bibles and "historical" Bibles. The abridged Bibles were older. The first recorded example was in Carpentras about 1473-74. This may have been the first book ever printed in the French language.[13] Abridged Bibles were still being published until 1545; they were distributed from Lyon, Paris, and Normandy. This popular Bible was that of common sense and of simple souls "who do not understand Latin." A medieval compilation of the Old Testament, from Genesis to Job, ended with the division of universal history into seven distinct eras. *The Bible Translated from Latin into French,*[14] published in Caen about 1535, was presented as a gigantic paraphrase; in its first pages the two stories of creation in Genesis are fused into one. Adam appears on the sixth day, without other proceedings. The different books of the Bible lose their identity in this immense interpolation. Each section or chapter is introduced, in the most schoolmasterly fashion, by the formula "How." Thus one finds the headings "How God created the heavens and the earth," "How the deluge came on the earth," "How Esau sold Jacob his birthright," etc. The book ends, in the form of a prognostication, with the description of the "seven ages" of the world, identified with Adam, Noah, Abraham, Moses, David, the Babylonian exile, and finally the birth of Jesus Christ.[15] The Gospels hardly appear. The teachings of Christ are summed up in a few clumsy formulas: "I do not desire the death of the sinner; I want him to be converted to me by penitence so he may have life in heaven." In short, this was a sacred history much more than a Bible, more a book of stories than a manual of piety.

The historical Bibles did not abandon this type of interrogation. *How* was still the operative question, much more than *why*. Tables are presented, as in a quasi-encyclopedic syllabus. The object is a presentation that is not fundamentally different from that of the *Shepherds' Calculator and Calendar,*[16] the famous almanac. The will to understand prevails over piety and devotion. One learns "how the heavens and the earth were created, and all the other elements,"

---

partement des livres imprimés, *Catalogue des ouvrages anonymes des xvie-xviie-xviiie siècles* (in process). See also G. Bedouelle and B. Roussel, eds., *Le temps des Réformes et la Bible* (Paris: Beauchesne, Bible de tous les temps, 1989).

12. B. T. Chambers, *Bibliography of French Bibles: Fifteenth- and Sixteenth-Century French-Language Editions of the Scriptures* (Geneva: Droz, 1983), pp. xi-xii.

13. The editor was Guillaume Le Roy of Lyon, working for Barthélemy Buyer. The translation was the work of two Augustinians of Lyon, Julien Macho and Pierre Farget.

14. *La Bible translatée de latin en françoys.*

15. A *Bible des sept états du monde* [Bible of the seven ages of the world] by Geoffroi de Paris dated back to 1243.

16. *Le Compost et kalendrier des Bergers.*

and in conclusion, "how on the day of judgment the good will be in eternal glory, and the wicked eternally in hell."

One of the best-known examples of this Bible was printed in Paris around 1494-96. Charles VIII entrusted the task of publishing the text to his confessor, Jean de Rély. This historical Bible remained dependent on earlier medieval versions.[17] Carefully prepared in the workshop of Antoine Vérard, the work was adorned with picturesque vignettes inserted in the columns of text.[18] A simple and vivid introduction explained the meaning of Scripture:

> An emperor or a king should have in his palace three rooms, that is, an audience hall, a salon, and a bedchamber. A hall for rendering justice, a salon for drinking and eating, and a bedchamber for repose. In the same manner our Lord God, who is the true emperor and king, commanding the winds and the sea, has in his palace the world for his audience hall, where he gives his commands and judgments. For his bedchamber he has the soul of the just man, where he takes his delight and repose. And for his salon he has the holy Scriptures, where his followers take their meals. This salon has three parts, foundation, wall, and ceiling. History is the foundation, allegory its walls, tropology is the ceiling. History is Scripture that recounts his deeds, and facts worthy of being remembered that occurred in a year, month, or day. If it recounts his deeds of a month it is called a calendar, and if it recounts his deeds of a day it is called an ephemeris. . . . Allegory, which is the wall built on this foundation which we call history, says that Jerusalem is the city where Jesus Christ was judged and died. And allegory gives us to understand that Jerusalem is the church militant, that is the congregation and union of all good Christians and true Catholics. Tropology, which is the ceiling of this salon, makes clearly understood what allegory says obscurely.[19]

There were some twenty editions of French Bibles in this period. To these abridged and historical Bibles should be added certain very rare works, exposi-

---

17. The historical Bible was a medieval genre based on the *Historia scolastica* of Peter Comestor (d. ca. 1180). This historical paraphrase was translated into French by Guyart des Moulins in the thirteenth century, and supplemented by reference to the Latin of the Vulgate.

18. F. Dupuigrenet Desroussilles, *Dieu en son royaume. La Bible dans la France d'autrefois, xiiie-xviiie siècles* (Paris: Bibliothèque nationale et éditions du Cerf, 1991), p. 22.

19. *Le Premier volume de la Bible en françoys* (Lyon: P. Bailly, 1521), unpaginated. The four senses of Scripture in medieval exegesis were the literal or historical sense, the allegorical sense (for faith), the tropological or moral sense, and the anagogical sense (concerning final ends).

tions of the Bible or extracts of it that also circulated. They disappeared after 1545-46, overtaken by the progress of learning. The phenomenon occurred across Europe; within twenty years, from 1520 to 1540, the Scriptures became accessible in all the major languages of western Europe.[20] One may understand the importance of this development by thinking of all the literature that gave its tone to the piety of the time: *The Life of Our Lord Jesus Christ* by Jean Ursin, reprinted continuously from 1485 on; *Meditations on the Life of Jesus Christ*[21] by Ludolphe the Carthusian;[22] not to mention *The Golden Legend* and its many offshoots, to the limit of prosopopoeia and of the pharmacopoeia, where holiness comes to the rescue of health.

In France the true break occurred with Lefèvre d'Étaples, already the translator of the New Testament in 1523. In 1530 Martin Lempereur of Antwerp issued *The Holy Bible in French, translated according to the pure and complete translation of Saint Jerome, compared and entirely revised according to the most ancient and correct copies.*[23] The first few pages were occupied by a perpetual calendar. The dates of movable feasts, Easter in particular, depended on these subtle calculations, which shows the scope of the work. But piety thereafter dominated every other aim: "[Saint Paul] magnificently praised the divine Scriptures because they have God for their author, who is all-powerful, all-knowing, and completely beneficent. And also because above all human things they are proper and useful for achieving eternal happiness, since they drive away and refute all errors and render their true hearers perfect, instructed, and prepared for every good work."

The Bible is an object of piety, and not a collection of stories. It is not a mirror of the world, but the Word of God. The Reformations of the sixteenth century brought about a narrowing of devotion. The Word suffices; God speaks. It is useless to add interminable litanies or the numberless codifications of a tariff religion. This is the spirit of reform: a return to the sources. A return

20. *Il Nuovo Testamento di Greco nuovamente tradotto in linqua Toscana per A. Brucioli* (Venice, 1530); *Die ganze Bibel der ursprünglichen Ebraischen und Griechischen waarheyt nach, auffs aller treüwlichest verteüschet* (Zürich, 1531); *Biblia, das ist, die gantze Heilige Schrifft Deutsch* (Wittenberg, 1534) (Luther's version); *Biblia beider Alt und Newen Testamenten* (Mainz, 1534) (a German Catholic version prepared by Johann Dietenberger); *The Bible, that Is, the Holy Scripture* (1535) (M. Coverdale version); etc.

21. *Vie de Notre Seigneur Jésus-Christ* and *Méditations sur la vie de Jésus-Christ.*

22. L. Febvre, *Au coeur religieux du xvie siècle* (Paris: SEVPEN, 1968), p. 44. This *Vita Christi* of the fourteenth century enjoyed extraordinary popularity from 1490 on in the French translation by the Franciscan Guillaume Le Menand. This work was a composite one in which apocryphal works were mixed with quotations from the saints, particularly Saint Bernard.

23. *La saincte Bible en françoys, translatée selon la pure et entiere traduction de sainct Hierome, conferee et entierement revisitee selon les plus anciens et plus correctz exemplaires....*

to the living waters of the Word, and as a consequence the relativizing of all other devotion. The Bible, henceforth, is at the center of piety.

But this Word, handed over to laymen who did not understand Latin, did it not risk arousing quarrels among its hearers? Lefèvre admitted this freely; Calvin would not deny this. The sixteenth century did not know the principle of free inquiry, and distrusted spontaneous or naive reading. The Bible is a difficult text that disturbs and scandalizes; its reading requires certain intellectual preparation. Lefèvre asserted in his prologue: "If in certain passages some difficulties are found . . . and some statements which at first glance seem contradictory, nevertheless one should not suddenly weaken on reading them, or imagine for himself some ill-advised gloss or explanation of the words of Scripture . . . , but the obscure passages must be clarified by others that agree and are more evident. And to do this, and to make a good beginning in the understanding of the Scriptures, it is very useful first to consider the appropriateness of their language, according as each language has its own manner of speaking."

The Bible of Olivétan, 1535

> It is as difficult . . . to make the French language speak with the eloquence of Hebrew or Greek (since it is only barbarity in comparison with them) as if one wanted to teach the sweet nightingale to sing the song of the hoarse crow.
>
> OLIVÉTAN, "TRANSLATOR'S APOLOGY"

Unfortunately, Lefèvre's magnificent translation remained dependent on Latin versions of the Bible. It nevertheless enjoyed an enormous success, carried forward by numerous reprintings, principally in Antwerp and Lyon. But a complete recasting remained necessary, based on the Hebrew and Greek of the original texts. This was the work of Olivétan, the first author of a Protestant Bible in French, which appeared in Neuchâtel in 1535: *The Bible, which Is All the Holy Scriptures. In which are contained the Old Testament and the New, translated into French. The Old from Hebrew, and the New from Greek.*[24]

"Hear, O heavens, and give ear, O earth, for the LORD hath spoken."[25] This quotation from Isaiah served as a motto for the new Bible. The two central affirmations of the Protestant Reformation are clearly stated here: God speaks;

---

24. *La Bible Qui est toute la Saincte escriture. En laquelle sont contenus, le Vieil Testament et le Nouveau, translatez en Françoys. Le Vieil, de Lebrieu: et le Nouveau, du Grec.*
25. Isa. 1:2.

the Bible contains his Word. The very title given to the translation was far from anodyne: the Bible is "All the Holy Scriptures." If the Bible is "all," nothing can be taken away from it, and it would also be presumptuous to add anything whatsoever to it.

This Bible was made possible by the close cooperation of several people. The editor, Pierre de Vingle, expelled from Lyon and a refugee in Neuchâtel, had collaborated with the famous Marcourt, author of the Placards. The author, Pierre Robert, alias Olivétan (ca. 1506–ca. 1538), a cousin of Calvin, also from Noyon, owed his nickname to the olive-oil lamp that burned all evening to permit him to work. In the current slang of the preparatory schools, we would say he was a *chiadeur,* a "workaholic." A certain amount of foolhardiness or of courage, in fact of both, was needed to produce at age twenty-nine a complete version of the Bible.

The two young men had been fellow students in Orléans, but Olivétan's precise influence on Calvin remains difficult to ascertain. He adopted Reformed ideas earlier than Calvin; he was obliged to flee to Strasbourg in 1528, and received the aid of his Waldensian friends four years later.[26]

What are the chief merits of this version? One would have to be a specialist in ancient languages to answer. Olivétan invented a formula, repeated in the most Protestant Bibles in French until recent years; he translated the Hebrew tetragrammaton YHWH as "the Eternal" *(l'Éternel).* In the New Testament he rendered the Greek *presbyteros* "elder" and not "priest." This distrust of the clergy echoes the very spirit of the Reform; if Christ alone is a priest, why restrict the priesthood to a few? Indeed, one could claim that every believer receives some sort of "universal priesthood," since priesthood itself has disappeared. Olivétan likewise rejected the terms "apostles," "bishops," "deacons," "mystery," and "apocalypse," for which he sought French equivalents. He rgave fulsome praise to the "college of three languages," the future Collège de France, mentioning "the clear and pure water of truth brought and led from the living fountain of the living source through clean and sound pipes, disgorging it in abundance as far as the Gallic language extends, to irrigate and renew the flowers of our hope."

"The flowers of our hope" — on the whole, the freshly gathered metaphor smells sweet. An Alpine fragrance, a mountain charm pervades Olivétan's Bible. This text, rough as a torrent, nevertheless underwent incessant revisions.

---

26. The Waldensians, savagely persecuted, were the transition from the evangelical movement of the Middle Ages to the Protestant Reformation of the sixteenth century. Many were refugees in the valleys of Piedmont, where in 1532 they rallied to the Reform preached by Guillaume Farel. See in particular G. Audisio, *Le barbe et l'inquisiteur* (Aix-en-Provence: Édisud, 1979).

The first edition became obsolete very quickly; revised several times, it ended as the "Geneva Bible," which dominated French-speaking Protestantism for two centuries.[27]

Was Calvin entirely satisfied with this version? We doubt it. But his misgivings do not seem to stem from theological reasons. The true difference between the two men was more linguistic than ideological. Calvin was the champion of the French language, one of its foremost practitioners. All his success stemmed from this accomplishment. Olivétan was, as he himself admitted, a "hoarse crow."

But how could Calvin not acclaim the first translation of the Scriptures taken from the original Greek and Hebrew? Although associating himself with the project, he continued to distance himself from it. "Olivétan's positions did not necessarily reflect Calvin's ideas and wishes," the specialist notes shrewdly.[28] The Reformer participated in the Genevan revisions of Olivétan's Bible. In his preface to the 1546 edition of the Geneva Bible, "Calvin expressed publicly certain reservations about his cousin's work." "Honoring his memory and his 'labors,' worthy of 'great praise,' [Calvin] nevertheless criticized 'his language, rough and somewhat different from the common and accepted forms.' But 'a man was found [this refers to Calvin himself] who took pains to refine it, not only by polishing it, but also by adapting it to make it more easily understood by everyone.'"

Calvin's dissatisfaction with Olivétan's work following the latter's death concerned one particular point: Calvin could not admit that French was a barbarous language. Intelligibility was more important than literal meaning; Calvin's French, like the later language of Rousseau, succumbed to the illusion of transparency.

Olivétan's preface[29] followed Calvin's Latin privilege, introduced by a majestic and fraternal *Salutem*. Paying homage to his Waldensian friends, Olivétan compared the "poor little church" of Christ to the visible church, "this church, triumphing in pomp and riches," "warlike." The true people of God are the Waldensians. Certainly, they are a people "expelled and banished," "scattered to the four corners of Gaul," "reputed, wrongly and without cause however, for the

---

27. It was revised in 1536, 1538, 1539, 1540, and in 1543 under the nominal supervision of Calvin, who continued his work of adaptation in 1546 and 1551. Louis Budé and Theodore Beza henceforth assisted Calvin, and the result of their common efforts was the Bible published in Geneva by Robert Estienne in 1553. This was again revised, in particular in 1560 and in 1588.

28. O. Millet, *Calvin et la dynamique de la Parole. Essai de rhétorique réformée* (Paris: H. Champion, 1992), p. 779.

29. This preface, dated "from the Alps, February 12, 1535," is reproduced in G. Casalis and B. Roussel, eds., *Olivétan, traducteur de la Bible. Actes du colloque Olivétan, Noyon, mai 1985* (Paris: Le Cerf, 1987), pp. 169-89.

name of Christ and according to his promise, the most wicked, execrable, and ignominious that ever was."

This Waldensian allusion came to be applied to all the authentic Christians; they could not help being in a minority and persecuted. Olivétan then delivered himself of a sort of Rabelaisian enumeration of all the torments inflicted on the true disciples of Christ: "Insulted, blamed, driven out, denounced, disavowed, abandoned, excommunicated, anathematized, confiscated, imprisoned, tortured, banished, hung on ladders, mitered, spat on, shown on scaffolds, cropped in the ears, tortured with pincers, branded, shot, dragged through the streets, grilled, roasted, stoned, burned, drowned, decapitated, dismembered, and other similar glorious and magnificent titles to the kingdom of heaven."

The work was dedicated to the true church, the bride of Christ. The Bible is addressed to it, to edify it during its suffering. "Now therefore, O noble and worthy church, fortunate bride of the son of the King, accept and receive this word, promise, and testament, which you find written here word for word, and not elsewhere; where you can see the will of Christ your spouse and of God his father, according to which you will govern your family. Thus you will be called the best-loved in the place where it seemed you were nothing to Him."

Olivétan was an artisan, a poetical theologian, still fascinated by the soil. His text is a field. Impressed by the grace of his text, he had a humble awareness of his weakness. This is the theme of his "translator's apology," which follows the preface. Olivétan recalls Erasmus's metaphor of the plowman to describe himself. "I have toiled and dug as deeply as I could in the living mine of pure truth to draw from it the offering I bring for the decoration and ornamenting of the holy temple of God."

Through well-chosen words he also compares the gospel to an organ, no doubt composed of a multitude of tongues that all participate in the "melody" of the whole. But his own tongue does not join in. He finds himself unskillful, and holds that French is desperately impoverished when compared with the riches of Greek or Hebrew. He is resigned. The text must be carried to the people, even by speaking "barbarously to the barbarians." What a sorry language French is, moans Olivétan, cursing on his part this "common patois and flat language, avoiding any attempt to use poorly concealed and unaccustomed terms, which are introduced from Latin." French, then, is a sub-Latin, and Latin no doubt is a sub-Greek or a sub-Hebrew. French is a dialect of Latin, or rather French does not exist. There are only assorted dialects. "But to pursue the character of the French language, it is so diverse according to the countries and regions, or even the towns of the same diocese, that it is very difficult to satisfy all ears and to speak to all intelligibly. For we see that what pleases one displeases another; one uses one expression, another rejects it and does not approve of it. The man from the Île de France speaks one way, the Picard another; the Burgundian, the Norman, the Provençal, the Gascon, the Languedocian, the Limousin, the Auvergnat, the Savoyard, the Lorrainer each has his particular way of speaking, different from the others."

Does this mean that Olivétan took no interest in French culture or literature? We have a piece of conflicting evidence: the book was also ornamented with a prefatory Latin poem by Bonaventure des Périers. Des Périers deplored that French literature did not make more references to Holy Scripture. The Bible was therefore logically called in to fertilize French letters.

Olivétan's reservations about the French language set him in opposition to his cousin. The mature Calvin, preacher or author, took the opposite tack; he used both Latin and French with the same ease. In following him one can hardly find any indication of the least inferiority in the French language. And without advancing any theory whatever here, one may remark that Calvin is still easy to read in our time, while Olivétan's language offers more resistance to the reader.

Get Out!

Whosoever shall be ashamed of me and of my words, of him shall the Son of man be ashamed, when he shall come in his own glory, and in his Father's, and of the holy angels.

LUKE 9:26

It was undoubtedly at Basel that Calvin wrote the two introductory texts for his cousin Olivétan's Bible, the Latin letter to the reader and the address to the "lovers of Jesus Christ." The Affair of the Placards and the Bible of Olivétan were two sides of the same coin. The church had split. Calvin took note of the rupture; there was no point in pretending that compromise was still possible. No, henceforth there must be separation.

Calvin therefore went first of all to Basel, where he settled in January 1535. The Reformation there had been the work chiefly of Johannes Oecolampadius (†1531), who had been succeeded by Oswald Myconius. In March 1536 Calvin set out again and went to Ferrara in Italy in the company of Louis du Tillet. Renée de France, the daughter of Louis XII, had married Ercole Borgia, the duke of Ferrara. A patron of the arts, the duke had welcomed Benvenuto Cellini, while his wife established around herself an atmosphere favorable to evangelism. But suddenly in April Calvin had to leave again, and he went to Paris.

101

Two texts enable us to examine Calvin's mental state at that pivotal moment when he left France. They are generally known under the Latin title *Epistolae*. These *epistolae* are two Latin letters that were later taken up again in polemical treatises. They deal respectively with the necessity of fleeing Roman impiety and with the papistic priesthood.[30]

The first condemns participation in Catholic rites. It was addressed to Nicolas Duchemin, Calvin's former fellow student in Orléans. Now official to the bishop of Mans, he had admitted his scruples to Calvin in a letter since lost. Calvin explained to his "much loved brother" that the Mass and the Roman rites, those "unclean forms of impiety," plunge the faithful into captivity. One must depart Egypt at once to preserve oneself from all impure rites. Many evangelicals, in fact, even now that they have "conceived some taste for God," allow themselves to be seduced by weakness and accept compromises, sacrificing themselves to "idolatry."[31] One must follow the steps of Saint Cyprian by preferring martyrdom to sacrificing to idols. This letter was the source of the *Short Treatise* of 1543, which repeated the same injunctions from Geneva.

The rhetorical apparatus of this treatise was fairly simple. It was based on a takeoff from Exodus: France has become a land of captivity. The letter discusses the question of idolatry on the basis of the Old and New Testaments. Under the new covenant, the body of the faithful itself becomes the body of the Lord. Whence the need asserted by the primitive church to "preserve all parts of the body from every sacrilegious rite."[32] All the more should the faithful henceforth turn away from the Mass, the mere watching of which is sufficient to pollute them. The Mass is an impure spectacle. The letter then ends with an invocation to Duchemin, very Senecan in tone. Just as Israel departed from Egypt, the faithful should flee the contagion of popery and abstain from idolatry. France henceforth is Egypt. And reciprocally, to flee one's native land to become a refugee in a country conquered by the Reformation becomes an obligation. "Exile was indeed the first remedy proposed by John Calvin. His cleverness was . . . in inverting the terms and, by comparing staying in France to the captivity in Egypt or Babylon, to make it understood that the true exile was to be in a Catholic country."[33]

The second *epistola* would later be translated into French[34] under the title

30. See J. Calvin, *Opera Selecta*, ed. P. Barth, 5 vols. (Münster: C. Kaiser, 1926-36), 1:287-362, for these two texts: *De fugiendis impiorum illicitis sacris . . .* (pp. 289-328) and *De Christiani hominis officio in sacerdotiis Papalis ecclesiae . . .* (pp. 329-62).

31. Calvin, *De fugiendis impiorum illicitis sacris . . .* , pp. 289-90.

32. Calvin, *De fugiendis impiorum illicitis sacris . . .* , p. 302.

33. T. Wanegffelen, "Des Chrétiens entre Rome et Genève. Une histoire du choix religieux en France, vers 1520-vers 1610" (*thèse* at the University of Paris I [Panthéon-Sorbonne], November 12, 1994; typescript, 2 vols., 913 pp.), p. 100.

34. By Nicolas Des Gallars?

Treatise on Benefices (1554).[35] It dealt with the question of the Catholic priest-hood, and was based on two citations from Revelation that condemn the "luke-warm," otherwise called moderates, who refuse to choose either camp.[36] Very rare for Calvin, this reference to Revelation took a moving, indeed prophetic turn, reinforced by a reference to Isaiah.

Calvin condemned the possession of ecclesiastical benefices in the Roman Church. He took aim at Gérard Roussel, bishop of Oloron since February 1536. It was the end of an almost fraternal friendship. "Recognize with me the true nature of your charge according to the Word of God."[37] Calvin defines the functions of an ideal pastor according to Scripture: to teach the Word, defend the church against Satan, and lead an exemplary life. He opposes this ideal to the Roman reality; curés, regulars, and monks appear equally corrupt to him. Calvin challenges Roussel, "What sacrilege under heaven is more execrable than the Mass? And nevertheless you initiate priests into these criminal ceremonies. . . . You take delight in this sort of crime."[38] He then recalls the maledictions of Isaiah: "In mine ears said the LORD of hosts, Of a truth many houses shall be desolate, even great and fair, without inhabitant."[39] Calvin adopts a prophetic style to predict the destruction of a world, in this case the Christian church, that has betrayed its calling:

> We are before a spectacle exactly like that of a city struck by a severe epidemic and taken by assault by an enemy, that is sinking under the simultaneous impact of the double carnage and is being utterly consumed in a single fire. Blow your trumpet, watchman! To arms, shepherd! What? You do nothing? What? You remain inactive? What? You sleep? Now, when there is murder everywhere? . . . You must render an account to the Lord of so many dead, wretched man; you are a homicide so many times, you are guilty of the blood shed, every drop of which the Lord will reclaim from your own hand. . . . But it is still not enough to call you a homicide and traitor to your own people. Behold a crime too great for any branding to punish: as far as it depends on you, you sell Christ over again and crucify him anew.[40]

35. *Traité des bénéfices.*
36. Rev. 3:1: "I know thy works, that thou hast a name, that thou livest, and art dead." Rev. 3:15-16: "I know thy works, that thou art neither cold nor hot; I would thou wert cold or hot. So then because thou art lukewarm, and neither cold nor hot, I will spue thee out of my mouth."
37. Calvin, *De Christiani hominis officio in sacerdotiis Papalis ecclesiae . . .* , p. 332.
38. Calvin, *De Christiani hominis officio in sacerdotiis Papalis ecclesiae . . .* , pp. 338-39.
39. Isa. 5:9.
40. Calvin, *De Christiani hominis officio in sacerdotiis Papalis ecclesiae . . .* , pp. 340-41.

Calvin was not yet thirty, and it was impossible for him to remain in his homeland. Henceforth he would become the voice that from Basel, Strasbourg, and Geneva incited Frenchmen to resistance. The Reformation triumphed only through conflict, and not thanks to accommodation. A new Protestant church was called to be born and to develop on the fringes of Catholicism. This was Calvin's task during the last thirty years of his life.

PART II

ORGANIZATION AND RESISTANCE

CHAPTER 6

From Basel to Geneva: 1536-38

Before Calvin was in this city we drank good wine.

ANTI-CALVINIST REMARK, 1553[1]

We have those in Geneva who would like to make themselves bishops if they were not kept from it.

TABLE CONVERSATION, 1554[2]

The overlap of two destinies, of a man and of his chosen city, should not mask in hindsight the part that chance and coincidence had in this providential encounter. The love affair between Calvin and Geneva was never devoid of impatience, indeed of suspicion and exasperation, not to speak of open rejection at times. The legend of a Jovian or Olympian Calvin, imposing his sovereign law on Geneva, is hardly valid.[3] Though Calvin finally retained Geneva, and Geneva kept Calvin, other choices were offered to the Reformer: Basel, in the first place, where he published the first Latin version of his *Institutes*;[4] then

---

1. *Annales Calviniani, Opera Calvini* (hereafter cited as *OC*) 21, col. 555. Remarks attributed to a certain Vulliodi, Thursday, October 19, 1553. The *Annales Calviniani* (*OC* 21, cols. 181-818) draw especially on the Registers of the Geneva Council, 1536-1564, vols. 29-58, Geneva archives, as well as the Registers of the Acts of the Consistory and those of the Venerable Company of Pastors.

2. *Annales Calviniani, OC* 21, col. 566.

3. Amédée Roget (†1883), *L'Église et l'État à Genève du temps de Calvin. Étude d'histoire politico-ecclésiastique* (Geneva: J. Jullien, 1867), p. 87.

4. This first edition was published by Thomas Platter the elder, for whom see the re-

Strasbourg, from which Calvin tore himself away only with regret in 1541 to settle finally on the shores of the Leman. Going from Basel to Strasbourg and ending up in Geneva again mirror a spiritual itinerary. Basel was the city from which the genius of Erasmus shone out for fifteen years,[5] the city of early humanism, covered up by the contribution of the Reformation.[6] From Basel to Geneva Calvin followed a route of initiation that led from great literature to the Reformation. Strasbourg was much more than a stopping place; it was the city of the dream-like utopia of a city upon the hill, given to man and to God. It was in Strasbourg that Calvin became a Calvinist; Protestantism there was a fact of civilization. For the adversaries of the Reformation at the end of the century, the identification was total: they carped endlessly, in a somber litany, at that "collection of brigands and thieves, hiding in the city of Geneva." It was to that place, in fact, that "there have fled from all parts of the world, as to an asylum and place of safety, all the criminals and evildoers, lost and abandoned people, thieves, robbers, brigands, homicides, murderers, assassins, sorcerers, enchanters, poisoners, arsonists, counterfeiters, and the whole band of outlaws and pillagers, because no other country has been willing to endure them, either among the Christians or even among the Turks."[7]

From the Frontier to the Refuge

Basel, Strasbourg, Geneva — or rather, more accurately, as it doubtless must be written, Basel, Geneva, then Strasbourg, and finally Geneva — these three crucial points have in common their (relative) geographical proximity. They are located generally northeast of the present French territory, in a frontier zone between the France, Germany, and Switzerland of today. Linguistically the same is true; the area is more or less on the border between French and German speech, and even on that of Italian to the south. Calvinism is inseparable from the myth of the frontier. It established itself in an undecided space; on the edge of the kingdom, it marked a threshold, a hope, and an expectation of the restoration of the true faith, embracing all hearts and all souls in the renewed announcement of the gospel.

Calvin's Geneva often showed itself reticent and stubborn, even frankly rebellious. But is not ingratitude to their rulers common among populations?

---

cent book by E. Le Roy Ladurie, *Le siècle des Platter, 1499-1628* (Paris: Fayard); three volumes planned; vol. 1, *Le mendiant et le professeur* (1995), in particular pp. 190ff.

5. Erasmus returned to Basel to die there on July 12, 1536.

6. Johannes Oecolampadius was the best-known Basel Reformer.

7. Anonymous, *Le boutefeu des calvinistes* (Frankfurt, 1584), p. 6.

In the course of his treatise on Genevan institutions, a chronicler recalled the Jews: "The Jews were the people chosen by God, to whom he had given so many gifts and benefits, and yet what ingratitude they showed to him! How many complaints they made against him and his servant Moses, whom he had given them for their leader!"[8]

To call Calvin a new Moses, however, is an imperfect comparison. There was certainly something of the legislator about him, but all the same his city was not theocratic. The pastor was distinct from the magistrate; the ancient division of duties between the spiritual and the temporal was never questioned by the Reformer. Unlike Moses, Calvin did not truly direct the people, but rather guided them. He was a new Aaron more than a new Moses.

The Calvinist city still maintained itself only on the margins of its powerful neighbors: France of course, but also Lorraine and Savoy, and the nebulous Holy Roman Empire. It was in the true sense a city of refuge, to which flowed the unsatisfied, the insatiable, the lovers of Jesus Christ, desirous of building an ideal Christian society, still inaccessible fifteen centuries after the preaching of Jesus Christ.

This refuge also took on a metaphysical character; exile was a foretaste of the final separation, that of death. Thus Anne de la Vacquerie, wife of Laurent de Normandie, the former mayor of Noyon, rejoiced on being in this refuge on the eve of her death (April 1549): "Oh, I am joyful at having left that accursed Babylonian captivity and that I am going to be delivered from my final prison! Alas, how it would be if I were now in Noyon, where I would not dare open my mouth to confess my faith frankly, even while the priests and monks vomited out all their blasphemies around me! And here I not only have liberty to give glory to my Savior so as to appear boldly before him, but I am guided there by the good exhortations you give me."[9]

This refuge furnished a foretaste of eternal life. Calvin declared with respect to this Christian death, "She forthwith magnified the grace of Jesus Christ, and there had her refuge."[10]

---

8. François Bonivard, *Advis et devis de l'ancienne et nouvelle police de Genève, suivis des advis et devis de noblesse et de ses offices ou degrez et des III estats monarchiques, aristocratiques et démocratiques* . . . (Geneva: J. G. Fick, 1865), p. 149.

9. J. Calvin, *Des scandales*, ed. O. Fatio (Geneva: Droz, 1984), pp. 49-50.

10. Calvin, *Des scandales*, p. 50.

The *Institutes,* First Version (1536)

I did not then bring out the book as it is now, copious and the product of great labor; but it was only a small booklet containing summarily the principal points.

JOHN CALVIN[11]

With these words Calvin recalled the first version of the *Institutes of the Christian Religion,* which appeared in March 1536. The author mentioned his stay in Basel, during which time "they burned many faithful and holy people in France." He spoke of them as "holy martyrs." Royal policy in France wavered between accommodation and repression. Following the excitement stemming from the Affair of the Placards, the Edict of Coucy marked a turn toward appeasement (July 16, 1535).[12] The Lutherans were offered a cessation of prosecutions provided they lived "as good and true Catholic Christians should." Moreover, they must renounce "their said errors, which they will be required to abjure canonically within six months hereafter." The edict was also designed to oppose the threat of the depopulation of the kingdom by raising the issue of the "fugitive religionaries." This measure was extended the following year, but in December 1538 the Edict of Coucy was revoked. Hostilities resumed, and in June 1539 a new edict envisaged the extirpation of the heresy. A year later the Edict of Fontainebleau charged the royal officers of justice with personally overseeing the denunciation of heretics. The policy of *détente* lasted about three years, from 1535 to 1538.[13]

Francis I's deeply held beliefs remain unclear. It is essential to analyze the king's views to understand Calvin's attitude. From 1536 to 1538 France was engaged in its third war with Charles V and had need of Protestant allies, both in Germany and in Switzerland. But peace was hardly concluded with the empire when the measures of clemency enacted at Coucy were canceled. Thus the future of the French Reformation seemed to depend on the personal attitude of Francis I. The Strasbourger Johann Sturm wrote to Bucer on March 4, 1535: "I have never better understood this passage of the holy Scriptures, 'The king's heart is in the hand of God,' than at the present time; for in the midst of the stakes [for burning heretics] he dreams of a reform of the church."[14]

Bullinger, in a letter to Bucer on March 28, 1535, mentioned Francis I's

---

11. J. Calvin, preface to *Commentaire des psaumes* (1557), *OC* 31, col. 24.

12. J. Jacquart, *François Ier* (Paris: Fayard, 1981), p. 271.

13. Considerations of international politics partly explain this clemency from Francis I, who was engaged in negotiations with the German Lutheran princes. This was also the time of Pope Paul III's ascent to the pontifical throne. The new sovereign pontiff elevated Jacopo Sadoleto and Jean du Bellay, both enlightened humanists, to the cardinalate.

14. *OC* 3, col. xviii.

cooperation with the German Lutherans while still persecuting them in France, and concluded, "[Francis I] rides on two saddles at once."[15]

It is in this troubled context that we should place the appearance in Basel of the Latin version of the *Institutes* in 1536. It was a response to the attacks of Guillaume Budé. His *Movement from Hellenism to Christianity* had appeared a year before, almost to the day, in March 1535 (see chap. 4 above). Calvin took up the challenge and intervened as a lawyer, addressing his brief to the king. The dedication of the *Institutes* to the king attempted to put the activity of Reform under the high and enlightened protection of Francis I, whose responsibilities included the administration of justice.[16] The "most excellent king" was warned, according to approved rhetoric, against the evil counselors who filled his "ears and his heart" with their "false calumnies."[17] Every monarchy, in fact, should be inspired by the royalty of Jesus Christ, "whom the Father made king with dominion from sea to sea, and from the rivers unto the ends of the earth."

But the *Institutes* did not deal only with existing circumstances. A profoundly original theology was introduced; it was elaborated during the following years, separating itself more and more clearly from Lutheranism. It was a matter of culture as much as of philosophy; Calvin had a French passion for clarity, reinforced by his legal education. He took care to defend the antiquity of the restored faith, in those times when longevity and legitimacy went hand in hand. He claimed that the Reformed faith was not novel, but was based on the apostolic preaching and through it conformed to the teaching of the Fathers. It did not set aside the patristic doctrines, but was inspired by them in a critical fashion. Some anticlerical comments accompanied the argument, as when the author talked about the "idle bellies" of the monks, whose cloisters he compared to "brothels" where people gorged on the "substance of others." (The chaste Calvin always gave his imagination free rein when he described the behavior in the monasteries.)

In fact, this polemical preface was a veritable doctrinal defense and legal plea, as if Calvin hoped that Francis I, if in a hurry, would read at least the first few pages of his treatise. "This preface has as it were the grandeur of a complete defense, although I made no claim to provide a defense in it but only to soften your heart to give a hearing to our cause."

Thus, the first version of Calvin's masterpiece, his *Institutes of the Christian Religion*, was published in Basel. The text itself was still, in many respects, a

15. *OC* 3, col. xix.

16. J. Bohatec, *Budé und Calvin. Studien zur Gedankenwelt des franzözischen Humanismus* (Graz: Böhlaus, 1950).

17. See J. Calvin, *Institution de la religion chrétienne*, ed. J. Pannier, 4 vols. (Paris: Belles Lettres, 1961), I, pp. 7-36, for the rest of this dedication.

pleading *pro domo,* a defense of himself.[18] Extensively recast and enlarged on several occasions, the work deserves to be dealt with at greater length (see chap. 14). But it is possible to point out its immediate importance: the *Institutes* crossed "a historical threshold." It put "an end to the period of Lutheranizing, mysticizing, and evangelical wanderings" and furnished those who doubted the established church with "a body of precise dogmatic definitions," while in due time proposing "an effective church organization." Thus numerous dissidents, separated from Catholicism, were "progressively won over to the doctrines of John Calvin, thanks to the establishment of a network of direct or indirect correspondence with the city of Geneva, where the Reformer settled permanently in September 1541." In a word, the French Reformation, from "various empirical searches for the Truth, thus evolved toward a state of orthodoxy. It tended to assemble all those who were aware of the need for a re-formation of the people of God under the paradigm of the biblical people of the Covenant."[19]

Moreover, the *Institutes* appeared opportunely at the moment when the royal repression increased, and thus "accompanied a veritable unleashing of the phenomenon of conversion."[20] What did these people feel but an intense conviction of being chosen by God, the beginning of that theory of predestination that Calvin would develop? Yes, "after centuries of forgetfulness of God, those men and women who were the first in a hostile and blind world to be illuminated by the Word could consider themselves among the elect."[21]

These were the "institutes," then, of the Christian religion, and not merely a "summa theologica" in the Thomist tradition or a philosophical treatise. Calvin used the word "summa" in his exposition, but he opted for another title, "institutes." The Calvinist word *"institution,"* in the classical tradition, described a pedagogical activity, whence the modern French word *instituteur,* "schoolteacher." Thus, paralleling Quintilian's *Institutes of Oratory (Institutio oratoria),* Erasmus had issued his own *Education of a Christian Prince (Institutio principis christiani),* imitated by Budé.[22] The "education *(institutio)* of a

---

18. T. H. L. Parker speaks, in a concise formula, of an "apologia pro fide sua." *John Calvin: A Biography* (London: J. M. Dent & Sons, 1975), p. 34.

19. D. Crouzet, *La nuit de la Saint-Barthélemy. Un rêve perdu de la Renaissance* (Paris: Fayard, 1994), p. 19.

20. Crouzet, p. 20.

21. Crouzet, p. 21.

22. Born about A.D. 30, Quintilian wrote his *Institutio* between 93 and 96. This manual stresses pedagogy and education, mentioning the preparation of the child from its first book on. Quintilian, *Institution oratoire,* ed. J. Cousin, 5 vols. (Paris: Belles Lettres, 1975-78). Erasmus's *Institutio principis christiani* appeared in Louvain and Basel in 1516, with a dedicatory letter to the future Charles V, who was then still only archduke of Austria; worth does not depend on age.

prince" was a current topic in the sixteenth century.[23] Moreover, the *Institutes* also recalled the most popular manual of law of the period.[24] With his legal education Calvin could not have been unaware of this when giving his theology the form of an *institutio*. The pedagogical meaning was therefore evident in the language of the time. However, we can add an additional point: Calvin contributed to giving the word "institution" its modern meaning. Society, the church, the state were not for him facts of nature, but of culture. These "institutions" have as their principal end the controlling of fallen human nature; they are collective organisms whose existence inevitably derives from a founding act. The ultimate Christian institution is the city. It acquires this title by the will of the governed and is subject to the rule of law.[25] In other words, the Christian city does not exist spontaneously; it appears as the fruit of a culture, of a pedagogy, of a history, indeed of a political process. The word "institution" "designates the foundation, the base, the principles of all organizations." It also refers to "the doctrines designed to furnish a firm basis for an organization." Calvin's work describes primarily "the organization of the society of the followers of Jesus Christ," or the church. But the term came to be applied to "the organization of the city of men." It is not astonishing from this standpoint that the Calvinist city, from Hobbes to Locke or Rousseau, ended in the theory of a social contract. The concern with "civil government," the respect due to the "magistracy," are the counterparts of a separate "ecclesiastical" government. The Christian institution has no theocratic character; it depends, on the contrary, on the separation of the political and religious powers. The *Institutes of the Christian Religion* cannot, however, be confined within these secular perspectives; according to Calvin, "the state, like the church, should obey the will of God."[26] To reform,

23. For example, Guillaume Budé, *L'institution du prince* (ca. 1515-22), text given in full in C. Bontemps, L. P. Raybaud, and J. P. Brancourt, eds., *Le Prince dans la France des xvie et xviie siècles* (Paris: PUF, 1965), pp. 77-139. The title *"institution"* was certainly not from Budé himself, but it harked back to well-attested usage. Huguet's *Dictionnaire de la langue française du seizième siècle* still gives the word *institution* the meanings only of "education," "formation," and "instruction." Furetière's dictionary already gives a definition closer to contemporary usage: "*Institution* is generally used for everything invented or established by men. It is opposed to *nature*." But it was the eighteenth century that vulgarized the word in the plural, *les institutions,* to describe those organizations concerned with public affairs.

24. Parker, p. 14.

25. B. Cottret, *The Huguenots in England* (New York: Cambridge University Press, 1991), p. 231.

26. J. Boisset, "La Réforme et les Pères de l'Église: les références patristiques dans l'institution de la religion chrétienne de J. Calvin," in *Migne et le renouveau des études patristiques. Actes du colloque de Saint-Flour (juillet 1975),* ed. A. Mandouze and J. Fouilheron (Paris: Beauchesne, 1985), p. 40.

from this standpoint, is to transform the relations among men, to cleanse or moralize them in the name of a Christian ideal full of distrust for a nature fallen through sin.

The Geneva Calvin Found

This holy evangelical law and Word of God.

THE GENERAL COUNCIL'S ACCEPTANCE
OF THE REFORMATION, MAY 21, 1536[27]

Post tenebras lux. After darkness, light. The motto of the Calvinist Reformation was also that of a city, Geneva, where the spirit of Calvin triumphed. However, the situation was not that simple; the Genevan Reformation in fact *preceded* Calvin's arrival. Moreover, without wanting to minimize the importance of religious factors, the Reformation also had considerable political importance, by providing a city with the key to its independence. In 1500 Geneva still revolved around Savoy; in 1555 Calvinism triumphed within the walls of an independent city, profoundly remodeled by its role as the Protestant capital. What had happened in the meantime?

A brief recapitulation is necessary here. While remaining nominally part of the Holy Roman (German) Empire, Switzerland in fact separated itself more and more from it in the course of the fifteenth and sixteenth centuries.[28] Three entities then emerged: the Confederation, the Valais, and the Three Leagues of the Rhaetian Alps. The Confederation included Zürich, Bern, Lucerne, Basel, and Fribourg — thirteen cantons in all. Increasingly independent, the Republic of Geneva was properly only an ally, not a full member of the Confederation.

We must avoid the simplistic idea of a religious reformation controlling the civil power to erect a theocratic, indeed fundamentalist state. In fact, it was almost the opposite, as the chronology demonstrates. Two revolutions took place in the sixteenth century, a political transformation and a religious reformation. These did not entirely coincide in time. "Geneva is the very type of a city-state, constantly threatened in its independence and in the integrity of its laws, constantly on the *qui-vive*, with the fragility of a political system that was

---

27. A. Roget, *Histoire du peuple de Genève depuis la Réforme jusqu'à l'escalade,* 7 vols. (Geneva: John, Jullien, 1870), 1:2.

28. It refused to submit to the reform of the empire in 1495. The Swiss cantons wished to be sovereign in judicial, military, and financial matters. The Peace of Westphalia in 1648 ratified the separation of the Swiss from the empire.

apparently doomed during the period of the formation of the great territorial states."[29]

Two parties opposed each other in Geneva: the Mammelus, or conservatives, and the Eidguenots, opposed to Savoy. The word *Eidguenots* derives from a German word meaning "confederates" and may be the origin of the word *huguenot*, later used to designate the French Protestants. As for *Mammelu*, the allusion is clear enough: it refers to the Oriental Mamelukes. The pejorative meaning of the term was insisted on at the time to describe those who loved "better to be serfs and slaves than to live in liberty, like the soldiers of the Sultan of Egypt, who to obtain wages have made themselves serfs and slaves of the said sultan."[30]

The duke of Savoy would no longer endure this challenge to his authority. Charles III entered Geneva in 1524 and convoked the "Council of the Halberds," which affirmed the authority of the bishop and of Savoy over the restive city. Two years later, in 1526, the union, or *combourgeoisie*, with Bern and Fribourg clearly marked the city's Swiss preference.[31] The Reformation played no role in these events. "In its initial phase the Genevan revolution had no confessional causes; directed against the power of the prince-bishop, it was essentially a political movement."[32] The religious reformation in fact followed the political revolution.

Bern greatly encouraged the movement. Several evangelicals came together in Geneva.[33] The first Protestant services were celebrated on Good Friday in the year of grace 1533. A public debate followed in January 1534, in which Guillaume Farel confronted a Dominican, Guy Furbity. Farel was born in Gap in 1489, at the border of Upper Provence and the Dauphiné. This redhead, permanently influenced by Lefèvre d'Étaples, had untiringly preached the Word in Neuchâtel and in the Vaud district.[34]

29. Jean-François Bergier, *Les foires de Genève et l'économie européenne de la Renaissance* (Paris: SEVPEN, 1963), p. 9.

30. Bonivard, p. 19.

31. Fribourg, remaining Catholic, later withdrew from the *combourgeoisie*.

32. W. E. Monter, "De l'évêché à la Rome protestante," in *Histoire de Genève*, ed. Paul Guichonnet (Toulouse: Privat; Lausanne: Payot, 1974), p. 133.

33. Claude Bernard, Baudichon de la Maisonneuve, Étienne Dada, Pierre and Robert Vandel, Claude Roset, Jean Goulaz, and of course Ami Perrin, who will be discussed later.

34. Farel also wrote the very first Reformed works in the French language: *Le Pater Noster et le Credo en françoys* (Basel: A. Cratander, 1524); *Sommaire et briefve déclaration* (Lyon, 1529); with Pierre Viret, *De la très saincte Cène de nostre Seigneur Jésus* (Basel, 1532?). The second edition of the *Pater Noster*, appearing under the title *L'Oraison de Jésuchrist* (Paris: S. de Colines, 1525), also included some extracts from Luther. For Farel, consult *Guillaume Farel* (Neuchâtel, 1930); P. Barthel, R. Scheurer, and R. Stauffer, eds., *Actes du colloque G. Farel 1980, Cahiers de la Revue de Théologie et de Philosophie* 9 (1983).

The population of Geneva had driven out its last bishop, Pierre de la Baume. Bishop of Geneva since 1522, "believing it a sovereign obligation of a prelate to set a full and dainty table, with good wines,"[35] this unfortunate dignitary saw clouds gathering on the horizon. It was still necessary to wait some months before the Reformation became official in 1535. The Small Council provisionally suspended the celebration of the Mass, while the regulars fled, with the exception of a few Franciscans. The clergy had been an important presence in Geneva, about 5 percent of a population of a little over 10,000. One should add to these members of the clergy the equally large number of laymen who worked in their service.[36] A few weeks later coins were solemnly struck, giving the city its definitive motto, "After darkness, light." A chronicle reports: "Because their old motto had been *Post tenebras spero lucem* [After darkness I hope for light], they put on one side of the said coins *Post tenebras lux,* saying that they had attained the light, and on the other *Deus noster pugnat pro nobis* [Our God fights for us]."[37]

The magistracy replaced the bishop. No representative of the clergy seriously influenced the changeover; there was a total "eclipse of the old ecclesiastical personnel."[38] The religious reformation followed a civil reformation. It was in every respect a reformation "from above." As for Farel, taking advantage of this ecclesiastical void, he concentrated "for a time in his own person all the attributes of the clergy."[39]

Should a date be proposed to mark the beginning of the reformation? Things accelerated in the spring of 1536. On Friday, March 10, *Master Guillaume Farel* gave "an exhortation that in the parishes subject to this city provision should be made that the Word of God be preached." The city council agreed: "It was decided and resolved that the subjects should be exhorted and that everywhere proclamations should be made similar to those in the city concerning obedience and abstinence from fornication and blasphemy."[40] The proclamation of the Word and the struggle against dissolute morals — these two objectives would be constants in the time of Calvin. Without further delay

---

35. A contemporary judgment reported by Monter, p. 130. Pierre de la Baume, a cardinal in 1539, became archbishop of Besançon in 1544.

36. H. Naef, *Les origines de la Réforme à Genève,* 2 vols. (Geneva: Droz, 1968), 1:22-25. G. Cadier, "Dans l'ombre de la Réforme: les membres de l'ancien clergé demeurés à Genève (1536-1558)," *Bulletin de la Société d'Histoire et d'Archéologie de Genève* 18 (1987): 367-88.

37. Bonivard, p. 135.

38. Roget, *L'Église et l'État,* p. 9.

39. Roget, *L'Église et l'État,* p. 12.

40. *Annales Calviniani, OC* 21, col. 197, Registres du Conseil de Genève 29, fol. 43.

a campaign began against young girls who did not cover their heads. It was the parents' duty "to cover the heads of virgins."[41]

But what to do with the old clergy? Ecclesiastics were suspect. On Monday, April 3, all the priests were assembled to be instructed as to what conduct to adopt from then on. "We have asked you here by a resolution of our council to know from you whether you wish to live according to evangelical doctrine and also to correct you because, against the prohibitions given you by us, you have said Mass and given other papal sacraments against the ordinance of God, which displeases us."[42] The priests answered that of course they agreed to follow the gospel, but continued, "We pray you that it may please you to let us live as we have said we would and as our neighbors do; and we are people who want to obey in everything. Our forefathers were good men, and we want to follow them. Nevertheless, when we see our neighbors changing their manner of living we will do likewise."

The pressure mounted; there was a complaint about Georges Putex, curé of Satigny, who possessed "books by which he seduces the people." The terrified priests were given a whole month to convert. They must announce that "the evangelical doctrine preached in this city is the holy doctrine of the truth." While waiting they should not "meddle in saying Mass, baptize, confess, marry," or conduct a single papal rite. Also all the parishioners should be exhorted to go to "the sermons to hear the Gospel." Farel accompanied the measure with many explanations of the will of God and the true contents of the Holy Scriptures. On April 5 the canons were also convoked and also asked not "to say Mass any more or make other papal sacrifices."[43] Finally, on Sunday, May 21, a day of joyful memory in the Geneva Protestant chronicles, the people, assembled in general council, adhered unanimously to the religious reformation: "With a single voice it was generally ordered, concluded, promised, and sworn to God by the raising of hands in the air that we all, unanimously, with the aid of God, wish to live in this holy evangelical law and Word of God as it is announced to us, wishing to abandon all Masses and other papal ceremonies and abuses, images, and idols, to live in union and obedience to justice."[44]

How to get rid of "images and idols"? The Reformation was accompanied by the first manifestations of iconoclasm in 1532, the work of Bernese soldiers. Although the Council prohibited such destruction in 1534, breaking of images increased. In December 1535 the last vestiges of the Catholic cult were sold or suppressed.

41. *Annales Calviniani, OC* 21, col. 199, Registres du Conseil 29, fol. 92v.
42. *Annales Calviniani, OC* 21, col. 198, Registres du Conseil 29, fol. 65.
43. *Annales Calviniani, OC* 21, col. 199, Registres du Conseil 29, fol. 70.
44. Roget, *Histoire du peuple,* 1:2.

These manifestations took place in a confused atmosphere. In 1532 an image of the Virgin bled from the wounds inflicted on it. Carried to the Church of La Madeleine in Geneva, it became the object of a worship surprising in those times of reformation. Or again, on May 1, 1534, a statue of Saint Anthony was mutilated, its eyes being deliberately torn out. On August 8, 1535, there was a scene of truly collective frenzy when several young men destroyed images and religious objects, crying, "We have the gods of the priests, do you want them?" The crowd then seized fifty consecrated hosts and gave them to a dog for food. "If they are really God, they will not let themselves be eaten by a dog." These scenes of profanation and sacrilege depended, as a recent historian has pointed out, on a "contradictory logic that at the same time denied and assumed that the objects had some special power."[45]

This unrestrained behavior cannot by itself sum up the Genevan Reformation. Let us first make an observation: the legal, indeed sententious character of the Genevan Reformation contrasted with the festive and disorderly air of this theatrical iconoclasm, which never found favor in the eyes of the Reformers. Moreover, repeated resistance appeared among the population. In June 1536 the Council abolished the celebration of feasts, except for Sunday. This passion for law, for legality, for the very ordinances, was shown by the vocabulary used; the expression "the law of Christ" came to designate the new regime. Moreover, Calvin was still not in Geneva, and was undoubtedly unaware that he would be called to end his days there. He therefore played no role during the early period of the Genevan Reformation. He arrived in the summer of 1536 by one of those providential accidents in which he would detect the will of God.

Installation in Geneva

Master Guillaume Farel kept me in Geneva, not so much by advice and exhortation as by a dreadful adjuration, as if God from on high had extended his hand over me to stop me.

JOHN CALVIN, 1557

The view taken by faith is often retrospective. It makes it possible after the flight of the years to take into account hidden coherencies and internal rhythms that

---

45. Jérôme Cottin, *Le regard et la parole. Une théologie protestante de l'image* (Geneva: Labor et Fides, 1994), p. 257. See also Carlos M. N. Eire, *War against the Idols: The Reformation of Worship from Erasmus to Calvin* (Cambridge: Cambridge University Press, 1986), and Olivier Christin, *Une révolution symbolique. L'iconoclasme huguenot et la reconstruction catholique* (Paris: Minuit, 1991).

are bound up with the story. This intrusion of meaning, this grammar of behavior, this renewed attention to grace fill the pages in which Calvin describes his arrival in Geneva. The context of this first entry into the city on the Leman was rather simple. Calvin, who was in Ferrara in the spring of 1536, returned to Basel. He then took the road to Paris, taking advantage of the lull in persecution that followed the Edict of Coucy to return to France. He had to settle certain family affairs, and he signed a procuration for his two brothers in June.[46] The next month he set out for Strasbourg, accompanied by his brother Antoine and his sister Marie. But the road was blocked because of the tensions between Francis I and Charles V. In place of taking the simplest route to the east, Calvin made a very wide detour to the south; it was thus that he found himself in Geneva, fortuitously, and heard Farel's call there. Over the years Farel's curse took on for him prophetic overtones. The author of the *Institutes* was not afraid to set a stage for himself by insisting on the modesty of his position. He wanted discreetly to avoid all publicity.

> Now, that I did not have any desire to display myself and make a noise I made evident, because immediately afterwards I went away from there, and also because no one there knew I was the author, nor had I appeared as such anywhere else; and I had intended to continue in the same way, until finally Master Guillaume Farel kept me in Geneva, not so much by advice and exhortation as by a dreadful adjuration, as if God from on high had extended his hand over me to stop me. Because the most direct route to Strasbourg, to which I wanted to withdraw myself, was closed by the wars, I had planned to pass by there [Geneva] quickly, without stopping more than one night in the town. Now a little earlier the papacy had been driven out of there by means of that good person I named and of Master Pierre Viret; but things had not yet been put in good order, and there were divisions there and bad and dangerous factions among those of the town. Then an individual, who has now villainously revolted and returned to the papists, discovered me and made me known to others. On which Farel (since he burned with a marvelous zeal to advance the Gospel) immediately made every effort to retain me. And after having learned that there were certain particular studies for which I wanted to keep myself free, when he saw that he gained nothing by prayers, he came to imprecations, that it might please God to curse my repose and the tranquility for study I was seeking if in a time of great necessity I withdrew myself and refused to give aid and succor. Which saying so frightened and shook me that I gave up the journey I had undertaken; but nevertheless, feeling my shy-

---

46. This concerned the sale of an eight-*setier* field to the prior of Mont-Saint-Louis, near Noyon, for the sum of 144 livres.

ness and timidity, I did not want to be obliged to carry out any specific duty.[47]

The Calvin to whom Farel addressed himself was still only twenty-six. Farel, for his part, was forty-seven. But he had immediately realized the ability of this timid and frail young man. His summons to Calvin took the tone of a divine vocation. Calvin hesitated, Calvin was afraid, Calvin was timid. Farel's summons was irreversible, just as irresistible as his "sudden conversion" three years before. Possibly in this autobiographical account one can perceive an echo of Jesus' prediction to the apostle Peter in the Gospel of John: "Verily, verily, I say unto thee, When thou wast young, thou girdedst thyself, and walkedst whither thou wouldest; but when thou shalt be old, thou shalt stretch forth thy hands, and another shall gird thee, and carry thee whither thou wouldest not."[48] This tragic prophecy of the resurrected Christ found its realization in Peter's execution. Although Calvin did not find martyrdom — far from it — his whole life was impregnated with the idea of it. Did he not cry out, when called upon by the Catholics to justify his vocation, that he was "ready to defend it with my own blood"?[49] Undeniably the Protestant sixteenth century gave to conversion, to the "true faith," a heroic character. For Calvin, humanist and scholar, thinker and writer, to become a public character was an agonizing decision. Just as every intellectual is at some time faced with the question of involvement, this man, still young, found himself suddenly confronted with a political task that terrified him, after the relative comfort of the study and the conviviality of the symposium. A certain terminological vagueness existed at the time; Calvin found himself called a "reader" at first, but after some months the words "preacher" or "pastor" were used with respect to him. One thing is certain: Calvin never received any pastoral consecration. The fact was far from soothing; it consecrated the rupture with the ministries of the Roman Church. The pastorate was defined by its function and not by any power whatever conferred by ordination.

47. Calvin, preface to *Commentaire des psaumes,* pp. 25-26.
48. John 21:18.
49. J. Calvin, *Épître à Sadolet* (1539), in *La vraie piété,* ed. I. Backus and C. Chimelli (Geneva: Labor et Fides, 1986), pp. 71-83.

The Lausanne Disputation and Synod, October 1536 to May 1537

The disputation is dangerous to this particular church.

CATHOLIC CHAPTER OF LAUSANNE, OCTOBER 1, 1536[50]

Should one say the church or the churches? The question is not purely grammatical. Nowadays, Protestants speak freely of "the churches," in the plural, while Catholics generally stick to the singular, "the church." The situation is still more complex if we recall that Calvin, for his part, used "the church," in the singular, to designate the community of the faithful united to Jesus Christ.[51] The plural, as Marc Bloch taught us, is the "grammatical form of relativity."[52] There is the church and there are the churches, the "local churches," as the Catholic detractors of the Reformation described them, adding that the local churches are placed under the oversight of the universal church. From this standpoint, what could an assembly of theologians decide on its own authority, apart from the Roman supremacy, or at least the conciliar supremacy, if indeed the general council, more than the pope, was the leaven of Catholic unity in the sixteenth century?

Three months after his contentious establishment in Geneva, the Lausanne Disputation marked Calvin's entry into public life. The Reformers took a bold step by solemnly deciding to hold a theological debate to decide the future of the town of Lausanne. They broke the umbilical connection with ecclesiastical authority. Along with Farel and numerous other theologians (including Caroli), our young man represented the Reformed faith against the adherents of the other confession. But serious cracks also appeared among the Reformers, and Calvin was accused by Caroli.

50. A. Piaget, ed., *Les actes de la dispute de Lausanne, 1536* (Neuchâtel: Secrétariat de l'Université, Mémoires de l'Université de Lausanne VI, 1928), pp. 24-25.

51. This incontestable attachment of Calvin's to the unitary concept of the church is to be ascribed to his insistence on the catholicity, in the sense of universality, of the Western tradition. According to Calvin, the problem was still to reform the church and not to establish it all over again. As Jacques Courvoisier wrote, "It was not a question for him [Calvin] of restarting or re-creating this church, as the Anabaptists believed necessary, since at its historical origin there were the apostles and Pentecost. This was not in question, because there is no more a re-baptism than there is a re-Pentecost. . . . Striving that the church, one in its essence in Christ, might also be one on earth in reality, Calvin was never more 'catholic' than when he acted as a 'reformer.'" "La dialectique dans l'ecclésiologie de Calvin," in *Regards contemporains sur Jean Calvin. Actes du colloque Calvin,* Strasbourg, 1964 (Paris: PUF, 1965), pp. 101-2.

52. M. Bloch, *Apologie pour l'histoire ou métier d'historien* (Paris: A. Colin, Cahiers des Annales, 1967), p. 4.

The disputation was held October 1-8, 1536, in the Cathedral of Notre-Dame in Lausanne. The Bernese, as German speakers, had planned the encounter to serve their own interests. The movement to the Reformation in Lausanne, as in Neuchâtel and Geneva, was not without a political purpose; the Bernese had directly encouraged Farel in his reforming enterprise. In 1530 Bern had come to the aid of Geneva, occupied by the Savoyards; in 1536 the Bernese again relieved the city on the Leman, then under blockade, and seized in the process the whole of the Vaud district.[53] In convoking the disputation, the Bernese mentioned "our lands, which by the grace of God we have justly conquered."[54] The conquest of the Vaud district, interpreted as a providential call to conversion, should logically lead to the adoption of the evangelical "true faith" by the population. But how could one demonstrate in a striking fashion the superiority of the Reformation? A grand public "disputation" was in order. The old clergy and the whole population were therefore summoned to declare the need for a religious reformation entirely based on Scripture.

This was not a new procedure. The Lausanne Disputation followed a series of similar confrontations that began in 1523. The determining character of disputations, although attested elsewhere, was one of the characteristic features of the Swiss Reformation. Zürich in 1523 and Bern in 1528 had also held disputations (*Gemeinschwörungen*). Just as in Zürich, so also in Bern and Lausanne, "the disputations were the founding acts of the Reformation."[55] A crowd of 600 attended the January 1523 Zürich disputation, a debate between Zwingli and the envoys of the bishop of Constance. In Bern five years later, Zwingli also carried the day, this time supported by Bucer and Wolfgang Capito from Strasbourg.

The model of a reforming disputation thus went back to Zwingli and the Reformation in Zürich. How was it distinguished from previous theological disputations? Luther had participated in similar jousts; the encounter in Leipzig between Johann Eck and the German Reformer in June and July 1519 demonstrated the existence of irreconcilable positions and the ineluctable character of the division between the churches. But the Lutheran *disputatio* was still part of the medieval pattern; this exercise in Latin rhetoric permitted students or their masters to contend intellectually with each other to determine the truth of a proposition. Things changed with Zwingli.

---

53. É. Junod, ed., *La dispute de Lausanne, 1536. La théologie réformée après Zwingli et avant Calvin* (Lausanne: Bibliothèque historique vaudois, 1988), pp. 14-15. Acts of the colloquy held from September 29 to October 1, 1986, by the faculty of theology of Lausanne on the same site as the disputation of 1536.

54. Piaget, p. 3.

55. Junod, p. 18.

In four respects the Zwinglian disputation overturned the pattern and the conditions of the traditional disputation. In the first place, it was no longer a doctor of theology who convoked the disputation, but the magistracy, that is the civil and political authorities. Second, the disputation was not held within the closed bounds of a university. It took place in front of the people in a building open to the public. Third, it was not conducted in Latin, but in the vernacular language (in German in Zürich and Bern, in French in Lausanne); the people had to be able to follow and understand. Fourth, the only arguments recognized, the only authority admitted was the Scriptures (and the Fathers, in Zürich). Tradition, the authority of the doctors, and reason could not be the foundation for the establishment of the truth; only Scripture could be invoked for this purpose.

The objective of such a disputation was evident. The government created conditions permitting a public demonstration of evangelical truth.[56]

The stakes in the Lutheran or Zwinglian disputation were considerable. It was not designed solely to verify the truth or falsity of a proposition; the future of Christianity depended on it. In a short time the disputations in Zürich, Bern, and Lausanne led to "an effective reformation of faith and worship."[57]

Everything began with the publication of ten theses. Highly Protestant in inspiration, they were posted in the churches in July 1536. They were the work chiefly of Pierre Viret (1511-71), the Reformer of the Vaud region. Shamefaced and confused, the Catholic clergy were relatively at a loss in these circumstances; in Lausanne they had recourse to a reproachful silence, hardly broken by a few timid interventions. In their appeal, the "lords of the chapter" were bent on emphasizing: "The disputation cannot be carried out without contention, rivalry, and discord, injurious to the peace."[58] The Catholic clergy therefore fell back on the universal church and its "holy general councils," where the powerful "infusion of the blessed Holy Spirit" made itself felt. It was incumbent on them to be as silent as possible while waiting for the next general council (October 1).

The Reformers, in this close duel, had the choice weapons: the Scriptures, only the Scriptures, and the vernacular. Moreover, there was little doubt about the outcome of the battle; the Reform party could not help emerging as victor in a debate it had itself convoked. But division loomed in the reformist camp. Their opposition to the Catholics, evident in the plenary assemblies in the Cathedral of Notre-Dame, did not prevent the ministers from sniping at each other in the

56. Junod, p. 18.
57. Junod, p. 19.
58. Piaget, pp. 24-25.

Church of the Franciscans. A later book, undoubtedly sponsored by Calvin, related the facts of the synod of Lausanne, the following year, without cordiality. "We arrived in Lausanne in May 1537; the synod met in the Church of the Franciscans. There were present more than 100 ministers of the Word from the territory of Bern, a score from the county of Neuchâtel, and only three from the church of Geneva."[59] An incident then occurred: Pierre Caroli accused the representatives of Geneva, Calvin, Farel, and Courand, of not believing in the dogma of the Trinity. The accuser then began to "declaim the Nicene Creed, then that of Athanasius, with such extravagant movements of his whole body, such incongruous shakings of his head, and such impetuosity in his voice that he raised a general laugh."[60] Calvin answered this "extravagant mountebank." He rose and cried: "Caroli opens a prosecution against us over the question of the nature of God and the distinction of the persons of God. I myself start higher up; I ask him whether he believes there is one God. I call God and men to witness that he has no more faith than a dog or a pig. And nevertheless this Epicurean who does not have the least pious feeling simulates zeal for God, causing us vexation over questions that are useless today. What need is there, in fact, to call a debate over points about which there is perfect unanimity among us?"[61]

Then follows a perfectly trinitarian confession of Calvin's faith: "We recognize, in the essence of God, eternal, spiritual, infinite . . . the Father and the Word, without however confounding the Father with the Word or the Word with the Spirit."[62] The gentle, modest, timid Calvin revealed himself here in broad daylight: he possessed a spirit of fire when he was attacked or his convictions were put in doubt. The intractable enemy of Servetus already loomed be-

---

59. J. Calvin (attributed to), *Défense de Guillaume Farel et de ses collègues contre les calomnies du théologastre Pierre Caroli par Nicolas Des Gallars*, ed. F. Gounelle (Paris: PUF, Études d'histoire et de philosophie religieuses, 1994), p. 57. The fact that this source was written eight years after the incidents it relates undoubtedly burdens its testimony with an element of reconstruction.

60. Along with the Apostles' Creed, the Nicene-Constantinopolitan Creed and the so-called Athanasian Creed, less often mentioned today, enjoyed great authority in the sixteenth century. See the excellent presentation by O. Fatio et al., eds., *Confessions et catéchismes de la foi réformée* (Geneva: Labor et Fides, 1986), pp. 17-23.

61. Calvin, *Défense de Guillaume Farel*, p. 58.

62. Calvin, *Défense de Guillaume Farel*, p. 61. Calvin also mentioned the "two natures" of the Council of Chalcedon (451) and denounced the errors of Sabellius, Arius, and Nestorius. Nevertheless, one can see the care he took to distinguish the "two natures" in a radical fashion. "These properties must be considered separately." Thus, speaking of "God's blood" is only a trope or figure of speech (p. 62). Lutheran theology, for example, was less absolute in this distinction between the two natures of Christ, truly God and truly man. Whence came the accepted formula to designate this theology of dissociation in Calvin, the *extra Calvinisticum*.

hind the opponent of Caroli. A strange person this Pierre Caroli (ca. 1480–ca. 1550). Originally from Rozay-en-Brie, he had been a member of Briçonnet's coterie in Meaux. First pastor in Lausanne at the end of 1536, he set himself up against Calvin and Farel, denouncing them to Bern as heretics. The two men would have to deliver themselves from his accusations by testifying to the orthodoxy of their faith in Jesus Christ. In August 1537, in fact, they were summoned to state their full and complete acceptance of the terms "Trinity" and "person," in the sense of one God in three distinct persons.[63] But Caroli in turn scandalized the Reformers by defending prayers for the dead. Caroli was to go back and forth several times between the confessions; he undoubtedly was "never truly converted to the church he rejoined."[64] For Calvin this spiritual itinerary was scandalous, especially when it accompanied insinuations about his own convictions. A terrible suspicion, however, dogged Calvin throughout his life, that of Arianism. The heresies that encumber the history of Christianity are like beetles; one can only marvel at their colors and their variety. Condemned by the Council of Nicea in 325, Arius made the Son the first of creatures, superior to men but inferior to the Father.[65] But the term was used, incorrectly no doubt, to describe the various heterodox opinions that appeared concerning the divinity of the Savior. Thus Erasmus also found himself accused of Arianism as a result of his Greek edition of the New Testament.[66] It must be said that Erasmus did not fail in return to criticize the accepted definition of the Trinity. In 1523 he explained his thinking: "The indiscreet subtleties of the Arians led the church to a more precise formulation. . . . We can forgive the ancients, but we, what excuse do we have for raising importunate, not to say impious, questions on subjects that are also remote from our own nature?"[67]

63. Calvin, *Défense de Guillaume Farel*, pp. 12-13.

64. T. Wanegffelen, "Des Chrétiens entre Rome et Genève. Une histoire du choix religieux en France, vers 1520-vers 1610" (*thèse* at the University of Paris I [Panthéon-Sorbonne], November 12, 1994; typescript, 2 vols., 913 pp.), p. 86.

65. B. Cottret, *Le Christ des Lumières. Jésus de Newton à Voltaire (1680-1760)* (Paris: Le Cerf, 1990), p. 21.

66. Erasmus was attacked by Zúñiga for his Greek edition of the New Testament. In particular, Erasmus suppressed the apocryphal addition to 1 John 5:7: "For there are three that bear record in heaven, the Father, the Word, and the Holy Spirit, and these three are one." This addition, commonly found in the Vulgate, is generally known as the *Comma Johanneum*. It does not occur in any of the earliest manuscripts and seems to have been unknown to the Fathers.

67. R. H. Bainton, *Hunted Heretic: The Life and Death of Michael Servetus, 1511-1553* (Boston: Beacon Press, 1953). Erasmus continued (pp. 34-35): "We define so many things which may be left in ignorance or in doubt without loss of salvation. Is it not possible to have fellowship with the Father, Son, and Holy Spirit without being able to explain philosophically the distinction betwen them and between the nativity of the Son and the

Erasmus the Arian? Calvin the Arian? The debate was not merely doctrinal; it raised a double question that would haunt Calvin for the rest of his days. Is the Trinity demonstrable from the sole standpoint of Scripture? Does the principle of *sola Scriptura,* of decisive recourse to the Bible as the fountainhead of authority, allow one to avoid ambiguity? How else can the role of the church and its ministry be defined? What credit should be given to the early councils officially recognized by the Reformers? No one should expect an answer to these questions from us; as a historian, we merely highlight the persistent difficulty that Calvin encountered when he was accused of Arianism. It was a shaken man who emerged as victor from his confrontation with Caroli.

The Confession of Faith and the Articles of 1537

Since there is no greater division than that in faith, we ask you to command that all inhabitants of your city be required to make confession and give an account of their belief, so that one may recognize those

---

procession of the Holy Ghost? If I believe the tradition that there are three of one nature, what is the use of labored disputation? If I do not believe, I shall not be persuaded by any human reasons. . . . You will not be damned if you do not know whether the Spirit proceeding from the Father and the Son has one or two beginnings, but you will not escape damnation, if you do not cultivate the fruits of the Spirit which are love, joy, peace, patience, kindness, goodness, long-suffering, mercy, faith, modesty, continence, and chastity. . . . The sum of our religion is peace and unanimity, but these can scarcely stand unless we define as little as possible, and in many things leave each one free to follow his own judgment, because there is great obscurity in many matters, and man suffers from this almost congenital disease that he will not give in when once a controversy is started, and after he is heated he regards as absolutely true that which he began to sponsor quite casually. . . . Many problems are now reserved for an ecumenical council. It would be better to defer questions of this sort to the time when, no longer in a glass darkly, we see God face to face. . . . Formerly, faith was in life rather than in the profession of creeds. Presently, necessity required that articles be drawn up, but only a few with apostolic sobriety. Then the depravity of the heretics exacted a more precise scrutiny of the divine books. . . . When faith came to be in writings rather than in hearts, then there were almost as many faiths as men. Articles increased and sincerity decreased. Contention grew hot and love grew cold. The doctrine of Christ, which at first knew no hairsplitting, came to depend on the aid of philosophy. This was the first stage in the decline of the church. . . . The injection of the authority of the emperor into this affair did not greatly aid the sincerity of faith. . . . When faith is in the mouth rather than in the heart, when the solid knowledge of Sacred Scripture fails us, nevertheless by terrorization we drive men to believe what they do not believe, to love what they do not love, to know what they do not know. That which is forced cannot be sincere, and that which is not voluntary cannot please Christ."

126

who hold to the Gospel and those who prefer to be of the kingdom of the Pope than of the kingdom of Jesus Christ.

PETITION OF THE REFORMERS TO
THE SMALL COUNCIL, END OF 1536[68]

Before 1914 German religious sociology tirelessly furnished historians with their most useful concepts — thus the idea offered by Max Weber of a connection between Protestant ethics and the spirit of capitalism, or again the distinction proposed by Ernst Troeltsch between communities of the sect type and of the church type.[69] A "church" tends to blend into the rest of society, while a "sect" requires withdrawal; the one is institutional, the other voluntary and based on entirely individual adherence. Finally, a "church" is organized from above, a "sect" from below.[70] "Above" and "below" refer to the social scale; they reflect a hierarchy of power or of knowledge that sees competence as the key to success. Thus Calvinism rested totally, entirely on a plan for a church; it required the education of the masses, without in any circumstances leaving them to their own devices. Calvin led an unremitting war against the "sects," which he described by the general term "Anabaptists."

Who were these "Anabaptists"? Ancestors of modern Baptists, they constituted a movement that opposed the administration of baptism to infants, "pedobaptism," in favor of that of adults. But this doctrine was quickly charged with radical political connotations. Several Anabaptists from the Netherlands were in fact found in Geneva at this time. Among these were Herman de Gerbihan and Benoît d'Anglen, banished during the winter of 1537 with some of their disciples. In Calvin's writings the term inevitably assumed an insulting tone.

The Protestant Reformation was intimately linked to a pedagogy; did it not proclaim itself an "institution" under Calvin, in the sense we have ex-

---

68. Cited in Backus and Chimelli, p. 41.

69. B. Cottret, "Max Weber Revisited. Le puritanisme anglais: de la réussite économique au salut," *Americana* 4 (1989): 75-96.

70. E. Troeltsch, *Die soziallehren der Christlichen Kirchen und Gruppen* (1911); English version, *The Social Teaching of the Christian Churches,* 2 vols. (London: G. Allen & Unwin, 1956), 1:331ff. Calvin attached himself exclusively to the "church" model and totally rejected the "sect" model. "It was not a question for him [Calvin] of restarting or re-creating this church, as the Anabaptists believed necessary, since at its historical origin there were the apostles and Pentecost. This was not in question, because there is no more a re-baptism than there is a re-Pentecost. Despite its decline, this church having had the apostles for its origin, the prescription advanced by Tertullian retained all its value." Courvoisier, p. 100.

plained previously? It was designed to guide these Genevans, still described in May 1536 as "people cold in the faith of God,"[71] to the evangelical truth. A first catechism, a confession of faith, and various articles, all proposed by Calvin, were intended to make it possible to inculcate in the population the evangelical principles they lacked.[72]

Guillaume Farel's chief activity in the fall of 1536 was the drafting of a confession of faith, officially presented on November 10. It came from the press of the German printer Wigand Köln. Its title confirmed the existence of a political project of vast amplitude; it was intended to get every inhabitant of Geneva to subscribe to the declaration. The title was: *Confession of Faith, which all bourgeois and inhabitants of Geneva and subjects in its territories should swear to keep to and hold.*[73] A score of articles rapidly dealt with the authority of the Word of God, the Decalogue, salvation through Christ as sole intercessor, the existence of two sacraments (baptism and Holy Communion), and the possibility of excommunication for all "manifest idolaters, blasphemers, murderers, thieves, fornicators, false witnesses, seditious people, quarrelers, slanderers, batterers, drunkards," and "wasters of goods." Finally, as was obligatory, the prerogative of the "ministers of the Word" and of the "magistrates," called to "feed the sheep," or to protect the innocent by chastising the guilty, was affirmed.

On January 16, 1537, the Geneva authorities approved the Confession of Faith, as well as the separate articles presented by Calvin. The Reformer did not carry all his points, however; he favored a monthly celebration of the Lord's Supper, "in view of the great consolation the faithful receive from it."[74] This insistence on Communion, moreover, should be considered in parallel with the disciplinary power of the churches. Calvin asked for excommunication without fail of "fornicators, avaricious people, idolaters, slanderers, and drunkards, devoted to plunder."[75] In the sixteenth century, far from being simple spiritual acts, the Lord's Supper and its complement, excommunication, were powerful levers for directing public morality. In a "face-to-face civilization," where everyone was under another's eye, not to have access to the holy table was equivalent to ostracism. Calvin was moreover very aware of the "ignorance of the people,"

---

71. *Annales Calviniani, OC* 21, col. 199, Registres du Conseil 29, fol. 111.

72. The *Instruction et confession de foi dont on use en l'Église de Genève* begins by affirming that the knowledge of God is the purpose of humanity. Then, following the order "the law, the faith, the prayer," one finds successively commentaries on the Decalogue, the creed, and the Lord's Prayer. A. Rilliet and T. Dufour, eds., *Le catéchisme français de Calvin, publié en 1537* . . . (Geneva: H. Georg, 1878), p. 3.

73. *Confession de foi laquelle tous bourgeois et habitants de Genève et sujets du pays doivent jurer de garder et tenir.*

74. J. Calvin, *Calvin, homme d'Église* (Geneva: Labor et Fides, 1971), p. 3.

75. Calvin, *Calvin, homme d'Église*, p. 6.

and asked that everyone be made to profess his faith publicly. The singing of psalms, the teaching of children, and the regulation of marriages also received his attention.

Calvin only partially attained his objectives, no doubt because his hearers seized on the political stakes of the Lord's Supper and excommunication. The Lord's Supper would be celebrated only four times a year, according to Bernese practice. Baptism, however, would have to be performed before the congregation, and banns of marriages be published for three Sundays in advance. On the same day, it was decreed that business would cease on Sunday during preaching, as soon as the last toll of the bell was rung. Also, pious images, preserved by certain people in their houses, must be ruthlessly destroyed. In March the Anabaptists were banished. In April, at Calvin's instigation, a syndic was commanded to go from house to house, accompanied by the captains of quarters and the *dizainiers* (district wardens). It was necessary to ensure that the inhabitants subscribed to the Confession of Faith. But on May 1 the Council took note of the difficulty of this undertaking, calmly admitting that they would do "the best they could" — leaving it to be understood that the task presented numerous difficulties.[76] The first official divergences from Calvin were appearing.

Bern encouraged Farel's Reforming vocation. In return, Bern naturally attempted to influence the Geneva Reformation. But Calvin had too much originality of thought merely to apply measures taken elsewhere. As a man of the church, he rejected too strict a control by the civil power. Moreover, his position remained precarious. After some months he found himself the butt of attacks by the Anabaptists and by a "vicious apostate," no doubt Caroli. Specifically, "Although I acknowledge myself to be timid, soft, and cowardly by nature, nevertheless I had from the very beginning to encounter these raging floods."[77]

In Geneva the Reformation went on apace. The civil power and the church collaborated. In June it was announced that Sunday was the only holiday, and that no other day of the year could be sanctified by stopping work. At the end of July, after Farel, Calvin, and Courand were heard, it was decided to interrogate each *dizainier* on his faith and to admonish him to live according to the principles he professed publicly. Moreover, he was entrusted with regulating the faith of the inhabitants of his quarter. In due time each quarter was to be assembled in the Cathedral of Saint-Pierre solemnly to accept the Confession of Faith and to take an oath of fidelity to the city. On October 30 there was an attempt to wring a profession of faith from all those hesitating. Finally, on November 12 all recalcitrants were ordered to leave the city: "Here it is stated how yesterday the people were asked *dizaine* by *dizaine* whether they had yet taken

76. Roget, *L'Église et l'État*, p. 15.
77. Calvin, preface to *Commentaire des psaumes*, p. 26.

the Reformation oath; some came and others not, and likewise those from the Rue des Allemands, of whom not one came. It was decided that if they do not wish to swear to the Reformation they be commanded to leave the city and go to live elsewhere, where they may live at their own pleasure."[78]

Departure from Geneva, April 1538

A double problem, however, existed for Calvin in Geneva: he had to watch over the adoption of a confession of faith, and in return claimed to exercise a dogmatic control that would extend to excommunication. That a Frenchman, and therefore a foreigner, could arrogate to himself the right to excommunicate respectable Genevans seemed highly presumptuous. Did it belong to the church to refuse the sacrament of the Lord's Supper to inhabitants of the city, and even to institute civil proceedings against them? The boundary line between the spiritual and the temporal was the site of many frontier conflicts. The debate permanently influenced Calvin's life.

The pressure mounted against Farel in the General Council of November 25, 1537. The right of preachers to banish people judged unworthy from the Lord's Supper was hotly contested. On January 4, 1538, the Council decreed "that the Lord's Supper not be refused to anyone." In a letter to Bullinger Calvin said he feared that the holy practice of excommunication would fall into oblivion.[79] Moreover, on February 3 four new syndics,[80] all hostile to Calvin, were elected as the executive power of the city. Their reservations with regard to the Frenchman cannot, however, be interpreted as any disavowal whatever of the Reformation. No, it was possible not to love Calvin and yet to show oneself favorable to religious change. The political overturn was confirmed the next day on the renewing of the Small Council. In March the Council was amazed at the liberty of speech of the preachers, who were ordered not to meddle anymore in civil affairs. The next month Courand was called before the Council for impertinence in his sermons; he was imprisoned for having called the Genevan state a "kingdom of the frogs" and the magistrates "drunkards."[81] The situation thereafter became more venomous; Calvin and Farel refused to celebrate the Lord's Supper according to the form adopted in Bern, using unleavened bread. The two men felt themselves in solidarity with their comrade Courand.[82] They were

---

78. *Annales Calviniani, OC* 21, col. 16.
79. *OC* 10, cols. 153-54, February 20, 1538.
80. Claude Richardet, Jean Philippe, Jean Lullin, and Ami de Chapeaurouge.
81. Calvin, preface to *Commentaire des psaumes,* p. 22.
82. Courand died of plague in October 1538.

ordered to cease all preaching, and refused to comply. When they were reproached for this, Calvin answered, "If we served men, we would be badly rewarded. But we serve a great master, who will recompense us."[83] Calvin and Farel violated the interdiction the next Sunday, April 21. They spoke publicly, the former in Saint-Pierre, the latter in Saint-Gervais. The Council of Two Hundred, and then the General Council, issued orders of expulsion against them, on April 22 and 23, respectively. They had only three days to leave Geneva! How can this hostility be explained? The pride of the Genevans had been wounded when someone dared to criticize their city and speak ill of a city that welcomed him. Calvin, on his part, promised himself that he would not be brought back there again. He went to Bern, then to Zürich with Farel; the two men attended a synod there at the end of April where they had the opportunity to defend their view of ecclesiastical discipline. The last attempts at reconciliation with Geneva failed in May; despite the mediation of Bernese delegates, access to the city remained forbidden to them. Calvin went provisionally to Basel, expecting to be able to drown his bitter defeat in fine literature. But far from it; it would be Strasbourg for him.

83. *Annales Calviniani, OC* 21, cols. 226-27, Registres du Conseil 32, fol. 36.

CHAPTER 7

Geneva or Strasbourg? 1538-41

It was in Strasbourg that Calvin became "Calvin."[1] Or more exactly, at the beginning of his thirtieth year Calvin invented a Reformation that was distinct from that of his predecessors. At first it was a matter of style more than of doctrine, a matter of style and temperament; Calvinism carried to its highest point the balance of thought and form. It proceeded from a literary passion. A new, thoroughly revised edition of the *Institutes,* which appeared in 1539-41,[2] showed clearly the emergence of a current of thought different from Lutheranism. But the best indication of this change is to be found in the *Commentary on the Epistle to the Romans* (1539),[3] in which Calvin proclaimed clearly to the world that he was neither Melanchthon, nor Bucer, nor Bullinger, but simply Calvin. Finally, Calvin's endorsement by Bucer, the Reformer of Strasbourg, confirmed his sense of an exceptional vocation, already recognized by Farel. Yes, Calvin undoubtedly spent the happiest years of his life in Strasbourg.

Not that Calvin had any intention at first of settling in Strasbourg. In 1538, returning from Geneva, Calvin intended to live in Basel, but he stopped in Strasbourg. He wanted to resume his studies, but he became a Reformer. Always this same obliquity. His vocation always took an indirect route; it was not a natural bent, fashioned by habit or for comfort, but a sudden eruption, imperative and peremptory, a calling he could not shirk. God decidedly contra-

1. J. Courvoisier, "Les catéchismes de Genève et de Strasbourg. Étude sur le développement de la pensée de Calvin," *Bulletin de la Société de l'Histoire du Protestantisme Français* 84 (1935): 107.

2. Latin version in 1539, French in 1541.

3. *Commentaire de l'épître aux Romains.*

dicted Calvin; he led him precisely where he did not want to go — to return him finally to his point of departure. Geneva or Basel, Strasbourg or Geneva: the Reformer was on a predestined trajectory.

For the moment it would be Strasbourg. Calvin arrived there in July, vaguely uncertain; Farel was in Neuchâtel. Calvin was dazzled by an offer to direct a French parish. Strasbourg was German-speaking, but its proximity to France had allowed for the establishment of a community of refugees. The city had undergone rapid changes in the space of a few years. An edict of December 1523 commanded the clergy "not to preach anything other than the holy Gospel." In February 1529 the Mass was abolished. A set of ecclesiastical ordinances completed the structure in 1534; the showpiece of the system was the establishment of lay ecclesiastical administrators. These *Kirchenpfleger,* some twenty of them, divided among them the inspection of the seven parishes of the city. Control of the pastors, oversight of the faithful, lay participation in the life of the church — was not this conception of the ministry based on the theology of universal priesthood?[4] His experience in Strasbourg did not leave Calvin so much with a transferrable ecclesiastical model as with an ambition; Protestantism was called to become, as well as a theology, a fact of civilization.

Several notable personalities influenced the Reformation in Strasbourg. Matthias Zell (1477-1548), curé of the cathedral, showed himself from the beginning an ardent propagator of evangelical ideas. He was joined in 1523 by Bucer and Capito. Martin Bucer (1491-1551), a former Dominican, was originally from Sélestat. He deserves a place by the side of the great Reformers like Luther and Calvin for the vigor of his thought and his action. In particular, he tried to resolve the inevitable tension that existed at the heart of Christianity between the confession and the institution, the spiritual church and the visible community.[5] Wolgang Köpfel, called Capito (1478-1541), was above all an intellectual, a collaborator of Erasmus's, who admired his mastery of Hebrew. Two laymen also gave their city an unequaled prestige. At the head of the city the *Stettmeister,* Jacob Sturm (1489-1553), was the author of a revolution that took power from the bishop to confer it on the burghers. At the same time, Johann Sturm (1507-89) founded a model college, the *Gymnasium* of Strasbourg. Theology, politics, pedagogy — here indeed were the three pillars of Reformed Protestantism. This is especially true if we add that for Calvin, politics,

4. F. Wendel (1905-72), *L'Église de Strasbourg, sa constitution et son organisation, 1532-1535* (Paris: PUF, 1942), p. 189. This work is indispensable. For a recent view, refer to Marc Lienhard, ed., *Un temps, une ville, une Réforme* (Aldershot: Variorum, 1990).

5. G. Hamman, *Entre la secte et la cité. Le projet d'Église du Réformateur Martin Bucer (1491-1551)* (Geneva: Labor et Fides, 1984), pp. 165 and 262.

in the strong sense of concern for the community, was directly dependent on a pedagogy.

From Farel to Bucer, the Elder Statesmen

From the summer of 1538 to that of 1541, Calvin spent the three best years of his life in Strasbourg. The distinguished patronage of Bucer helped him to carry out his vocation. Calvin, however, had not spared him his criticism, firm but courteous, in a letter of January 1538; Bucer's moderation irritated the fiery Picard.[6] But, with the patience that comes with maturity, Bucer chose not to be upset. Much more, he immediately saw the great advantages "his" Strasbourg Reformation could gain from the presence of the talented Calvin. It only remained for him to play the noble father, the prophet, or the rebuker so that Calvin, impressed, would accept the direction of the French parish. After some years' interval, it was the same scenario as in Geneva. Bucer addressed himself to Calvin, as Farel had done before him. "That excellent servant of Christ Martin Bucer, with a remonstrance and declaration similar to those Farel had made before, recalled me to another position. Appalled by the example of Jonah, which he suggested to me, I still persevered in the duty of teaching."[7]

Calvin would not be Jonah. He would go directly to carry the word of the Lord. Calvin did not lack courage, but he backed his way into things. Why was it necessary that he be detained permanently in Geneva or in Strasbourg? He expressed his reluctance: "My timidity . . . presented me with many reasons to excuse myself, so as not to take such a heavy burden on my shoulders again."

Strasbourg fortunately was not Geneva. The French community was a chosen society that gave Calvin the welcome he deserved. He apparently delivered his first sermon to them in September. The French met at first in the Church of Saint-Nicolas-des-Ondes, then in the Chapel of the Pénitentes de Sainte-Madeleine, and finally in the choir of the Church of the Dominicans. (This high place later housed the famous public library, destroyed during the Franco-Prussian War.) These assemblies were renowned for the beauty of their singing. A traveling student described the worship in his own words:

> No creature could believe the joy one feels at singing the praises and marvels of God in one's native tongue. I had been there only five or six days when I saw this small assembly, which had been expelled from every country for having maintained the honor of God and the Gospel. I began to cry, not from

6. *Opera Calvini* (hereafter cited as *OC*) 10b, cols. 137-44.
7. Preface to *Commentaire des psaumes* (1557), *OC* 31, cols. 26-27.

sadness but for joy, on hearing them sing with such a good heart as they did. You could not hear any voice interfere with another; each had a music book in his hand, men and women, and each praised the Lord. There are those here who left behind seven or eight thousand florins of income and came here to nothing at all, giving thanks to the Lord that it has pleased him to bring them to a place where his name is honored. . . . And here one's conscience is at rest when one is where the Word of God is purely preached and the sacraments purely distributed.[8]

The "music book" everyone had "in his hand" undoubtedly was the Huguenot psalter, the first edition of which goes back to 1539. This book, *Some Psalms and Canticles Put to Music*,[9] still included only eighteen psalms, sung in unison by the assembly of the faithful. The tunes apparently came from the repertory of Strasbourg.[10]

Calvin had a large following in Strasbourg, and various young men sometimes shared his house. He exhorted them to embrace the pastoral ministry. The household was crowded and the environment was a little like student life; a frank conviviality reigned among the young men. Michel Mulot came from Montbéliard to study at Calvin's side, and he was not alone. The Breton Jean Curie; Gaspard Carmel, a cousin of Farel's; and Jacques Sorel and Robert Louvat from Brie gathered around the Reformer, before being sent back into France, the mission field. Sebastian Castellio would follow their example in May 1540. We will encounter him again thirteen years later among Calvin's Protestant opponents, attacking him for religious intolerance. Calvin's lodging thus took on the attractions of a clubhouse. Calvin spent happy days in Strasbourg, in a fraternal society of the elect, men of faith and learning. His young entourage was undoubtedly fascinated by the personality of the older man, already recognized as the author of the *Institutes*. Calvin put all his hopes on a young scholar, Claude Feray, who lived beside him, with three of his students, Louis and Charles de Richebourg and their relative or friend Malherbe.

Was Calvin entirely accepted in Strasbourg? Certainly the pastor received its bourgeoisie in July 1539. But a particularly painful episode took place upon the arrival of Caroli in October. Caroli's movements back and forth between Catholicism and Protestantism had made him suspect as a turncoat, and he attempted to gain Bucer's pity. In essence, he claimed that his conscience had

8. Cited by Ferdinand Buisson, *Sébastien Castellion. Sa vie et son oeuvre (1515-1563)* (Paris: Hachette, 1892), 1:107. A. Erichson, *L'Église française de Strasbourg au xvie siècle* (Strasbourg: F. Bull, 1886), pp. 15 and 22.

9. *Aucuns psaumes et cantiques mis en chant.*

10. E. Weber, *La musique protestante de langue française* (Paris: H. Champion, 1979), p. 28.

been troubled by Calvin and Farel. Calvin was summoned to a humiliating encounter in which he had to render an account of his faith. Several articles, no doubt drawn up with Caroli's blessing, were presented to him. Calvin flew into a rage; he would rather die than submit himself to this infuriating ritual. The good Bucer, acting as a mediator, tried to appease him. On his return home Calvin had a veritable nervous breakdown: sighs, sobs, trembling of the body. Calvin acknowledged his sin; he had let himself be consumed by anger. But there was good reason for it.[11]

Calvin, a Robinson Crusoe? Calvin's "Extraordinary" Vocation

I doubt that you . . . have had your vocation there from God, having been called there only by men.

LOUIS DU TILLET TO CALVIN, SEPTEMBER 1538[12]

What understanding did Calvin have of his mission? In comparing himself to the prophet Jonah when he decided to remain in Strasbourg, Calvin in part answered this question. Jonah was the man with an irresistible calling, with a tormenting vocation that hemmed him in, pressed him, and badgered him even when he was cast into the sea. Even in the belly of the great fish that, for three days and three nights, held him swallowed up as in the tomb, Jonah continued his dialogue with his creator. In good Calvinist logic, Jonah was the very type of the predestined soul; it was God who chose him, not he who chose God, God who pursued him and tirelessly addressed his Word to him.

The theme of shipwreck, moreover, had remarkable standing. For Calvin it was inseparable from the idea of "vocation" or "calling." Noah, Jonah, even Moses during the crossing of the Red Sea were confronted with the menacing presence of the sea.[13] Later Protestant culture would combine these situations with the story of Robinson Crusoe. What was Robinson Crusoe on his island but a man surrounded by the sea? In Daniel Defoe's novel, the new Jonah, or

11. *OC* 10b, cols. 396ff., to Farel, October 8, 1539.
12. J. Calvin, *Correspondance française avec Louis du Tillet,* ed. A. Crottet (Geneva: Cherruliez, 1850), September 7, 1538, p. 53.
13. The image was applied in particular to the church. "The servitude in Egypt continued after that time, which was like a general shipwreck." The more complete image combined the idea of the deluge with that of the Egyptian captivity, another test God imposed on his people. "It can be clearly seen that the church has not been delivered from one deluge only, but, floating among various waves, it has endured many ages as it were in the midst of the sea." J. Calvin, *Des scandales,* ed. O. Fatio (Geneva: Droz, 1984), p. 100.

prodigal son of the parable, Crusoe was also called by God, and also unfaithful before being saved.

The figure of Calvin and the exceptional character of the calling he received were strongly emphasized at the beginning of the seventeenth century by Pierre du Moulin in his treatise *On the Vocation of Pastors* (1618). This work throws some light on the question of the refounding of the church. The author distinguishes between "ordinary" and "extraordinary vocations." By an "ordinary calling" is meant "one that, being instituted by God, should always be continued in the Christian church."[14] But du Moulin points out the possibility of discontinuities, during persecutions for example. Hence the existence of "extraordinary callings." These extraordinary callings themselves are of "two sorts"; some have no successors — this is the case with Moses, John the Baptist, the apostles, and Saint Paul — while others are periodically renewed; God can raise up new prophets in every age. Where should one place Calvin? Or more generally, what was a Protestant Reformer? Was he a prophet or an apostle, a new Isaiah or a new Saint Paul? For my part I will answer that he was a Robinson Crusoe:

> Let us then pose the case that some faithful Christian is carried alone, by shipwreck or otherwise, into some barbarous island, and that he becomes used to it from necessity, and that having learned the language he undertakes to instruct the barbarians in the Christian religion, and that through his words many are converted. There being then a question of establishing a church among these people to preach the Gospel and administer the sacraments, and there being no means of finding pastors elsewhere because the island has no use of navigation or contact by word of mouth, I see no other means than these: that is, that all the Christians in the island meet in one place and, after invoking the name of God, elect that one among them who will be most proper for the work of the minister. And if the one who is elected can travel to a country where he can receive the imposition of hands according to customary usage, he will do wisely to travel there to avoid the possibility of discord. But there being neither ships nor ability nor health for making such a voyage, I believe he would offend God greatly if, for lack of a formality, he abandoned the work of God.[15]

Missionary activity is basic to Christianity. It does not only aim at distant lands or the "Fridays" of the Pacific; it also looks to the immediate neigh-

14. P. du Moulin, *De la vocation des pasteurs* (Sedan, Ardennes: Jean Jannon, 1618), p. 17.

15. Du Moulin, p. 33.

borhood. The Protestant Reformation aimed at a complete transformation of the sense of community; Calvin in Strasbourg or Geneva was also a mission-ary, an envoy. His vocation was clearly assigned to him by the voice of Farel or Bucer. But we also possess a more intimate testimony indirectly through his correspondence.

A strange epistolary exchange is laid out in the letters exchanged from January to December 1538 between Calvin and his old comrade du Tillet; they tell the story of a disappointed friendship. Louis du Tillet finally rejoined the Catholic Church, the church of his fathers,[16] but the conflict, the debate, and the estrangement between these two men provide a vantage point for anyone who wants to understand, in all impartiality, the stakes of a vocation. Du Tillet and Calvin, even when they confronted each other, remained essentially faith-ful, even under torment, to their intimate convictions.

The two men were still young; they had preserved the intrepid character of adolescence; they adopted pen names to foil the censors. Calvin signed his letters Charles d'Espeville.[17] This aristocratic, almost military surname in fact derived from one of the properties attached to La Gésine, young Calvin's first ecclesiastical benefice. In his turn du Tillet became Haultmont. How long would these two young men in quest of an identity still dream of deceiv-ing everyone? At the outset Calvin deplored the tepidness of his friend; he feared having offended him by not always observing the proper "modesty."[18] Du Tillet described the "afflictions" of his conscience, his "languidness." De-spite that which henceforward would separate them, he wanted Calvin to maintain his friendship for him. Moreover, du Tillet did not renounce justifi-cation by faith in the least, and admitted the need for a *reformatio*, but one in-ternal to the universal church.[19]

On July 10, 1538, from Strasbourg, Calvin took up the central question of his own vocation. He had the greatest difficulty in concealing his anger at the Genevan "Fridays": "The Lord will direct us. I fear above all things to return to the duties from which I have been delivered, considering what perplexities I was in at the time when I was immersed in them. For although then I felt the vocation from God that held me bound, with which I consoled myself, now, on

---

16. Louis du Tillet belonged to a family from Angoulême that had been ennobled in the fifteenth century. His brother Jean became bishop of Saint-Brieuc and of Meaux, and he himself became a canon of Angoulême.

17. Calvin took the same pseudonym again twenty years later in his correspondence with the church of Paris. J. Calvin, *Lettres françaises*, ed. J. Bonnet, 2 vols. (Paris: Meyrueis, 1854), 2:126, letter of March 15, 1557.

18. Calvin, *Correspondance française avec Louis du Tillet*, p. 24, January 31, 1537.

19. Calvin, *Correspondance française avec Louis du Tillet*, pp. 29-49, March 10, 1537.

the contrary, I fear to tempt him if I again take up such a burden, which I have known to be unbearable to me."[20]

The task was sometimes too heavy. An extraordinary confidence emanates from a hesitant Calvin, waiting for God to manifest himself, to show himself only to indicate to him what road to follow. In his own happiness at having returned to Catholicism, du Tillet sought to find a weakness in his armor; he took up the whole question of Calvin's vocation again. On September 7 he wrote, "I doubt that you have had your vocation there from God, having been called there only by men . . . , who have driven you away from there, just as they received you by their sole authority."[21] Or again in December, in a letter he did not expect an answer to, "I would conclude resolutely that you did not have a calling from God to the ministry."[22]

Had Calvin, solicited by Farel and then by Bucer, been the dupe of that calling that he felt in the center of his being? Calvin the Reformer showed plainly that he owed his pastoral vocation only to God; he had not received and would never receive any anointment or laying on of hands. God alone called him; God called him through men, certainly, but it was no one's business to confer on him or to contest a mission he owed to the Highest.

Connubial Bliss

Marriage does not approach the life of the cloisters as regards pleasure of the flesh.

JOHN CALVIN[23]

This semiconfidence of Calvin's in 1550 leaves some lingering doubts about the attraction the matrimonial state had for the Reformer. This impression is confirmed, moreover, by Theodore Beza: "[Calvin] lived in marriage for about nine years in perfect chastity."[24] It was in Strasbourg that an important change occurred in Calvin's life: he married. The happy woman? A widow who did not lack a certain charm, if not a charm that was certain. Idelette de Bure was the result of a good action and a conquest. A poor woman, she had married a Jean Stordeur of Liège. The two had tasted the murky delights of Anabaptism, charitably giving Calvin occasion to practice his ministry in turning them from this

20. Calvin, *Correspondance française avec Louis du Tillet*, pp. 50-51, July 10, 1538.
21. Calvin, *Correspondance française avec Louis du Tillet*, p. 53.
22. Calvin, *Correspondance française avec Louis du Tillet*, p. 70, December 1, 1538.
23. Calvin, *Des scandales*, p. 206.
24. T. Beza, *L'histoire de la vie et mort de Calvin* (1565), *OC* 21, col. 37.

evil road. Jean Stordeur died opportunely of plague in Strasbourg. Idelette herself, in delicate health, was to die in March 1549 without having given Calvin any living children.[25]

The union was most probably celebrated in August 1540 by Guillaume Farel in Strasbourg. Calvin was thirty-one; it was high time for him to take a wife. Celibacy was hardly proper for a preacher of the gospel; it was important to set oneself apart from the old clergy by visibly embracing the life of ordinary laymen. (Farel, tormented by the flesh, was to marry at sixty-nine rather than burn — provoking the astonishment of more than one friend.) Besides, how could one run a household or take care of oneself without a wife? This prosaic argument seems to have been the determining one for the chaste Calvin, afflicted during his whole life by a thousand worries about his health. Calvin wrote to a correspondent: "I, who have the air of being so hostile to celibacy, I am still not married and do not know whether I ever will be. If I take a wife it will be because, being better freed from numerous worries, I can devote myself to the Lord."[26]

God, as was well known, created women so that men could devote themselves to the Lord. They were the necessary intermediaries between the external world and their husbands; through them the outdoor uproar was transmitted, muted, attenuated, and as it were disinfected. Like fairies, they constantly watched over the household. Discretion was their first and most enduring virtue. Beginning on May 1, 1539, Calvin saw himself allotted one florin a week in Strasbourg. It was decidedly high time to marry. Some days later he took Farel to witness that he was not of the "insane race" of lovers. The repose of the warrior held no place among his projects. He explained to his correspondent with frank masculine clumsiness: "Remember well what I seek for in her. I am not of the insane race of those lovers who, once taken by a woman's beauty, cherish even her faults. The only beauty that seduces me is that of a woman who is chaste, considerate, modest, economical, patient; who I can hope, finally, will be attentive to my health."[27]

His sales pitch belongs to an employment office as much as to a matrimonial announcement. "Preacher of the gospel seeks chaste woman for caregiving, and possibly more. Only serious woman wanted." The offer, in itself, was terribly lacking in attraction. Calvin was disconsolate. He found no one. Should one be surprised?

25. Examining a portrait of Calvin's wife preserved in the museum of Douai, N. Weiss evokes their first meeting, which would have been in March 1537 in Geneva. N. Weiss, "Un portrait de la femme de Calvin," *Bulletin de la Société de l'Histoire du Protestantisme Français* 56 (1907): 222-33.

26. *OC* 10-1, col. 228. Cited by R. Stauffer, from whom we have taken the rest of these quotations. *L'humanité de Calvin* (Neuchâtel: Delachaux & Niestlé, 1964), p. 19.

27. *OC* 10-2, col. 348, May 19, 1539.

On February 6, 1540, the happy choice had still not appeared, despite the efforts made by Calvin and his entourage. He confided to his dear Farel during the first weeks of 1540: "I was offered a young girl of a noble family and whose dowry surpassed my condition. Two reasons dissuaded me from this marriage: she did not speak our language, and I feared that she would remember her birth and her education too much. Her brother, a man of great piety, insisted, and without a strong motive, unless, blinded by his love for me, he was neglecting his own interest. Animated by the same zeal, his wife fought beside him so well that I would almost have been reduced to declaring myself beaten if the Lord had not delivered me."[28]

The Lord was unavoidably one of the parties. He delivered the terrified Calvin from the burden that threatened him. He suggested a subterfuge to Calvin, that he ask the young girl first to learn French. What an effort for a poor girl of Strasbourg in the sixteenth century! *Kinder, Kirche, Küche*; children, church, kitchen — all part of the arrangement, and perfectly acceptable. Let us also add sewing and the care of the household — that is still all right. But to learn French! Really? Ah, Calvin had escaped her; he was free. Courageous but not rash, he took advantage of the young girl's hesitations to sneak away.

He then commissioned his brother Antoine to ask on his behalf the hand of a third woman who, it was said, had no attractions other than her beautiful soul and her moral qualities. No more was needed to inflame Calvin. "If she is equal to her reputation she will bring, without any fortune, a dowry that is fine enough. In fact she is recommended in a most flattering manner by those who know her. . . . If, as I firmly hope, she welcomes my offer, the marriage will not be delayed beyond next March 10."

But this fine match apparently eluded the solicitations of the Reformer. The former family took advantage of this to try again; they assailed Calvin with their favors. The poor man desperately prayed the Lord to "deliver him from this difficulty."[29]

As much as Calvin feared solitude, he was frightened by this sudden abundance of wealth. Fearing to fall from Scylla into Charybdis, he tried successfully to use one match to defeat the other. He concluded by becoming engaged to the poor but honest girl, to ask himself finally whether her honesty was complete — and to break the engagement. Behold him returning to his starting point: "I have still not found a wife, and I doubt that I should look for one any more," he sighed on June 21.[30]

Barely two months later Calvin was happily married. His wife was "actu-

28. *OC* 11, col. 12.
29. *OC* 11, col. 30.
30. *OC* 11, col. 52.

ally pretty," Farel noted incredulously, while praising her respectability and honesty.[31] The conquest of Idelette de Bure, moreover, included itself naturally among Calvin's pastoral tasks. Brought back to the true faith, her first husband gone, nothing more remained for the lovely Idelette than to marry her benefactor. She had had two children by her first marriage, a boy whose name, even, we do not know, and a girl, Judith.

The honeymoon was short; after six weeks the Lord sent a providential illness to the couple so they would not sink into hedonism. "In truth, out of fear that our marriage would be too happy, the Lord from the beginning moderated our joy," said Calvin, explaining that one must know how to keep one's countenance.[32]

But illness hovered over the city as well. In July 1540, while Calvin was at the Diet of Hagenau, his servant Jean Chevant took to his bed, never again to get up. In March 1541 Calvin was in Regensburg when he learned that the plague had again broken out in Strasbourg.[33] His house was infected; Claude Feray, the talented young Hellenist whom Calvin destined to the pastoral ministry, died after a few days. Antoine Calvin and three other inmates took refuge at a boarding house, abandoning the house struck by illness. But the plague pursued and caught them, snatching away young Louis de Richebourg. The youngest of the group, Malherbe, was at death's door and watched night and day. As for Idelette and her two children, they had sought asylum from a brother outside the city. Calvin, detained far away, let his anguish break out. "My wife is in my thoughts day and night, deprived of counsel because she is deprived of her master."[34] Calvin returned to Strasbourg in July. He would stay there only a few weeks before departing for Geneva. He received his successor in Strasbourg, Pierre Brully, a former Dominican who had tried in vain to preach the Reform in Metz.[35]

---

31. *OC* 11, col. 78.

32. *OC* 11, col. 83.

33. The Diet of Hagenau in 1540 and that of Regensburg the following year strove in vain for the rapprochement between "Catholics" and "Protestants" desired by Charles V. Gasparo Contarini represented the pope in Regensburg, while the opposing party delegated Bucer and Melanchthon. Calvin, looking on, distrusted accommodation; he rejected the ambiguity of the proposed eucharistic formulas. One must not be satisfied with half of Christ (*OC* 11, col. 127). Calvin would never again participate in this sort of meeting between Catholics and Protestants.

34. *OC* 11, col. 175.

35. Arrested in Tournai in present-day Belgium, he died at the stake in February 1545.

Calvin the Calvinist?
The *Commentary on the Epistle to the Romans*

The principal virtue of a commentator is an easy brevity that does not involve obscurity.

JOHN CALVIN[36]

The *Institutes* appeared again in August 1539 in a considerably enlarged version; the book had tripled in length. Without repudiating the internal aspect of faith, the institutional church had gained in consistency (see chap. 14 below). The version of 1536 had remained dependent in its arrangement on the Lutheran catechism: the law, the creed, the Lord's Prayer, the sacraments, and finally the "false" (Catholic) sacraments and Christian liberty. The new edition stressed the knowledge of God and self-knowledge; it also contained substantial development of predestination and of providence. One may legitimately conclude from this that his experience in Strasbourg had contributed to Calvin's theological maturity.

A *Commentary on the Epistle to the Romans* appeared characteristically in the fall. This Latin work likely resulted from a course in exegesis taught by Calvin in Johann Sturm's *Gymnasium*.[37] Following Luther, Saint Paul's Epistle to the Romans became one of the obligatory reference points of the Reformation. Was not that affirmation of justification by faith found there on which the whole Protestant movement has based its legitimacy down to the present day? If faith alone saves and justifies, the church is defined still more as a community of believers than as a judicial system. Works, like the sacraments, have meaning only with reference to the faith that produces them, and have no autonomous power in themselves. Luther meditated at length on the epistle, first in a course in Wittenberg in 1515-16, and then for the rest of his life. Was it not "the masterpiece of the New Testament, the purest Gospel of all"?[38]

Calvin transformed an obligatory action into a masterstroke; he also wrote a commentary, but wrote it in French. He loved conciseness, limpidity, clarity; he found the Germans, or at least the German speakers, to be long-winded, diffuse, and bombastic:

36. J. Calvin, *Commentaires sur le Nouveau Testament,* 4 vols. (Toulouse: Société des livres religieux, 1894), 3:1. The dedicatory letter to Simon Grynaeus is dated from Strasbourg on October 18, 1539. The book appeared in March 1540.

37. Calvin had analyzed the Gospel of John and several Pauline epistles, including the two epistles to the Corinthians. See F. Wendel, *Calvin, sources et évolution de sa pensée religieuse* (1950; Geneva: Labor et Fides, 1985), p. 38.

38. Martin Luther, *Werke,* Weimarer Ausgabe, vol. 6, p. 10.

Since that variety which is seen to be natural to the spirits of men causes some to take pleasure in one thing, others in another, we leave everyone his free judgment in this matter, provided no one wants to compel all the others to his own preference and to that which he finds good. This means that on the one hand we who prefer brevity will not reject or despise the labors of those who are long and copious in the interpretation of the books of holy Scripture, and on the other hand that they also will bear with us mutually, although it seems to them that we are too brief and concise.[39]

This is not a declaration of war — far from it — but rather a declaration of independence. Calvin takes account of his own originality. "Calvinism" was, to begin with, a question of style, of writing; Calvin was a thinker because he was a writer. Certainly he did not fail to cite his great predecessors, Melanchthon, Bullinger, and Bucer. He recognized with humility their great merits, but he was eager to compare himself with them.

Philip Melanchthon, with the excellent doctrine, industry, and dexterity he has in all sciences, has greatly clarified the matters treated in this, beyond the others who have thrown light on some things. But because his purpose has apparently been to treat only the most notable points, while he stops short at these he deliberately puts aside many things which might give some difficulty to those who are not among the greatest minds. Next comes Bullinger, who also rightly has gained great praise, since he also has had a skill in doctrine which has made it very agreeable. Finally, Bucer, bringing his labors to the light, has in a manner of speaking carried the work to completion. For this person, as you know, besides his profound knowledge and wide acquaintance with many things, besides his subtlety of mind and great reading, and many other and various virtues in which there is hardly one today who surpasses him and very few who compare with him — on the contrary, he surpasses many — has that praise that is proper and particular to him, that no other in our times has employed himself in the interpretation of Scripture with greater diligence. Since therefore I confess it would be a perverse and exorbitant emulation to want to try to take the prize from such persons, it was never my intention to take from them the smallest particle of their praise. May the grace and authority which they have merited by the common judgment of all respectable people remain to them safe and intact. Nevertheless I hope this point will be granted to me, that there has never been anything so well accomplished by men that the industry of their successors could not be found always employed either in polishing their work or arranging it or clarifying it.

39. Calvin, *Commentaires sur le Nouveau Testament,* 3:1.

As for me, I dare say nothing about it except that it has seemed to me that this labor of mine would not be useless, and there has not been any reason that induced me to undertake it other than the public welfare of the church. Besides, I thought that the distinct manner of proceeding which I proposed to myself here would be sufficient to purge me of all charges or suspicion of emulation, which was the thing I had most to fear.[40]

Philipp Schwarzerde, or Melanchthon (1497-1560), acquired a reputation as a moderate; he remained celebrated for the distinction he drew between indifferent matters *(adiaphora)* and articles necessary to salvation. Heinrich Bullinger (1514-75) was Calvin's junior by some years. At a young age he had succeeded Zwingli in Zürich. He remained attached to a purely symbolic conception of the Lord's Supper, while Calvin was to admit a real but spiritual presence of the Savior in the elements. Bucer, Melanchthon, and Bullinger were the thinking heads of a Reforming movement in which Calvin, growing bold, demanded a place. The author of the *Commentary* listed the omissions of his predecessors. Melanchthon "achieved what he intended, that is to make clear the most necessary points. And if, having stopped at these principal points, he has omitted many other things that should not be despised, he has not wished to prevent others from amusing themselves by examining them also." So much for Melanchthon. He writes admirably, but after reading him one realizes that everything remains to be said. His subtlety and doctrinal liberalism leave the reader hungry. On shutting his book one does not know what to think. Bucer represents almost the opposite tendency. "Bucer is too long." Too "long"? The word was out; everyone understood. Calvin reconsidered, and corrected his audacity: "Bucer is too long to be read in haste." Whew! There might have been a mistake. Calvin continued: numerous readers "are distracted by other occupations." They might be understood to be occupied with other things than reading Bucer. Bucer, in fact, is "too high to be easily understood by the low and by those who do not consider things too closely."

What audacity, Calvin, toward your host in Strasbourg! But Calvin had begun, and he continued, "The moment he undertakes to treat a subject, whatever it is, his incredible fertility of mind furnishes him with so many things to say that he cannot cut himself off and make an end." Calvin concluded, "The one has not treated all the issues, and the other has worked them out too fully to be read in a short time."

Calvin, however, had better things to do than strike a courteous balance. Saint Paul's Epistle to the Romans was a living spring where he quenched his thirst. "This epistle, besides many other and singular graces found in it, has one

40. Calvin, *Commentaires sur le Nouveau Testament*, 3:2, for the citations that follow.

proper and peculiar to it, which can never be sufficiently prized and esteemed; this is that anyone who has achieved a true understanding of it has as it were an open door through which to enter into the most secret treasures of Scripture."[41]

Why choose Saint Paul? For theological reasons, certainly. But also for historical ones: the Epistle to the Romans was part of the designated route that led, inevitably it was thought, to the Reformation. But the Apostle to the Gentiles, like the Reformers, exercised an extraordinary ministry; he owed his vocation directly to the Resurrected One. He who had not known the historical Jesus was a disciple of the glorified Christ. His sudden conversion permitted him to cut short any appearance of succession whatever. "Having begun with the proof of his apostolate, he goes on to the praise of the Gospel. And because this matter cannot be treated without discussing faith he begins to speak of that, following the thread of his discourse word by word. Thus he enters on the chief point of the whole epistle, which is that we are justified by faith; which he follows to the end of the fifth chapter. This then is the subject of these five chapters, that men have no other justification than the mercy of God in Christ."

Maintenance of Relations with Geneva

After we had been expelled, the audacity of Satan and his acolytes was seen to increase in Geneva.

CALVIN AND FAREL TO BULLINGER[42]

The affront had been severe. Calvin and Farel could not think of Geneva without bitterness. "You cannot figure out," they continued, "with what license and what insolence the impious there plunge themselves into all sorts of vices, with what effrontery they insult the servants of God, with what brutality they laugh at the Gospel, with what extravagance they behave on every occasion." In conclusion, in an aggrieved tone bordering on a curse: "Bad luck to him by whom such a scandal was produced! Bad luck to those who gave their hands to this criminal design!"

With the naïveté of pouting children, the two men had a tendency to think that the world had fallen apart in their absence. This picture hardly corresponded to reality. Certainly, thanks to Calvin's exile, the councils reestab-

---

41. Calvin, *Commentaires sur le Nouveau Testament*, 3:4, for the citations that follow.

42. A. Roget, *Histoire du peuple de Genève depuis la Réforme jusqu'à l'escalade,* 7 vols. (Geneva: John Jullien, 1870), 1:116.

lished the Bernese rites and ordered the celebration of the four great feasts they had abolished in 1536, Ascension, Circumcision, Annunciation, and Christmas.[43] But one cannot speak of laxity — far from it. An iron discipline continued in theory to govern the town: compulsory attendance at Sunday services and taking of the Lord's Supper, prosecution of Catholics and Anabaptists, expulsion of refractory foreigners. On March 18, 1539, the public space was moralized by prohibiting gambling and driving out vagabonds and beggars — who would be assisted, provided they stopped importuning passersby. In all this, continuity is evident. The absence of Calvin from 1538 to 1541 did not bring about any moral or doctrinal relaxation. Two new pastors replaced Calvin and Farel, respectively Jean Morand and Antoine Marcourt, the author of the Placards. Two Genevans, Henri de la Marre and Jacques Bernard, worked alongside them.

Calvin's enemies, who triumphed at his departure in 1538, were known by the picturesque name of the party of the "Artichokes" or "Articulants." Their leader, Captain General Jean Philippe, was executed in June 1540. Among Calvin's partisans was in particular Ami Perrin, who subsequently became the most energetic of his adversaries. Calvin did not give up all contact with Geneva. Once his anger had been forgotten, he described the still-painful past with moderation and calm. Thus, on July 10, 1538, to Louis du Tillet he wrote: "The Lord will direct us. I fear above all things to return to the duties from which I have been delivered, considering what perplexities I was in at the time when I was immersed in them. For although then I felt the vocation from God that held me bound, with which I consoled myself, now, on the contrary, I fear to tempt him if I again take up such a burden, which I have known to be insupportable to me."[44]

This dispassionate viewpoint culminated in the apostolic letter, very Pauline in tone, that Calvin sent on October 3, 1538, to his "beloved brethren in Our Lord who are the remnant of the dispersal of the church of Geneva." The metaphor of a "plague" set the tone for the letter; it was all the stronger because epidemics were a persistent scourge. Evil and suffering exist only to test the faithful servants of God. "The punishments he sends to his servants are for their good and salvation."[45] God authorizes evil, moral or physical. "You must think that these things did not happen to you without the dispensation of the Lord, who also acts through the unrighteous, according to the counsel of his own will."[46] Calvin had no doubts, in retrospect, about the validity of his voca-

43. The ordinance of 1536 would be reenacted, however, in November 1550.
44. Calvin, *Correspondance française avec Louis du Tillet*, pp. 50-51.
45. Calvin, *Lettres françaises*, 1:16-17.
46. Calvin, *Lettres françaises*, 1:14.

tion; God had indeed chosen him to exercise his ministry in Geneva. "Our conscience is well assured before God that it was by his vocation that we were once joined with you."[47]

When he was forced to flee, his partisans (and Farel's) were known in Geneva under the name of "Guillermins," from Farel's first name, Guillaume. But Farel took great care not to appear as a member of a party. "Nothing weighs so much on the heart as ingratitude, giving evil for good and hate for the affection one bears, death and confusion for the life and honor one has obtained." Or again, "Do not cry out against this one or that, but each one against himself; take all the guilt to yourself, so that your mouth says nothing but good of others." He exhorted everyone to penitence. "Cry out, weep, lift up your voice, so that your cry from the depths of this horrible and detestable calamity may come to the ears of God."[48]

Calvin likewise advised moderation to those who remained. One of them, Antoine Saunier, wanted to know whether he should partake of the Lord's Supper in the midst of unworthy people. Calvin tried to remove these scruples. He explained to Farel on October 24, 1538:

> There should be among Christians such a hatred of schism that they will avoid it as much as they can. There must be such a respect for the ministry and the sacraments that everywhere that they are seen to exist, there is held to be a church there. When therefore it happens, by the permission of God, that the church is run by these who are what they are, if the Christians perceive in them the marks of the church it is preferable that they not separate themselves from its Communion. It is not an obstacle if certain impure dogmas are taught there; there is hardly any church that does not preserve some remnant of ignorance. It is sufficient for us that the doctrine which is the foundation of the church of Christ has and preserves its place.[49]

After Calvin's departure the bourgeois feared for their good reputation. Thus on September 17, 1538, it was reported that "Several preachers are spreading words that are greatly to the disadvantage of the Gospel, saying the Mass is sung in the city and that supporters of the Gospel are rejected."[50] On December 27 it was noted with anger that many Genevans and foreigners had not come to partake of the Lord's Supper on Christmas Day. They were called to order:

47. Calvin, *Lettres françaises,* 1:12.

48. Roget, 1:136-39. Farel's letters are dated June 19, August 7, and November 8, 1538.

49. *OC* 10, col. 275.

50. *Annales Calviniani, OC* 21, col. 236, Registres du Conseil de Genève 32, fol. 149.

There is talk of foreigners who do not want to live according to the customs of the city or take Communion as has been ordered in the Small, Large, and General Councils, but are the cause of dissension among many. Be it resolved that all foreigners not wanting to live according to the customs, ordinances, and edicts of the city and who did not take Communion last Christmas Day like most of the city should leave the city, they and their households, and go to live elsewhere in their own fashion.

Also it is said that many of the city did not come to take Communion on Christmas Day, who also do not live according to the commands of the Small, Large, and General Councils and of the Synod of Lausanne, as we have ordered all in general to live.[51]

In February 1539 the election of new syndics testified to a reversal, or at least a recapturing of public opinion.[52] Calvin followed events in Geneva closely, but he hardly dreamed of returning. In April he wrote, not without rancor, that his return would certainly be a "satisfaction" to his self-respect, but that it would hardly advance the "cause" he and Farel represented.[53] In May he said to Farel, "Go to Geneva, you say to me. . . . Why do you not rather tell me to take up my cross?"[54] He returned to the same idea some months later, when he declared to the same person that he would prefer "a hundred deaths to this cross."[55] Calvin repeated his instructions to the faithful on June 25, 1539:

Beloved brethren:

Nothing has made me sadder, after the troubles that have so unfortunately dispersed and almost overturned your church, than to learn of your differences and disputes with the ministers who have succeeded us. Although the irregularity that attended their installation and that still subsists today could rightly have offended you, I cannot hear without great and profound horror that there is a great schism in the church, whatever may be the occasion. . . . But now, at the moment when I hear, to the contrary of what I expected, that the reconciliation between your pastors and the neighboring churches, a reconciliation arranged by Farel in person and approved by me, was not able to unite you, by a sincere feeling of friendship

51. *Annales Calviniani*, OC 21, col. 236, Registres du Conseil 32, fol. 253ff., for the rest of this discussion.

52. Girardin de la Rive, Antoine Chiccand, Hudriod du Mollard, and Jean Coquet. Chiccand, indeed, was strongly favorable to Calvin.

53. Roget, 1:289.

54. Roget, 1:290.

55. Letter to Farel, March 25, 1540, OC 11, col. 30.

and by the bond of a legitimate connection, to your pastors, to whom the care of your souls is entrusted, I see myself obliged to write to you to attempt to the extent possible to provide a remedy for this evil. . . . I only wish that with regard to those who exercise in some measure the function of pastor in such a way that they are endurable you will behave like Christians, and that you will thus concern yourselves more with what you owe to others than with what others owe to you.[56]

At the end of the year a major reversal occurred; the deterioration of relations with Bern resulted in an edict against treason, presented to the Council of Two Hundred on November 14: "That all citizens, bourgeois, sworn subjects, and inhabitants of Geneva who may speak, procure, or act either secretly or openly to alienate or transfer the principality, lordship, and city of Geneva, whatever their authority may be, shall be taken, and within three days, being legitimately convicted of such practices, have their heads cut from above their shoulders in the middle of the Place du Mollard, without any mercy. Their bodies shall be cut into four quarters and their goods be adjudicated by the government."[57]

This terrible punishment was applied fifteen years later, in May 1555. The peace agreement with Bern was made on February 1, 1540. New syndics were elected eight days later.[58] The trial of the Articulants, accused of friendship with Bern, followed in May. Their leaders were condemned to death *in absentia,* and one of their partisans, Jean Philippe, was tortured and then decapitated as a result of an altercation in the middle of the city. This shedding of blood tragically sealed the destiny of the Artichokes, until then Calvin's adversaries. Their Guillermin opponents decisively took power.

In October 1540 the return of Calvin as a preacher was called for. Louis Dufour, a member of the Two Hundred, was sent to Strasbourg to carry a message dated October 22, declaring in substance, "On behalf of our Small, Large, and General Councils . . . we beg you very affectionately to decide to come to us and return to your former place and ministry."[59] But Calvin had wind of these preparations. Even before receiving the letter he had responded by courteously declining this offer. He was bound by his commitments to his parish in Strasbourg: "When Our Lord makes a man pastor in a church to instruct it in his Word . . . he should consider himself attached to the government of it, so as

---

56. *OC* 10-2, cols. 351-52.

57. Roget, 1:197.

58. Étienne de Chapeaurouge, Étienne Dadaz, Jean Phiippin, and Antoine Gerbel. The first two, close to the Articulants, would be deposed as a result of their condemnation.

59. Roget, 1:292.

not to withdraw from it easily without having certainty in his heart and testimony before the faithful that the Lord has discharged him from it."[60]

Why were the Genevans so insistent on Calvin's return? They needed someone to counsel and edify them. Two of their pastors, Morand and Marcourt, had left them. In their disarray the inhabitants of the city suffered, among other things, doctrinal hesitations over the meaning of the Lord's Supper. On December 25, 1540, for example, "Master Champereaux stated today in his sermon that through baptism we have remission of sins and that in Communion the body of Christ is in the bread and his blood in the wine. Nevertheless he apologized for this, answering that he did not intend it this way and that tomorrow he would explain it better to the people."[61]

In January 1541 the secretary Roset was dispatched to seek out Calvin. But Calvin explained courteously that he still could not come. Finally in September 1541 the great news arrived: Calvin was in Neuchâtel, en route, and would be arriving shortly. The house of Sieur de Freynevile was prepared for him; the Genevans hoped Calvin's wife would soon join him. The Strasbourgers were congratulated; they should be glad to receive from the Genevans the "letter of thanks" that confirmed that John Calvin was "very propitious for this church, and is retained in it."[62] Calvin was back. The Genevans magnanimously hastened to pardon him of all the injury they had done him. The great man reentered Geneva on September 13, 1541. The Calvin who came back to Geneva had changed greatly; his experience in Strasbourg had been very enriching; he was now married; and finally, the *Institutes* had come out in a second Latin version in 1539. At the end of January 1542 he commented on events: "When I went before the people to preach everyone was prey to great curiosity. But passing over in complete silence the events which everyone assuredly expected me to mention, I stated in a few words the principles of my ministry, then with brevity and discretion recalled the faith and integrity that animated me. After this introduction I chose the text to comment on in the same place where I had stopped before. I wanted to show by this that, rather than having laid down the duty of teaching, I had been interrupted in it for a time."[63]

60. Calvin, *Lettres françaises*, 1:30.

61. *Annales Calviniani, OC* 21, col. 273, Registres du Conseil 34, fol. 538v.

62. *Annales Calviniani, OC* 21, col. 283, Registres du Conseil 35, fol. 327, September 16, 1541.

63. *OC* 11, cols. 365-66.

"Cardinal, Greetings." The *Letter to Sadoleto*

We proceed in this common faith of the church and in the observance of its laws and commandments.

JACOPO SADOLETO[64]

Nothing better demonstrates the interest Calvin continued to take in Genevan affairs than his magnificent *Letter to Sadoleto*. The occasion for it was provided by a letter from the cardinal presented to the Small Council of Geneva by Jean Durand, a citizen of Carpentras, on March 26, 1539. Calvin's answer, first published in Latin, promptly appeared in French, in the good city of Geneva, on September 5, 1540. It therefore is a central piece of evidence for analyzing Calvin's return to the city on the Leman.

Jacopo Sadoleto (1477-1547) was the ideal type of Renaissance humanist. This prelate, despite his blatant anti-Semitism, showed remarkable clemency with respect to the enemies of the faith, whom he preferred to convert by his teaching rather than by the fear of torture, at least in this world,[65] since he evidently promised them the flames of hell in the hereafter. Thus to Cardinal Farnese, who had asked him to use more severity toward the Lutherans, he replied with compunction: "The weapons I prefer to use against them may appear softer, but they are stronger; it is not terror or torture, it is the truth itself, it is extreme clemency that will make them admit their errors not with the mouth only, but in the heart. . . . I am the pastor of these people and not their hireling. I am moved as much as anyone by indignation against the wicked, but even more by compassion for the unfortunate."[66]

Titular bishop of Carpentras from 1517 on, Sadoleto deigned to reside for some months in the midst of the Provençals seven years later, before establishing himself for ten years in the midst of his flock.[67] This "reforming"[68] prelate and friend of common people had persuaded Clement VII to recognize the authenticity of the holy nail called the Holy Bit of Carpentras, "with a plenary in-

---

64. In *La vraie piété*, ed. I. Backus and C. Chimelli (Geneva: Labor et Fides, 1986), p. 71.

65. Sadoleto was disturbed by the tolerance the Jews enjoyed in pontifical territories. [Translator: This included Carpentras.] On February 1, 1525, he wrote from Rome to the consuls of the city to explain that he had asked the pope to revoke these privileges.

66. July 28, 1539. Cited by Buisson, 1:76.

67. In 1527 the bishop returned to establish himself in Carpentras. Residence of bishops was one of the major themes of this humanist reforming movement. He remained there without interruption until 1536.

68. M. Venard, *Réforme protestante, Réforme catholique dans la province d'Avignon, xvie siècle* (Paris: Le Cerf, 1993), p. 272.

dulgence for the faithful who came to venerate it on Saint Siffrein's day."[69] He preferred to indulge the piety of the humble, as he confided to Erasmus several times. It was important not to collide with "the deep-rooted ideas of the people, as long as they are not incompatible with true piety." Or again, it was necessary not "to oppose popular devotions, since everyone cannot raise himself to more sublime ideas."

A cardinal versus a Reformer? Why not? Calvin acquired his reputation by appearing as the champion of Geneva. Luther followed the passage of arms with interest: "I have read the treatise with singular delight. I wish Sadoleto believed God was the creator of men outside of Italy."[70] Calvin, barely recovered from the wounds to his self-esteem, defended Geneva, which had received him so badly. Past ingratitude was forgotten in the face of this common enemy, the papist hydra, always ready to draw poor strays into its net. The Geneva edition did not fail to reproduce Sadoleto's letter in order to attach Calvin's response to it, giving the undertaking the character of an open letter, permitting all, citizens, bourgeois, or mere inhabitants, to form an opinion. Its title was: *Letter of Jacques Sadolet, Cardinal, Sent to the Senate and People of Geneva; by which he seeks to reduce them under the power of the Bishop of Rome. With the answer of John Calvin. Translated from Latin into French*. It was printed in Geneva by Michel Dubois, 1540.[71]

Sadoleto's letter was dated March 18, 1539, from Carpentras. The author introduces himself in a few words: "Jacopo Sadoleto, priest, cardinal of the holy Roman church named after Saint Calixtus," to "his beloved brethren the syndics, Council, and citizens of Geneva." Sadoleto craftily flatters the Genevans, with all the condescension of a prince of the church addressing himself to provincials. He mentions the "nobility" of the city, the "order and discipline" of the republic, the "excellence of the citizens," and above all their "exquisite and praiseworthy humanity" toward foreigners. He puts them on guard against "the enemies of Christian union and peace," who by their innovations try to turn the peoples away from concord.[72] One must beware, in fact, of intellectual vanity. "Christian doctrine . . . is not based or founded on syllogisms or deceptive words, but on humility, piety, and obedience to the Lord."[73]

His optimistic humanism was no doubt inspired by antique models in his divinization of the God-man. Christ was the apotheosis of man. "God descended

---

69. Venard, p. 275.

70. *OC* 10-2, col. 402, Luther to Bucer.

71. *Épître de Jacques Sadolet, cardinal, envoyée au sénat et peuple de Genève: par laquelle il tâche les réduire sous la puissance de l'évêque de Rome. Avec la réponse de Jean Calvin. Translatée de latin en français*. In Backus and Chimelli, pp. 55-119.

72. Backus and Chimelli, p. 66.

73. Backus and Chimelli, p. 67.

to earth to be made a man, and man mounted to heaven to be made equal to God."[74] Sadoleto also criticizes justification by faith and insists on the importance of works. Faith, he insists, includes "charity." It is not simply "credulity or persuasion," but "hope."[75] Various themes of classical Catholicism now appear: the Eucharist, the confession of sins, prayers for the dead. While still threatening the Reformers with "eternal perdition,"[76] Sadoleto offers them the consolation of a "mild" God, ready to grant his "clemency and mercy" to repentant sinners.[77]

Sadoleto certainly admits the ecclesiastical disorders of the church, but maintains its doctrinal correctness. Although a sinner, the church endures; it is a ship assailed by the waves of sin, but it alone avoids the reefs to guide into a safe harbour souls concerned for their salvation.[78] Finally, Sadoleto's argument enters into a judicial vein. God is a "sovereign judge,"[79] and the unfortunate Reformers will not find any interceding advocate who will permit them to avoid the "outer darkness" where there is "weeping and gnashing of teeth."[80]

Addressed "from Strasbourg, the first day of September, 1539,"[81] Calvin's response blazed, magnificent in its fire and its impudence. He courteously greeted the cardinal, whose knowledge he praised, expressing the "great admiration and esteem" of his contemporaries. Hyperbolical and flattering, the tone is still that of Renaissance humanism, sometimes carried to the point of sycophancy. "Between learned men," Calvin wrote, we ought to understand each other. Do we not share the same love of "good literature"?[82]

This ironical opening introduced one of the best efforts of Calvin the pamphleteer. It was the defiance of the strong by the weak, of the man of the church by the prophet. Calvin's ministry was "founded and confirmed by the vocation of the Lord."[83] "The vocation of the Lord"; again the obsession with a

---

74. Backus and Chimelli, p. 69.

75. Backus and Chimelli, p. 70. Calvin refuted this thesis; faith cannot be confounded with charity. "Whenever Saint Paul attributes the power to justify to faith, he limits and restricts it to the gratuitous promises of the benevolence of God, separating it entirely from trust in and consideration of works" (p. 96).

76. Backus and Chimelli, p. 73.

77. Backus and Chimelli, p. 76.

78. Backus and Chimelli, p. 72.

79. Backus and Chimelli, p. 75.

80. Backus and Chimelli, p. 78. Along with the epidictic and the deliberative, the judicial was one of the chief genres of classical rhetoric recognized by Aristotle and Cicero. But here it refers to a Christian judiciary; God recapitulates men's past actions to pronounce a final judgment on them that will consign some to "infinite misery" and grant others "eternal felicity" (p. 75).

81. Backus and Chimelli, p. 119.

82. Backus and Chimelli, p. 81.

83. Backus and Chimelli, p. 82.

calling. Calvin drew all his legitimacy "from Christ," as he explained in a very Pauline manner.[84] And naturally he was willing to submit himself to that judgment of God mentioned by his adversary. Calvin's tone here anticipates that of Rousseau at the beginning of his *Confessions*. "Let the trumpet of the last judgment sound when it will; I shall come with this book in my hand to present myself before the sovereign judge. I shall say proudly, Here is what I have done, what I have thought, what I was."[85] Calvin, ordinarily so reserved, so discreet about himself, breaks away from his habitual modesty: "For my part, my Lord, I have experienced how difficult and troublesome it is to sustain against men the envious accusations I have been oppressed with on earth. But with the same confidence with which I have always called on and appealed to your tribunal, for this also I should now appear before you, knowing that the truth reigns in your judgment."[86]

This equivalence between the book and the judgment had deep roots. It was drawn from the Bible; in Daniel, and later in the Christian Revelation, the vision of the Book of Life announces the imminence of the last judgment. Calvin therefore draws up an assessment of his life; he has not egotistically sought to serve his own interest. By taste and by temperament he would have preferred "to pursue his studies in some respectable and free condition."[87] The author of the *Commentary on Seneca*, in fact, could have simply gone on writing humanist books, without encumbering himself with defending the cause of the gospel. As on every occasion when he evokes the peaceful existence of a scholar that he should have led, Calvin lets a ray of nostalgia pierce through. He therefore accepts the confrontation with Sadoleto before the "judgment seat of God." What dogmatic argument does he have to oppose to the cardinal? The purity and rectitude of his conscience. "As regards doctrine, our conscience is so assured that it does not fear that celestial judge from whom it knows for certain that that doctrine descended."[88] This preeminence of conscience, however, is not equivalent to a defense of inspiration. Far from it. The pope and the Anabaptists, those two "sects," according to Calvin, had in common precisely their spiritual pretensions. "When they vaunt themselves so arrogantly about the Spirit, they certainly aim at nothing else . . . except to give scope to their lies."[89]

The central question is therefore that of Christian authenticity. How to recognize the true church? The essential criterion is not antiquity, as the cardinal seemed to claim, but the preaching of the Word. Certainly the Reformed

84. Backus and Chimelli, p. 83.
85. J.-J. Rousseau, *Confessions*, in *Oeuvres complètes* (Paris: NRF, Pléiade, 1959), 1:5.
86. Backus and Chimelli, p. 108.
87. Backus and Chimelli, p. 85.
88. Backus and Chimelli, p. 108.
89. Backus and Chimelli, p. 90.

churches had not recovered the perfection of the primitive church, but they approached it. Moreover, the Catholic assemblies, according to Calvin, merited the name of "churches of Christ," but they were dominated by the pope and the "false bishops," described as "very cruel and dangerous wolves."[90]

Calvin understood very well the cardinal's blackmail, his use of fear of the hereafter to bring the Reformers back into the Roman orbit. He rejected this argument. "The business of a Christian is to rise higher than to seek and achieve only the salvation of his soul."[91] To the terrors instilled by the priests into the souls of the faithful he preferred the certainty produced by the assurance of salvation. "The consciences of the faithful . . . have only begun to repose on and trust in the bounty and mercy of God, which formerly were in constant anxiety and perturbation."[92]

90. Backus and Chimelli, p. 103.
91. Backus and Chimelli, p. 88.
92. Backus and Chimelli, p. 100.

CHAPTER 8

Geneva, a City of God?
The Middle Years of the Century

Calvin in Geneva was a Frenchman who dreamed of his country.

JOHN VIÉNOT (1859-1933)[1]

May the confidence God commands us to have in his grace and his virtue always be to you an invincible fortress.

CALVIN, "LETTER TO THE FAITHFUL IN FRANCE," 1547[2]

Calvin was the man of a calling and of uncompromising resistance. In Geneva's insularity he found a refuge and an asylum; from there he drew his energy, his inspiration, his reasons for hope. He also directed against the native Genevans his coldest and most inextinguishable anger.

The Reformer arrived in Geneva in mid-September 1541. He left Strasbourg with regret, carrying with him his right of bourgeoisie. A scalded cat fears even cold water, and Calvin was not really sure of remaining among the Genevans. For years afterward he would consider himself a temporary guest, ready at the slightest alarm to abandon the town he obstinately distrusted.

1. J. Viénot, *Histoire de la Réforme française,* 2 vols. (Paris: Fischbacher, 1926-34), 1:268.
2. J. Calvin, *Lettres françaises,* ed. J. Bonnet, 2 vols. (Paris: Meyrueis, 1854), 1:216, July 24, 1547.

There was great instability in the church; Morand and Marcourt, the two pastors who had replaced him and Farel in 1538, were no longer there to welcome him. There were three active ministers: Aimé Champereaux, who withdrew some weeks later; Jacques Bernard; and Henri de la Mare. Calvin drew a hasty picture of these last two: "The first, of a touchy, or rather savage, character, was not amenable to good counsel; the other, wily and sly, was inflated with lies and trickery; both were ignorant as well as vain. To the lack of knowledge was added the lack of care and of solicitude, for they had not thought, even in dreams, about what it means to direct a church."[3]

An impatient Calvin reveals to us one of the driving forces of his character. "I knew well what it would cost me, and that I must buy peace at the price of many concessions, which as you know is not precisely my natural bent. I did violence to myself, however; by my moderation I contained their malice and prevented it from breaking loose out of doors."

Harboring a fiery, indeed intransigent temperament under an appearance of placidity, this man of thirty-two, with a sharpened intelligence and a bitter spirit, already did not support his colleagues. Did they understand this? This appears plausible, as the two men left Geneva as soon as possible, in 1542 and 1543. Calvin's pastoral duties were crushing; his painstaking, profound sermons were based on rigorous exegetical labor. They were in fact veritable university lectures, embellished for effect with strong and picturesque images designed to rivet the attention of the humble. In the sixteenth century a pastor was neither a social worker nor a talk-show host. He was judged not so much on his kindness as on his ability. Calvin preached twice on Sundays, and in some weeks gave several weekday sermons besides (see chap. 13).

But Calvin understood that he also had to reorganize the church, defend its autonomy with regard to the temporal power, regulate the doctrine and morals of the faithful, and finally add an international dimension to his mission. In all these roles he was primarily a man of the Word; as preacher or writer, he employed his considerable energy in the service of that vocation that haunted him, lived in him, undermined him, drove him to despair sometimes — before he recovered his confidence. His correspondence shows us the hidden face of the ecclesiastical organizer — nervous, sensitive, troubled, and also ironical. He was also a stylist, who used writing to recover that peacefulness of soul that lucidity produces.

3. *Opera Calvini* (hereafter cited as *OC*) 11, col. 364, January 1542.

A City in Active Change

Calvin's relationship with Geneva includes an uninterrupted series of frictions, sometimes carried to the point of hatred, and has given rise to numerous misunderstandings. To begin with, there is a danger in retrospectively identifying a great man, in this case Calvin, with the society that surrounds him. Calvin's influence on Geneva is undeniable, but it occurred within a general evolution of which we would like to provide a glimpse.

Let us begin by eliminating one source of confusion. Calvin was a Reformer. This does not imply that he was always followed. Some of his ideas, even in the ecclesiastical field, remained dead letters, for example his preference for monthly and not quarterly celebration of the Lord's Supper. In civil matters he was neither an omniscient dictator nor a demiurge, nor even a great legislator who endowed his adopted city with its laws and institutions. His role remained more modest; he accompanied more often than initiated the evolution of the city. If one accepts the label "Calvinism" to describe the changes occurring, one must be careful not to ascribe everything to the will of one man.

Geneva, in fact, was never a theocracy. Although they interpenetrated each other more than today, the religious and political powers, the ministry and the magistracy, were never one and the same. Calvin indeed had to fight step-by-step to maintain the autonomy of the church against the ascendancy of the councils. The question of excommunication was at the center of the debate. Was it a religious action, as Calvin maintained, or did it come under civil jurisdiction, as his adversaries wished? To sum up, Calvin did not take over the state; he was neither a commanding general nor an ayatollah. On the contrary, he only wanted to guarantee a minimum of liberty of action to the church.[4]

In many respects Geneva was located at the intersection between northern Europe and a southern world, to which its Franco-Provençal speech and the role of the vineyards linked it in the beginning. The sixteenth century marked its emancipation from the guardianship of Savoy and its entrance onto the international stage, of which the migratory movements furnish the most spectacular illustration. A rapid calculation enables us to measure the scale of the phenomenon. With nearly 10,000 inhabitants on average in the second half of the century, Geneva exceeded in importance its closest neighbors, Fribourg, Bern, and Zürich. Only Basel could pretend to rival Geneva in population, with be-

---

4. As A. Roget wrote in the nineteenth century, "The Genevan church . . . meddled with matters we would consider today as not within its province. But it has not been noticed that the opposite phenomenon was manifested in a still more pronounced way, and that the state did not hesitate to intrude into a number of matters that we rank today among the attributes of the church." A. Roget, *L'Église et l'État à Genève du temps de Calvin. Étude d'histoire politico-ecclésiastique* (Geneva: J. Jullien, 1867), p. 5.

tween 9,000 and 10,000 inhabitants. But the chief characteristic of Geneva's de-mography was the fluctuation of its population. Geneva exceeded 13,000 souls in 1550, reached a peak of 21,400 in 1560, then went down again in the follow-ing years. These zigzag movements continued: 17,300 in 1580, 14,400 in 1590. These peaks recurred a century later; the Genevan population reached its low-water mark in 1650, at 12,300, and did not return to 17,500 until 1700.[5] This demographic singularity was bound up with the religious choices of the city: "The middle of the sixteenth century was a decisive turning-point in the his-tory of Geneva. With the adoption of the Reformation in 1536 the ancient eco-nomic center became the city of refuge, home to the incontestable beacon of Calvin's name, and also a geographical reality. One must refer to a map of Euro-pean religion to understand better the strategic importance of this small city, an outpost of Protestantism thrust like the head of a lance into Catholic Europe."[6]

Around 1550-60 the first wave of immigration coincided with the religious flight. The increase of population was startling. It was accompanied by a xeno-phobia that hardly spared Calvin, often the first target of anti-French campaigns. However, the importance of these feelings of resentment must not be exagger-ated; the graft of the Protestant refugees onto the ancient Genevan stock was a success. The overture had begun some years earlier, about 1542, at the very time Calvin settled permanently in Geneva. This human tide was impressive; within ten years more than 5,000 refugees, with their wives and children, came to crowd themselves into a city "that until then had housed hardly more than 10-12,000 people." This rate of increase was "obviously inflationary; 5% per year, possibly more." And, Alfred Perrenoud continues, "in some ten years Geneva had almost doubled. Around 1560, with more than 20,000 inhabitants, the town reached a peak, also a point of saturation and of pressure hard to endure; and very quickly, as shown by marriages and births, the population declined."

This fall itself probably corresponded to a drop in the number of the ref-ugees. However, this unstable contribution remained statistically negligible; these arrivals-followed-by-departures did not change the long-term profile of the city. The contribution was therefore more qualitative than quantitative. Otherwise the demography of Geneva followed the annual rhythms character-istic of traditional societies. "Everything obeyed the seasons; winter was the time for marriages, spring that for conceptions, summer that for death."[7]

5. A. Perrenoud, *La population de Genève du seizième au début du dix-neuvième siècle. Étude démographique* (Geneva: Société d'histoire et d'archéologie, 1979), p. 37. To set a scale of size, Strasbourg had about 20,000 inhabitants in 1580, and Paris 300,000 to 400,000 in 1600.

6. Perrenoud, p. 41, for this citation and those following.

7. Martin Körner, "Réformes, ruptures, croissances, 1515-1648," in *Nouvelle histoire de la Suisse et des Suisses* (Lausanne: Payot, 1986), pp. 333-496, p. 341.

The importance of deaths during summer was principally due to epidemics — no less than thirteen of plague alone occurred from 1500 to 1640. Calvin, like all his contemporaries, dreaded the assaults of the scourge that periodically plunged him into terror — fear of seeing his closest friends disappear, instinctive fear before the spread of the prowling death that drove the preacher to urge conversion. The phenomenon was not restricted to Protestantism. How much did the Reformation affect the behavior of the population? To this question one can give only a subtle answer:

> Canon law forbade the celebration of marriages before Easter (during Lent), as well as during Advent, and with a few exceptions these rules were generally respected in the sixteenth and seventeenth centuries in the Catholic areas of the country. In Geneva, on the other hand, the Reformation in the space of a single generation eliminated these practices linked to the liturgical calendar, removing the interdiction of November and December even more rapidly than that of March. But in place of the Catholic interdictions appeared almost immediately, and surprisingly for Calvin's city, a ban derived from a popular custom stamped with paganism which prohibited marriage during May.[8]

The influx of Frenchmen and Italians favored a spirit of enterprise that transformed Geneva economically during the sixteenth century, introducing clock making, weaving, and the silk industry. It also accelerated the adoption of French at the expense of the native Franco-Provençal.[9]

The Original Institutions

The most renowned philosophers who have written well and wisely about civil institutions hold that a republic should be tempered between the rule of the honorable people and chief men of a city and popular rule.

G. CONTARINI, *ON THE MAGISTRATES AND REPUBLIC OF VENICE*, 1543[10]

8. Körner, pp. 337-38.

9. Jaakko Ahokas, *Essai d'un glossaire genevois d'après les registres du Conseil de la ville de 1409 à 1536* (Helsinki: Société néophilologique, 1959), pp. 7-9.

10. G. Contarini (1483-1542), *Des magistratz & république de Venise*, ed. J. Charnier (Paris: G. Du Pré, 1544). The original was from 1543.

In their own fashion the Genevans are insular. Their identity presents a subtle mixture of external contributions and indigenous development. The city was indeed an island in the sixteenth century. In its language and culture it was close to its French-speaking neighbors, but it was differentiated by its religion. With the exception of the Vaud and Neuchâtel, won over to the Reformation, French-speaking Protestantism was a minority element. Similarly, Geneva resembled its German neighbors in religion but was distinguished from them in language and mentality. Its relations with Bern, a blend of suspicion and mutual help, sufficiently demonstrate this.

Geneva, therefore, shone through its uniqueness. François Bonivard (†1570), former prior of Saint-Victor, chronicler and prolific writer, was the author of a remarkable treatise, *Description and Estimate of the Old and New Regulation of Geneva,* which long remained unpublished. It concerned the "regulation" *(police)* of Geneva, meaning its political and constitutional organization. Dazzled by his subject, the author discovered in it the prodigious wisdom of the ancients. Like ancient Sparta, and in imitation of Venice, Geneva had a "mixed" government which included the three pure political forms, monarchy, aristocracy, and democracy. The author tried to demonstrate the existence of three "estates" in sixteenth-century Geneva, each represented by its own council.[11]

The city was endowed with several councils, the Small or Narrow Council, the Council of Sixty (whose functions were mainly diplomatic), and the Council of Two Hundred or Large Council. The Large Council, among other things, was responsible for the election of the Small Council. The General Council (or Commune) played a more and more tenuous role. To see these as representing a monarchy, an aristocracy, and a democracy required an extravagant imagination. There was also a more and more rigorous distinction drawn between citizenship and bourgeoisie. Citizenship required birth and baptism in the city; bourgeoisie, on the other hand, could be granted to newcomers. A few years before his death, Calvin acquired the enviable title "bourgeois of Geneva." But offices were restricted to "citizens." Finally, there was a third group of foreigners and "natives" (sons of foreigners residing in Geneva). Bonivard cheerfully describes this Genevan political life:

> In the time of the papacy a Mass of the Holy Spirit was said before an election, and afterwards one went to the cloister, where elections were held. Nowadays one goes to a sermon, where the minister exhorts the people to elect

11. F. Bonivard, *Advis et devis de l'ancienne et nouvelle police de Genève, suivis des advis et devis de noblesse et de ses offices ou degrez et des III estats monarchiques, aristocratiques et démocratiques* . . . (Geneva: J. G. Fick, 1865).

magistrates who are faithful and God-fearing, and after the sermon he offers prayers which the people follow, and then they go to the cloister, where they bow the knee in prayer. . . . The next day the four new syndics convoke the Two Hundred to the ringing of the bell; but no one of the Narrow Council goes in with them except the four former syndics, the treasurer, and the secretary. . . .

.These new and former syndics depose half of the sixteen councilors who remain and elect as many new ones, and afterwards [do the same for] the other eight. But those elected must all be citizens, born and baptized in the city, for these only are called citizens; the others who were born elsewhere are called only bourgeois or inhabitants; which bourgeois can indeed belong to the General Council, also the Two Hundred, or even the Sixty, but the mere inhabitants, no. No one, also, who is not a citizen can hold office.[12]

Bonivard explains: "It is about thirty-two years that the difference among these terms has existed. For previously there was no difference either in name or in fact, and on the Narrow Council, or even among the syndics, there could be found those who were natives of other places or countries."

The four syndics more or less wielded the executive power in the city, with the aid of the Small Council. In referring to the latter, one often says simply "the Council." Along with the *lieutenant de justice* (criminal judge) and the treasurer, they were subject to an annual election. Until 1555 the army was under the command of a captain general. For purposes of defense the city was carefully divided into *dizaines* (literally, "tens"), *bandes* (bands), and quarters, commanded by *dizainiers, banderets,* and captains.

Moses and Aaron: The Ordinances of 1541

Two biblical personages, Moses and Aaron, represented complementary facets of power. Their brotherhood dissolved in their differences. Moses was both the liberator of his people and their chief legislator, in the Hellenistic tradition;[13] Aaron assumed the duties of the priesthood. Now the Reformation broke the links traditionally maintained between the temporal and spiritual powers in the West. Should the restoration of "true religion" lead to a strengthening of the state or to a higher status for the church? The question was far from being resolved in the sixteenth century. One thing is certain: Geneva was never a theoc-

12. Bonivard, pp. 24-25.
13. Philo of Alexandria, *De aeternitate mundi,* ed. R. Arnaldez and J. Pouilloux, *Oeuvres* (Paris: Le Cerf, 1969), III, 87.

racy. Not only did the spiritual and temporal remain distinct, not only did Calvin not rule the city, but the Reformation still had to fight inch by inch to maintain the independence of the decisions of the church against the encroachments of the Council. Myconius of Basel put Calvin on his guard against this drift toward the temporal: "The laymen put forward a truly anarchical dogma; the Council, they say, is the church *(Senatus Ecclesia est)*. They have even usurped the right of excommunication. All the power that the Pope formerly enjoyed they strive to claim for the magistrate. They claim that Moses, a secular prince, gave orders to his brother Aaron, that David and the other pious kings also commanded the Levites. Why, they say, should things not go the same way under the government of the New Testament?"[14]

Myconius's description of Basel testifies to the very plain risk that the Reformers feared: a total annexation of the church by the state, a secularization of theology for the benefit of political ideology, a dilution, finally, of the ecclesiastical dignity within the civil hierarchy. The risk appeared clearly to Calvin. In a letter to Farel he exclaimed: "See what a sad precedent our brethren would establish if they came to recognize the head of the state as the judge of doctrine. Certainly, if we permit the yoke to be imposed on us in this way, we betray the holy ministry."[15]

This difficulty was overcome by forestalling it. A veritable race began: in September 1541 Calvin suggested to the Council the drafting of ecclesiastical ordinances. The legislative work extended over several sessions: discussion in the Council beginning on September 27, adoption by the Council of Two Hundred on November 9 and by the General Council on the twentieth. What in substance did these Ordinances of 1541 say in their final version?

> In the name of Almighty God, we the syndics, Small and Large Council, assembled with our people at the sound of the trumpet and the great bell following our ancient customs, having considered that it is a thing worthy of attention above all others that the doctrine of the holy Gospel of Our Lord be preserved in its purity and the Christian church be properly maintained, that young people in the future be faithfully taught and the hospital be kept in good condition for the maintenance of the poor, which cannot be done unless there is a definite rule and pattern for living by which each estate may understand the duties of its position; for this reason it has seemed good to us that the spiritual government, as Our Lord revealed and established it by his Word, be reduced to good order to take its place and be observed among us. And thus we have ordered and established to be followed and preserved in

14. *OC* 11, cols. 368-69, Myconius to Calvin, February 10, 1542.
15. Roget, *L'Église et l'État*, p. 35.

our city and territory the following ecclesiastical discipline, as we see that it is taken from the Gospel of Jesus Christ.[16]

Picturesque in form, this prefatory text laid down a certain number of fundamental principles. To begin with, it stipulated the existence of a distinct religious sphere, with its own "discipline." The civil government was therefore distinguished from the church, and many duties still fell to the spiritual power. The gospel was always a field of expectation common to the whole of society; the instruction of youth and the care of the poor derived from its precepts. One could not therefore speak of "secularism" in the sense this term later acquired in our modern societies, but there was nevertheless not a fusion of the church and the civil society. Great care must be taken to specify that the pastors exerted "no civil jurisdiction and used only the spiritual sword of the Word of God, as Saint Paul ordered them to."[17] The vocation proper to each "estate" was also clearly affirmed; all secular activity was itself a calling, a vocation.

The church was then divided into four offices: pastors, doctors, elders, and deacons. The pastors preach and distribute the sacraments, the doctors teach, the elders "amicably admonish those they see are at fault and leading a disorderly life."[18] As for the deacons, they watch over the poor and the sick. Begging, moreover, was rigorously forbidden. These distinct ministries, equally worthy of respect, were one of the characteristic elements of Calvinist civilization. They were not restricted to Calvinism — Bucer's views were hardly different — but they found their highest degree of systematization in the work of the French Reformer.[19]

The moralizing of social life, the work ethic, the prohibition of begging, aid to the poor — these are some distinguishing traits of the Calvinist city. The

16. Roget, *L'Église et l'État*, pp. 27-28. These Ordinances of 1541 were revised in 1561, and again in 1576 after Calvin's death.

17. Roget, *L'Église et l'État*, p. 45.

18. Roget, *L'Église et l'État*, p. 35.

19. François Wendel, *L'Église de Strasbourg, sa constitution et son organisation, 1532-1535* (Paris: PUF, 1942), p. 189: "For a long time the division of ecclesiastical functions into a certain number of ministries distinct in their jurisdiction and also, to a certain extent, in their dignity, was attributed to Calvin. Recent research has enabled us to find its source in the third edition of Bucer's *Commentaire évangélique*. But we believe it would be possible to find still older testimony both in Bucer and in Capito. The principle of plurality, originally based on the theory of universal priesthood, is clearly enunciated in the Tetrapolitan." Bucer already listed four ministries, preachers, elders, deacons, and doctors, but for him this was scarcely a "definitive enumeration" (p. 191). The Strasbourg ordinance of 1534 did not recognize the diaconate, but there were pastors and elders, or *Kirchenpfleger*, as well as doctors.

centerpiece of the system was undoubtedly the consistory. This ecclesiastical court, half-lay, half-pastoral, watched over the morals and beliefs of the faithful. The consistory met on Thursdays. Besides the ministers, it included twelve lay members appointed by the civil authority.[20] It called people before it like a court but was not part of the civil jurisdiction; it pronounced spiritual penalties, including excommunication, much dreaded in that face-to-face civilization. Not to be solemnly admitted to partake of the Lord's Supper during its four annual celebrations was a terrible humiliation. Communion, contrary to Calvin's original wishes, was distributed only on Christmas, Easter, Pentecost, and the first Sunday in September. It marked a strongpoint in social solidarity, since it demanded, ideally, cessation of scandalous behavior, reconciliation, and mutual pardon. The first appearances of people before the consistory occurred on December 20. Calvin defined its role as follows: "The consistory has been established to regulate morals. It has no civil jurisdiction, but only the right to reprove according to the Word of God, and the most severe decision it can take is excommunication."[21]

In practice the civil power always contested this ecclesiastical jurisdiction. Thus, on March 19, 1543: "In the Council of Sixty it was discussed whether the consistory has the power to prohibit the unqualified from receiving the Communion of Our Lord or not; regarding which, resolved that the consistory has neither jurisdiction nor power to prohibit Communion, but only to admonish and then give a report to the Council, so that the government may judge delinquents according to their faults."[22]

The consistory therefore could not inflict any penalties; it had only limited doctrinal competence. The double role of permitting or of prosecuting heresy belonged to the Council. Calvin described the consistory as a "sort of ecclesiastical court."[23] It basically possessed only an admonishing role, the lords of the Council being charged with penal prosecutions if needed. Without penalties, could the consistory be sure that transgressors regretted their sins? There was some hesitation on this point; in 1547 the Council informed Calvin that "a remand before the consistory" would only apply to the "rebellious" and "obstinate"; others would go "in peace."[24]

In 1542, in parallel with the ecclesiastical ordinances, the city revised its

20. Two members of the consistory came from the Small Council, four from the Sixty, and six from the Two Hundred. They were named by the Small Council and approved by the Two Hundred.

21. Roget, *L'Église et l'État*, p. 31.

22. Roget, *L'Église et l'État*, p. 37.

23. *OC* 11, cols. 376ff., letter to Myconius, March 14, 1542. Oswald Geisshaüser, called Myconius (1488-1552), was Oecolampadius's successor in Basel.

24. Roget, *L'Église et l'État*, p. 41, March 29, 1547.

constitution. Calvin played a rather secondary role in this work, which involved specifying the method of electing the syndics, the councils, and the various officers and defining their functions. A Genevan historian described this activity as follows:

> The regulations it entailed dealt with a variety of topics and entered into the most minute details. Thus all the duties of the town crier, the bell-ringers, the gate-keepers, the building inspector, the inspector of the artillery, the rules to follow in case of fire, were given with great precision.
>
> But it is exactly the entirely municipal character of these regulations that makes us believe that the Reformer did nothing but select from, coordinate, and amend a draft of the old ordinances. They would certainly not have waited for Calvin to regulate the roads or the police in Geneva.[25]

He concludes that Calvin played the role of an "editor" and not of a "legislator."[26] Moses and Aaron remained separate. Appearing the same year as the ordinances, the *Short Treatise on the Lord's Supper*[27] laid the foundations of a doctrinal Calvinism that was distinct both from Lutheranism and from the doctrines of Zwingli. All the Reformers were in agreement on one point: Communion was a commemoration of the Last Supper eaten by Christ on the eve of his death, and in no case a sacrifice. But their interpretations varied considerably. Luther preserved a real presence of Christ in the elements while postulating the existence of distinct substances, the bread and the wine on one side, the body and the blood on the other. Zwingli, with the "sacramentarian" party, interpreted the Lord's Supper in a purely symbolic fashion. It remained for Calvin to attempt a synthesis of these apparently irreconcilable points of view by postulating a spiritual but not material participation in the body and blood of the Savior. "We therefore confess with one voice that in receiving the sacrament faithfully according to the ordinance of the Lord we are truly made participants in the very substance of the body and the blood of Jesus Christ."[28] This led Calvin to reject both the local presence of Christ — for which he reproached Luther — and the purely symbolic version of the sacrament: "On the one hand it behooves us, in order to exclude all carnal fantasies, to elevate our hearts to heaven, not thinking that the Lord Jesus could be abased to the point of being enclosed by any corruptible ele-

25. A. Roget, *Histoire du peuple de Genève depuis la Réforme jusqu'à l'escalade*, 7 vols. (Geneva: John Jullien, 1870), 2:66.

26. Roget, *Histoire du peuple*, 2:68.

27. *Petit traité de la sainte Cène*.

28. I. Backus and C. Chimelli, eds., *La vraie piété* (Geneva: Labor et Fides, 1986), p. 151.

ments. On the other hand, so as not to belittle the effectiveness of this holy mystery, we must think this is done by the secret and miraculous power of God and that the Spirit of God is the link in this participation, for which reason it is called spiritual."

Written in French, the *Short Treatise* obviously goes back to Calvin's period in Strasbourg. It is addressed to the humble, the ignorant, and the *illiterati*, who were also invited to the Lord's Supper. Calvin would give a more elaborate form to his eucharistic theology in the *Consensus Tigurinus* of 1549.

We confine ourselves for the moment to saying that, by 1541, Calvinism was already endowed with a politics and a theology distinct from the other Protestant confessions. The Latin *Institutes* of 1539 had certainly marked a first break, but it had reached mainly the world of scholarship. In 1541, strengthened by his Strasbourg experience, within a few months Calvin imparted to the church of Geneva his double plan, doctrinal and institutional. The fundamental question remained the transmission and popularization of his ideas; the catechism marked the decisive move in this process.

The Catechism of 1542

When you explain the articles of faith to them let it be in the form of direct instruction, and not by questions and answers. They should never answer anything other than what they think themselves, and not what someone has dictated to them. All the answers in the catechism are backwards; it is the student who instructs the teacher. They are nothing but lies in the mouths of children, since they explain what they do not understand and affirm what they are far from believing.

JEAN-JACQUES ROUSSEAU[29]

In dialogue form and yet predictable, leaving no question unanswered, a catechism, as generally envisaged, has become by antiphrasis the very symbol of received ideas, as when one speaks of a "revolutionary" or "Stalinist catechism."[30] Catechisms go back to the sixteenth century. They are the joint fruit of the two Reformations, Catholic and Protestant, although the Protestants seem to have

---

29. J.-J. Rousseau, *L'Émile* (1762), *Oeuvres complètes* (Paris: NRF, Pléiade, 1969), 4:722.

30. F. Furet, *Penser la Révolution française* (Paris: NRF, 1978), p. 113.

taken the initiative in creating a codified form that was adopted later in the Roman Church.

These catechisms were certainly based on a pedagogical duplicity whose parroted repetition and deceitful character were denounced by Jean-Jacques Rousseau. The master and the student have a ventriloquial relationship. The play of questions and answers appears to entrust to the child, and not to the instructor, the duty of affirming in a thin voice an orthodoxy to which one can only bow down. In the mouths of the humble the official doctrine of the churches thus takes on an extraordinary prominence. This inversion of roles, while it guarantees learning, also assumes a symbolic value in a religion addressed especially to the poor and to children — while keeping them in scrutinized liberty.

The student, in the Calvinist catechism of 1542, speaks in the first-person plural; the master plays the role of the "tempter." In his questions he is careful to refer implicitly to future "errors" that will have to be corrected.[31] The word "catechism" comes from a Greek word meaning literally "to cause to resound." It refers to transmitting the good news so that its echo may spread to infinity. Catechizing repeats a technique of diffusion as well as its contents. The expression was originally applied to the initiation that preceded baptism. But this catechumenate declined during the fifth to eighth centuries with the development of precocious infant baptism in the bosom of a Christianity henceforth identified with society as a whole. The Fourth Lateran Council in 1215 prescribed annual confession of sins and Easter Communion. The Sunday sermon henceforth became the preferred instrument for the diffusion of Christian teaching, alongside ritual, that catechism "before catechisms."[32] In the thirteenth century instructions to priests and synodal statutes prescribed the dogmatic instruction priests should transmit to the faithful: instruction in the Apostles' Creed, the Decalogue, and the sacraments. The septenary form aided memorization: seven deadly sins,[33] seven beatitudes, and finally seven sacraments.

Jean Gerson, chancellor of the University of Paris, at the beginning of the fifteenth century emphasized the teaching given to children and the humble in his *ABC for Simple People*.[34] Gerson played an essential role in Western Christianity by insisting, as the Reformers did later, on the Ten Commandments, destined to replace in the following century the seven deadly sins of the medieval era. A French translation of the Decalogue, inspired by his work, found a place

31. O. Millet, "Rendre raison de la foi: le Catéchisme de Calvin (1542)," in *Aux origines du catéchisme en France* (Paris: Desclée, 1988), p. 199.

32. N. Lemaitre, "Le catéchisme avant les catéchismes, dans les rituels," in *Aux origines du catéchisme en France*, pp. 28-44.

33. Pride, envy, anger, avarice, gluttony, sloth, and lust.

34. *ABC des simples gens*.

from 1491 on in the *Shepherds' Calculator and Calendar*.[35] But the Ten Commandments "that God gave to Moses on Mount Sinai" nevertheless did not replace the seven deadly sins. "The book aimed to be an encyclopedia for simple people. The shepherd who was supposed to have written this illustrated almanac gave his readers all sorts of useful information about new moons and eclipses, 'physic and healthy diet,' 'the astrology of the signs, stars, and planets and the physiognomy of shepherds.' But more than a third of this very didactic calendar was devoted to 'the tree of vices, the tree of virtues, and the pictured tower of wisdom.'"[36]

The modern catechism was born in the sixteenth century from the confrontation between the rival churches. Luther took the initiative. In 1529 he published two complementary manuals, the *Large German Catechism* and the *Small Catechism, for the Use of Pastors and Poorly Educated Preachers.* . . .

"That which led me to shorten the catechism," Luther explains, "was the desolate state of the church. . . . Almighty God! Of what miseries have I not been the witness! The country people, above all, know nothing at all of the Christian doctrines; a great number of pastors, alas, are themselves incapable of teaching them. All call themselves Christians, are baptized, and receive the sacraments; and they know neither the Lord's Prayer, nor the creed, nor the Ten Commandments. They live like brutes and pigs."[37] The two Lutheran catechisms followed a prescribed order: the Ten Commandments, the contents of the faith, the Lord's Prayer, baptism, and Communion. The Pauline complementarity of law and grace thus appears in the order of instruction itself.

During his first stay in Geneva, Calvin composed a *Course of Instruction and Confession of Faith Used in the Church of Geneva* (1537). On his return he published his *Catechism of the Church of Geneva; that is, the formulas for instructing children in Christianity* in 1542.[38] The catechism combined a double

---

35. The *Compost et kalendrier des Bergers*. J. Bossy, "Moral Arithmetic: Seven Sins into Ten Commandments," in *Conscience and Casuistry in Early Modern Europe*, ed. E. Leites (Cambridge: Cambridge University Press, 1988), p. 222.

36. J. Delumeau, *Le péché et la peur* (Paris: Fayard, 1983), p. 229. Also consult B. Guégan, ed., *Grand Kalendrier . . .* (Paris: Siloë, 1976).

37. E. Germain, *Langages de la foi à travers l'histoire. Approche d'une étude des mentalités* (Paris: Fayard-Mame, 1972), p. 32.

38. *Instruction et confession de foi dont on use dans l'Église de Genève*; and *Catéchisme de l'Église de Genève, c'est-à-dire, le formulaire d'instruire les enfants en la chrétienté*. O. Fatio et al., eds., *Confessions et catéchismes de la foi réformée* (Geneva: Labor et Fides, 1986), pp. 25-110. Other catechisms circulated at the time, such as the Latin catechism of the Alsatian Leo Jud, those of Bucer, and the *Exposition chrétienne des Dix commandements . . . réglée et modérée selon la capacité et l'entendement des enfants* (1537) by Gaspard Grossman, called Megander. The German original of this work came out in 1533. Megander had to leave Bern in 1537 because of his differences from Lutheran or-

heritage, of arcane academics and practical pedagogy. It corresponded to a revival of interest in childhood.[39] The title "catechism" was in a sense deceitful; one needs to bear in mind the "very great semantic extension of the term . . . during the first decades of the Reformation."[40] From this standpoint, does not the *Institutes of the Christian Religion* also stem from catechizing, like so many other works of Calvin?

The work follows this order: creed, law, Lord's Prayer, thus reversing the first two parts of the Lutheran exposition.[41] From this viewpoint everything distinguishes the two Calvinist catechisms of 1537 and 1542. The first catechism followed the plan of Luther's *Large German Catechism*. The lessons were still in the form of discourse and not of questions and answers. "It is a pedagogical arrangement. The Law is there to reveal to us the existence of our sins; it is, following the expression of Saint Paul, a teacher to lead us to Christ. Next comes Faith, which teaches us that Jesus having died for our sins, anyone who believes in him has eternal life."[42] In 1542, however, "to the scheme Law, Faith, Prayer succeeded the scheme Faith, Law, Prayer. The pedagogical arrangement was superseded by a theological one."[43]

---

thodoxy concerning the Eucharist; he became a pastor in Zürich. See Francis Higman, "La réfutation par P. Doré du catéchisme de Megander," in *Aux origines du catéchisme en France*, pp. 55-66. For his part Bucer published a first German catechism in 1534 and a summary of it in 1537, which was in turn translated into French *(Institution puérile de la doctrine chrestienne . . .).*

39. M. Venard, introduction to *Aux origines du catéchisme en France,* p. 10.

40. Millet, p. 189.

41. The Catholics did not remain silent; various catechisms appeared in the German language. They culminated in the works of the Dutchman Peter Canisius (1521-97). Established in Vienna during the 1550s, this Jesuit published in Latin a *Summary of Christian Doctrine in Questions and Answers* (1555), followed in the next two years by a *Catechismus minimus* and a *Catechismus minor.* Ten years later Pius V promulgated the *Roman Catechism,* which in 1566 incorporated the dogmatic decisions of the Council of Trent. In 1563 Father Edmond Auger (1515-91) published in Lyon a *Catéchisme et sommaire de la doctrine chrétienne* designed to counter Calvin.

42. J. Courvoisier, "Les catéchismes de Genève et de Strasbourg. Étude sur le développement de la pensée de Calvin," *Bulletin de la Société de l'Histoire du Protestantisme Français* 84 (1935): 106, for this citation and that following.

43. The second catechism was inspired by that of Bucer of 1534, *Kurze Schrifftliche Erklärung.* The latter followed the plan of a previous work by Capito in 1527, from which it borrowed the dialogue form.

The Psalter of 1543: The Besieged Fortress

When Israel went out of Egypt . . .

PSALM 114, TRANSLATED BY C. MAROT

To leave Egypt and to take the road to the Holy Land — this in itself is a double itinerary, both geographical and religious — and is comparable to Calvin's own, to depart France and to establish himself in Geneva. For Calvin's contemporaries who intoned the psalm, the allusion was evident. The terrestrial journey was paralleled by a spiritual one, to the beat of the Huguenot psalter. The psalter *was* the French Reformation. The first Reformers ignored the proliferation of hymns; they were content with singing in a full voice to carefully measured martial tunes the love of God for his people, the crushing of the wicked, and the beauty of the world. The singing of psalms was to the French Reformation what the chorale was to the German Reformation. Music was an intimate part of Calvinist culture. It involved the replacement, according to an admirable formula, of "the music of the spheres" by that "inexplicable world" where "the arbitrary action of grace and of reprobation" reigned supreme.[44]

Having become emblematic of the French Reformation, Psalm 114 was cited by Rabelais at the beginning of his *Fourth Book* (1548-52). Was this the insolence of a polemicist, or an evangelical leaning? Rabelais and Calvin were indeed the polar opposites of each other, and the pronounced antipathy of the two men broke out exactly during these years, culminating in Calvin's fulminations against this "boor" who used to lampoon the Holy Scriptures.[45]

Clément Marot, and later Theodore Beza, were the authors of the versified translation of the psalms that occupy an entire book of the Bible. Psalm 6 appeared with Marguerite de Navarre's *Mirror of a Sinful Soul.* The use of sacred song in church services was clearly attested by the publishing in 1539 in Strasbourg of *Some Psalms and Canticles Put to Music.* The work included some of the psalms, the Canticle of Simeon, the Ten Commandments, and a confession of faith. The *Order of Prayers,*[46] published in Geneva in 1542, added more translations done by Marot, but it was not until 1543 that a separate collection was assembled, entitled *Fifty Psalms.* The complete translation of the psalms

---

44. Gisèle Venet, "Bible et musique sacrée en Angleterre au xviie siècle," in *La Bible dans le monde anglo-américain aux xviie et xviiie siècles* (Nanterre: University of Paris X, 1984), p. 84.

45. *OC* 27, col. 261, sermon on Deut. 13:6-11.

46. *Forme des prières.*

with their musical accompaniment was not accomplished until 1562, two years before Calvin's death.[47]

The purpose of the psalter was clearly defined by Calvin in 1543: "It would be merely juggling to amuse the people with symbols whose significance is not revealed to them."[48] In the very depths of his being Calvin had a most in-timate awareness of the power of music. He feared and relished it at the same time. It possessed an ascendancy over souls and bodies that could either capture them by its evil spells or liberate them by its beauty: "Among the things that are proper to divert a man and give him pleasure, music is either the first or one of the most important. . . . For there is hardly anything in this world that can more readily bend the manners of men this way and that, as Plato sensibly judged. And in fact we find by experience that it has a secret and almost incredible ability to move hearts one way or another."[49]

Music, that deceitful power, should be put to the service of the text and of the Word, illustrating them and not obscuring their meaning. "All evil speech . . . when accompanied by music, pierces the heart much more strongly and enters into it in such a way that, just as wine is poured into a vessel from a funnel, so also venom and corruption are distilled to the bottom of the heart by melody."[50] The attitude of the Reformers toward music remained profoundly ambivalent. Was not music the "science of proportions," capable of elevating the soul by recalling the harmony that presided at the creation of the universe? But did not music by its "mysterious powers" also risk escaping the control of the reason?[51] Did it not conduct one as easily to superstition as to the worship of the One?

Calvin could not talk of music without emotion. "Spiritual songs cannot be sung well except with the heart."[52] Handled without precaution, it reveals itself as a deceitful power, a form of illusion; in short, it already participates in that imaginary world the classics warn against. Music should guarantee the in-

---

47. See É. Weber, *La musique protestante de langue française* (Paris: H. Champion, 1979), pp. 12 and 31. In its definitive form in 1562, the Huguenot psalter would include all 150 psalms, a third of them adapted by Clément Marot and the other two-thirds by Theodore Beza. To these were added the Ten Commandments, the Canticle of Simeon *(Nunc dimittis)*, prayers to be said before and after meals, the Lord's Prayer, the articles of faith, and some rare canticles. The musical harmonization was entrusted to Claude Goudimel; it appeared from 1564 to 1580.

48. *OC* 6, cols. 167-68.

49. *OC* 6, cols. 169-70.

50. *OC* 6, cols. 169-70.

51. M. Vignaux, "L'influence de la Réforme sur la nature et la fonction de la musique dans la liturgie anglicane," *Foi et Vie* 91, no. 2 (1992): 81-83.

52. *OC* 6, cols. 171-72.

telligibility of the text, and not distract the senses; this requirement reappeared in the Catholic Reformation, in Palestrina, for example.[53] "Calvin," a specialist in the sixteenth century explains, "analyzed the double potential effect of music, at once destructive and creative, on a sensibility whose dangerous instability he perceived, an instability that would shortly reveal itself to be fundamental to baroque psychology."[54]

Calvinist Acculturation?

Pedagogy was the key to the Calvinist enterprise. The catechism, preaching, and the admonitions of the consistory had no other end but to profoundly transform mentalities by sowing the good seed of the gospel in men's hearts. The distinction between popular culture and educated culture tended to be reduced by the same process; all superstitions, all magical practices, indeed all remnants of Catholicism were ruthlessly pursued as idolatry. "Popery" was a special target for Calvin, who directly inspired the consistory. In the spring of 1542 a certain Jeanne Petreman appeared before the consistory. She did not partake of the Lord's Supper; worse yet, she attended Mass outside Geneva and said her Pater in the "Roman" tongue. Monsieur Calvin admonished her; the poor wretch held tenets of consummate popery. "She said that the Virgin Mary is her advocate. She said the Virgin Mary is the friend of God and that the Virgin Mary is the daughter and mother of Jesus Christ." She was recalcitrant, refused to recognize her errors, was stubborn, and defied her hearers. "She said her faith was good and that she has never had any faith other than the faith of Jesus Christ, and that Our Lady is a blessed woman." The guilty woman herself had put herself outside the church; one could only hope that "the Lord would touch her heart" and that she would recognize her errors.[55] Monsieur Jacques Symont, in May of the same year, communicated in the Protestant church without doubts on his part, while admitting that he still prayed to the Virgin Mary. Interrogated about the papist Mass, he recognized its idolatrous character, and when asked what he thought about the Lord's Supper, he replied adroitly that he "believes as is now believed among us."[56] Jeanne Bergeon, in November 1542, still recited her Ave Maria as her father and mother had taught her, as well as various other improper prayers in Latin. It was not rare, moreover, for these remnants of idolatry to be accompanied by dissolute words. Thus Jean Dalphin, butcher, took

---

53. J. Samson, *Palestrina ou la poésie de l'exactitude* (Geneva: Henn, 1950).
54. Venet, p. 85.
55. *Annales Calviniani*, OC 21, cols. 292-94.
56. *Annales Calviniani*, OC 21, col. 296.

advantage of his professional activity to deliver all sorts of anatomical pleasant-ries in doubtful taste. "There appeared . . . Jean Dalphin, butcher, to whom were given remonstrances that in selling his meat he speaks very improperly in inde-cent words and blasphemes God. Asked to say the prayer, he could not say it in French, and said it in Latin, also the *Ave Maria,* the *Credo,* the *Benedicite,* with-out knowing how to pronounce anything" (November 3, 1545).[57] But it did not stop there: "He also said grace in Latin and *Animae fidelium defunctorum requiescant in pace,* which is a terrible and detestable thing." A similar affair took place in February 1548, when it was learned that during a burial several women had thrown earth on the coffin while crying, "*Requiescat in pace. Amen.*"[58] But there were still worse things: "Monsieur Curtet's sister, Lucrèce, to whom remonstrances were given because she went with some money to have masses sung in Annecy, to the nuns of Saint Claire. Asked to say whether she does not have scruples [doubts], to speak up. Answered that her father and mother brought her up in another law than there is here; nevertheless she does not despise the law there is now. Asked when the feast of Saint Felix was, an-swered that it was yesterday. Asked whether she did not fast, answered that she fasts when she is free. Asked whether she does not wish to pray to only one God, answered yes. Asked whether she does not pray to Saint Felix, answered that she prays to Saint Felix and the other saints who pray for her. She is very obstinate." Her punishment? "To go to whatever minister she wishes and every day to the sermon and to be forbidden the Lord's Supper" (Tuesday, August 31, 1546).[59]

Or again, on Thursday, September 2, 1546, there appeared a brave Fran-ciscan, brought in for walking through the town, asking for food "in the name of God and of the Virgin Mary" — which was perfectly unseemly in Reformed Geneva. The mendicant friar was freed, being judged inoffensive. Obviously he understood nothing of the Holy Scriptures, and since he was content to impor-tune papists beyond the frontiers, the Genevans had nothing to fear from him.

Matrimonial alliances also occupied Genevan consciences. Ami Andrion, apothecary, married his daughter Françoise to a Piedmontese. Tension mount-ed in the consistory; the daughter, whom they were trying to get to oppose her parents, was asked whether she was going with a light heart to embrace idolatry. She was not overawed. Since this good Piedmontese match had lent money to her parents, they were accused of "selling their daughter." In the battle against exogamy they were sent before the Company of Pastors, while being suspended from the Lord's Supper.

Did not women risk having their heads turned by a rich papist, young

57. *Annales Calviniani, OC* 21, col. 366.
58. *Annales Calviniani, OC* 21, col. 422.
59. *Annales Calviniani, OC* 21, col. 387.

and handsome, or by the misty attraction of Latin prayers they did not understand? In May 1550 Claudine and Bertholomée, respectively niece and wife of Jean Achard, maintained Catholic practices. Young Claudine did not know her prayers except in Latin and admitted having fasted on Good Friday. The women tried to excuse themselves by explaining that they were Savoyards and not Genevans. As for the husband, he explained that he had not succeeded in turning the two women away from papal heresies.[60] Some weeks later the goldsmith Mallard apologized for having made objects of idolatry, such as a Catholic chalice, but explained, more like a merchant than a believer, that he had to get his living "in some way."[61] Should artisans respond with indifference to the requests of their clientele? A barber was reproved in April 1557 for having "made a papal crown on a priest" — in other words, for having cut a tonsure on the top of his head.[62] But the profits were not small, and certain Genevan merchants were called to order in October 1559 for having sold rosaries at the fair of Briançon: "Since they marketed these instruments of idolatry and knew well that they were doing wrong and that it was against the edicts of our lords, they should be commanded to have all the rosaries of theirs remaining in the said place of Briançon brought and should bring with them all those they still have in their shop there, which they should confirm under oath, and the rosaries should all be burned."[63]

In March 1556, access to the holy table was forbidden to a group of merry fellows, guilty of having followed the custom of sharing the "cake of the kings" on the day of Epiphany. There was no excuse for this culinary popery. They also carried their presumption to the point of electing a queen to profane cries of "The queen drinks, the queen drinks!"[64]

The following year Nicolas André, a cobbler by trade and "said to be a citizen of Geneva," claimed "that the pope maintains justice and relieves poverty." It seemed to him that in these respects he was a "decent man." André admitted that he was not perfect for all that, but he refused to specify his "wicked deeds."[65]

Sometimes this resistance to Protestant acculturation was not Catholic but bluntly anti-Christian. Thus Louis Le Barbier, in March 1548, "When he was summoned to know what his faith was, he declared that he does not hold the religion we hold and that he could not adhere to it or receive Communion with us."[66] The consistory was uncertain "whether it would be expedient for

---

60. *Annales Calviniani, OC* 21, cols. 464-65.

61. *Annales Calviniani, OC* 21, col. 466.

62. *Annales Calviniani, OC* 21, col. 658, Registres du Conseil de Genève 53, fol. 99.

63. *Annales Calviniani, OC* 21, col. 722.

64. *Annales Calviniani, OC* 21, col. 662.

65. *Annales Calviniani, OC* 21, col. 669.

66. *Annales Calviniani, OC* 21, col. 422.

the common profit of the city to endure people of all sorts of religions." Le Barbier also possessed several works of his own composition, full of scoffing. "A book was found issued from his hand, full of enchantments, sorceries, and also of execrable blasphemies, such as the Ten Commandments of the Virgin, mocking those of God, and the Twelve Articles of Faith of the Virgins, to mock the faith and creed of Christians." These lewd jottings apparently did not amuse the members of the consistory, who saw clearly how sarcasm at Marian piety overflowed here to strike at the rest of revelation, beginning with the Decalogue. However, Le Barbier escaped prosecution for a long time.

The acculturation of Geneva also applied to the giving of first names at baptism. Calvin was explicit: the name must figure in the Bible. On November 9, 1546, the parishioners of Saint-Gervais expressed their anger when the pastor tried to dissuade them from calling a young boy Aimé or Martin.[67] Calvin also did not like the name Claude, no doubt because of the risk of superstitious outbreaks, in view of the proximity of the town of Saint-Claude. He drew up an edict on names at baptism on November 22, 1546:

> There follow the names that seem not to be proper to impose at baptism:
>
> First the names of the idols that have reigned in the country, because superstition could still be present in them, and also because they are a reminder of the idolatry from which it has pleased God to deliver the country through his grace: Suaire, Claude, Mama. . . .
>
> Also the names of offices [Baptistes, Juge, Évangéliste].
>
> Also names belonging to God alone or to Our Lord Jesus Christ [Dieu le Fils, Espoir, Emmanuel, Sauveur, Jésus].
>
> Also clumsy names in which there is some absurdity that can be mocked [Sépulcre, Croix, Noël, Pâques, Chrétien].
>
> Double Names.
>
> And other similar ones that sound bad [Gomin, Mermet, Allemande].
>
> Also corrupted names like Tyvan and Thévenot in place of Étienne, or Monet in place of Simon.[68]

Luxury and ostentation were also suspect. On May 25, 1547, the need for moderation in clothing was recalled. "All clothing that is made, except for necessity, [is] superfluous."[69] This rejection of superfluity, common to all moralists, found in Calvin a supplementary justification. Geneva ought to be an exemplary city. A close friend of Calvin's, Nicolas Des Gallars, led a great campaign at the end

---

67. *Annales Calviniani, OC* 21, col. 389, Registres du Conseil 41, fol. 238.
68. *OC* 10, I, col. 49.
69. *Annales Calviniani, OC* 21, col. 405, Registres du Conseil 42, fol. 118v.

of September 1558, "because superfluities and excess increase among us rather than diminishing, so that by this means great scandal is given to those others who, thinking to find us Christians, on seeing such excesses are scandalized. Against these excesses no remonstrances have served, but the said excesses increase from day to day, as much in clothing as in banquets and foods." Women were particularly awful with their gewgaws and their "twisting of their hair and other novelties," in which they delighted.[70] Self-love and romance crept in through bad books; some copies of *Amadis of Gaul*, found with a merchant, were burned. These romances could only "corrupt and deprave the young." And besides, it was explained, they contained only "lies and fantasies."[71]

The Spreaders of Plague[72]

The plague we have in our city is a scourge of God, and we confess that he justly punishes and chastises us for our sins and faults.

JOHN CALVIN, LETTER TO A CERTAIN CURÉ, 1542[73]

Plague was endemic. Calvin had seen the effects of this terrible illness on his entourage in Strasbourg in 1541, and in 1542 he found himself confronted with the evil in Geneva. The pastors were particularly exposed, since the dying required their pastoral attention. Calvin did not hide his fears. Until now he had delegated this crushing responsibility to one of his colleagues. But how long would he be safe?

> The plague here is beginning to be more severe, and of those it infects few recover. We have had to designate one of our colleagues to attend the sick. Pierre Blanchet having offered himself, all easily consented to let him go. If he comes to harm I fear that after him it will be my duty to expose myself to the danger. As you say, if we are debtors to each individual member of the church, we cannot default to those among them who lay claim to our ministry. Nevertheless I am not of the opinion that, to render service to one part of the church, we should abandon the church altogether.[74]

70. *Annales Calviniani, OC* 21, col. 705, Registres du Conseil 53, fol. 295v.
71. *Annales Calviniani, OC* 21, col. 712.
72. See Roget, *Histoire du peuple*, 2:156ff.
73. Calvin, *Lettres françaises*, 1:68-69.
74. *OC* 11, col. 457, to Pierre Viret, October 1542.

Calvin plainly was afraid of sickness and death. Aware of his importance, he avoided exposing himself uselessly. Although a man of duty, he did not hide the fears that assailed him. Pierre Viret in Lausanne encountered the same difficulties; in May 1543 he confided to Calvin: "If the epidemic continues to rage I have decided to visit the sick, at least if it is not possible to find any other solution. I prefer this rather than to have someone come from elsewhere or to force someone to accept it unwillingly. Our deacon, if I am not mistaken, would not refuse it, but I fear strongly for his life; he is very gravely ill at this moment."[75]

The Council was disturbed the next year in Geneva by the lack of haste of the ministers when it came to going to see the dying, and also by their willingness, for once, to delegate their pastoral duties to laymen. In May 1543 the recalcitrant pastors were threatened with dismissal; Pierre Blanchet, who had already volunteered the year before, heroically accepted the task again. He was offered ten florins per month in addition to his regular salary. He died on June 1, a victim of duty. It was therefore necessary to fill again the post of almoner of the hospital in Plainpalais, outside the city. Monsieur Calvin was excluded from this office from the first by the Council; he was rendering too much service by his skill in preaching to be exposed to the risk.

The ministers were therefore asked to designate a volunteer from among themselves. On Tuesday, June 5, the pastors were assembled "to learn which of them might wish to perform his office and help and console the said poor infected people." Naturally, "Monsieur Calvin was not included with the others, because he is busy serving in the church and responding to all those passing by." Not counting Calvin, there remained five pastors, all natives of France: Mathieu de Geneston, Philippe Osias (called De Ecclesia), Louis Treppereaux, Abel Poupin, and Aimé Champereaux. They were told "that it was part of their office, not only in times of prosperity, but in times of war and of plague and other emergencies, to serve the Christian church." The poor pastors admitted "that it is true that it is their office," but they flatly refused, offering as a pretext that "God has still not given them the grace to have the strength and constancy to go to the said hospital." Only M. de Geneston appeared flexible, but he demanded a drawing of lots. His frightened colleagues prayed God "to give them more constancy in the future." And they courageously proposed Simon Moreau of Tours to replace them. The latter remained five long months with the sick, from June to October 1543. His successor in the following year, Mathieu de Geneston, was carried out on August 11.[76]

The horrors increased. The plague was followed by famine in 1544. The

75. *OC* 11, col. 563, P. Viret to Calvin, May 29, 1543.
76. We have borrowed our account of these developments from F. Buisson, *Sébastien Castellion. Sa vie et son oeuvre (1515-1563)* (Paris: Hachette, 1892), 1:186-90.

respite during the winter of 1544-45 was followed by an irrational determination to punish the fomenters of the evil. It was discovered that a certain Bernard
Dallinges and his confederate Dunant, nicknamed Freckles *(Lentillé)*, had applied "plague venom" to a foot removed from the body of a hanged man. This
was then smeared on the locks of several houses. Unfortunately Freckles died
under torture in February 1545 without admitting his crimes. His torturers
were terribly clumsy, and they provoked a fatal hemorrhage in their zeal for
well-doing. Despite everything, the body was dragged to the middle of town, in
order not to deprive the inhabitants of the fine burning they had a right to. Sorcerers, like heretics, as was well known, were characterized by their combustible
qualities. Far from settling men's minds, this salutary diversion provoked a
panic. The poisoners, greasers of locks, were watched for with anxiety. Several
were apprehended, men and women, not to mention a barber and a hospital
supervisor who had made a pact with the devil.

Two women were executed on March 7, 1545. Calvin humanely interceded the same day to keep the poisoners from being forced to languish in
prison. The Council followed this happy directive and urged the executioner
henceforth to "be more diligent in cutting off the hands of malefactors." Moreover, the quality of the spectacle — there's nothing like a good fire — did not
necessarily require that the sorcerer still be alive. It was just as easy to strangle
the condemned person beforehand, if only the means could be found. A simple
garrote, of the sort used for cats, did the trick.

The executions continued. Yet those detained refused to confess; the tortures were combined skillfully to avoid killing the guilty foolishly: torture of the
strappado, with pincers. Most of those tortured, no doubt aided by Satan, overcame these tests without admitting the obvious. Must they be immured alive so
they would finally talk? By varying the means of death a little, one or two sorcerers were decapitated "for having composed a plaster which included plague
grease and other villainous things and having thus caused several people to
die."

Some committed suicide in their cells to avoid torture, so they were put in
handcuffs. No matter. One of the arrested women threw herself from a window.
The last execution took place on May 16. Seven men and twenty-four women
died in the affair; others fled. The phenomenon was not new — Geneva had
previously punished spreaders of plague in 1530 — but in 1545 the scale was
unprecedented. The fear revived in 1568, and even later. Calvin, for his part,
was grieved, provided no one poisoned his door also. "The Lord tests us in a
surprising manner. A conspiracy has just been discovered of men and women
who for three years employed themselves in spreading the plague in the city by
means of sorcery whose nature I do not know. Fifteen women have already
been burned, and the men have been punished still more rigorously. Twenty-

five of these criminals are still shut up in the prisons, and nevertheless they do not cease from smearing the locks of doors every day. So far God has preserved our house."[77]

Calvin therefore shared in all respects the fantasies of his entourage. He found occasion to exhort his contemporaries to pursue sorcerers in order to "extirpate such a race," as he proclaimed in November in a neat formula.[78] A pair of these henchmen of Satan had just been burned the previous month. Another sorcerer had admitted his association with the devil, only to retract, although the greatest care had been taken to grill the soles of his feet. The unfortunate man got away with his life, but was banished in perpetuity from the city.

Calvinism was not rationalism. Its stress on education, its pedagogy, and its determination to eradicate idolatry and superstition did not prevent the support in broad daylight of behavior all the more shocking because it appears archaic to us. Calvin was not fully and entirely a modern. Fear of sorcery and of heretics entailed their retinue of hasty, indeed barbarous remedies: imprisonment, torture, the stake.

Ancient demons assailed Calvin and his contemporaries; they were born from the close association of life and death and from the weakness of the moment. Affliction and illness remained unexplained and possibly inexplicable; they were both a call to conversion and a punishment of sins. In August 1545 Calvin referred repeatedly to the plague, endemic in these summer months. "It is because we are looking for Jesus Christ that we must expect to find him crucified everywhere we go in this world."[79] Christ, dead and resurrected; Christ in his glory, seated at the right hand of the Father; Christ, whose sacrifice does not allow any repetition, did not prevent the scandal of an ever present evil. And Calvin, strangely, appears here to anticipate Pascal: "Jesus will be in agony until the end of the world."[80]

77. *OC* 12, col. 55, letter to Myconius, March 27, 1545.

78. Roget, *Histoire du peuple,* 2:179.

79. J. Calvin, *Lettres à Monsieur et Madame de Falais,* ed. F. Bonali-Fiquet (Geneva: Droz, 1991), p. 66, August 5, 1545.

80. B. Pascal, *Pensées,* 736 [87]; *Oeuvre* (Paris: NRF, 1950), p. 1060.

CHAPTER 9

The Somber Years: 1547-55

You must remember . . . that wherever we go the cross of Jesus Christ will follow us.

JOHN CALVIN, JUNE 1549[1]

Where, then, is the brilliant young man we left in his blissful years? What has happened to this lover of Jesus Christ? What has become of the brilliant writer, the humanist, the orator, excited by the announcement of the gospel? What remained ten years later of the hopes formed in Strasbourg in 1538-41? Calvin's maturity in Geneva can be recognized by its nostalgia. Doubts henceforth gripped him and gnawed at him. What doubts? Would Calvin doubt God? Of course not. But he doubted nonetheless and questioned himself endlessly. He told his friends, "If I had thought only of my own life and my private interests I would have immediately gone elsewhere. But when I think of the importance of this corner of the earth for the propagation of the kingdom of Christ, it is with reason that I occupy myself with defending it."[2] He held nothing back from his hearers on the occasion of a sermon on Jeremiah. "Behold what is done today; I do not mean in the papacy, but in Geneva. How do the wretches receive the sermons that are given to them? . . . 'Oh, we do not want this Gospel here, go look for a different one.'"[3]

1. J. Calvin, *Lettres françaises*, ed. J. Bonnet, 2 vols. (Paris: Meyrueis, 1854), 1:303, June 10, 1549.
2. *Opera Calvini* (hereafter cited as *OC*) 13, col. 1187, letter to Bullinger, May 7, 1549.
3. J. Calvin, *Supplementa Calviniana* (Neukirchen-Vluyn: Neukirchener Verlag, 1971), 6:19-20, sermon of June 24, 1549, on Jer. 15:1-6.

Bereavements and Whisperings

The Reformer's private life was permanently marred during his lasting stay in Geneva. Idelette, his wife, led an existence of complete devotion, divided among reverence for the gospel, the care of her husband, and domestic worries. On July 28, 1542, she gave birth to a son, Jacques. But the child was premature and survived only briefly. In these sad circumstances Calvin turned again, as always, to his God. "The Lord inflicted on us a grave and painful wound in the death of our beloved son. But he is our Father; he knew what was good for his children" (August 19, 1542).[4]

In spite of the extreme reserve that surrounds Calvin's personal life, this bereavement seems to have borne immense symbolic importance for the Reformer, as also did the illness and death of his wife. As late as 1562 he explained, "The Lord gave me a young son; he took him away. . . . Throughout Christendom I have ten thousand children."[5] Following on the loss of his only son, Idelette fell ill in 1545. She died on March 29, 1549. Calvin suffered terribly from her passing. He expressed his sorrow in two letters, to Farel and to Viret. In the former, on April 2, he confided: "I try as much as possible not to be entirely beaten down by grief. Moreover, my friends gather around me and neglect nothing to bring some solace to the sadness of my soul. . . . I devour my sorrow to such an extent that I have not interrupted my work at all. . . . Farewell, brother and faithful friend. . . . May the Lord Jesus fortify you with his spirit, and me also in this great misfortune, which certainly would have broken me if he had not extended his hand from heaven, he whose office is to raise up the fallen, to strengthen the weak, to revive the weary."[6] And on April 7, to Viret: "Although the death of my wife was very cruel to me, I try as much as possible to moderate my grief, and my friends compete in doing their duty. But I declare that they and I, we achieve fewer results than one might wish. . . . I was deprived of the excellent companion of my life, who, if misfortune had come, would have been my voluntary companion, not only in exile and in misery, but even in death."[7]

Calvin did not remarry. He nevertheless refused to idealize this celibacy, as he explained five years later in a sermon: "I do not want it attributed to me as a virtue that I am not married. . . . I knew my weakness, that perhaps a wife would not do well with me. However that may be, I refrain from it only so as to

---

4. *OC* 11, col. 430.

5. J. Calvin, *Réponse . . . aux injures de Balduin* (1562), *Opuscules,* p. 1987. Cited by R. Stauffer, *L'humanité de Calvin* (Neuchâtel: Delachaux & Niestlé, 1964), pp. 26-27.

6. *OC* 13, cols. 228-29.

7. *OC* 13, col. 230.

be more free to serve God. And this is not because I think myself more virtuous than my brothers."[8]

The virtue of his brothers was not, alas, in question. It might indeed be wished that it had been a little more. Antoine, Calvin's brother, was afflicted with a wife of ardent temperament. Her lush nature gave some disquiet to her cuckolded husband. On Thursday, September 27, 1548, Calvin brought up his fears in the consistory. "M. John Calvin stated that last Sunday he was told of a scandal which has greatly afflicted his heart. It is a suspicion of adultery between the wife of his brother Antoine — Anne, daughter of Nicolas Lefer[9] — and Jean, son of Jean Chautemps."[10]

Naturally, Calvin thought to himself, these vicious rumors were devoid of foundation. Someone wanted to compromise his sister-in-law by causing trouble in a respectable family. The offense was all the sharper because all the Calvins lived together in the same house on the Rue des Chanoines. Anne, Antoine's wife, was said to have resisted like a Stoic under trial the dishonest advances of Jean Chautemps. The latter ended by confessing that he "urged dishonor on the said Anne last Sunday, and he repents of it." But the distressed wife fortunately must have been able to preserve her good sense before the advances of the young man. "If the said Anne had been as foolish as he, things would have gone badly." However, Chautemps did everything to seduce her, going so far as to enter her bedroom at night while Antoine was in Burgundy. Apparently suspicions persisted, and the two lovers were detained for having fornicated villainously.[11] Anne was freed on October 16. On the eighteenth, in all solemnity, she had to kneel and ask for forgiveness from her husband, Antoine, as well as from John Calvin himself, injured through her.

Indeed a guilty wife. The wretch relapsed less than ten years later. In January 1557 Anne was imprisoned for having sinned with Pierre Daguet, a hunchbacked servant of her husband's. The latter asked for a divorce and accused Daguet of several thefts.[12] Thus no shame was spared to an honorable family, sorely tried.

With good reason, Calvin felt himself to be the butt of Genevan society. In March 1551 he complained that people were playing tennis (or were engaged in other profane activities that he preferred to be silent about) in front of the Cathedral of Saint-Pierre while he was preaching inside. Tension rose, and Calvin saw red when anyone dared answer him back. On September 10, 1552, he

8. *OC* 53, col. 255, twenty-first sermon on 1 Timothy, fall 1554.

9. Originally from France, his father, Nicolas Lefer, received the bourgeoisie of Geneva in 1555.

10. *Annales Calviniani, OC* 21, col. 435.

11. *Annales Calviniani, OC* 21, col. 437.

12. *Annales Calviniani, OC* 21, cols. 658-59.

warned against the game of skittles, particularly noxious, especially when it was played on days when the Lord's Supper was celebrated.[13]

On September 19, 1552, Calvin referred to musicians who deliberately sang "lewd songs" to sacred psalm tunes.[14] Calvin's personality and his sexual austerity brought down on him all the gossip of the taverns, where they did not hesitate to call him a "bugger."[15] On November 24, 1552, it was reported that a barber apparently had grown tired of the importance given to Calvin and his writings; was there in fact "any need for so many books, apart from the Bible and the New Testament"? And, he added fiercely, "Monsieur Calvin should not let anyone call him Monsieur Calvin or Master Calvin."[16]

The Reformer, however, was able to base his reputation solidly on well-written polemical works in which he had learnedly analyzed, with the skill of a churchman, the different heresies and doctrinal perversions that lay in wait for his contemporaries. Nicodemism, Anabaptism, spiritual libertinism, and judicial astrology no longer held any secrets from him. Several works had followed each other from his pen: *A Short Treatise Showing what a Faithful Man Should Do . . . when He Is among the Papists* (1543); *Apology to the Nicodemites* and *Brief Instruction to Arm all Good Believers against the Errors of the Anabaptists* (1544); an essay *Against the Fantastic Sect of Libertines Who Call Themselves Spiritual* (1545). We must add the *Treatise on Relics* (1543) and the *Warning against the Astrology Called Judicial* (1549).[17] All these texts culminated in the *Treatise on Scandals* of 1550. We might also add the admirable *Consensus Tigurinus*, which in 1549 systematized Reformed positions on Communion, and must not forget, naturally, the impact of the *Institutes*. Calvin was indeed the author of a confessional construction, and in a sense, according to Émile Léonard's description, the "founder of a civilization."[18] His nimble mind and his gifts as a polemicist (dealt with in chap. 12) made him an extraordinary propagandist, who left to the modern world an appreciable fraction of his ideas, or who at least systematized their use. The word "institution," henceforth, did not apply only to the education of princes; it passed from humanist pedagogy

---

13. *Annales Calviniani, OC* 21, col. 517.

14. *Annales Calviniani, OC* 21, col. 518.

15. *Annales Calviniani, OC* 21, col. 523.

16. *Annales Calviniani, OC* 21, col. 527.

17. *Petit traité montrant que c'est que doit faire un homme fidèle . . . quand il est entre les papistes; Excuse à Messieurs les Nicodémites; Brève instruction, pour armer tous bons fidèles contre les erreurs des Anabaptistes; Contre la secte fantastique des libertins qui se nomment spirituels; Traité des reliques; Avertissement contre l'astrologie qu'on appelle judiciaire.*

18. É. G. Léonard, *Histoire générale du protestantisme*, 3 vols. (Paris: PUF, 1961-64), 1:258ff.

to the field of politics. Similarly the word "libertinism," or at least the recognition of "libertines," owes much to the language of Calvin.

The legacy he left was a strange one. "Spiritual libertines," according to Calvin, were not so much debauched people as liberated spirits who, in the name of the grace given for their salvation, felt themselves emancipated from the law (biblical) and the laws (civil). The word "Nicodemite," by contrast, belonged to the language of scholars; a Nicodemite was one who, internally convinced of the vanity of Catholic usages, externally pretended to submit to them. In reality Calvin did not speak so much of Nicodemites as of alleged Nicodemites who, inspired by the example of Nicodemus, who came to Jesus in secret, did not reveal their convictions openly. As for "judicial" astrology, Calvin took great care to distinguish it from scientific astrology, which we would call astronomy. Finally, his reflections on the Bible and on the sacraments led to an investigation of their language. Calvinism was largely dependent on a rhetoric; its attention to grammar and to the development of forms and figures of speech was already laying the foundations of French classicism. Reciprocally, it was from anti-Calvinist controversy that the Jesuits and Jansenists, and more generally the Catholic Counter-Reformation, derived in reaction their greatest originality. Calvinism was not a religion; the religion was Christianity, "reformed" Christianity or Christianity "pretending to be reformed," depending on whether one partook of its ideas or not. Calvinism, for its part, was a culture.

"These people," Bossuet exclaimed, not without reason, "were humanists and grammarians." Bossuet the polemicist, Bossuet the critic of Calvin, emphasized better than any other thinker of the seventeenth century the rhetorical character of the Reformed movement.[19] Confronted with mystery, Calvin acted in many ways as a logician or a grammarian, careful to make the language of faith transparent and drive all useless obscurity from it.[20]

---

19. Bossuet, *Histoire des variations des Églises protestantes*, 2 vols. (1688; Paris: Garnier, n.d.), 1:94.

20. Bossuet perceived the theological implications of the Reformed eucharistic doctrine. He formulated a number of objections, as much methodological as more strictly theological, based largely, moreover, on Luther as against Calvin. In the first place, why employ such a complicated rhetoric? "Luther could never persuade himself either that Jesus Christ deliberately wanted to obscure the institution of his sacrament or that such simple words were susceptible of such far-fetched figures" (Bossuet, 1:58). It was in fact the role given to Jesus Christ that disquieted Bossuet; was not the union of the two natures, Jesus true God and true man, at issue in Communion? Similarly, if the term "substance" disappeared from the eucharistic definition, could it be preserved in the formula of the Trinity? How can you have one God in three persons endowed with the same "substance" and refuse to speak of "substance" in the case of the Eucharist (pp. 118-19)? These possible objections no doubt explain in turn Calvin's insistence on the dogma of the two natures and on the Trinity, which he was always suspected of not preserving. A recent author insists on

Calvin, moreover, never claimed to be the founder of a religion. Such a perspective would have frightened him by its sacrilegious audacity. But he certainly left to the modern world, directly or indirectly, with the help of his imitators and his detractors, an appreciable fraction of his references. To begin with, the disenchantment of the universe and denunciation of "superstition," taken up by all clergy before free thinkers took over the attack.

Accursed Frenchmen

I see well that you are French; you other Frenchmen come to make synagogues here after having driven out the honest men who told the truth; but before long you will be sent to make your synagogues elsewhere.

NOVEMBER 1546[21]

Partly directed against Calvin, anti-French sentiment mounted in Geneva. Pierre Ameaux was arrested at the end of January 1546 for having cursed the great man, this "Picard" who preached "false doctrine."[22] Being a maker of playing cards by trade, Ameaux had no reason to appreciate Calvinist strictness. Two and a half months later, on April 8, he was severely chastised for his temerity; he was condemned to "make a circuit of the city in his shirt, his head bare, a lighted torch in his hand."[23]

About the same time, Claude, wife of Durbin, said that "these Frenchmen are already numerous, and the Gospel is also everywhere in their own country" (January 7, 1546).[24] Or again, in June 1547 the watchman François Mestrat came to the rapid conclusion that the Frenchmen ought to be thrown into the Rhone River.[25] On January 26, 1548, Nicole Bromet was of the opinion that they should "take a boat and put all the Frenchmen and banished people in it to

---

the difficulty Calvin found in thinking out the incarnation of Christ or the two natures while emphasizing the distance that separates man from God, banished to his solitude. P. Le Gal, *Le droit canonique dans la pensée dialectique de Jean Calvin* (Fribourg: Éditions Interuniversitaires, 1984), p. 103. The reproach is in fact very old; it goes back to his Lutheran opponents, who accused Calvin of not preserving the possibility of a real union between the humanity and the divinity of the Savior — which was called, in a standard formula, the *extra Calvinisticum.*

21. *Annales Calviniani, OC* 21, col. 390.
22. *Annales Calviniani, OC* 21, col. 368, Registres du Conseil de Genève 40, fol. 359.
23. *Annales Calviniani, OC* 21, col. 377, Registres du Conseil 41, fol. 68.
24. *Annales Calviniani, OC* 21, col. 367.
25. *Annales Calviniani, OC* 21, col. 407.

send them down the Rhone"[26] — in other words, to assemble them in one vessel that would drift down the course of the Rhone. In March, Millon, from Auvergne, was driven from the city for having composed ballads against Calvin. The same month dame Grante, mother of Ami Perrin, sharply criticized Calvin. The old woman no longer had much to lose, and with the daring of old age she persevered before the consistory:

> She continued to hurl great insults at the said M. Calvin, among which are those that follow: that he came to Geneva to throw us into debates and wars, and that since he has been here there has been neither profit nor peace. . . . Moreover, she reproached him that he did not live as he preached, and that she has never found love in him, but he has always hated her. Also that she has never been able to get a word of consolation from him. And because he remonstrated with her for her rebellion against God and his church, telling her that she hardly knew what Christianity was, she answered that she was a better Christian than he and that she belonged to the church at a time when he was still in the taverns. And she gave many other insults to some of the members, and committed so many insolences that there was great trouble and confusion in the consistory.[27]

This deterioration extended to the sermons themselves. Calvin and his colleagues had accused the Council of moral laxity: "They have preached that there is no justice done against fornicators; now if they learn that there is some fornication or other sinister thing in the city, before anything else they should come reveal it to the magistrates without thus publishing it from the pulpit, on account of the audience, both local and foreigners."[28]

On May 21, 1548, it was reported that Calvin had complained that the "magistrates permitted many insolences." He was asked to explain. The same persistent rumor surfaced again in July when it was said that Calvin had exclaimed in the pulpit that the "Children of Geneva wanted directly to cast down the Gospel and drive out the ministers." The point at issue was a stupid quarrel about clothes: many Genevans would not endure being reproached for the crosses they wore on their doublets. These in fact had nothing to do with idolatry or superstition; they were Swiss insignia. In October Calvin was sharply reprimanded by the Council, which begged him "to do his duty better another

---

26. *Annales Calviniani, OC* 21, col. 420.

27. *Annales Calviniani, OC* 21, col. 423.

28. Amédée Roget, *L'Église et l'État à Genève du temps de Calvin. Étude d'histoire politico-ecclésiastique* (Geneva: J. Jullien, 1867), pp. 43-44, for this citation and that following.

time."[29] In fact, a letter of Calvin's had been intercepted some weeks earlier, revealing that the Reformer had disparaged the Genevans.

How can one explain these tensions between native Genevans and Frenchmen? On the other hand, what were the Frenchmen, "refugees for the faith," seeking? The printer Robert Estienne (1503-59) was a good example of these exiles. Along with Nicolas Cop, Laurent de Normandie, and François and Louis Budé, the sons of the great Guillaume, he belonged to Calvin's French entourage during these troubled years. What did Geneva offer him? The "light" of the gospel after the "darkness" of the papacy:

> I ask you, could one believe that the darkness of Egypt was thicker than that with which these good theologians obscure, or rather enchant, the understandings of men, removing their souls from Christ, who is the only savior, spreading in place of him the darkness of their thoughts? — being entirely similar to the scribes and pharisees who by their fallacies ruined the Jewish people. Now where is there a greater light than in the church of Christ, in which is administered every day not what men have thought and contrived but the pure Word of God, which reveals the impieties of men and their sins, returns to the road those who are wandering and vagabonds, points out the salvation that was ordained by God before all time in Christ the sole redeemer, and brings us to and confirms us in the certain hope of eternal life; where there is also the pure and legitimate administration of the sacraments according to the usage ordered by the Master?[30]

These pious remarks evidently did not prevent internal quarrels. In the treatise *On Scandals* (1550), there is an echo of the internal conflicts of Geneva. Calvin mentions "those who make war on us every day" because they are angry that someone takes away their liberty to live according to their own will. He concludes that these people, described in the passage as "fornicators, debauched and dissolute," are in the pay of the pope.[31]

A case involving women set off the explosion. On Thursday, June 23, 1547, several women appeared before the consistory for having danced. Among them was Françoise Favre, second wife of Ami Perrin. She had already had dealings with the consistory a year before (April 1546), when, refusing to testify against several friends of hers who were guilty of having danced, she stood up

---

29. Roget, p. 47.

30. R. Estienne, *Les censures des théologiens de Paris, par lesquelles ils avoyent faussement condamné les Bibles imprimées par Robert Estienne imprimeur du Roy: avec la responce d'iceluy Robert Estienne* (1552), pp. 3-4.

31. J. Calvin, *Des scandales*, ed. O. Fatio (Geneva: Droz, 1984), pp. 193-94.

to Calvin, thus incurring several days' incarceration. This time she was determined to resist. She calmly refused to be talked to about it and sharply told the elders that it was not for them to admonish her. This noble task belonged at most to her husband. Her "fierce and rebellious words" and "gross blasphemies" cast a certain chill.[32] The next day the pastor Abel Poupin let his anger break out in turn, and Françoise Perrin was ordered imprisoned under the control of the watchman Jean Blanc. Ami Perrin, the poor husband of this unfortunate pleasure-seeker, was in France on assigned service, representing his city before Henry II, who succeeded Francis I that spring. Several relatives, including Pierre Tissot and Louis Bernard, interceded for the wife. But it was no use. Excitement mounted in the town, where various vicious rumors against Calvin circulated; a placard written in Geneva dialect was even posted on the pulpit of Saint-Pierre. There Abel Poupin was described bluntly as a "big lard-belly," while the venerable pastors appeared as "fucking renegade priests" who, barely quit of their "monkeries," intended to "blow smoke in the eyes" of everyone. In the middle of all this Ami Perrin returned from his journey in September; he hurried to the Council "in great anger." He displayed his affliction, and played the *grand seigneur*, greeting the august assembly nobly. Putting one leg forward, he exclaimed:

Most honored lords!

I understand that you are considering imprisoning my father-in-law and my wife. My said father-in-law is old, my wife is ill; by imprisoning them you will shorten their days, to my great regret, which I have not deserved from you and which would be to give me poor recompense for the services I have done you. Therefore I beg you not to imprison them. If they have done wrong I will bring them here to make such amends that you will have reason to be content. I pray you to grant me this, since if you put them in prison God will aid me to avenge myself for it.[33]

But they remained cold to the supplications of poor Perrin. It was a time of repression. The author of the placard posted in Saint-Pierre against Calvin was also arrested. Jacques Gruet admitted his crime under torture. He was immediately executed at the end of July. A strange person, this Gruet, whose materialist arguments could be validly considered a declaration of atheism. His papers reveal original thoughts abounding in denials of Christianity. "If I want to

---

32. *Annales Calviniani, OC* 21, col. 407.

33. F. Bonivard, *Advis et devis de l'ancienne et nouvelle police de Genève, suivis des advis et devis de noblesse et de ses offices ou degrez et des III estats monarchiques, aristocratiques et démocratiques* . . . (Geneva: J. G. Fick, 1865), p. 73.

dance, leap, lead a joyful life, what business is it of the law?" Or again, "The world had no beginning and will have no end." "The one who was called Christ, who said he was the son of God, why did he endure his passion?" "I believe that when a man is dead there is no hope of his living." And so on. Calvin tore into Gruet, and his writings were publicly burned in a joyful auto-da-fé in 1550. Was Gruet an atheist? Probably. But he was also Gruet, a companion of the Favres and Perrins, Gruet the Genevan, exasperated by Calvin and the moral order he incarnated, against and opposed to everything.[34] Many Genevan families, including many leading ones, endured more and more restively the supervision of the great man. These were the Perrins, the Favres, the Septs, and the Bertheliers, the hard core of the opposition to Calvin. They adopted the revealing title of "Children of Geneva." They were maliciously called "libertines," the title under which they have passed to posterity.

Ami Perrin

[Ami Perrin] wanted to be elaborately dressed and to live well, and was not merely dainty in his eating, which means to desire little but of the best, but dainty and gluttonous together, since he must have plenty of the best.

F. BONIVARD[35]

Ami Perrin loved life. "Our comic Caesar" — it was thus that Calvin later described this bitter enemy, alluding rudely to his braggart character.[36] We must expand our picture of this troublesome character. His father was originally a dealer in wooden vessels, but he soon added a second shop for selling cloth. This Perrin married the daughter of a thriving Piedmontese apothecary. They had only one son, whom they fawned on and spoiled excessively, as the story goes.

One may easily imagine Ami Perrin, more a glutton than a gourmet, devoted to clothes and good cheer. It is not surprising that his connection with Calvin was rather short-lived. A partisan of Calvin's during the 1530s and a convinced "Guillermin," Perrin thought himself poorly rewarded for his support. Calvin had given him to understand that he should expect no favorable

34. For this man see the article by F. Berriot from which we have borrowed the whole of our information, "Un procès d'athéisme à Genève: l'affaire Gruet (1547-1550)," *Bulletin de la Société de l'Histoire du Protestantisme Français* 125 (1979): 577-92.

35. Bonivard, p. 56.

36. *OC* 14, col. 657, letter to Farel, October 26, 1553.

treatment from him.[37] Too many things divided the two men; and then Perrin added to his insatiable appetite a boasting side, versatile and sparkling, that lent itself to rhyme:

> Our captain is so angry
> That his blood runs red
> In his face before the battle;
> But when he comes to blows, this passes off.

Or again:

> Equipped like a brave Saint George
> And armed to the teeth,
> Our captain shows himself
> In person at the muster.[38]

How could the prudish Calvin get along with this Sir John Falstaff, whose high words and rich attire concealed a legendary cowardice? Calvin himself was thin as a lath, said only what he knew, and detested bluster. Perrin was not alone; for several years Calvin was to incur the enmity of a veritable family clan. The patriarch of the family, François Favre, father of the woman who liked to dance, was a former Eidguenot, recently very active on the Council. Born about 1480, the merchant draper was still vigorous; had he not been reproached for his escapades in 1546, while his son Gaspard acquired a dreadful reputation for playing skittles during sermons?

Feelings grew more bitter. On September 23, 1547, François Favre was prosecuted for having said that Calvin had proclaimed himself bishop of Geneva. He also said the French had reduced his city to slavery and that Calvin had reintroduced a form of auricular confession: "One must go to him to recount one's sins and make a reverence."[39] The aged Favre, Perrin, and his wife

---

37. *OC* 12, cols. 338ff., Calvin to Perrin, April 1546. Calvin left no doubt about his intention to make the discipline of the church prevail without regard for persons. Let us remember that Ami Perrin began by being the firmest supporter of the Reformer, the chief of the "Guillermins," that is of the partisans of Guillaume Farel and John Calvin after the crisis of 1538, and that it was he who played the chief role in the recall of Calvin to Geneva. The good understanding between the two men should have endured some years longer. It was Perrin's wife, the terrible Françoise Favre, who was responsible for the irremediable estrangement, and after her the Favre clan, her father and brother, as a result of their quarrels with the consistory. Henri Meylan, "Calvin et les hommes d'affaires," in *Regards contemporains sur Jean Calvin* (Paris: PUF, 1965), p. 164.

38. Bonivard, p. 58.

39. *Annales Calviniani, OC* 21, col. 413.

found themselves again in prison, along with Laurent Mégret, called "the Magnifico." Very heavy charges were made against Mégret and Perrin, who were suspected of having betrayed Geneva for the benefit of France. On October 9 Perrin was deprived of his rank of captain general. Mutiny also loomed among the overworked ministers, who complained that they were treated like "stableboys." All the more because they were asked to preach every morning, at the expense, it is true, of shortening their sermons (October 1548). In December the city was on the brink of an uprising; on the sixteenth Calvin intervened courageously between the mob and the Council.

On Christmas Eve all hatreds and grudges were supposed to be reconciled. Perrin and his group were expected to pardon the salutary humiliations they had received and participate solemnly in the Lord's Supper. Nothing doing. Perrin said he was troubled in his conscience and courteously declined Communion, standing back from it. The gesture was interpreted as a threat.[40] As for Mégret, he was not freed until January, also losing his rights of bourgeoisie. The worst fears were justified. A year later, on January 18, 1549, the Council published a proclamation that struck at the pastors in passing:

> Following the example of the good kings of the ancient church and also of the Christian princes, lords, and magistrates who are governed by the Word of God, we declare to the citizens, bourgeois, and inhabitants of our city that we are very angry and displeased that the holy admonitions and remonstrances that have been given to them through the Word of God, which is preached to them daily, have not been better observed, as they should have been, and also that the commands we have given have not been better followed and put into effect; in which the ministers of the Word of God have been negligent and have not done their duty in carrying out their office, in admonishing and reproving vice and setting a good example, as they are obliged to do and their vocation requires.[41]

Some days later Perrin became first syndic. In a paranoid atmosphere Calvin complained in March that people came to listen to his sermons in order to denounce him afterward. The affair of Philippe de Ecclesia furnished a *casus belli*. De Ecclesia, whose true name was Philippe Osias, was pastor of Vandoeuvres. Since March 1549 the ministers, with Calvin at their head, had obstinately demanded the removal of this man, their colleague, with that charming penchant for denunciation that periodically grips simple souls, protectors of their flocks. But the Council refused until January 1553. However, his brother pastors did not

40. *Annales Calviniani, OC* 21, col. 443.
41. Roget, pp. 47-48.

stint their criticisms of him: usury, mistreatment of his wife, and, naturally, erroneous opinions. The Genevans were indeed in need of pastors. In September Calvin let drop the following: "Some murmur because there are so many preachers in this city; now even if there were many it would be with good cause, since there is a greater need of them in this city than in any other."[42]

Mounting Danger, 1552-55

If it were up to me, I would want God to remove me from this world, and that I should not have to live here three days in such disorder as there is here.

CALVIN, DECEMBER 1554[43]

The tension increased on the shores of Lake Leman, culminating in the riots of May 1555, which were severely repressed. Calvin was the symbol of an evolution that was vigorously criticized. Although he finally emerged strengthened by the trial, Calvin lived his most somber days in the fall of 1553. Faced by his unpopularity, he asked himself whether he would be forced into a second exile. As in 1538, after a gap of fifteen years, would he have to leave Geneva again? From 1552 on his authority was contested on two fronts. In the disciplinary field Philibert Berthelier refused to accept his excommunication, which was rapidly transformed into a cause célèbre by his partisans. Berthelier's hatred of Calvin had originally had the air of a juvenile prank; when he was reproached for his untimely coughing fits during the sermon, he threatened, without theological subtlety, "Calvin doesn't want us to cough? We'll fart and belch!"[44] But also in the doctrinal field, a former monk, Jean Trolliet, called predestination into question. Calvin asked whether he was being maliciously described as a prophet. If so, he would take no notice; he was content with announcing the Word of God, like Ezekiel and so many others before him. "There are those who say today, 'Behold Calvin, who makes himself a prophet when he says they shall know that there has been a prophet among us. He means himself. And is he a prophet?' Now since it is the doctrine of God that I announce, I must indeed use this language. Since what we hear here from Ezekiel is the Word of God, I do not want to conceal what he said, since it was not only for him personally that this was said, but in general for everyone."[45]

42. Roget, p. 49.
43. *OC* 53, col. 316, twenty-sixth sermon on 1 Timothy.
44. *OC* 21, col. 417.
45. Twenty-first sermon on Daniel. Reference is to Ezek. 2:5. Cited by Richard

The real debate, however, was over excommunication. Calvin defended the importance of this action, which consisted in refusing Communion to a hardened sinner, known for the scandal he provoked around him. It concerned the dignity of the sacrament itself. "I who am nothing but His servant, indeed a poor earthworm, I will not allow Him thus to be mocked and defamed; yes, and nevertheless I declare that I am here, that I will not on my life suffer the temple of God to be turned into a pigsty."[46]

The situation worsened the next year; in February 1553 Perrin was again elected first syndic, as in 1549. The Favres, Perrins, Septs, and Bertheliers prepared to take their revenge. A rash of anticlericalism broke out in the town; some pastors were reproached for attending the General Council. The good ministers marveled, through Calvin's mouth, that anyone dared to compare them to the Catholic priests, while they did not ask for any ecclesiastical privileges and submitted themselves to "temporal judges."[47] The Council of Two Hundred declared their exclusion from political assemblies. On April 15 the Council summoned several ministers, following complaints from various inhabitants who were tired of the admonitions of the consistory.

The standing cause of confrontation, however, was the question of suspension from the Lord's Supper. Philibert Berthelier, a member of the Perrin clan, was not allowed to communicate, despite the authorization he obtained from the Council (summer 1553). What was more, Berthelier belonged to an old Geneva family that had become famous during the revolution, furnishing the city with one of the first martyrs to its liberty. What should we say about him? He enjoyed, like Perrin, a rather murky reputation as a young wastrel. To begin with, his mother, we are assured, was "a great hypocrite and dissembler." As for his own vices, he would have considered them virtues.[48] On Saturday, September 2, before an extraordinary assembly, Calvin refused to yield. Fearing a disturbance, someone secretly warned Berthelier not to appear for the Lord's Supper the next day. Calvin seems not to have known this. With that impassibility that he always showed in times of crisis, he prepared to preach on this Sunday, September 3, 1553, what might be his last sermon, at least in Geneva. The Reformer mounted the pulpit with a lump in his throat from emotion. He raised his voice, and discovered in himself reserves of assurance and determination. He would not yield; God was directing him: "As for me, while God keeps me here, since he has given me constancy and I have taken it from

Stauffer, "Les discours à la première personne dans les sermons de Calvin," in *Regards contemporains*, p. 216.

46. *OC* 52, col. 153, forty-sixth sermon on Daniel.

47. *OC* 52, col. 55.

48. Bonivard, p. 65.

him, I will use it, whatever happens, and will govern myself only by the rules of my master, which are entirely clear and obvious to me. Since we should now receive the Holy Communion of Our Lord Jesus Christ, if anyone wants to intrude at this holy table to whom it has been forbidden by the consistory, it is certain that I will show myself, at the risk of my life, what I should be."[49]

He was also to add, "As for me . . . I would rather have been killed than have offered the holy things of God with this hand to those declared guilty as scorners."[50] Berthelier did not appear. Calvin's firmness had paid off. But had he lost all his doubts, for all that? It seems not. In the afternoon he preached on Saint Paul's farewell address to the elders of Ephesus. The choice of text owed nothing to chance. "Ye know . . . after what manner I have been with you at all seasons, serving the Lord with all humility . . . ; neither count I my life dear unto myself, so that I might finish my course . . . and the ministry, which I have received of the Lord Jesus."[51] Calvin, the new Saint Paul, laid bare the meaning of this text. He seems to have said in substance: "I must declare to you that I do not know whether this is the last sermon I shall give in Geneva. Not that I shall take leave of my own accord. It does not please God that I should want to leave this place on my own authority. But when intolerable conditions are imposed on me I shall not resist those who hold the power."[52]

Calvin, the good apostle, complained of the ingratitude of men. In this sad fall of 1553, while the churchman was dejected, Servetus already was no more. His still-warm stake, the acrid wood smoke, the cries of the condemned man, the terrible odor of burning human flesh were so many united testimonies to the fanaticism a Christian society is capable of, whether it be Reformed or not. Where were you, Calvin, on this Friday, October 27, 1553, when Servetus went to the stake?

Plainly Calvin had made himself a noble soul. His pious protestations, his defense of ecclesiastical rights, and his arguments for excommunication filled pages of correspondence. As he assured Bullinger on November 6, he was ready to offer his resignation rather than yield to the civil authorities. His position did not lack appeal or courage. Calvin would perhaps have made a good and holy martyr had he been given the chance. But he lacked opportunity. He made a final attempt to blackmail the Genevans; he was ready to leave, he could not

49. Stauffer, "Les discours à la première personne dans les sermons de Calvin," p. 217. The author employs Gautier's *Histoire de Genève*, dating from the beginning of the eighteenth century. The original of this work disappeared during the nineteenth century.

50. After Theodore Beza, still cited from Stauffer, "Les discours à la première personne dans les sermons de Calvin," p. 218.

51. Acts 20:18ff.

52. Stauffer, "Les discours à la première personne dans les sermons de Calvin," p. 218.

permit the authority of the consistory to be trampled under foot by distributing the Lord's Supper to manifest scorners who merely mocked at pastoral admonitions.[53] The Small Council continued to defend its prerogative in the case of Berthelier. "When it is decided here in Council that Communion should be given to someone, this should take place without being referred back to the consistory" (November 7).[54] In other words, the consistory could not reverse a case heard by the Council. The Two Hundred, convened the next day, supported this decision. Calvin wrote to his colleagues in Zürich on November 26 to complain of the small regard the gospel was held in. Could the doctrine of Christ thus be flouted by preventing the just excommunication of scandalous persons?[55]

This month of November was one of general humiliation. Farel himself, the founding father of the Reformation, had to apologize for having spoken negatively about Genevan youth. However, the Council ended, against all expectations, by drawing back; after having reaffirmed its right of examination, it did not admit Berthelier to the Lord's Supper in December 1553. Calvin had won; the bread and wine of Communion would not touch the impious man's mouth.

In January 1554 the Council tried to reconcile Perrin and Calvin. At the end of the month a fraternal banquet of reconciliation even took place. A heavy and suspicious atmosphere weighed on the city; in June Calvin thought himself defamed by insulting writings. Excommunication was still, as always, at the heart of the debate; the Council should settle it. Could a consistory deprive a church member of Communion? Philibert Berthelier felt himself permanently wronged by the refusal of the ministers to admit him to the Lord's Supper. The affair dragged on. Calvin's strictness against Berthelier and other similar cases appeared clearly in a sermon in January 1555. "If I see a fool, and I have tried to win him by fair means, and I have struggled with him, and in the end he is clearly hopeless, and also he breaks all bounds and blasphemes against God, what shall I do? Shall I speak to him as if he had good judgment? Not at all, but rather I shall mock at his stupidity. And indeed if I see him rise to still greater pride I shall have to make use of threats."[56]

Was the world divided into pious souls, recognized by Calvin, and hopeless "fools" or hardened sinners? Did one have no other alternative than to sing psalms with a contrite air or be marched through the city with a torch in one's hand? Had not Pierre Ameaux been forced to carry out this expiatory rite eight or nine years earlier, in April 1546 (see above)? The young people were the first

53. *OC* 14, col. 655.
54. Roget, p. 59.
55. *OC* 14, cols. 674-78.
56. *OC* 35, col. 201, 134th sermon on Job.

to react heedlessly. Some sort of nocturnal disturbance occurred one night in January 1555. Several young people paraded through the streets of the city with torches in hand, mocking the psalms. Calvin was furious at this defiance of his authority. The next Sunday he let his anger erupt from the height of the pulpit: "Alas! Our Lord has indeed given occasion to weep and moan, both to you, children of Geneva, and to me with you, for it is needful that a pastor, when there is some scandal in the church, should be the first to cry out to ask pardon of God, so that all the people may follow him."[57]

The following Sunday he said: "I would like to be far from Geneva. And might it please God that I should never have to approach within a hundred leagues to please them, provided there were people who desired their salvation" (January 20, 1555).[58]

The elections of February 1555 were favorable to Calvin, thanks mainly to the increasing pressure of the new bourgeois of foreign origin. The four new syndics supported him, and Calvin's partisans outweighed Perrin's Children of Geneva. Would the Perrinists make headway again? Would they manage to recapture, by a revolution, the power they had lost? There was a riot in the merry month of May. On Thursday, the sixteenth, a great "tumult and sedition" arose against Syndic Henri Aulbert. Swords were drawn. Numerous inhabitants were roused by cries of "Arise, arise, someone is killed at the Mollard!" Perrin then did the irreparable: he seized the baton, the emblem of his office, from Syndic Pierre Bonna. This insidious symbolic gesture had the appearance of a coup d'état. During the following days poor Perrin fled, along with Philibert Berthelier.

After the incidents of May 16, 1555, Calvin called for repression. He exclaimed publicly: "There are those who will complain, as soon as one talks of doing justice, that one is bloodthirsty, that there is nothing but cruelty. . . . And not only will the gallows-birds talk so — I speak of those whose sins and crimes are manifest — but their henchmen in the taverns, who imitate the preachers. Oh, they know how to invoke humanity and mercy, and it seems to them that I spare blood no more than they do wine, which they swill and guzzle without measure or judgment. But such blasphemies are addressed to God and not to men."[59]

Certainly the spectacle of evil leads one to interrogate oneself about one's own sins. But this is done to praise the Lord for being saved. Was Calvin talking about himself or proposing an ideal example of a repentant sinner when he cried, during a sermon of this same period, "By nature I was no better than

---

57. *OC* 53, col. 405, thirty-third sermon on 1 Timothy.
58. *OC* 53, col. 438, thirty-sixth sermon on 1 Timothy.
59. *OC* 26, col. 501, fifty-first sermon on Deuteronomy.

those whom I see to be entirely against God"? He continued, "I was rather his mortal enemy; there was no nerve in me that tended to his obedience, but I was full of fury, full of malice, full of presumption and of a diabolical determination to resist God and to engulf myself in eternal death."[60]

On Monday, June 3, 1555, the guilty were judged *in absentia;* Perrin (if taken) was condemned to have "the hand of his right arm with which he attempted the syndical baton cut off." His accomplices[61] and he himself should also be decapitated. Then, "the heads and the said hand [should be] nailed to the gibbet and the bodies cut into four quarters."[62] The same sentence fell on the two brothers Comparet, condemned to have "their heads cut off . . . and their bodies quartered." As for Claude Galloys, he should carry a torch and ask for mercy. He would no longer have the right to carry a sword, and would be put in the *colard,* a sort of pillory, along with Girard Thomas, in two different parts of the city.

With the exception of those who fled, the accused were executed. The Genevan chronicle has preserved the memory of these macabre ceremonies, so shocking to our modern sensibility. Who would have said that Geneva would one day be one of the capitals of humanitarianism?

One after the other four of these seditious people were decapitated, the two Comparets, one two weeks after the other, who after having their heads cut off were quartered and the quarters each hung from a gallows in the four corners of the territories of the city, and the head of each with one of the fore-quarters; one was put next to the Arve Bridge, always in view of their companions, if they wished, who daily frequented the lodging-houses of the said bridge. The fore-quarter and head of the other were carried across the Rhone and hung at the edge of the Geneva border, which, as we already said above, is not three paces from the Perrin house, so that he might have in seeing them a constant reminder of his companions. [François] Berthelier and the Bastard only had their heads cut off, without being quartered; Berthelier's head and his body remained on the gibbet, and so did the body of the Bastard, but his head was nailed to a rafter over the wall of the Mollard, and this epitaph was made for him:

> For having fallen into the misfortune
> Of loving a man more than God
> Claude de Genève has his head
> Nailed up in this place.[63]

60. *OC* 54, col. 212, eighteenth sermon on 2 Timothy.
61. Balthésard, Chabod, Vernat, and Michalet.
62. *Annales Calviniani, OC* 21, col. 608, Registres du Conseil 49, fol. 96.
63. Bonivard, pp. 146-47.

François-Daniel Berthelier, brother of Philibert, was among the victims of repression. Calvin really let himself go in the fall. He evoked the "henchmen of Satan" whose "various sects" had troubled Geneva for eighteen years. The allusion was to the presence of the Anabaptists gathered around Herman de Gerbihan and Audry Benoît d'Anglen in 1537.[64] He also justified the severity of the sentence passed on the Perrinists: "Those who do not correct evil when they can do so and their office requires it are guilty of it. Just as, if a preacher dissimulates the reigning vices, it is certain that he is a traitor and disloyal, since he should keep a good watch and awaken those who are in danger of perdition. If then I support evil knowingly or by indifference, I shall be the first to be condemned. Similarly, if those who have the sword of justice do not employ the severity they should to correct faults, it is certain that the anger of God will fall on them forever."[65]

The Treatise *On Scandals*

Jesus Christ . . . would not have been the Savior of the world, the foundation of the church, or the true Christ if he had not been a stumbling block.

JOHN CALVIN, 1550[66]

It was in this troubled context that there appeared in 1550 from the press of Jean Crespin in Geneva the treatise *On the Scandals that Today Prevent Many People from Coming to the Pure Doctrine of the Gospel and Ruin Others*. This major work, however, was in no way a product of the moment. It was certainly "one of the texts in which Calvin was most personally involved."[67] Calvin carried this book in his mind for almost four years. He wrote the Latin version, and then the French version after some months' interval, the former in July-August, the latter in the fall.

Its writing coincided with a moment of stabilization and even of retreat for the Reformation on the international scene. In particular, there is an allusion to the defeat of Mühlberg that allowed Charles V to crush the Lutherans in

---

64. Stauffer, "Les discours à la première personne dans les sermons de Calvin," p. 225.

65. *OC* 27, col. 271.

66. J. Calvin, *Des scandales qui empeschent aujourd'huy beaucoup de gens de venir à la pure doctrine de l'Évangile, & en desbauchent d'autres* (Geneva: Jehan Crespin, 1550). Calvin, *Des scandales*, ed. Fatio, p. 58. Citations are from this edition.

67. O. Millet, *Calvin et la dynamique de la Parole. Essai de rhétorique réformée* (Paris: H. Champion, 1992), p. 517.

April 1547. "A Gospel that was too triumphant would have made us insolent beyond measure."[68] The pamphlet also took up again the analysis sketched out in a letter to M. de Falais on July 14 of this disastrous year. "I recognize that Our Lord wants to take this triumphant Gospel entirely away from us to force us to fight under the cross of Our Lord."[69] The France of Henry II, for its part, was carried away by a repressive movement on a vast scale, with the creation of the Chambre Ardente, the regulation of bookselling, and the interdiction of numerous authors, including Calvin.[70]

Another danger, finally, was the impiety of men of letters. Back in 1542 Antoine Fumée, a counselor of the Parlement of Paris, had called the attention of the cold-prone and migrainous Calvin to the existence of "Achristians." After the Nicodemites, the Anabaptists, and the spiritual libertines, previously denounced, these furnished one of the targets of the treatise On Scandals. Calvin, in his commentary on the Epistle to the Galatians in 1548, judged the Epicureans to be more dangerous than the papists: "And there is no kind of persecution more mortal than when someone attacks the salvation of the soul. The swords of the wicked do not reach us who are delivered from the tyranny of the Pope. But how witless we are if we are not moved by this spiritual persecution, when they try in every way they can to extinguish this doctrine from which we take and hold our lives, when by their blasphemies they assail our faith, and even shake the faith of some who are infirm. As for me, truly the rage of the Epicureans causes me greater distress than that of the papists."[71]

Calvin described these adversaries in Latin as "Epicureans" or "Lucianites"; they were the latter-day disciples of Lucian, the Greek poet who satirized

---

68. Calvin, Des scandales, p. 114. In the empire the Schmalkaldic League, commanded by Johann Friedrich of Saxony, had been defeated at Mühlberg by Charles V on April 24, 1547. On May 15, 1548, the "Augsburg Interim" became the law of the empire. While a complete religious reconciliation was awaited (in the "interim"), two concessions were offered to the Protestants: marriage of the clergy and Communion in both kinds for the laity. In a letter to Bucer in October of 1549 Calvin exclaimed: "Oh, if I could relieve a little the distress of your soul and the cares with which I see you tormented! We all beg you not to let yourself become uselessly depressed. Not that we would desire to see you happy and contented when you have such diverse and numerous reasons for being afflicted; this is not demanded of your piety; this is not desirable. You should merely constrain yourself to the extent possible to preserve yourself for the Lord and for the church." OC 13, col. 437.

69. J. Calvin, Lettres à Monsieur et Madame de Falais, ed. F. Bonali-Fiquet (Geneva: Droz, 1991), p. 157.

70. F. H. Higman, Censorship and the Sorbonne: A Bibliographical Study of Books in French Censured by the Faculty of Theology of the University of Paris, 1520-1551 (Geneva: Droz, 1979).

71. J. Calvin, Commentaires sur le Nouveau Testament, 4 vols. (Paris: C. Meyrueis, 1855), 3:726.

the gods, and of Epicurus.[72] But for Calvin the scandal also assumed metaphysical significance. The last lines of the treatise show how the mystery of the cross is inseparable from the idea of scandal: "Certainly if Saint Paul had wanted to do away with the scandal of the cross, it would have been easy for him to invent subtle means for doing so. Now he was so far from this that he argued strongly and firmly that it would not be serving Jesus Christ if he should want to separate his preaching from such a scandal."[73]

The work was dedicated to "Master Laurent de Normandie" (1510-69). This former mayor of Noyon, a refugee in Geneva in 1548, had just been cruelly hit by a series of deaths at the time when Calvin took up his pen; his father, his wife, and his daughter had followed each other to the tomb. This fate had led to the recollection of the trials of Job, the biblical figure who was the brother of all the afflicted. Calvin saw it as a "great accumulation of scandals" sent by Satan.

What was a scandal for Calvin? The Reformer stuck close to the etymology; in its Greek meaning, a scandal is a stumbling block. The same idea is found in the Hebrew word.[74] Figuratively a scandal is the occasion for a sin. The perception of scandal remained profoundly ambivalent for Calvin. Did not God in fact know how "to change evil into good"?[75] How can this enigmatic remark be understood? How could Christ present himself as an object of scandal? Calvin took advantage of this to identify a *positive* meaning of the word "scandal": "[Jesus] knew that in fact there are many things in the doctrine of the Gospel and its profession that are contrary to human wisdom, and also that Satan in his cleverness would soon devise various scandals and obstacles to make it hateful or suspect to the world. And also it was necessary that what the Holy Spirit had said about Jesus Christ be accomplished, that is that he would be a stone of scandal and a stumbling block."[76]

He thus came to the paradox that "He whom we know to be the gate of eternal life" is also "called a stumbling block and a scandal." Likewise the gospel, "the doctrine of peace and concord," provoked "many troubles."[77] The Reformation period also became connected with scandal; this was the paradoxical

---

72. See M. Lienhard, "Les Épicuriens à Strasbourg entre 1530 et 1550 et le problème de l'Épicurisme au xvie siècle," in *Croyants et sceptiques au xvie siècle* (Strasbourg, 1981), pp. 17-45.

73. Calvin, *Des scandales*, p. 229.

74. The Greek word *skandalon* was used in the Septuagint to translate the Hebrew word *mikechôl*, which also carried the idea of stumbling.

75. Calvin, *Des scandales*, pp. 117-18.

76. Calvin, *Des scandales*, pp. 53-54.

77. Calvin, *Des scandales*, pp. 54-55.

mark of its Christian authenticity. Some, "to avoid scandal," refused "to receive the pure doctrine of the Gospel that we profess."[78]

Calvin criticized the wits who reproached the Bible for its "coarse and simple language."[79] Certainly the Scriptures were written neither in the language of Cicero nor in that of Demosthenes. They are of a "rude and simple fashion," while pedants "want to have their ears tickled with sweet and melodious language."[80] This criticism of those admirers of antique beauty who despised Christianity reflected on a whole philosophy of classical language: the principle of economy, rejection of affectation, etc. It also had a metaphysical content. "God, who created the language of men, wants to stammer with us" — a marvelous description of a revelation that speaks to the humble and whose profundity does not depend on artifice. "However, in stammering, he confounds us, and has a gravity as high and eminent for subduing human spirits as if the most elegant rhetorician who ever lived deployed all the beautiful adornments that can be found in art."[81]

The mystery of Christ enabled the development of these reflections on language. Calvin's conception of language was directly linked to his theology of the incarnation. Certainly the scandal of the cross, here compared to a gibbet, remains incomprehensible.[82] Moreover, the weakness of the true church in itself constitutes another scandal, after the humble birth in a manger and the infamous death on a cross. Yes, the kingdom of God is more than ever a spiritual reality: "And in fact as things are today people should not be astonished if the state of the true church, poor as it is, repels them, and the great pomp displayed by our adversaries dazzles their eyes. Nevertheless no one will stumble over this stone or be held back by this scandal except those who do not know that the reign of Christ is spiritual. For those who are not deterred from adoring him as their king either by the stable in which Jesus Christ was born or by the cross on which he was hung will not hold in disdain the base condition and smallness of his church."[83]

The cross of Christ becomes a call to mortification for every believer. "It is necessary that our fierceness be subdued and humbled under the discipline of the cross." This individual destiny — everyone in turn is called to carry his cross — is also found on a collective level. The true church itself is under the cross. "We see how the church has flourished in all spiritual virtues during its

78. Calvin, *Des scandales*, p. 58.
79. Calvin, *Des scandales*, p. 64.
80. Calvin, *Des scandales*, pp. 66-67.
81. Calvin, *Des scandales*, p. 67.
82. Calvin, *Des scandales*, p. 71.
83. Calvin, *Des scandales*, p. 85.

afflictions, and when there has been great worldly prosperity how it has melted away like snow in the sun."[84]

What exactly is the church? "The church" does not only describe the Christian community as it was constituted after the resurrection of Christ and in the expectation of his return. No, "the church" came to be applied by Calvin to the people of Israel, and even to the whole of humanity. The church is the community of believers; the contract signed between man and God, the initial pact, goes back to creation. "It is clear that the continual revolts of men broke the course of God's grace, which left to itself would have endured forever. And this can be seen as though from the beginning of the world."[85] "The church," from this standpoint, describes the community of the just as it was gathered around Noah, that small band of eight people called to repeople the earth.[86] Now the children of Noah offended God, just as later the lineage of Abraham and of Moses or the subjects of David and of Solomon would rebel in their turn. This cyclical character of human history continued after the coming of Jesus Christ. One arrives at the paradox that Jesus Christ, come as prince of peace, sowed war and discord: "At the time when Jesus Christ was born all was peaceful. Forty years or so later his Gospel was sown in various countries. After it had been clearly preached far and wide, things changed, and marvelous troubles arose everywhere."[87]

"Marvelous troubles" must be understood as troubles that provoked stupor or astonishment. This agreement between Calvin and Matthew can be explained by an identity of situation. Calvin himself was accused by one party of Genevans of having brought war and not peace to their city. More fundamentally, the Reformation renewed its ties to the primitive period of Christianity. From then on the difficulties it experienced in establishing itself became the evidence of its authenticity. Only the purest Christianity provoked these troubles and confrontations to which Jesus Christ himself, the Christ of Matthew, had drawn attention. The good news was decidedly not identified with peace.

84. Calvin, *Des scandales*, p. 114.
85. Calvin, *Des scandales*, p. 89.
86. Noah, Shem, Ham, Japheth, and their wives.
87. Calvin, *Des scandales*, p. 93. This is an implicit reference to the Gospel of Matthew: "And the brother shall deliver up the brother to death, and the father the child: and the children shall rise up against their parents, and cause them to be put to death" (10:21). And again, "Think not that I am come to send peace on earth: I came not to send peace, but a sword" (10:34).

CHAPTER 10

The Trail of the Heretics:
Bolsec, Servetus, Castellio

Calvin and his henchmen, watched for by the law,
In Paris went to execution in effigy.
Servetus was immolated in person by Calvin.
If Servetus had been sovereign in Geneva
He would, as an argument against his adversaries,
Have had the necks of the Trinitarians squeezed in nooses.

VOLTAIRE, *POEM ON NATURAL LAW* (1756)[1]

Calvin *and* Servetus or Calvin *or* Servetus — must one choose? Michael
Servetus had the "singular misfortune to be burned twice: in effigy by the Catholics, and by the Protestants in flesh and blood."[2] The omen was auspicious. Executed in Calvin's Geneva in 1553, Servetus was an outcast who fell victim to a
Christian civilization that left no room for ecstatics. In his *Christian Dialogues*
in 1760, Voltaire gave voices to a Protestant minister and a Catholic priest. The
former explains to his papist colleague: "It is true that our ideas about the
means for spreading the faith are different; but we also have had some of those

---

1. Voltaire, *Mélanges* (Paris: NRF, Pléiade, 1961), pp. 282-83.
2. R. H. Bainton, *Hunted Heretic: The Life and Death of Michael Servetus, 1511-1553*
(Boston: Beacon Press, 1953), p. 7. For the importance of this debate down to recent times,
see V. Zuber, "Pour en finir avec Michel Servet. Les protestants du début du xxe siècle entre
mémoire et histoire," *Bulletin de la Société de l'Histoire du Protestantisme Français* 140
(1995): 97-120.

brilliant moments you regret, and the execution of Servetus ought to excite your admiration and envy."[3]

The Protestants were no better than the Catholics. This seemed obvious to Voltaire, who advocated a form of free thought that would find its end in natural religion. According to Voltaire, the revealed religions, Judaism, Islam, and Christianity in all its lines, Catholic, Protestant, or Orthodox, all presented the same distressing spectacle. The Christians themselves are in turn victims and executioners: persecute them, and they supply martyrs; give them power, and they persecute in their turn. The controversy between the Jesuits and Jansenists in the France of his day seemed to Voltaire to epitomize this cross fire of intolerance and sectarianism.

So thought the author of *Candide,* using those flippant sallies that the volatile French usually take for granted. At some centuries' distance, we see clearly that the most secular societies have in their turn given birth to monstrosities and that atheistic totalitarianism has undoubtedly surpassed all revealed religions in horror.

Calvin or Servetus? Following Voltaire's steps, we shall not choose, not from lack of humanity, but for the sake of historical precision — and in the first place, from a wish to exclude all anachronism from our judgments. For neither the word "tolerance" nor the concept existed in the sixteenth century. Philosophical tolerance, which Voltaire was trading in, was an imported article which the French seized on with their customary love of new products. Tolerance was born in the 1680s, at the beginning of the Enlightenment; it developed in a single area, that of northwestern Europe, England and the United Provinces. Finally, it was the work of one man in particular, John Locke, to whom the eighteenth century devoted faithful worship.[4]

Tolerance, then, did not exist in the sixteenth century. In fact, it appeared impious. Is an example wanted? Thomas More, the author of *Utopia,* who was faithful to the end to his ideal of Catholic humanism, preferring the ignominious death of a traitor to renouncing his principles — the great Thomas More accepted the stake for heretics. Indeed, he could not very well see what one could do with heretics other than burn them.[5]

---

3. Voltaire, p. 363.

4. Between things prescribed and things proscribed, tolerance defines an intermediate region, that of things indifferent, from which it banishes constraint. From this standpoint Locke's tolerance is radically distinguished from Bayle's "liberty of conscience," which is based on the right to be in error. In the strict sense liberty of conscience does not admit any restrictions, in contrast with tolerance, which is based on the judgment of society. See B. Cottret, "Tolérance ou liberté de conscience? Épistémologie et politique à l'aube des Lumières," *Études Théologiques et Religieuses* 65 (1990): 333-50.

5. B. Cottret, "Traducteurs et divulgateurs clandestins de la Réforme dans l'An-

Derived from Latin, the French words *tolérer* and *tolérance* at first were not applied to religious dissidence. They designated a provisional measure of conciliation, more pragmatic than philosophical. To tolerate was to suffer and permit, at most, what one could not manage to destroy.[6] In short, tolerance was a lesser evil and had no positive value of its own.

Calvin was scarcely tolerant. But in any case, could he have been?[7] It would be equally fallacious to see all Calvin's adversaries as consistently "declared champions of tolerance, of individual liberty, and of the rights of civilized society."[8] Certainly, in the absence of tolerance in the philosophical sense, various conciliatory attitudes remained theoretically possible: "ecclesiastical concord," irenicism, advocacy of peace among Christians, and finally indifference, which permits coexistence. But neither clemency, nor mildness, nor lassitude, nor indifference merits the name of tolerance.[9] In any case Calvin's program, his dogmatic system, and his exhortations to resistance ruled out all these solutions. No, by definition the Calvinist enterprise could not envisage the least compromise, which was immediately perceived as a compromise with conscience. Calvin's logic could no more accommodate a contradiction than his conscience could a business arrangement.[10] Various of his opponents had to bear the cost, and among them Michael Servetus.

Theodore Beza emphasized Calvin's clemency: only one execution of a heretic, that of Servetus. Calvinism in this respect showed itself clearly less productive than the Roman Church, and indeed than the other Protestant confessions:

> There are few towns in Switzerland or Germany where Anabaptists have not been put to death, and rightly; here we have been content with banishment. Here Bolsec blasphemed against the providence of God, here Sebastian Castellio derogated the very books of the holy Scriptures, here Valentin blas-

---

gleterre henricienne, 1520-1535," *Revue d'Histoire Moderne et Contemporaine* 28 (1981): 472.

6. W. H. Huseman, "A Lexicological Study of the Expression of Toleration in French at the Time of the Colloquy of Poissy (1559-1565)," *Cahiers de Lexicologie*, no. 48 (1986): 96-97.

7. On the other hand, the attention he gave to the Christian conscience led him to approve, up to a certain point, "liberty of conscience." See O. Millet, "Le thème de la conscience libre chez Calvin," in *La liberté de conscience (xvie-xviie siècles)* (Geneva: Droz, 1991), pp. 21-37.

8. A. Roget, *L'Église et l'État à Genève du temps de Calvin. Étude d'histoire politico-ecclésiastique* (Geneva: J. Jullien, 1867), pp. 4-5.

9. F. Buisson, *Sébastien Castellion. Sa vie et son oeuvre (1515-1563)* (Paris: Hachette, 1892), 1:viii.

10. Buisson, *Sébastien Castellion,* 1:205.

phemed against the divine essence. None of these is dead; two were only banished, the third got off with formal amends to God and the government. Where is this cruelty? Servetus alone was sent to the fire. And who was ever more worthy of it than this wretch, who for the space of thirty years in so many ways blasphemed against the eternity of the Son of God, gave the name of Cerberus to the Trinity of three persons in a single divine essence, reduced to nothing the baptism of small children, gathered the greater part of all the foulness that Satan ever vomited against the truth of God, seduced an infinity of persons, and as the climax of his curse never wished either to repent, giving way to the truth by which he had been so many times overcome, or to give hope of conversion?[11]

Bolsec and "Fucking Predestination," 1551

Have Christians become tyrannical?
Do Christians show pharisaical zeal?
Have Christians lost their fine morals?
Are the sheep of Christ so cruel?
Oh savage assaults, oh mortal alarms,
That consume my heart with tears!

COMPLAINT OF JÉRÔME BOLSEC,
IN PRISON IN GENEVA, TO THE TUNE OF THE PSALM
"MY GOD FEEDS ME UNDER HIS HIGH POWER"[12]

While he shared the prejudices of his contemporaries against sorcerers, Calvin the churchman remained devoted to one of the church's principal missions, the denunciation of heresy and the condemnation of heretics. For Calvin the greatest heretics were the Anabaptists. They were the internal enemy, as against the papists, who threatened the development of the "true faith" from outside. Papists, moreover, were not heretics in the strict sense; their errors were predictable, almost programmed, and less dangerous on the whole than those original thoughts that risked affecting the Reformed world itself. In 1545 the Anabaptist Belot held that the Old Testament was abolished by the New. This point of view might be debatable theologically, but did it justify the torture inflicted on poor Belot after he was chained and his invectives against Calvin were laughed at?[13]

11. T. Beza, *L'histoire de la vie et mort de Calvin* (1565), *Opera Calvini* (hereafter cited as *OC*) 21, col. 39. For this Valentin Gentilis, see the following chapter.
12. *OC* 8, col. 226. This is Psalm 23, in Clément Marot's version.
13. *OC* 12, col. 256, Calvin to Farel, January 21, 1546.

Some years later Jérôme-Hermès Bolsec brought up another issue. This former Carmelite at first rallied to the Reformation, only to turn against Calvin. A man of certainty more than a specialist in nuances, Theodore Beza related the episode in his own fashion:

[A certain Carmelite] named Hiérome Bolsec of Paris — who had suddenly turned from a theologian into a doctor — to make himself important, thinking he was in his cloister and not in a church of God (of which he had never known anything except by hearsay), and also being urged by certain rascals . . . began in open congregation to criticize the doctrine of providence and eternal predestination, as though we made God the author of sin and guilty of the condemnation of the wicked. Calvin took the field against this disguised wolf and answered him so well in speech in public and in private, and then also in writing, that truly nothing remained to his adversary except a monkish impudence that rendered and still renders him today noxious to every man with any good feeling. . . . This wretch, who had deserved punishment for a seditious act, being treated by the magistrates with all clemency because it was thought that some remedy would soon be found for his sophistical ignorance, after having raised all the scandals and troubles he could in the neighboring churches and having seen himself driven out of the lands of the lords of Bern three times, finally, being intolerable to everyone, gave glory to God, acknowledging his errors and especially his bad conscience in Orléans before the general synod of the French churches in 1562, so that one might have hoped for something from him. But later, being repossessed by the same evil spirit, he returned to his former errors, and being driven away by all as he deserved, still serves today in all the places he goes to as a testimony to the anger of God against those who resist the truth.[14]

Despite its prejudice, this account is not incorrect as to the facts. This former Parisian Carmelite indeed established himself as a practitioner in Geneva. Already in May 1551 he had had to answer for his errors concerning predestination and free will.[15] Predestination quickly became one of the most disputed dogmas of Calvinist doctrine. God chose to save certain people and to damn the rest — no doubt a shocking proposition in its blunt form, it appeared only within the context of a broader theology.

Bolsec indeed had the imprudence and impudence to attack Calvin publicly in the "congregation" of October 16. These congregations involved preach-

---

14. Beza, *L'histoire de la vie et mort de Calvin*, pp. 23-24.
15. *Annales Calviniani, OC* 21, col. 481, Friday, May 15, 1551.

ing and what we would call today a Bible-reading society, permitting an exchange of views. (We shall examine this oratorical genre further in chap. 13.)

Jean de Saint-André, pastor of Jussy, expounded chapter 8 of the Fourth Gospel, notably verse 47, "He that is of God heareth God's words." Farel added a few words. Calvin was absent. Then Bolsec, seizing the opportunity, argued against the predestinationist explanation, citing Saint Augustine at length. Calvin, he claimed, made God the author of sin. According to Bolsec, in fact, "One should not recognize any other election or reprobation except that which is seen in believing or not believing, and those who put an eternal will in God by which he has ordained some to life and others to death make him a tyrant, indeed an idol, like that the pagans made of Jupiter."[16]

Calvin entered without being seen; for an hour he improvised brilliantly in defense of his thesis. On leaving, Bolsec was conducted to the prison of the Évêché to await his trial. He was interrogated on the spot. The civil authorities, it must be acknowledged, had great difficulty in following these highly technical debates on predestination. In October, discussing the oratorical battles that continued between Bolsec, shut up in the Évêché, and the ministers, the councillors timidly let fall the remark, "The things they talk and dispute about are vast and difficult."[17]

Bolsec remained firm in face of Calvin; to him predestination seemed an absurd doctrine. It made God the author of sin, he concluded, to the great indignation of Calvin, who rejected this consequence of his theory. If in fact God irremediably chooses the good and the wicked, the good cannot be anything but good, and the wicked wicked. From which it would follow "that the direct will of eternal God is the cause of the sins committed by the wicked and of their perdition."[18] This at least in substance was the metaphysical puzzle that Bolsec presented to Calvin. It was titled "Articles Proposed by Jérôme Bolsec to Master John Calvin, so he may answer him categorically and without human arguments or vain similitudes, but simply by the Word of God."[19]

Calvin had the susceptibilities of an author or an offended scholar. Bolsec plainly had not read him, or still worse, had not read him carefully, since he would otherwise know that Calvin had never written that God was the author of sin. A dialogue was impossible between these two stubborn men. "As for me,

16. *OC* 8, col. 145. Extract from the registers of the Venerable Company of Pastors. For the rest of the Bolsec affair, see R. Kingdon and J.-F. Bergier, eds., *Registre de la compagnie des pasteurs de Genève,* 12 vols. (Geneva: Droz, 1964-95), 1:80-131.

17. *OC* 8, col. 176. Extract from Registres du Conseil de Genève, October 27, 1553.

18. *OC* 8, col. 178.

19. "Articles proposés par Jérôme Bolsec à Maître Jean Calvin, afin qu'il lui réponde catégoriquement et sans raisons humaines ne vaines similitudes, mais simplement par la parole de Dieu."

he slanders me falsely," Calvin declared, "saying I have written that God necessitates men to sin." Then, sarcastically, "This word, that God 'necessitates,' is not my language, but the jargon of monks, which I have never used."[20]

Poor Bolsec composed from his prison a defense brief that did not lack spirit. As a physician, he also agreed magnanimously to care for Monsieur Du Falais, who at the approach of the rigors of winter sought the heretic's medical care once again, after having asked the Council's permission. But the preparations for the trial continued; the sister churches of Bern, Basel, and Zürich were consulted and were taken aback by Bolsec's boldness. On December 23 a sentence of banishment was finally pronounced: "You, Jérôme Bolsec, we condemn to be perpetually banished, and we banish you from this our city and its lands, to leave it within twenty-four hours and never to return, on pain of being retaken and whipped through the crossroads of this city in the customary manner. And this to give an example to others who may wish to commit such an act."[21]

The severity of the sentence is understood if we bear in mind that Bolsec was undoubtedly not the only one to contest Calvin's dogmatic authority. Reservations regarding predestination surfaced again in the city. In October 1552 these questions of doctrine came to be discussed even in the taverns, where someone exclaimed that Calvin "makes God the author of sin."[22] In July 1553 a certain Robert Lemoine, a native of Honfleur in Normandy, appeared before the consistory for his very individual ideas. "Jesus Christ did not redeem us from sin, but it was from ourselves and not from hell. And there is no devil in hell." As for "fucking" predestination, to repeat his words, he characterized it bluntly as "heretical." According to him, this dogma implies that God is the author of evil — repeating Bolsec's idea. As for the priority given to Scripture, he judged it equally severely. The "true Scripture," according to our Norman, already a follower of Rousseau without knowing it, is "the heart." The rest is only "paper and ink."[23] Some days later he was reproached for his excesses of language, and in particular for the term "fucking" predestination, held to be particularly improper. Certainly, Lemoine admitted, but he came from "a country where they talk that way."[24] Moreover, according to him, the Calvinist dogma harmed the Protestant Reformation more than it helped it. "Many people from France have come here who have immediately returned when they heard about the said predestination." Lemoine also held advanced ideas about other subjects, although he showed himself ready to retract them. Thus he had only con-

20. *OC* 8, col. 182.
21. *OC* 8, col. 247.
22. *Annales Calviniani, OC* 21, col. 523.
23. *Annales Calviniani, OC* 21, col. 544.
24. *Annales Calviniani, OC* 21, col. 545.

tempt for belief in the devil, mocking his contemporaries who "depict him with horns, and others with a tail." In conclusion, "There is no devil other than man."[25] Or again, he said "that in this world all men should be equal, and the one who has more goods in this world should give to the other who does not have as much." Belief in a primitive and original communism seems to be attested throughout history.[26]

A little later Jean Baudoin was reprimanded for statements no less subversive and mocking. He said the resurrected Jesus Christ was nothing but a vulgar phantom, a lover, appearing to holy women to announce his passion. Did Baudoin believe in only one God? No doubt, but it was in the one who makes "the hay and vines sprout and bloom." As for the Holy Scriptures, he saw in them only "blank paper" on which people wrote what they wanted to.[27]

The ministers themselves joined the fray. In 1555 André Zébédée,[28] pastor of Nyon, and his colleague Jean Lange, from Bursin, preached against Calvin's ideas. The opposition to the Calvinist theses took shape in Bern, under Bolsec's urging. Geneva was disturbed, and Bern was asked to proscribe any polemics on the subject of predestination. The lords of Bern, however, gave only very limited support to the Reformer, whom they suspected of criticizing Zwingli. It was desirable not to write anything more "concerning such high matters as the providence of God, or his secrets, which tend rather to scandal than to edification." Their object was not to enter into the quarrel, but to guarantee the public peace.[29] The city of Bern banished Calvin's opponents, in particular Sébastien Foncellet, the author of an epigram describing Geneva as Sodom and abusing the Reformer. Also Pierreson was imprisoned for three days. In April 1556 Jean Trolliet, a former monk, was accused of having written in Burgundy to condemn predestination. In doing so he had tarnished the reputation of the city. The accused denied all the insinuations completely.[30] Calvin, more and more suspicious, described the misunderstandings that threatened his theology: "Because I affirm and maintain that the world is conducted and governed by a secret providence of God, a gang of ar-

25. *Annales Calviniani, OC* 21, col. 546.

26. On this subject see Christopher Hill, *The World Turned Upside Down: Radical Ideas during the English Revolution* (London: Temple Smith, 1972).

27. *OC* 21, col. 548, Thursday and Friday, August 3-4, 1553.

28. This "red-haired, proud man," a native of Brabant, had been pastor at Orbe. At first fascinated by Calvin, he had turned away from him, transferring his admiration to Zwingli. He had then lost his chair in the College of Lausanne, being transferred to Yverdon as pastor.

29. *OC* 21, col. 601, Registres du Conseil 49, fol. 44v. "They say that it is not the business of the said lords to approve or disapprove the said books of M. Calvin, but they do not want there to be a dispute about them in their country; therefore they forbid it."

30. For Jean Trolliet, see p. 194 above.

rogant people rise up, babbling that by this account God would be the author of sin. This is a frivolous calumny which would have easily vanished by itself if it had not encountered people with sharp ears who take pleasure in sucking in such statements."[31]

Saint Servetus, Heretic and Martyr (1553)

I do not separate Christ from God any more than a voice from the speaker or a ray from the sun. . . . He and the Father are one as the ray and the sun are one light.

Christ walketh upon the wings of the wind and sitteth upon the circle of the earth. He measureth the heavens with a span and the waters of the sea in his hand.

M. SERVETUS[32]

Born about 1511 in Villanueva, 160 miles upriver from Zaragoza, Servetus was Calvin's close contemporary. But the two men had dissimilar destinies, part of which, no doubt, can be attributed to geography. The pseudonym "Villeneuve" which Servetus assumed, derived from Villanueva, sufficiently indicates his Iberian roots. Spain at that time had a large number of *marranos*, Jews who had converted to Christianity without always adopting all its principles. Thus Spaniards were often suspected of not adhering to the Trinity. One God in three distinct persons? This belief was unnecessary, according to Servetus, who deplored the fact that this doctrine divided Christianity from the other monotheisms, Judaism and Islam. Moreover, he denied that this dogma was found in the Bible, Old or New Testament. Was Servetus a Jew? He always denied it. But the evidence suggests that he possessed a knowledge of Judaism that surpassed that of the best Christian scholars.[33] His Judaizing was not just methodological; it also had doctrinal repercussions. For Servetus "one basis of determining the validity of a Christian view was whether or not Jewish sources would have accepted that point of dogma." The "restoration" of authentic Christianity, corrupted since the Council of Nicea in the fourth century, required a constant confrontation

31. J. Calvin, preface to *Commentaire des psaumes* (1557), *OC* 31, col. 32.
32. Michael Servetus, *De trinitatis erroribus* (1531) and *Dialogorum de trinitate libri duo* (1532), cited in Bainton, pp. 49 and 65.
33. Servetus denied being a Jew as such; *OC* 8, col. 767. On this question see the works by Jerome Friedman, "Michael Servetus: The Case for a Jewish Christianity," *Sixteenth Century Journal* 4 (1973) and *Michael Servetus: A Case Study in Total Heresy* (Geneva: Droz, 1978).

with the rabbinical sources that preceded the New Testament.[34] The attempt to found Christianity on Judaism was undoubtedly doomed to defeat. In Servetus the three great monotheistic religions that had colonized the Iberian Peninsula, Judaism, Christianity, and Islam, coexisted. Servetus was above all the representative of a mystical longing and nostalgia for a vanished Spain.

It would be vain to try to lock this man up retrospectively within any orthodoxy; divided between provocation and his internal illumination, his impossible synthesis had a strong emotional and personal tone. This did not prevent him from boldly criticizing Christian dogma. The Trinity? It was a mere sophistry, invented by the Council of Nicea in 325. The two natures of the Savior, defined by the Council of Chalcedon in 451? Servetus accepted the formula, but when he explained himself, his readers tore their hair. It was above all for his ideas about Christ that Servetus was reproached.[35] This Spaniard was completely, abominably heretical; his obstinacy, his nimble mind, and his feeling for a retort never abandoned him. He had an answer for everything, and he bothered and disconcerted people. Calvin, prey to headaches, emerged exhausted from his encounters with him.

In July 1530 Servetus was in Basel, the city where Erasmus had stayed so long. He was received by Oecolampadius, who at last took offense at his ideas; was he not dishonoring "Jesus, the son of God"? In fact, "by denying that the Son is eternal, you necessarily also deny that the Father is eternal. You have submitted a confession of faith that the simple and innocent might approve, but I abominate your subterfuges."[36] In a second letter Oecolampadius summoned

---

34. J. Friedman, *The Most Ancient Testimony: Sixteenth-Century Christian Hebraica in the Age of Renaissance Nostalgia* (Athens: Ohio University Press, 1983), pp. 55-56.

35. Bainton, pp. 47-49: "Divinity and humanity, then, are not mutually exclusive and Jesus could be God without ceasing to be man. His relationship to God, since it was not that of other men, remained to be more precisely defined. For Servetus the Word was eternal, a mode of God's self-expression, ever-latent in the Being of God. The Word became flesh. . . . Before his incarnation He was called the Word. After His union with the man Jesus, He was called the Son. The Word, therefore, was eternal. The Son was not eternal. With regard to the Trinity one may concede, with Tertullian, a Trinity of dispensations or administrations. . . . The Spirit is simply God's spirit moving within our hearts." Now, this thought is more complex than one might think. "Thus far the thought of Servetus seems clear enough. There is one God who manifests himself in diverse ways. His spirit enters into the hearts of men and they are capable of union with him. This was true in a unique measure of Jesus Christ, in whom God's Spirit or Logos or Word was preeminently manifest. But ambiguity enters, in that the term Christ is applied both to the man Jesus, the Son, and also to the pre-existent Logos, the Word. The reason may well be that for Servetus the man Jesus became so identified with the Word that thereafter no distinction could be drawn."

36. Bainton, p. 52.

Servetus, if he still wanted to be considered a Christian, to recognize Jesus as the Son of God, consubstantial with the Father.

Servetus had to leave Basel. No matter — he went to Strasbourg, where there was then great religious liberty. Many Anabaptists were active there, including Schwenckfeld and Melchior Hofmann. Servetus published a pamphlet against the dogma of the Trinity.[37] But Bucer publicly refuted this work, and it was banned, in Strasbourg as well as in Basel. Servetus broke out again the next year in *Dialogues* on the same burning subject.[38] There was a considerable sensation, as much among the Protestants as among the Catholics. Schwenckfeld thought the book "deserved to go to hell"; the mild Melanchthon found it at once "penetrating" and "confused," carrying its conclusions to the point of "fanaticism." As for the Holy Inquisition, it feverishly watched for the return of the prodigal son. Where could he go? All doors closed, one after the other. Miguel recalled, ten years later, his tribulations: "Oh Christ Jesus, Son of God, when I was a young man of hardly twenty, I was driven as by a divine impulsion . . . to embrace this cause. . . . Such was the blindness of the world that I was sought for up and down to be led to my death. . . . With Jonah I longed rather to flee to the sea or to one of the new isles."[39]

What America, however, would permit Servetus, the servant of Jesus, to find repose? Michel de Villeneuve, as he called himself henceforth, went to Paris, then capriciously on to Lyon and Montpellier, without managing to establish himself. He ended by returning to Lyon, working thereafter in the printing house of Melchior and Gaspar Trechsel. He edited an edition of Ptolemy and another of the Bible, issued in 1542. The preface to its third edition emphasized the value of the historical sense of Scripture for raising oneself to the hidden meaning of the text. This argument accompanied a defense of the superiority of the Hebrew.

Besides medicine and the pharmacopoeia, Servetus also cultivated geography and astrology. Insatiably curious about everything, he studied the origin of syphilis, the digestion of food, and the pulmonary circulation of the blood.

---

37. *De trinitatis erroribus* (1531).

38. *Dialogorum de trinitate libri duo* (1532). Bainton explains: "Whereas before Servetus had made Christ the Son of God, not by nature, but by grace, now to grace he would add nature, because to the Son *naturally* belongs the glory of the Father. He would admit two natures in Christ provided nature be understood to mean a *natural* property. Previously he had been unwilling to call the Holy Spirit a person. He would do so now in the sense that the Spirit after the departure of Christ became *personalized* by dwelling in us, though properly speaking there is no person in the Spirit. He had distinguished the incarnate Son from the pre-existent Word. Now he was prepared to say that the Word is Christ" (pp. 62-64).

39. Bainton, pp. 73-74.

After 1540 he settled in Vienne, in Dauphiné. He remained there a dozen years; editorial labors alternated with the practice of medicine. He wrote two works, a book about Christ that remained in manuscript,[40] and especially *The Restoration of Christianity*, which was striking in its audacity. Published belatedly in 1553, *Christianismi restitutio* was the cause of the tragic death of its author. Neoplatonist influence is evident in his definition of a God immanent in the world, bordering on pantheism. "God in wood is wood, in a stone he is stone."[41] The metaphysics of light influences the conception of Christ: "There is one brightness of the sun and another of the moon, another of fire, and still another splendor of water. All these were disposed in light by Christ, the architect of the world, who is the first principle in whom all things consist, celestial and terrestrial, corporeal and spiritual." Indeed, in the same poetic vein: "Christ fills all things. On account of him God made the world and by him the world is filled. He descends to the lowest depths and ascends to the loftiest heights and fills all things. He walks upon the wings of the wind, rides upon the air, and inhabits the place of angels. He sits upon the circle of the earth and measures the heavens with his span and the waters in the hollow of his hand."[42]

In Servetus's christology the Word that existed before the world is not strictly confounded with the Son. It was a form that was not fulfilled except by the incarnation. Moreover, he favored adult baptism, following the example of Jesus, baptized in his thirtieth year. Servetus rejected the preexistence of the Word except in an ideal fashion. The Word could only have been an idea; otherwise this would imply not one Son of God, but two. Calvin's later testimony clarifies this point. The heretic told the Reformer, "If something was really begotten, it was an incorporeal Son. Now by this not only is God torn in pieces, but two Sons are made, one corporeal and the other incorporeal."[43]

A strange mixture of fascination and repulsion haunted the relations between these two men. Many long years passed before the battle to the death began which ended in Servetus's burning. This historical encounter began, naturally, with an uncompleted action: according to Beza, Servetus and Calvin were supposed to meet in Paris in 1534, but Servetus was not there, having been prevented at the last minute.[44] Twelve years later, in 1546, the two men were again brought into contact by a Huguenot editor in Lyon, Jean Frellon.[45] Immediately a rather silly authors' quarrel began, accompanied by a theological debate. With an assurance close to impudence, Servetus immediately began giving Calvin

40. *Declarationis Jesu Christi filii Dei libri V.*
41. Bainton, p. 133.
42. Bainton, p. 136.
43. *OC* 8, col. 485.
44. *OC* 21, Theodore Beza, *Joanis Calvini vita* (1575), col. 123.
45. *OC* 8, cols. 834-35.

lessons in christology and the baptism of the newly born.[46] Calvin answered, but Servetus referred him to the manuscript of his *Restitutio*. Calvin, in turn, urged Servetus to read carefully and meditate on his own *Institutes*. Servetus complied and returned his copy of this work to Calvin, covered in the margin with his own critical annotations.

Calvin could not permit the *Institutes*, the work of his life, to be debated. He preferred, charitably, not to respond to this amateur theologian. Servetus persisted, but Calvin refused to continue corresponding with this bore, who sent him no less than thirty letters. Impassive, Calvin remained mute, and did not even deign to return the Latin manuscript of the *Restitutio* to the Spaniard. This apparent tranquillity was crossed by flashes of lightning, heralds of the storm to come. On February 13, 1547, Calvin allowed his anger to show in two letters, one to Jean Frellon, the other to Farel. He wrote to the former:

> Since my return, in the first leisure I have had, I have wished to satisfy your desire [for him to write to Servetus]; not that I have much hope of profiting by such a man as I see him disposed to be, but in order to try again to find some means of reducing him to sense, which will be only when God has so worked in him that he becomes entirely different. For he has written to me in such an arrogant spirit that I have indeed wanted to abate his pride a little, speaking to him more sharply than is my custom; but I have not been able to do otherwise with him. For I assure you that there is no lesson more necessary to him than to learn humility, which will come to him from the spirit of God, not otherwise. But we should also try our hands. If God gives such grace to him and to us that the present answer profits him, I will have reason to rejoice. If he continues in such a style as he does now you will lose your time in further soliciting me to labor with him, because I have other business that presses me more closely. And I would make it a matter of conscience to occupy myself with it any more, not doubting that this is a Satan sent to distract me from other more useful reading.[47]

In the second letter, written this same February 13, 1547, Calvin predicted to Guillaume Farel: "Servetus recently sent me with his letters a new volume of his ravings. . . . He would come here if I agreed. But I will not give him my word; for if he came, as far as my authority goes, I would not let him leave alive."[48]

---

46. *OC* 8, col. 482.

47. J. Calvin, *Lettres françaises*, ed. J. Bonnet, 2 vols. (Paris: Meyrueis, 1854), 1:140-41. The date of 1546 given for these letters is old style. The modern date is 1547.

48. *OC* 12, col. 767: "Servetus nuper ad me scripsit, ac literis adjunxit longum volumen suorum deliriorum. . . . Si mihi placeat, huc se venturum recipit. Sed nol fidem

Calvin manifestly did not accept Servetus the heretic. He did not denounce him to the Catholics, however — at least not yet. The correspondence between the two men now ceased. Servetus sank into apocalypticism, awaiting the end of the world. The Four Horsemen of the Apocalypse had already appeared: the papacy, the cardinals, the Dominicans, and the other mendicant orders. Michael Servetus saw himself as a squire to Saint Michael. He calculated the end of the world: 1,260 years[49] should pass between the accession of Constantine in 305 or the Council of Nicea in 325 and the end of time. These calculations gave two probable dates, 1565 and 1585. Servetus addressed himself spitefully to a colleague of Calvin's in Geneva, Abel Poupin, predicting his own approaching death and the end of time:

> Woe, woe, woe! This is the third letter I have written to warn you that you may know better. I will not do it again. It may shock you that I meddle in this battle of Michael's and that I want to involve you in it. Study this passage carefully, and you will see that they are men who will fight there, offering their souls to death in blood and for a testimony to Jesus Christ. Before the battle the world will be seduced. Then the battle will come, and the time will be near. . . .
>
> I know that I shall certainly find death on this account, but I do not lose the hope of being a disciple like the Master.[50]

The Burning of Servetus

Come, Lord Jesus.

REVELATION 22:20

Goodbye, and do not hope for more news of me. . . . I will see what He will say, for He will come, He will certainly come. He will not tarry any more.

MICHAEL SERVETUS[51]

The struggle between Calvin and Servetus was an authentic defiance of the strong by the weak. Calvin bearded Servetus by refusing to return him the

---

meam interponere, nam si venerit, modo valeat mea authoritas, vivum exire non patiar." The original is found in the Bibliothèque Nationale, Mss Dupuy 102, fol. 3.

49. The period of 1,260 years corresponded to the 1,260 days spent by the Woman in the desert in Revelation. See Bainton, pp. 146-47, for full details.

50. *OC* 8, col. 751, letter from Servetus to Abel Poupin.

51. *OC* 8, col. 751.

manuscript of his book; Servetus persisted in provoking Calvin. He considered himself a David confronting the Genevan Goliath; the future of the Reformation seemed to depend on the outcome of this single combat. At least, for this fevered reader of Revelation, every battle for the faith was cosmic and titanic. Calvin, for his part, played Cassandra. Emerging from his reserve, he called Christianity, threatened by its internal enemies, to witness. In 1550 he expressed publicly in his treatise *On Scandals* the repulsion Servetus inspired in him.

> There is a certain Spaniard named Michael Servetus who pretends to be a doctor, calling himself Villeneuve. This poor braggart, already inflated with the arrogance of Portugal, but bursting even more with his own pride, thought he could acquire great fame by overthrowing all the principles of Christianity. Thus everything we have from Scripture concerning the three persons who are in the one essence of God, and which has been held without contradiction since the times of the apostles, to him is nothing but a fable; and he is not content with this, but acts like a madman in crying out and storming against it. In the book he wrote he shows himself such a mad dog, barking and biting, without sense or reason, that it can be clearly seen what spirit drives him. When it comes to substance it can be seen even better that he is a man hungry for glory, who drinks in all the dreams he can find to get drunk on. He imagines that the eternal Word of God did not exist before the creation of the world because Moses says that God began to speak at that time, as though the Word had not existed before its effect and virtue were felt. But on the contrary, it was a rather strong demonstration of its eternal existence when the world was created by it. He makes the flesh of Jesus Christ so divine that he abolishes its human nature. Again, he makes the divinity of Jesus Christ entirely corporeal. However, he does not leave off openly calling Jesus Christ "God"; but to him this is only a phantom. Also he holds he was not the Son of God for any reason except because he was conceived by the Holy Spirit in the womb of the Virgin Mary. Meanwhile he assembles I do not know what speculations so clumsy and unsupported that there is no one of sound understanding who would not judge that there has never been a man who drivelled like this unless he was bewitched by foolish self-love.[52]

Servetus, having now become for Calvin the public enemy of Christendom, called a "dog"[53] and accused of all vices and guilty of all blasphemies, was

---

52. J. Calvin, *Des scandales,* ed. O. Fatio (Geneva: Droz, 1984), pp. 148-52.
53. The comparison between "blasphemers" and dogs seems to have been standard. It is also found in Calvin's sermons, where Servetus is again called an "accursed

not unaware of the monstrous hypocrisy of the churches. He did not fail to expose it. "Your Gospel is without God, without real faith, without good works. In place of God you have a Cerberus with three heads. For faith you have a fatalistic dream, and according to you good works are vain images."[54]

Far from being a happy bachelor — are bachelors ever happy? — he led an irreproachable life, an accident in his youth having freed him finally from those urgings of the flesh that men are subject to. Not the least lewdness, no fornication, no double life, no mistresses in his closet, Servetus offered nothing, absolutely nothing, for his opponents to lay hold of — he was totally irreproachable. In the midst of so many Christians who believed or thought they believed, his faith was indisputable, his motives were pure; he was, in short, a holy man who was mistaken in his beliefs. A heretic irritates all the more if he is virtuous. In this world of false pretenses and accommodations, denounced, moreover, by Calvin, Servetus offered the spectacle of his resolution. Where did he get his great confidence? No doubt from his faith, from his belief in his mission. Was that indeed all? Servetus was alone, certainly, but he received assistance. In the first place he enjoyed the support of his editors, Balthasar Arnoullet and Guillaume Guéroult, both Protestants, but both tired of Calvin. Guéroult, in particular, had had to leave Geneva because of a sexual peccadillo — youth must be served. Written in Vienne, the *Christianismi restitutio* came out in Lyon on January 3, 1553. Minds grew heated; the book even spread to Geneva. People were astonished that the French censors had let such a book get by, while five Bernese students were condemned to the stake in Lyon. Were there two standards in the kingdom of France? Would the publication of "heresy" be accepted when it injured Calvin, but forbidden when it did not serve such Machiavellian purposes? Moreover, by its very title, did not the *Restitutio* constitute a "criticism and antithesis" of Calvin's *Institutio?*[55]

It is at this point that one of the blackest episodes in the story occurred, the participation of the Calvinists in the prosecution of Servetus by the Catholic Church. How should this unnatural alliance be interpreted? No doubt it was a reflex of established churches against an outsider. This solidarity between rival churches unambiguously marks Calvin's intention of enjoying institutional recognition henceforward. To become fully acceptable among Christians, it was desirable for him in his turn to identify a heretic, a heresy, a blasphemer, an apostate. Bullinger saw at once the benefit that the whole of Protestantism could derive from the condemnation of Servetus. "God has given you an op-

---

dog." R. Stauffer, *Creator et rector mundi. Dieu, la création et la providence dans l'oeuvre homilétique de Calvin,* 2 vols. in 1 (Lille: Atelier de reproduction des thèses, 1978), 2:229.

54. *OC* 8, cols. 750-51.

55. A. Frank, *Vie de J. Calvin par T. de Bèze* (Paris: Cherbulliez, 1864), p. xxiii.

portunity to wash us all clean from the suspicion of being heretics or favoring heresy if you show yourselves vigilant and ready to prevent this poison from spreading further."[56] From this standpoint the burning of Servetus simply marks the respectability of the Genevan church and its entrance into the communion of saints. Reformed "Catholicism" had no need to envy the Roman Church in this matter.[57] As P. Imbart de la Tour justly wrote, "What Calvin sought to restore to the bosom of Protestantism, and in part against its will, were the Catholic ideas of universality and authority."[58] Calvin, fully at ease in this role, gave himself the airs of a Saint Augustine. He briefly referred to the bishop of Hippo: "As Saint Augustine said, it is the cause and not the suffering that makes the martyr."[59] To these institutional reasons it is proper to add personal motivations; by the condemnation of Servetus Calvin furnished a proof of his trinitarian orthodoxy. He divorced himself from the Arianism of which Caroli in particular had accused him more than fifteen years before (see chap. 6).[60] By his "intransigence against Servetus" Calvin therefore was trying to clear himself of the accusations that had hung over his own orthodoxy.[61]

A good heretic is a dead heretic. Calvin's conduct can also be explained, more prosaically, by his fear of a popish plot aimed at destabilizing his position in Geneva. Thus Servetus was treated by both sides as a sort of double agent that neither camp recognized as one of its own. Guillaume de Trie, a friend of Calvin's, wrote his Catholic cousin Antoine Arneys, living in Lyon, a letter that leaves no doubt about this (February 1553). The Reformers were at least as strict, said this inhabitant of Geneva in substance, as the Catholics. They did not endure heresy either, and they therefore behaved as good Christians when torturing heretics was in question. Yes, Servetus must be burned: "I am astonished that you dare to reproach me, among other things, that we have no ecclesiastical discipline or order. . . . And nevertheless I see, thanks to God, that vices are better corrected here than they are in all your officialities. . . . And I can give

56. *OC* 8, col. 558.

57. For the forms of "coexistence" between the rival confessions, see Thierry Wanegffelen, "Les chrétiens face aux Églises dans l'Europe moderne," *Nouvelle Revue du Seizième Siècle* 11 (1993): 37-53, and also his "La reconnaissance mutuelle du baptême entre confessions catholique et réformée au xvie siècle," *Études Théologiques et Religieuses* 69 (1994): 185-201.

58. P. Imbart de la Tour, *Les origines de la Réforme*, 4 vols. (Paris: Hachette, 1905-35), 4:53.

59. *OC* 8, col. 466: "Martyrem facit causa, non poena."

60. Calvin's sensitivity to this sort of accusation, even in 1545, has recently been demonstrated by F. Gounelle, who attributes to the Reformer a defense that appeared in 1545 under the name of Des Gallars, *Défense de Guillaume Farel*.

61. R. Stauffer, "Un Calvin méconnu: le prédicateur de Genève," *Bulletin de la Société de l'Histoire du Protestantisme Français* 123 (1977): 201.

you an example that is greatly to your confusion . . . ; it is that a heretic is supported there who well deserves to be burned wherever he may be."

"Here" referred to Geneva and "there" to Catholic territories. One might say, contradicting Montaigne, "Error here, and also error there." Heresy here remains heresy there; error in Geneva should also be chastised unremittingly in Lyon or Vienne. There was an admirable unanimity among the established churches with regard to defending the fundamental dogmas of Christianity, and among these the Trinity, that God in three persons, equal and distinct, in which Servetus, the mocker, saw a Cerberus, the demonic dog with three heads that guarded Hades:

> When I speak to you of a heretic, I mean a man who would be condemned by the papists as well as by us, or at least who ought to be.
>
> (1) Because, although we differ in many things, yet we have this in common, that in one essence of God there are three persons, and that the Father has begotten the Son, who is his eternal wisdom before all time, and that he has had his eternal power, which is his Holy Spirit.
>
> (2) Now when a man says that the Trinity, which we maintain, is a Cerberus and monster of hell, and vomits all the villainies it is possible to imagine against all that the Scriptures teach us about the eternal generation of the Father and of the Son, and laughs aloud at all that the ancient doctors said, I ask you, in what place and estimation will you hold him? . . .
>
> (3) Behold him who calls Jesus Christ an idol, who would destroy all the foundations of the faith, who collects all the dreams of the ancient heretics, who even condemns infant baptism. . . . The man of whom I tell you has been condemned in all the churches you reprove. However, he is suffered among you, even to the point of having his books printed, which are so full of blasphemies that I need say no more.

I have reconstructed the syllogism of the argument, with its implacable order. Major premise: all Christians adhere to the Trinity. Minor premise: now Servetus blasphemes against this belief. Conclusion: he therefore has no rights of citizenship. Socrates is a man, and therefore mortal; Servetus is a heretic, and therefore combustible. *QED.* The argument is accompanied by this terrible sentence: "One should not be content with simply killing such people, but should burn them cruelly."[62]

In March, Maugiron, lieutenant general of Dauphiné, opened an inquiry at the request of Cardinal De Tournon. Servetus, alias Michel de Villeneuve, appeared; his house was gone over with a fine-tooth comb, as well as the presses

---

62. Letter of February 26, 1533, now lost, cited by Bainton, pp. 152-53.

where the *Christianismi restitutio* must have been printed. But nothing was found — not the least evidence of guilt. What was more, the archbishop of Vienne, Pierre Palmier, vouched for Servetus.

Guillaume de Trie in Geneva was sought out again. He answered that it was necessary "to purge Christendom of such filth, indeed such deadly plagues." The term "Christendom" is illuminating: it postulates the existence of a common ground, beyond the rival confessions. De Trie, however, had to conquer Calvin's reluctance, as he explained in the same letter. "I have had great difficulty in obtaining what I send you from Monsieur Calvin." In fact, "It seems to him that his duty is to convict heresies by doctrine rather than pursue them by such a means, since he does not hold the sword of justice."[63]

Thus the proofs against Servetus were gathered in Geneva, in Calvin's very entourage. The latter, however, denied to the end having delivered up Servetus "as one throws a man to savage beasts."[64] At the beginning of April the Catholics were in possession of the compromising material that they had asked for, including part of the correspondence addressed to Calvin by Servetus. In the evening of April 5 Servetus's interrogation began before Matthieu Ory, Inquisitor General of the Faith in the kingdom of France. Michel Villeneuve, doctor of medicine, shamelessly denied being the said Servetus.

But Servetus contrived to escape over the rooftops on April 7. He was condemned *in absentia* on June 17. The sentence was executed by burning him in effigy along with five bales of blank paper, used to represent his works. Servetus's escape, however, was from Scylla into Charybdis; he passed through Geneva, where he was arrested on August 13 of the same year.

How are we to understand Servetus's appearance in Geneva? Our whole interpretation of Calvin's attitude depends on this preliminary question. For him, no doubt, Servetus's presence was hardly fortuitous; it was part of a gigantic conspiracy, at a moment when Calvin himself confronted the opposition of Berthelier and his partisans. This was the view that the pastor Musculus maintained when he gave Bullinger his version of the affair. "Servetus recently came to Geneva to take advantage of the rancor felt toward Calvin by the government."[65]

Servetus's interrogation brought the heretic and the Reformer into collision. Calvin reproached Servetus for his pantheistic positions, according to which "all" creatures are of the "same substance" as God. How absurd! ex-

63. Bainton, p. 156.
64. *OC* 8, col. 479.
65. *OC* 14, col. 628, September 28, 1553. Wolfgang Musculus (1497-1563) was a Reformer from Lorraine who ended his life in Bern after having fled Augsburg in the wake of the Interim.

claimed Calvin, who continued, with rather flat common sense, "What, wretch! Then every time one steps on the floor, must it also be said that he steps on his God?" The discussion turned to the devil: Is he also God in his substance? Certainly, retorted Servetus, "all things are a part and portion of God, and the nature of things is substantially the spirit of God."[66]

Servetus, still imprisoned, sent a moving petition to the Council (September 15). He complained of Calvin, "For his own pleasure [he] wants to make me rot here in prison."[67] Servetus also described his own unenviable state. "The lice eat me alive, my hose are torn and I have nothing to change into, neither doublet, nor any shirt but a wretched one." Touched, the Genevans promised to furnish him with new clothes — which were late in coming. The prisoner took heart; the best defense is attack. Servetus attacked Calvin and demanded his condemnation. He accused the Reformer of simony, the crime of using spiritual powers for temporal ends. He also said with an air that he would be content if in restitution he was given the goods of the said Calvin.[68]

Servetus advanced toward his destiny. His cause took on an exemplary aspect, as Zürich, Bern, Basel, and Schaffhausen were asked to pronounce on it. Advice was asked of the ministers and magistrates in particular, and there seems to have been a unanimous judgment against Servetus, with some rare exceptions. The pastor Vergerio admitted his fears; heretics should not be handled "with fire and sword."[69] And a former Dutch Anabaptist, David Joris, was indignant that the teaching of Christ, "Judge not that ye be not judged,"[70] was still ignored. But Calvin seems hardly to have shared this minority point of view. The Reformer regretted only the cruelty of the punishment reserved for Servetus. "He has been condemned unanimously. Tomorrow he will be led to the stake. We have tried to change the manner of his death, but without result."[71]

Calvin also went to see the condemned man. With touching care he has left us the account of his interview. Poor Servetus was indeed a hardened sinner whom Calvin's exhortations could not convince. His duty done, Calvin could return with the vast serenity of conscience that the spectacle of the vicissitudes of fortune has always provided to men of faith:

> I simply protested . . . that I had never pursued any personal grudge against him. . . . I reminded him gently how I spared no effort more than sixteen

66. *OC* 8, col. 496.
67. *OC* 8, col. 797.
68. *OC* 8, col. 806.
69. *OC* 8, col. 633, October 3, 1553.
70. Matt. 7:1. Bainton, pp. 206-7.
71. *OC* 14, col. 657.

years ago to win him to Our Lord, even to the point of hazarding my own life. . . .

Then afterwards, saying that I put aside everything that concerned me personally, I prayed him rather to think of begging mercy of God, whom he had so villainously blasphemed, wanting to efface the three persons who are in his essence and saying that those who recognize in one God the Father, the Son, and the Holy Spirit with a real distinction invent a three-headed hound of hell. I prayed him to devote his efforts to asking pardon of the Son of God, whom he had disfigured with his fantasies, denying that he had worn our flesh and that he was like us in his human nature, and whom by this means he had renounced as his Savior. Seeing that I gained nothing by exhortations, I did not want to be wiser than my master permitted me to be. Therefore, following the rule of Saint Paul, I withdrew from a self-condemned heretic who carried his mark and brand on his heart.[72]

Farel, not Calvin, attended Servetus during his last moments, on Friday, October 27, 1553.[73] But he did not obtain any complete confession of his errors from him. Servetus died, burned alive, on the plain of Champel at the gate of Geneva. He passed away after committing a terrible error in syntax; he cried out, "Oh Jesus, son of eternal God, have pity on me!" in place of saying, as was proper, "Oh Jesus, eternal son of God."[74] His punishment was due to the misplacing of a single adjective. Heresy is never anything but a question of grammar.

Castellio

[Castellio] advises everyone to believe whatever he wants, opening the door by this means to all heresies and false doctrines.

THEODORE BEZA[75]

What distinguishes a saint from a martyr in popular opinion? Did not the determination to make Servetus a heretic contribute, on the contrary, to plaiting him a crown? The remembrance of Servetus persisted in Geneva in the years that followed his death at Champel. In 1556 Matthieu Antoine was banished from the

---

72. *OC* 8, col. 826.

73. *OC* 14, cols. 692-95, letter from Farel to Blaarer, December 10, 1553, containing the account of the event.

74. The observation is from T. Beza, *De haereticis a civili magistratu puniendis libellus* (Geneva: O. R. Stephani, 1554), p. 100.

75. Beza, *L'histoire de la vie et mort de Calvin*, p. 27.

city for his words favorable to Servetus; two years later a gatekeeper named Jean Jacquemet mentioned the scandal that was still attached to his tragic end. Again, in 1559 Catherine Cop maintained that Servetus was a "martyr of Jesus." To fight against this influence, it was Calvin's task to deliver Servetus's funeral sermon in the face of posterity, and Theodore Beza's to draw the moral of his history. The former returned again to Servetus's "errors" in the last edition of the *Institutes* (1559-60), reaffirming the existence of the Word before the incarnation.[76] As for Beza, he would barely admit the humanity of Servetus, "that Spaniard of accursed memory," "not a man but rather a horrible monster, compounded of all heresies ancient and modern, and above all an execrable blasphemer against the Trinity, and especially against the eternity of the Son of God."[77]

The accusation of Servetus as a "blasphemer" took on increased importance posthumously. Indeed, it was not so much the heretic as the blasphemer who was put to death. What was a blasphemer in the case of Servetus? A scandalous heretic, injuring by his words the church and the state, which he risked destabilizing by disturbing the fundamental articles of the Christian faith. This feeling of a looming deadline explains Calvin's haste in writing his defense of the Trinity against the errors of Michael Servetus. The work came out at the beginning of 1554. It maintained "that it is lawful to punish heretics and that this wicked man [Servetus] was rightly executed by the law in the city of Geneva."[78]

76. "In our own time there has arisen a monster who is no less pernicious than the ancient heretics, namely Michael Servetus. . . . He denies that Jesus Christ was otherwise or for any other reason the Son of God except because he was engendered in the womb of the Virgin by the Holy Spirit. Now his cleverness aims at this, that by overturning the distinction between the two natures, Jesus Christ would be as it were a mixture composed of one portion of God and one portion of man, and nevertheless would not be reputed either God or man. For the result of these discourses is that, before Jesus Christ was manifest in the flesh, there were in God only shadows and figures, the truth and effect of which did not truly commence until the Word began to be the Son of God, according to the honor it was predestined to. . . . However . . . , the doctrine of the church remains firm; it is that he should be recognized as the Son of God because existing before all time, the Word begotten of the Father, he took our nature, uniting it with his divinity. The ancients called this hypostatic union, meaning by this that the two natures were combined in one person." *Institution de la religion chrétienne* (1560), II, chap. 14, §5, *OC* 3, cols. 551-52.

77. Beza, *L'histoire de la vie et mort de Calvin*, p. 23. Beza continues, "Having come to this city and been seized by the magistrates because of his blasphemies, he was so vigorously opposed that, for his whole defense, nothing remained to him but an indomitable obstinacy, by reason of which, by the just judgment of God and men, he ended in death by fire his miserable life and his blasphemies, which he had vomited from his mouth and in writing for the space of more than thirty years."

78. *Defensio orthodoxae fidei de sacra trinitate* . . . (Geneva, 1554); *Déclaration pour maintenir la vraye foy que tiennent tous Chrétiens de la Trinité des personnes en un seul Dieu. . . . Contre les erreurs de Michel Servet Espagnol* (Geneva: J. Crespin, February 1554).

One of the first to react was a Bernese magistrate, Chancellor Nicholas Zurkinden, who wrote to Calvin on February 10. Accustomed to human problems, the Bernese recalled with sound judicial sense the execution of a woman of eighty and her daughter merely for having rejected infant baptism. No, henceforth magistrates should not investigate consciences; they must be content with punishing reprehensible acts. But "the use of the sword" is hardly necessary in matters of faith.[79] Was this an isolated reaction? Nothing is less certain, for even among "his closest friends, his most zealous disciples, one would search in vain for frank and unreserved approbation."[80] Calvin wrote to Bullinger, "You at least, even in your criticisms, judge me with equity. Others attack me savagely, reproaching me with professing cruelty, with pursuing with my pen a man who died by my hand."[81]

One person was found to take up the challenge publicly. Sebastian Castellio, a former close friend of Calvin's in Geneva finally settled in Basel, whence he fired twin missiles in Latin and in French. Some weeks later *De haereticis* became a *Treatise on Heretics, that is whether they should be persecuted and how one should behave toward them, according to the advice, opinions, and judgments of various authors, both ancient and modern* (1554).[82] Calvin at once guessed where these shots came from: this Martinus Bellius, the signer of the work, could be no other than Sebastian Castellio.[83] The play on words is illuminating: Bellius comes from the Latin *bellum*, "war." The book opened a battle, taking up the challenge of the death of Servetus.

But before describing this important work, we must present its author. Who was this Castellio whose biting tone Calvin recognized immediately? Theodore Beza long afterward put him in company with those other monsters, Servetus and Bolsec. He summed up in a few words an existence rich in reversals:

> A man named Sebastian Castellio, who because he had some acquaintance with languages and also some dexterity in Latin was received here to conduct the school [the College of Geneva]. But his spirit being naturally inclined to be pleased with itself, he plunged so far into vanity that at last he drowned in it, because no one was ever able to win him over to taking the pains to read the *Commentaries* [of Calvin] and other writings to resolve his doubts. This

---

79. *OC* 15, cols. 19-22, letter from N. Zurkinden to Calvin, February 10, 1554.

80. F. Buisson, *Sébastien Castellion. Sa vie et son oeuvre (1515-1563)* (Paris: Hachette, 1892, 1:354.

81. *OC* 15, col. 124, to Bullinger, February 27, 1554.

82. *Traité des hérétiques, à savoir si on les doit persécuter, et comme on se doit conduire avec eux, selon l'avis, opinion et sentence de plusieurs auteurs tant anciens que modernes.*

83. *OC* 15, col. 96, to Bullinger, March 28, 1554.

was the cause why at one bound he condemned the Song of Songs as a filthy and unchaste book; and on being remonstrated with for this he publicly vomited a thousand insults against the pastors of this church. On which being commanded by the magistrates to justify his words, and being convicted of manifest malice and calumny, the judge ordered him to depart after acknowledging his fault. Having finally withdrawn to Basel, he lived there until, the trouble with Jérôme Bolsec about predestination having arisen, this man, who had always maintained the perfection of the Anabaptists, but secretly and with his friends, and moreover finding no difficulty in accommodating himself to anyone, and also being greatly irritated by the death of Servetus, revealed himself openly, first in a book he had printed in Latin and French under the false name of Martin Bellie, the errors and blasphemies of which I have answered. He added another treatise that he called in Latin *Theologia Germanica* under the name of Theophilus, and in French *Treatise on the Old and New Man*.[84] Finally, he turned, or rather overturned, the whole Bible from Latin into French with such villainous impudence and ignorance that it would be a marvel if men could be found who would be pleased with it, were it not that novelty is always agreeable to all ambitious spirits, for which today it is a better season than ever before. At the beginning of his translation he put a letter addressed to the late good King Edward of England, in which under a pretense of preaching charity he overthrew the authority of Scripture as obscure and imperfect, throwing us back on particular revelations, that is on the fantasies of the first dreamer who wishes to show himself. He made certain annotations on the ninth chapter of the Epistle to the Romans in which he manifestly established Pelagianism; and he recognized no decrees of God except concerning things that are good by nature, forging in God a permission contrary to his will, and falsely charging that we make God the author of sin.[85]

Sébastien Chatillon or Castellion (Castellio in the better-known Latin form of the name; 1515?–1563) was some years younger than Calvin. Born at Saint-Martin-du-Fresne, southwest of Nantua in Bresse, he studied at the Collège de la Trinité in Lyon. Around age twenty he indefatigably composed poems in Latin and Greek while walking along the banks of the Saône River. Apparently Castellio was "converted" about 1540, but the date remains unknown. He then went to Strasbourg, where the spirit of young Calvin, author of the *Institutes*, was blazing. He was immediately lodged with the Reformer (May 1540). After Calvin's return to Geneva, Castellio took over the job of principal

84. *Traité du vieil et nouvel homme.*
85. Beza, *L'histoire de la vie et mort de Calvin*, p. 26.

of the college in place of Maturin Cordier, who was retained in Neuchâtel and then in Lausanne. He was the author of bilingual *Sacred Dialogues* in Latin and French which combined classical learning with religious education. But the young master found his salary insufficient; he married without receiving the promised dowry, and undertook a translation of the New Testament, provoking Calvin's irritation.[86] In January 1544 Calvin removed Castellio from the direction of the school.[87] Partly for financial reasons, Castellio refused to continue his career in Geneva. But doctrinal doubts also explain why he was kept from the ministry: he admitted reservations about the Song of Songs, "a lascivious and obscene poem in which Solomon described his unchaste loves." Calvin signed a letter of discharge in the name of the ministers of Geneva in which he explained that no moral irregularity or impiety "concerning any capital point of the faith" could be imputed to Castellio.[88] But one detects the growth, behind this gentlemen's agreement, of a personal conflict between Castellio and Calvin. Calvin revealed his views to Pierre Viret. "I know well that he has it in his head that I have the desire to rule. Is it wrongly or rightly that he has this opinion of me? The Lord must judge."[89]

Sebastian Castellio, moreover, continued to behave as an *enfant terrible*.

86. *OC* 11, col. 439, to Viret, September 3, 1542. "Now hear the fantasies of our Sebastian [Castellio]; they will make you laugh and anger you. Three days ago he came to me. He asked me whether I would see any objection to his publishing his translation of the New Testament. I answered that it needed numerous corrections. He asked me to be more specific. I complied, using some chapters that he had previously communicated to me. He answered that he had worked with more care afterwards, and asked me again what I had decided. I answered that I did not want to prevent the printing, but that nevertheless I was disposed to keep my word to Jean Girard [the Geneva editor] by revising and correcting everything that required it. He rejected this condition, but offered to come read me his manuscript, if I would consent to name a time. I told him that I would never, even if he offered me a hundred crowns, agree to be held to meetings at a fixed time, only to haggle sometimes for two hours together over a single word.

"At this he took his leave, visibly hurt. And yet, judge for yourself the fidelity of his translation. Most of the time he errs through a desire to distinguish himself. Thus, to give you only one example, where it is simply written, 'the spirit of God who lives [*habite*] in us,' he adds, 'who haunts [*hante*] us.' Now '*hanter*' does not mean 'to inhabit' in French, but rather 'to frequent.' This schoolboy blunder would suffice by itself to discredit the rest of the work. Behold, however, the nonsense that I have to endure in silence."

87. *OC* 11, col. 673, to P. Viret, February 11, 1544. "Sebastian left for Lausanne with letters from us. I wish indeed that he knew better how to provide for his interests, or that we had some means of providing for him without detriment to the church! We would have left him his previous position intact; he did not want to keep to it without an increase of salary, and this increase could not be obtained from the Council."

88. *OC* 11, cols. 673-74, for the rest of this text.

89. *OC* 11, col. 691, letter of March 26, 1544.

He seized on a passage in the Second Epistle to the Corinthians — to wit: "Giving no offence in any thing, that the ministry be not blamed: but in all things approving ourselves as the ministers of God, in much patience . . ." (6:3-4) — to express aloud the criticisms he addressed to the pastors of Geneva. On which Castellio concluded, "Paul was a servant of God, we serve only ourselves; he was very patient, we are very impatient. He passed his nights consecrating himself to the building of the church, we pass the night in gambling; he was sober, we are drunk; he was threatened by seditions, and we raise them; he was chaste, we are debauched; he was shut up in prison, and we shut anyone up there who wounds us with a word. He used the power of God, we that of others. He suffered for the sake of others, we persecute the innocent."[90]

Calvin did not accept these outbursts and lodged a complaint against Sebastian before the Geneva civil authorities. Castellio, who had just been denied entry to the ministry, henceforth lost the right to preach. If he was not expelled from Geneva — as was long claimed on the authority of Theodore Beza[91] — he chose to leave the city. He was only twenty-nine.

He directed his steps to Basel. There he worked as a proofreader in the house of Oporin. He also encountered Thomas Platter, the famous publisher, and above all Francisco de Enzinas, better known under the name of Dryander, who, like him, had undertaken a translation of the Bible.[92] He was also connected with the great jurist Bonifacius Amerbach. About 1553, after a long sojourn in the desert, he was named Greek lecturer at the university.

Author of poems in Latin and Greek, Castellio also translated part of the Pentateuch under the title *Moses latinus* (1546), as well as the Psalms: *Psalterium* (1547). In treating Moses he entered on one of the great debates of the time: Was the law of Moses abrogated by that of Christ? He gave a negative answer, while distinguishing the "perfect laws" proclaimed by Moses from rites and precepts that had only a provisional value for a particular people or time.

In February 1551 he dedicated his Latin translation of the Bible to Edward VI, the young king of England. His attempt gave the distinction between the letter and the spirit a methodological significance; a good translation should respect the spirit even more than the letter of Scripture. This led him,

90. *OC* 11, cols. 719-22, for the rest of this long letter from Calvin to Farel on May 31, 1544. This scene took place at an "informal explanation" of Scripture, or "congregation," a sort of Bible reading, which was held on Friday, May 30, 1544.

91. Buisson established the facts, *Sébastien Castellion*, 1:214ff.

92. For T. Platter see E. Le Roy Ladurie, *Le siècle des Platter, 1499-1628* (Paris: Fayard); three volumes planned. Dryander had been thrown into prison in 1543 after submitting his project for a translation of the New Testament to Charles V. Having escaped, he took refuge in England, where he was appointed professor of Greek at Cambridge in 1548, only to depart for Basel and Strasbourg the following year. He died of plague in 1552.

for example, to add extracts from the Jewish historian Josephus to the biblical text. His French translation did not win unanimous approval.[93] His orthographical reforms, which led him to write "*êt*" in place of "*est*," burdened more than they assisted the reader. But the undertaking was damaged above all by the laudable desire to find equivalent words and adaptations. While one could defend his suggestion of translating "baptize" by "wash," "washing" is a poor equivalent for Christian baptism. Similarly, "foreskin" *(avant-peau)* is no doubt an excellent equivalent for "prepuce" (*prépuce* in French), but from this to render "uncircumcised" as "unskinned" is marginal. The speech of Canaan was invaded by borrowings from the dialect of Bresse in the sixteenth century, and by ridiculous approximations — the "*bailliages*" of the Philistines, the "*gendarmerie*" of Israel, or the touching "satyrs," "fawns," and "sylvans" of the forests of Judea, not to mention the "hay" that Castellio, good man, lavished generously on the oxen and hippopotamuses.

But it was the *Treatise on Heretics* of 1554 that raised the most emotion, and this while the coals of Servetus's stake were still smoldering in men's consciences. The book had two different prefaces: the Latin version was dedicated to the duke of Württemberg, the French edition to the landgrave of Hesse. Castellio argued the vanity of theology, insisting instead on the moral character of the teaching of Christ: "We dispute, not about the road by which we can go to Christ — which is to correct our lives — but about the status and office of Christ, that is where he is now, what he is doing, how he is seated at the right hand of the Father, how he is one with the Father. Also about the Trinity, predestination, free will, God, the angels, the status of souls after this life, and other similar things, which we do not greatly need to know to achieve salvation through faith, since without this knowledge the publicans and harlots were saved."[94]

And Castellio cites this sentence from the Beatitudes: "Blessed are the pure in heart: for they shall see God." Then this from the apostle Paul: "And though I . . . understand all mysteries, and all knowledge . . . , and have not charity, I am nothing."[95] Thus, according to the author, the evangelical ethic is opposed to the vain science of the theologians. This is a universal phenomenon. "There is no sect that does not condemn all the others and wish to reign en-

---

93. *La Bible nouvellement translatée, avec la suite de l'histoire depuis le temps d'Esdras jusqu'aux Maccabées: et depuis les Maccabées jusqu'à Christ* (Basel: Jean Hervage, 1555). For his linguistic work see the indispensable analyses of S. Baddeley, *L'orthographe française au temps de la Réforme* (Geneva: Droz, 1993), p. 285.

94. Castellio, Latin preface to the duke of Württemberg, cited at length by Buisson, *Sébastien Castellion,* 1:360-69. This duke, Christopher, had spent some time in Montbéliard and had a reputation for broad-mindedness.

95. Matt. 5:8; 1 Cor. 13:2.

tirely alone." All evils derive from this vanity, "banishments, exiles, bonds, imprisonments, burnings, gibbets, and this miserable rage for death and torment that is exercised daily." This cruelty itself is useless, for one cannot settle one way or the other these inexhaustible debates over "unknown things, already disputed among men for such a long space of time, and without any certain conclusion." Thus the "robe of Christ" is adorned with torture and degradation.

Castellio, full of fury, then asks what Christ will say when he returns, an allusion to the end of time. "What will Christ do when he comes?" The author, however, does not refuse to condemn heresy when it exists. But he warns against persecution: "There is hardly one of all the sects, which today are without number, which does not hold the others to be heretics. So that if in one city or region you are esteemed a true believer, in the next you will be esteemed a heretic. So that if anyone today wants to live he must have as many faiths and religions as there are cities or sects, just as a man who travels through the lands has to change his money from day to day, since that which is good here in another place is not current, unless his money is of gold."

Whence a fine metaphor. This gold money, which is accepted everywhere, is faith in "Almighty God the Father, the Son, and the Holy Spirit" and approval of the "commandments of true piety, which are contained in the holy Scriptures." It is therefore useless to exterminate each other in the name of speculative opinions; the same coexistence ought to reign among differing Christians that is observed with the Jews and the Turks. The French preface repeats the same idea. "It would be better to let a hundred, even a thousand heretics live than to put a decent man to death under the pretense of heresy."[96]

The book is then presented as a collection of authorities prohibiting the pursuit of heresy. This florilegium assembles the names of Luther, Erasmus, Sebastian Franck, Saint Augustine, Saint John Chrysostom, and Saint Jerome — indeed of Calvin himself, contradicting his own acts. To cover his tracks, Castellio added his own name to the list.

Theodore Beza, who was then teaching Greek in Lausanne, decided to respond to Castellio. His Latin work of 1554 was issued in a French version some years later, *Treatise on the Authority of the Magistrates in the Punishment of Heretics and on the Way to Proceed in This* (1560).[97] Here Beza responded affirmatively to three questions: Must heretics be punished? Is the repression of heresy properly under the jurisdiction of the magistrates, infringed by the ecclesiastical power? May capital punishment be used? Castellio did not remain quiet;

---

96. Buisson, *Sébastien Castellion*, 1:374.

97. *Traité de l'autorité du magistrat en la punition des hérétiques et du moyen d'y procéder.* T. Beza, *De haereticis*. The French translation is by Colladon.

conquered, he still resisted, and wrote a double manuscript in Latin and French that ended with this sentence, as a last defiance: "Arise, Oh God, plead thine own cause."[98]

98. Ps. 74:22. S. Castellio, *De l'impunité des hérétiques,* ed. B. Becker and M. Valkhoff (Geneva: Droz, 1971), p. 401. The author denies that magistrates may pursue heretics, but he nevertheless thinks it is their duty to punish blasphemy or irreligion.

CHAPTER 11

To Thee the Glory

[By killing Isaac] I would make God a liar,
Since he told me he would give me the good fortune
That from my son would issue
A great people who would fill the earth.

THEODORE BEZA, *ABRAHAM SACRIFICING* (1550)[1]

Did a great people issue from Calvin? The individual was gradually absorbed by the public character. Calvin dissolved into Calvinism: he was a man, and he became an ideology, a doctrine, almost a religion — at any rate, a culture. If the seed does not die. . . . Calvin's face grew more gaunt with the years, his breath thinned, his back bent; his suffering body was racked with fever. Incessantly subject to migraine, fever, hemorrhoids, kidney stones, and phthisis, his physical appearance called up images of Job. Brother of all in his humanity, subjected to all torments, Job furnished Calvin with the topic of his finest reflections. For Calvin death was the ultimate liberation. A death without relics, almost without a tomb, which had the imperious inevitability of the rivers that all run into the sea. A death that was itself an apotheosis, by establishing the separation of the man from the doctrine. Calvinism survived Calvin; it was a discipline, an asceticism, often pushed to the point of rigidity; it was also a style that permeated the French language.

---

1. T. Beza, *Abraham sacrifiant* (New York: Johnson Reprint, 1969), p. 43. See also Olivier Millet, "Exégèse évangélique et culture littéraire humaniste: entre Luther et Bèze, l'Abraham sacrifiant selon Calvin," *Études Théologiques et Religieuses* 69 (1994): 367-80.

Calvin did not enjoy his victory for long; his personal power lasted less than ten years, from 1555 to 1564. But it was practically uncontested. "After 1555," one of the best analysts of the period assures us, "no one any longer dared oppose the Reformer openly."[2] The crushing of his internal enemies (Ami Perrin) and the victory over the heretics (Servetus) left Calvin with a free hand, at least in Geneva. Calvin had won. He enjoyed international standing; the Reformation he impersonated, to the point of rigidity, appeared as an alternative form of Protestantism, distinct from German Lutheranism.

The controversy with Rabelais illustrates well the importance of inchoate Calvinism within French culture. The Reformer had attacked Master François Rabelais in his treatise *On Scandals,* classing him among the despisers of true religion.[3] The facetious author replied in his *Fourth Book* in 1552, referring to the "demoniacal Calvins, impostors of Geneva."[4] Calvin, not being conciliatory, would not let this bon mot go unpunished. In one of his sermons on Deuteronomy, delivered on October 16, 1555, he replied:

> This is a boor who issues villainous lampoons against the holy Scriptures, like this devil named Pantagruel, and all that filth and villainy; these people do not pretend to present any new religion, so one might say that they are deceived by their own foolish fantasies, but rather they are mad dogs who vomit their filth against the majesty of God and want to pervert all religion. Must they be spared? What about it? They have the cardinals for their henchmen, they are favored by them and support them; indeed, one sees the names of the cardinals emblazoned on these fine books, which mock God as much as they do Mohammed. It is all one, all this will be permitted; provided one applauds the cardinals it is enough, they are happy to be mentioned in this way, and it can be seen that they not only make fun of all religion, but that they want to abolish it entirely.[5]

2. A. Roget, *L'Église et l'État à Genève du temps de Calvin. Étude d'histoire politico-ecclésiastique* (Geneva: J. Jullien, 1867), p. 72.

3. J. Calvin, *Des scandales,* ed. O. Fatio (Geneva: Droz, 1984), p. 138.

4. Rabelais, *Oeuvres complètes,* ed. P. Jourda (Paris: Garnier, 1962), 2:137.

5. *Opera Calvini* (hereafter cited as *OC*) 27, cols. 261-62, sermon on Deut. 13:6-11. The anticlerical allusion to "cardinals" is aimed at Cardinal Odet de Châtillon, to whom the *Fourth Book* was dedicated and who joined the Reformation in 1564.

From Calvin to Calvinism

The faith is confirmed; go to those regions
That have not heard of our religions,
To Peru, Canada, Calicut, the Cannibals,
Show there in truth your virtues Calvinal.

PIERRE DE RONSARD, 1562[6]

That *cannibal* should rhyme with *calvinal* (as Ronsard tongue in cheek maintains) is a good illustration of sixteenth-century polemics. What secret connection, then, links the "Huguenot and the savage"?[7] The distant lands, and especially the New World, presented an authentic challenge to the West. Was America a domain of sin or innocence, hell or paradise lost?[8]

But being ruled by his sense of rhyme, Ronsard also suggests another adjectival form, *calvinien*. In this case *calvinien* was derived from *luthérien* (Lutheran).[9] Calvinism thus was defined by difference and similarity. It was distinguished from Lutheranism, but instead of showing a new civility, it unwittingly engaged in barbarism. Who was the cannibal? This rhetorical question took on an unexpected dimension during the years 1550-60. The accusation of cannibalism, traditionally cast by white men at extra-European cultures, was found transplanted to French soil. A Catholic, it was said maliciously, is a cannibal who eats his God. How did people arrive at this surprising invective?

An individual experience illustrates the misfortunes of Calvinism in the New World. The Burgundian Jean de Léry, a cobbler by trade, found temporary asylum in Geneva when he was not yet twenty. He left there for America in

6. P. de Ronsard, *Discours des misères de ce temps*, ed. F. Higman (Paris: Librairie générale française, Le Livre de Poche, 1993), "Continuation" (1562), p. 87.

7. F. Lestringant, *Le huguenot et le sauvage* (Paris: Aux amateurs de livres, 1990). Also, by the same author, "Genève et l'Amérique: le rêve du Refuge huguenot au temps des guerres de Religion (1555-1600)," *Revue de l'Histoire des Religions* 210 (1993): 331-47.

8. Lestringant, *Le huguenot et le sauvage*, p. 8: "From the Age of Discovery to the Century of Enlightenment, and from Columbus to Buffon, this continent unknown to Europe for millennia was interpreted in turn as a remnant of lost Eden whose inhabitants had preserved an ideal nudity and as an antechamber of hell where innumerable vices resided, where even cannibalism was sanctified by religion, where nature, finally, showed itself weaker in its products. Often, in fact, the two contradictory hypotheses coexisted in the same work, revealing the unstable European reaction to the New World."

9. Ronsard, *Discours des misères de ce temps*, "Remontrance au peuple de France" (1562), p. 99: "Now Lutheran, now Calvinist [*calvinien*]." The word "Calvinist" is found as a noun in A. Du Val, *Les contrarietez et contradicts, qui se trouvent en la doctrine de Jean Calvin, de Luther & autres nouveaux evangelistes de nostre temps* (Paris: N. Chesneau, 1561).

236

1556,[10] but his greatest work did not appear until much later. Published in Geneva in 1578, his *History of a Voyage to the Land of Brazil* recounted the young man's stay of ten months in Rio de Janeiro Bay, from March 7, 1557, to January 4, 1558.[11] The book is, on the word of Claude Lévi-Strauss, an authentic "breviary of an ethnologist."[12]

The author embarked in November 1556 for "France Antarctique," at the entrance to Rio de Janeiro Bay. A memorable religious controversy took place across the Atlantic in this country surrounded by Indians. Directed with a hand of iron by the Chevalier De Villegagnon, the colony had been founded at the instigation of Admiral De Coligny in November 1555. Transferred to a small island out of fear of the Tupinambas, the French population lost some of its members who were attracted to savage life. Villegagnon appealed to Calvin, his former fellow student in Orléans (January 1556). "I intend to establish a retreat there for the poor believers who are persecuted in France, in Spain, and elsewhere across the sea, so that without fear of king, emperor, or other potentate they may serve God there purely according to his will."[13]

Fourteen "Genevans," mostly recent immigrants, fourteen adventurers determined to take root and render worship only to God, disembarked on March 7, 1557, among them Jean de Léry and the ministers Chartier and Richer. These brothers in Christ solemnly took Holy Communion on March 21. But a serious theological rift appeared some weeks later, on Whit Sunday.

Nicolas Durant De Villegagnon, a Knight of Malta, clashed seriously with the Reformed minority sent by Calvin from Geneva. The debate concerned the

---

10. On returning to Europe, Jean de Léry (1536-1613) hesitated between his trade of cobbler, his wife's trade of innkeeper, and a pastoral vocation. Having been in Sancerre, in 1574 he published his *Histoire mémorable* of that town.

11. *Histoire d'un voyage fait en la terre du Brésil.* We may also mention, however, Léry's participation in Crespin's *Histoire des martyrs,* in the 1564 edition. Two notices from his pen deal with: (1) his stay with Villegagnon, then on the mainland in the midst of the cannibals; (2) the execution of three Reformers. These notices appeared in a separate edition in Geneva in 1561, *Histoire des choses mémorables advenues en la terre du Brésil . . .* A new abridged edition of it came out in 1565, *Brief recueil.* See F. Lestringant, "Calvinistes et cannibales I," *Bulletin de la Société de l'Histoire du Protestantisme Français* (1980): 11 and 24-26; J. Crespin, *Histoire des Martyrs* (Geneva: P. Aubert, 1619), bk. 7, pp. 432-38 and 452-57. See also M. de Certeau, *L'Écriture de l'Histoire* (Paris: Gallimard, 1975), pp. 215-48.

12. Jean de Léry, *Histoire d'un voyage en terre de Brésil, 1557,* ed. F. Lestringant (Paris and Montpellier: Max Chaleil, 1992), p. 9.

13. F. Lestringant, "Tristes tropiques: du Brésil à la France, une controverse à l'aube des guerres de religion," *Revue de l'Histoire des Religions* 202 (1985): 270-71. Also "Calvinistes et cannibales. Les écrits protestants sur le Brésil français (1555-1560). Deuxième partie: la 'Réfutation' de Pierre Richer," *Bulletin de la Société de l'Histoire du Protestantisme Français* (1980): 167-92.

interpretation of the eucharistic sacrament. Why did this fratricidal quarrel among Christians in the New World turn on the question of cannibalism? Was it a charming borrowing from local color? Did a suitable insult instigate the quarrel? Or was it a debate of theologians, cut to the quick? No doubt a little of all three. Villegagnon defended eucharistic realism; the body and the blood of Christ were really present in the bread and wine of Communion. That was anthropophagy, the Calvinists answered. But Villegagnon, who scarcely appreciated being thus called a cannibal, had the upper hand.[14] The Calvinist minority deserted the community and found asylum on the mainland. The "Genevans" finally left the colony in 1558, two years before its total collapse.

The debate reached Geneva. The pastor Pierre Richer found himself attacked by Villegagnon, who no longer spared Calvin, the chief instigator of the troubles shaking Christianity. His "artificial" language, his use of "certain words not common in the vulgar tongue, bombastic and specious," had created a new scholasticism. Villegagnon clearly questioned the use of grammar and rhetoric in explaining the eucharistic mystery.[15] Richer replied the same year, 1561, in his *Refutation of Foolish Dreams*.[16] Villegagnon was there rudely called a Cyclops. But above all, this text contains one of the favorite elements of Huguenot controversy, the merging of the Catholic with the cannibal. Does not the carnivorous Catholic eat his God raw in the Eucharist?[17] This gustatory confusion virtually provoked nausea, disgust, and anorexia. The accusation of cannibalism against the papists amounted to denying them all humanity, consigning them to barbarism. The procedure hardly differed from the list of animals regularly used by Calvin to confound his adversaries, who suddenly became monkeys, dogs, pigs, or wolves (see chap. 12). It reinforced a view of the world that opposed the low to the high, the spiritual to the material, man to beast, and soon the civilized man to the savage, Robinson Crusoe to Friday. By

14. Reformers versus Catholics? This interpretation has the air of an a posteriori reconstruction; Villegagnon would have had to accept the truth of the gospel, only to retract in the end. This attitude remains inexplicable according to our later confessional criteria. Thierry Wanegffelen has recently posed the questions that result. "And if Villegagnon was never, even temporarily, a Protestant?" T. Wanegffelen, "Des Chrétiens entre Rome et Genève. Une histoire du choix religieux en France, vers 1520-vers 1610" (*thèse* at the University of Paris I [Panthéon-Sorbonne], November 12, 1994; typescript, 2 vols., 913 pp.), p. 328.

15. N. Durant de Villegagnon, *Les Propositions contentieuses entre le chevalier de Villegaignon et maistre Jehan Calvin concernant la vérité de l'Eucharistie* (Paris: A Wechel, 1561; reissued 1562), pp. 4ff.

16. P. Richer (1506-80), *La Resfutation des folles resveries, exécrables blasphèmes, erreurs et mensonges de Nicolas Durand qui se nomme Villegaignon* (1561). A Latin version appeared the same year.

17. Lestringant, "Calvinistes et cannibales. . . . Deuxième partie," p. 173.

describing the Calvinists as cannibals, Ronsard was only returning the compliment. The sacrificial liturgy of the papists provoked a form of repugnance or of abasement among the Reformers. In opposition to the Catholics and the Lutherans, Calvin rejected the least physical presence of the Savior in the species. His glorified Christ remained in heaven, without being soiled by the mouths of communicating sinners. "This body that the Calvinists relegated to heaven, as far as possible from an earth reeking with butchered flesh and shed blood, the Catholics did not cease to offer in propitiatory sacrifice. This is incontestably the core of the cannibal controversy."[18]

The French Calvinists were not the ones who would conquer the New World. They turned this task over to the English Puritans. Another project detained them, the spiritual conquest of the kingdom of France. A land of exile to which refugees flocked, Geneva was rapidly transformed into a missionary center. Calvinism was born of the confrontation.

The term "Calvinist" appeared in 1552 in the writings of Joachim Westphal, a Lutheran pastor from Hamburg.[19] Calvin was the first to deplore this term. He took exception to it in 1563 on the eve of his death, in his Latin commentary on Jeremiah (1565 for the French version). He deplored the existence of "seditious shouters," "almost similar to those fanatics called zealots who are mentioned in Josephus." And he continued: "They find no greater insult to attach to us . . . than this word 'Calvinism,' but it is not hard to conjecture where such a mortal hate as they have for me comes from."[20]

The Exile and the Kingdom

Dearest lords and brethren, we glorify our God because he multiplies his seed in you.

CALVIN, "TO THE FAITHFUL IN LOUDUN," SEPTEMBER 1555[21]

18. Lestringant, *Le cannibale. Grandeur et décadence* (Paris: Perrin, 1994), p. 34.

19. O. Millet, "Les Églises réformées," in *Histoire du christianisme des origines à nos jours*, vol. 8, ed. J.-M. Mayeur, C. Piétri, André Vauchez, and M. Venard, 14 vols. (Paris: Desclée, 1992), p. 56. The word "Calvinist" was in fact used to stigmatize Calvin's views on Communion (*Farrago confusanearum et inter se dissidentium opinionum de Coena Domini ex Sacramentarium libris congesta*, 1552).

20. J. Calvin, *Leçons ou commentaires et expositions . . . tant sur les Révélations que sur les Lamentations du prophète Jérémie* (Lyon, 1565), unpaginated preface.

21. J. Calvin, *Lettres françaises*, ed. J. Bonnet, 2 vols. (Paris: Meyrueis, 1854), 2:73-74, September 9, 1555.

From 1549 onward Calvin was clearly aware of the role of England in the defense of the "true faith." The reign of young Edward VI, however, was only a parenthesis, from 1547 to 1553. The return to Catholicism under the reign of Mary Tudor obliterated the Reformers' hopes, before the Elizabethan period timidly renewed its ties to Protestantism. The Reformation, it was thought in Geneva, took a profoundly original course across the Channel by combining conservatism and renewal, the maintenance of the episcopate and the purification of doctrine. But did this suffice finally to eliminate all "superstitions"? Calvin exhorted Edward to continue his efforts. "Only with great difficulty, Sire, will you ever be able entirely to uproot all the evils that require correcting."[22]

A community of refugees was officially permitted to establish itself in London under Edward VI. This "experimental" church led a profoundly original life in the Continental manner; doctrinal Calvinism was fully established during the 1560s, thanks to Calvin's sending of the pastor Nicolas Des Gallars. The foreigners' church was then endowed with a system of discipline like that of the other Reformed churches.[23] Calvin, moreover, was able to congratulate Queen Elizabeth on her accession to power, while Geneva saw its English and Scottish colonies depart.[24]

The chronology of events in France reveals a succession of periods of repression and times of calm that alternated in the second half of the sixteenth century. We enter the era of the Wars of Religion (see app. 4). In 1555 the first Calvinist churches in France were organized in Paris, Meaux, Angers, Poitiers, and Loudun. Bourges, Orléans, Rouen, La Rochelle, Toulouse, Rennes, and Lyon followed during the next three years.

How were they to find their bearings in the restored "true faith"? Two million, perhaps more, gathered in hundreds of distinct churches. The Calvinist pastoral of exile reversed itself henceforward. Whereas fifteen or twenty years before, Calvin had exhorted the faithful to abandon France, the land of Egypt or new Babylon, the situation was reversed in 1555-62; one must remain in the kingdom to establish the evangelical life there.[25]

Jean Macar was one of the men sent directly by Calvin. With total devotion, with unfailing obedience, he scrupulously kept Calvin informed about the Parisian situation. He succeeded Nicolas Des Gallars as pastor in Paris at the beginning of 1558.[26] In the spring he exclaimed, in the name of the church of

---

22. Calvin, *Lettres françaises,* 1:327-38, January 1551.

23. B. Cottret, *The Huguenots in England* (New York: Cambridge University Press, 1991), pp. 46ff.

24. *OC* 17, p. 135, January 18, 1559.

25. T. Wanegffelen, *La France et les Français. xvie-milieu xviie siècles. La vie religieuse* (Gap: Ophrys, 1994), p. 35.

26. Born about 1520 in the vicinity of Laon, Jean Macar married a niece of the Reformer's in Geneva. He died in Geneva in 1560.

Paris, "The number of faithful increases in a marvelous fashion. Reapers are called for on all sides, but they are few in number."[27] Some weeks later it was the turn of the church of Bordeaux to ask for a "David" and a "Daniel" to oppose Goliath and the dragon. Similarly, Jean Macar declared, "The fire lit today in all parts of the kingdom could not be put out by all the waters of the sea. But God has hardened the hearts of Pharaoh and his counselors."[28]

On May 22, 1558, Jean Macar reported that as a result of the gathering in the Pré-aux-Clercs the day after Ascension, such assemblies had been forbidden in Paris on pain of death. D'Andelot, the brother of Admiral De Coligny, had been imprisoned. The pastor also admitted his reservations about the king of Navarre. Despite his commitment to the side of the Reformers, the latter spent his time in dancing all day with women of light virtue.[29]

Calvin distrusted Antoine de Bourbon, king of Navarre. Jeanne d'Albret's husband had not been "suddenly transformed into an austere Calvinist."[30] Calvin wrote the king on June 8 to explain to him very explicitly that he remained subject to the same moral law as the least of the faithful. It was also his duty to set an example. Calvin also scolded D'Andelot, Coligny's brother, who had had the weakness to attend Mass at the request of his wife, who was about to give birth. He also addressed Coligny in September; the latter had been a captive in Flanders since the disaster of Saint-Quentin.[31] This same year the expected peace between France and Spain was dreaded in Geneva. On May 13, 1558, Jean Macar wrote, "If the peace is concluded the two monarchs have promised the Duke of Savoy soldiers to take by assault the city that is the mother and nurse of

---

27. *OC* 17, col. 135, Macar to Calvin, April 12, 1558.

28. *OC* 17, cols. 158 and 162, May 6 and 9, 1558. The following pastors were sent by Calvin: in May 1558 Verax to Bourges, Chanourry to Blois, Corradon to Romorantin, Guy de Morranges to Issoudun; in July Charles Duplessis to Tours, Ambroise Faget to Orléans; in October Michel Mulot to Lyon; in December F. Chambelly to Le Havre, F. de Dureil to Bergerac, Lucas Aubé to Sainte-Foy, Gilles to Bordeaux, François de Morel to Paris in place of Jean Macar, Dupuis to Dieppe, and Paumier to Caen. The total number sent exceeded 100. R. M. Kingdon studied 88 cases, a third of whom were former practicing ministers. R. M. Kingdon, *Geneva and the Coming of the Wars of Religion in France, 1555-1563* (Geneva: Droz, 1956).

29. *OC* 17, col. 177.

30. L. Crété, *Coligny* (Paris: Fayard, 1985), p. 111.

31. In 1557 Philip II took advantage of the absence of François de Guise, who was in Piedmont, to attack France with his wife, Mary Tudor. On August 2, 1557, the town was attacked by some 10,000 to 12,000 cavalry and 35,000 to 40,000 infantry. The town received the support of Gaspard de Châtillon, Admiral De Coligny, who sneaked in. The French troops who came to the rescue on August 10 were cut to pieces. The town was invested on August 27. François de Guise returned from Italy and took Guînes and Calais (January 8, 1558), then Thionville the following June 22.

all errors."[32] The two belligerents in fact signed the Peace of Cateau-Cambrésis in April 1559.

During May 26-29, 1559, some thirty churches attended a national synod held in Paris. A common confession of faith and a system of ecclesiastical discipline were drafted. Calvin was a little worried about such haste. "This ardor displeases us," he confided on May 17, taking men and angels to witness.[33] And without delay the Reformer sent a proposed confession in thirty-five articles, which arrived on the last day of the conference. This text was immediately amended by the French. But they were a little afraid of the reactions of the irascible Calvin, and they minimized the changes made to the master's version. They politely informed him: "We have thought it good to make some additions to your confession, but changing only very few things in it."[34]

Few changes? This understatement should not deceive the historian. The new confession in fact included forty articles. Calvin had proposed only one prefatory article. There the Word of God appeared as the very foundation of the faith. The knowledge of God and salvation were only possible because God himself took the initiative.

> Because the foundation of belief, as Saint Paul says, is through the Word of God, we believe that the living God is manifest in his law and through his prophets, and finally in the Gospel, and there he has given testimony of his will insofar as is expedient for the salvation of men. Thus we hold the books of the holy Scriptures of the Old and New Testaments to be the summary of the one infallible truth proceeding from God, which it is not lawful to contradict. Also since the perfect rule of all wisdom is contained in it we believe that it is not lawful to add anything to it or take anything from it, but that everything in it must be acquiesced in throughout. Now since this doctrine does not take its authority from men or angels, but from God alone, we also believe (since it is a thing beyond all human reason to recognize that it is God who speaks) that he alone gives the certainty of this to his elect and seals it in our hearts by his Spirit.[35]

"It is God who speaks." This is undoubtedly the most perfect summary of Calvin's theology: God speaks, God chooses, God summons. But this message,

---

32. A. Roget, *Histoire du peuple de Genève depuis la Réforme jusqu'à l'escalade,* 7 vols. (Geneva: John Jullien, 1870), 5:193.

33. *OC* 17, col. 502.

34. *OC* 17, col. 538, Morel to Calvin, June 5, 1559.

35. *OC* 9, cols. 739-41.

by its audacity, escaped his contemporaries. While Calvin's theology had an existential or performative aspect, the Frenchmen's adaptation depended on a philosophy of essences. "We believe and confess that there is one God who is a single and simple spiritual essence, infinite, incomprehensible, and simple." For Calvin the Lord was the God who speaks; he became a simple body whom one defined with the help of some baseless adjectives. Theology gave place to schoolboys' observations. The final version of the confession of faith, ratified by the French, was relatively conventional. Its introduction replaced Calvin's one majestic article with five separate articles, clearly less original. One God (Article 1) is manifested to men (Article 2). The Scriptures are composed of various books (Article 3). These are the "rule" for all faith and cannot be changed in anything (Articles 4 and 5).[36] The two texts were published under the titles *Confession of Faith Established by Common Accord by the Churches that Are Scattered through France and that Abstain from Papal Idolatries* and *Confession of Faith Established by Common Accord by the French Who Desire to Live according to the Pure Gospel of Our Lord Jesus Christ.* This last version, in forty articles, is better known under the later name of Confession of La Rochelle, since it was confirmed by a synod held in that city in 1571.[37]

The influence of Geneva worried the French monarchy. On January 23, 1561, Charles IX complained of the presence of preachers. The Geneva authorities took fright, and Calvin was ordered to respond: "At seven o'clock in the morning the Council was assembled expressly to hear the letters of the King of France read and to respond to them. They contained in sum that having attained to the crown, he found in his council and state that the source of so many dissensions arisen and nourished in the said kingdom proceeded from the ministers who have been sent by the principal ministers of this city, and that to maintain his people in peace and prevent the troubles that might come from this, he begs that all the ministers who have been sent be recalled and summoned and that an order be given that in the future there be no more" (Tuesday, January 28, 1561).[38]

The answer emphasized that no one in Geneva was responsible for the civil troubles that divided France, but that when pastors were asked for to advance the cause of the gospel, it was not possible to stand aside. Calvin tried to

36. *OC* 9, cols. 731-52.

37. *Confession de foi faite d'un commun accord par les Églises dispersées en France, et s'abstiennent des idolâtries papales* and *Confession de foi faite d'un commun accord par les Français, qui désirent vivre selon la pureté de l'Évangile de notre Seigneur Jésus-Christ.* Other comparable confessions of faith existed at the time: the Confession of Paris of 1557, or the confession of Theodore Beza the next year. See O. Fatio et al., eds., *Confessions et catéchismes de la foi réformée* (Geneva: Labor et Fides, 1986), pp. 111ff.

38. *Annales Calviniani, OC* 21, col. 741, Registres du Conseil de Genève 56, fol. 137v.

reassure everyone of his peaceful intentions: "We would indeed desire that the doctrine by which our salvation is assured be spread everywhere. But we are well aware of our limits and do not presume so far as to wish to reform a great country, being sufficiently prevented as it is from maintaining ourselves peacefully in all humility in the lowly condition in which God has put us."[39]

The counterpart of the establishment of this international network was the development of denunciation. Calvin struggled to reinforce a contested image. Thus in September 1552, in his correspondence with the foreigners' church in London, the Reformer denounced the false idea according to which people wanted to transform him into an "idol" or metamorphose Geneva into a "Jerusalem." Similarly, three years later Calvin tried to reassure his audience that it must not be believed that everyone in Geneva "kissed his slippers."[40] This defense of himself was invariably accompanied in its turn by accusations. Bolsec, Castellio, and Trolliet were some of Calvin's targets in his letter to the church of Poitiers. "It is well that the dogs who bark at us so much cannot bite us."[41] Calvin was also grieved by the troubles that existed in the bosom of the church of Frankfurt.[42] He likewise sent a fraternal letter in December 1556 to the French church of Antwerp. "Since you love me, I do not doubt that my remembrance of you will make you rejoice."[43] He congratulated the faithful of Paris the following year. "May your good life serve as a buckler to repel all the slanders of your enemies."[44]

Again in 1558, in a letter to James Hamilton, earl of Arran, Calvin warned against "a certain young man" who, it might be feared, "would infect everything with his venom." This "serpent full of pride" was applying himself to "overthrowing and falsifying the whole truth of God."[45]

Martyrdom and the Impossible Reconciliation?

The last ten years of Calvin's life saw the development in France of "mass Protestantism." Émile Léonard described this evolution as a passage from a

39. Calvin, *Lettres françaises,* 2:375.

40. Calvin, *Lettres françaises,* 1:351, September 27, 1552, and 2:19, February 20, 1555.

41. Calvin, *Lettres françaises,* 2:20.

42. Calvin, *Lettres françaises,* 2:81ff., 1555-56; the conflict was about the choice of Valéran Poullain as pastor.

43. Calvin, *Lettres françaises,* 2:111, December 21, 1556.

44. Calvin, *Lettres françaises,* 2:123, March 15, 1557.

45. Calvin, *Lettres françaises,* 2:229, February 18, 1559. On the organization of international Calvinism, see M. Prestwich, ed., *International Calvinism, 1541-1715* (Oxford: Clarendon Press, 1985).

church "of converts" to churches "for conversion."[46] Now this change was also brought about and realized through violence — violence both suffered, that of martyrdom, and inflicted, when the Huguenots took up arms. As modern research establishes, "the strategy of martyrdom aimed at transforming a judicial humiliation into a divine providence."[47] An execution took on the nature of both a "spectacle" and a "ceremony."[48] In the last edition of the *Institutes* (1559-60), Calvin was led to explain the meaning of this supreme gift. The witness for Jesus Christ who is killed participates in the death and resurrection of the Crucified.[49] In a Calvinist context, however, martyrdom in itself has no efficacy; it is not a redemptive action. This death appears in the enigmatic and paradoxical light of a spiritual communion. Martyrdom cannot be confused with sacrifice.

If the Protestant Reformation did not do away with sacrifice, it conferred on it an exceptional, indeed unique, value, as the Placards of 1534 had already affirmed. The sacrifice of Christ cannot be repeated either by the martyr or by the priest at the altar. The Lord's Supper is a "commemoration," the Reformers insisted, at the precise moment when, from the Catholic side, the Council of Trent reaffirmed that the Mass is a sacrifice.

However, the voice of blood, Christian heroism carried to the point of torture or the stake, explains the necessity of justifying these tragic testimonies on a metaphysical level. Frank Lestringant has just vigorously raised the question, "How did people go from holy horror at the Mass to a morbid fascination with the death of the martyrs, that eloquent and spectacular death that had all the external appearance of a sacrifice?"[50] In fact, the same author points out, "The bodies of the martyrs were . . . very troublesome. What to do with this flesh, atrociously mutilated and as it were 'cooked' by the fire of the stakes that were lit everywhere in Europe? At the test of history the Reformed community was obliged to take account of a violence it had driven from its symbolic practices and that returned in strength through the gate of reality."

On August 23, 1554, the *Book of Martyrs* of Jean Crespin was submitted

---

46. É. G. Léonard, *Histoire générale du protestantisme*, 3 vols. (Paris: PUF, 1961-64), 2:87.

47. D. El Kenz, "Le roi de justice et le martyr réformé: État sacré et désacralisé, jusqu'à la veille de la première guerre de religion," *Bulletin de la Société de l'Histoire du Protestantisme Français* 140 (1995): 49.

48. D. Nicholls, "The Theatre of Martyrdom in the French Reformation," *Past and Present* 121 (1988): 49.

49. J. Calvin, *Institution de la religion chrétienne* (1560), ed. J. D. Benoît (Paris: Vrin, 1957), I, 177-78.

50. F. Lestringant, *La cause des martyrs* (Mont-de-Marsan, Landes: Éditions Interuniversitaires, 1991), p. 12.

for the approval of the Council of Geneva.[51] Huguenot martyrology increased in importance. In July 1555 Calvin felt the need to justify from the pulpit the apparently questioned use of the term "martyr." He returned to the subject repeatedly. Thus on September 4, 1557, worship took place in the house of Monsieur Barthélemy on the Rue Saint-Jacques in Paris, opposite the Collège de Plessis. More than 100 people were arrested, including many women. Seven victims were finally burned in the Place Maubert. Calvin addressed himself to the imprisoned women awaiting martyrdom. Women, like "manual workers," he explained, are called to salvation. The supreme gift, one's life, ought to be offered in complete serenity. "Since Jesus Christ died for you and you hope for salvation through him, having been baptized in his name, you must not be reluctant to render him the honor that belongs to him."[52] The same message was addressed to the faithful of France in June 1559. "The more the wicked seek to exterminate the memory of his name from the earth, the more power He will give to our blood to make it flourish."[53] Or to the church of Paris at the same moment: "You must raise your eyes to heaven, since without this it would be very difficult for us to leave the world, and there is nothing that can comfort us in all battles except for us to be well persuaded that this heritage cannot fail us. Therefore think of our head, the Son of God, who rose from the dead, so that it does us no harm to die with him so as to be participants in his celestial glory."[54]

It is indeed necessary "to live and die in the service of Him who died for us." Every believer is called to prepare himself mentally for this distinguished honor. "As for you, my brethren, hold in reverence the blood of the martyrs that is poured out as testimony to the truth, as dedicated and consecrated to the glory of our God. And apply it to your edification, inciting you to follow them."[55] This feeling of the imminence of persecution, moreover, did not spare those in exile. Calvin mentioned the dangers that the Peace of Cateau-Cambrésis, signed between France and Spain on April 3, 1559, would bring to Geneva. "It is true that at this time I speak from outside the battle, but not very far, and I do not know for how long, since as far as one can judge our turn is indeed near."[56] Even if Calvin, devoted to the law, preached submission to authority, the Huguenots were aware of their strength. In the last years

51. J. Crespin, Le livre des Martyrs qui est un recueil de plusieurs Martyrs qui ont enduré la mort pour le Nom de Nostre Seigneur Jésus-Christ, depuis Jean Hus jusqu'à cette année MDLIII (Geneva, 1554).

52. Calvin, Lettres françaises, 2:147, September 1557.

53. Calvin, Lettres françaises, 2:278, June 1559.

54. Calvin, Lettres françaises, 2:283, June 29, 1559.

55. Calvin, Lettres françaises, 2:305, to the faithful of France, November 1559.

56. Calvin, Lettres françaises, 2:310, to a prisoner, November 13, 1559.

of this period, they were led to renounce the "martyr complex" that was so common before 1559 and again after 1572. "Between these two dates, by contrast, there was a period when the Reform, instead of 'suffering,' became 'militant.'"[57]

Divided between sudden clear spells and episodes of cruelty, the second half of the sixteenth century was the time of the Wars of Religion.[58] Agreement proved impossible. A last important attempt at Poissy, west of Paris, was a failure.[59]

Calvin did not go to the conference; his shaky health, the attachment of the Genevans, and finally his unwavering sense of authority explain why Theodore Beza was preferred.[60] This noble Frenchman enjoyed a reputation as an orator and a diplomat that amply justified this choice. But in practice he proved even more Calvinist than Calvin. The chronology explains the political stakes in this dialogue between Catholics and Reformers. The Estates General of the kingdom and the assembly of the clergy sat in August 1561, respectively in Pontoise and in Poissy. The ecumenical colloquy that followed in September clearly marked the failure of the determination to achieve national reconciliation, clearly affirmed by Chancellor Michel de l'Hospital. The utopian dream of a kingdom in which the simple name of "Christian" would replace the names of parties haunted the imagination of the statesman. But could one ever manage

57. D. Richet, "Aspects socio-culturels des conflits religieux à Paris dans la seconde moitié du xvi⁰ siècle," *Annales ESC* 32 (1977): 785 n. 40.

58. First War of Religion, from the massacre of Wassy to the Pacification of Amboise, March 1562 to March 1563. Second War of Religion, from the ambush of Meaux to the Peace of Longjumeau, September 1567 to March 1568. Third War of Religion, August 1568 to August 1570 (Peace of Saint-Germain). Saint Bartholomew's Day Massacre, August 22, 1572. Fourth War of Religion, August 1572 to July 1573 (Edict of Boulogne). Fifth War of Religion, from the Huguenot assembly at Millau to the Peace of Monsieur, July 1574 to May 1576. Sixth War of Religion, August 1576 to September 1577. Seventh War of Religion, 1579-80. Eighth and last War of Religion, 1585-98.

59. B. Cottret, *1598. L'édit de Nantes* (Paris: Perrin, 1997), pp. 55-57.

60. This had not prevented the Reformer from furnishing some preliminary suggestions in his "Proposal for the Holding of a Council." This had been sent by Calvin to the Reformed churches of France in December 1560. Calvin explained: "The points of doctrine that are now in dispute concern the service of God, that is whether it should be regulated purely and simply by the holy Scriptures or whether men can enact laws for it, and whether their traditions can compel souls under pain of mortal sin. And under this are included vows, prohibition of marriage, confession, and similar things. After this it is a question of knowing on what our confidence in our salvation is based, and whether we are justified by the merit of our works or by the gratuitous mercy of God. On this depend the matters of free will, satisfaction, purgatory, and similar things. There is also the means of invoking God, which is combined with the certainty of the faith and carries with it the intercession of saints." *Lettres françaises*, 2:352, December 1560.

to supplant the words "Lutherans," "Huguenots," and "papists"? Did anyone really want to?

The sincerity or ultimate duplicity of the actors matters little. The historian leaves it to God to sound men's hearts. One thing is clear: Poissy marked the defeat of conciliation and the survival of Calvinism. What would a French Peace of Augsburg, which the cardinal of Lorraine dreamed of, have in fact meant? Charles de Guise, cardinal of Lorraine, did not fail to cite the Lutheran example.[61] In 1555 the Diet of Augsburg had officially recognized the existence of Catholic and Lutheran territories in the bosom of the Holy Roman Empire. The religion of the subjects should conform to that of their prince, according to the formula *cujus regio, ejus religio.* Such a compromise, facilitated by the marked diversity of the German principalities, was unthinkable in France. Moreover, Calvinism was clearly distinguished from Lutheranism by its eucharistic doctrine. Calvin admitted a spiritual presence of Christ in the elements, but in no circumstances a local presence in the bread and wine of the Lord's Supper. The Lutherans, on the other hand, believed in the existence of two substances, the bread and the body of Christ, the wine and his blood. Theodore Beza clearly scented the trap set at Poissy. In any case, here Calvinism confirmed its doctrinal existence.

The colloquy took place from September 9 to October 14. In his opening speech Michel de l'Hospital compared the king to Emperor Constantine at Nicea. On September 9 Theodore Beza expressed a very clear-cut point of view on the Eucharist. "The body of Christ is as far removed from the bread and wine as the highest heaven is from earth."[62] Beza's challenge was entirely deliberate. He simply argued that Christ, being in heaven, could not be found at the same time on the Communion table. Why this rejection of ubiquity? Why specify that a body cannot be in two places at the same time? What is the reason for applying this terrestrial physics to the celestial body of the Crucified? Beza chose his target knowingly, deliberately; he was refuting not only Catholic transubstantiation but also and above all Lutheran consubstantiation, the presence of two substances in the Eucharist. There was therefore no compromise possible. Beza's apparent intransigence permitted the survival of Calvinism.[63] An

61. Wanegffelen, "Des chrétiens entre Rome et Genève," pp. 228ff.

62. J. Delumeau, *Naissance et affirmation de la Réforme* (Paris: PUF, 1965); new edition, 1973, p. 150. G. Baum, É. Cunitz, and R. Reuss, eds., *Histoire ecclésiastique des Églises réformées au royaume de France,* 3 vols. (Paris: Fischbacher, 1883-89), 1:574.

63. Theodore Beza (1519-1605) was a Burgundian noble born in Vézelay. He studied law in Orléans from 1535 to 1539. He experienced a spiritual crisis in 1548 and went to Geneva, then to Lausanne, where he taught Greek. In 1554 he defended the execution of Servetus. He was at the Colloquy of Worms in 1557, then came to Geneva to teach Greek, and in 1564 theology also. He was Calvin's true successor in Geneva.

American historian has concluded, not without humor, that the Eucharist, "the sacrament of unity," was transformed into "an apple of discord."[64] This was all for the better in one respect: henceforth Calvinism clearly existed. It was neither a variety of Lutheranism nor an inverted Catholicism. Wittenberg, Rome, and Geneva thereafter defined the boundaries of a multipolar Western Christianity. Theological wealth existed only at the cost of diversity.

Calvinism, therefore, was not a Genevan ideology. Theodore Beza had clearly demonstrated this at Poissy. After Servetus, after Castellio, Calvin chose a new adversary, François Banduin or Baudoin. Enmity, like friendship, can be elective. Calvin knew how to choose his friends, and he defined his enemies with judgment. Baudoin was the perfect compromiser. Or at least he incarnated for Calvin that ideal of conciliation that implied the swift dilution of Reformed evangelism. For Calvin Baudoin was the very embodiment of the spirit of Poissy, which, had it succeeded, would have ended the Reformers' hopes.[65] Received in Geneva in 1545 after having been condemned for heresy in Arras, Baudoin had spent his life in a university career that led him successively from Bourges to Strasbourg, from Strasbourg to Heidelberg, and finally from Heidelberg to Douai. This former servant of Antoine de Navarre totally abjured Protestantism in 1563.

Baudoin had transmitted to the participants in the colloquy a conciliatory essay written by Georg Cassander, *On the Duty of a Pious Man, a True Lover of Public Tranquility, in the Present Religious Dissension.*[66] This Catholic theologian of Cologne appealed for more charity among Christians, rejecting the extremes of both laxity and severity.[67] Calvin attributed this work to Baudoin and without delay fired off his *Response to a Crafty Interloper Who under the Pretext of Making Peace Has Tried to Obstruct the Progress of the Gospel in France.*[68] The quarrel continued. Beza lost his temper, then calmed down finally

64. Donald Nugent, *Ecumenism in the Age of the Reformation: The Colloquy of Poissy* (Cambridge: Harvard University Press, 1974), pp. 125ff.

65. Calvin, T. Wanegffelen insists rightly, attracted Beza's attention to the peril presented by F. Baudoin. The correspondence between the two men in September 1561 is enlightening. "Des Chrétiens entre Rome et Genève," p. 181. On this complex individual see the fine *thèse* of M. Turchetti, *Concordia o tolleranza? F. Bauduin e i "Moyenneurs"* (Milan: F. Angeli, 1984).

66. *De officio pii ac publicae tranquillitatis vere amantis viri in hoc religionis desidio.* G. Cassander, *Opera* (Paris, 1616), pp. 780-97.

67. J. Lecler, *Histoire de la tolérance au siècle de la Réforme,* 2 vols. (Paris: Aubier, 1955), 1:267ff. Born near Bruges, G. Cassander (1513-66) taught theology in Cologne without ever receiving ordination.

68. *Responsio ad versipellem quendam mediatorem qui pacificandi specie rectum evangelii cursum in Gallia abrumpere molitus est, OC* 9, cols. 525ff. The French edition of 1566 is reprinted in *Recueil des opuscules* (Geneva), pp. 1885-1918.

when it was pointed out to him that anger is a bad counselor and risks injuring the cause he wished to serve.[69]

Calvin in Geneva

There are only two devils in hell, of whom the said Calvin is one.

REMARK REPORTED IN DECEMBER 1554[70]

I think that this city will soon be made a Rome, and M. Calvin an idol.

MAY 1561[71]

From 1555 to 1564 (and afterward) Calvinism achieved its international image. From the first churches organized in France to the Colloquy of Poissy, from Geneva to London, and soon to Heidelberg, in Scotland as in the Netherlands, Calvinism presented itself in its double aspect, doctrinal and ecclesiastical. This does not mean that Calvin forgot Geneva — far from it. His control of the city continued without weakening. It became the symbol and incarnation of that "other" Reformation that was not absorbed into Lutheranism or Anabaptism, still less into Roman Catholicism.

As for the Genevans themselves, anti-French outbreaks did not cease entirely. In May 1555 there was murmuring in Geneva against all the naturalizations of Frenchmen admitted to the bourgeoisie. In 1556 François Périssod appeared before the consistory for having said "to the poor Provençals who are in the hospital outside the city, what are they doing there, poor wretches that they are, and would they not be more at ease in their own country? To which they answered that they were happier in their poverty than kings and princes are under the papacy" (Thursday, December 31, 1556).[72]

Rowdiness remained the only weapon against Calvinist acculturation, once all recourses of argument were exhausted. The body, in disorderly movements, in anarchistic somersaults, remained one of the favorite bases of this resistance, more instinctive than calculated. In 1557, in Saint-Gervais, Jacques Pichard tried to interrupt the sermon by making unseemly noises with his seat.

69. P.-F. Geisendorf, *Théodore de Bèze* (Geneva: Labor et Fides, 1949), p. 238.

70. Geisendorf, p. 591.

71. *Annales Calviniani, OC* 21, col. 752. The statement was attributed to the Provençal Jean Carriche. On the Geneva consistory during these years, see E. W. Monter, *Enforcing Morality in Early Modern Europe* (London: Variorum Reprints, 1987), pp. 467ff.

72. *Annales Calviniani, OC* 21, col. 656.

But, faced with the impassiveness of the audience, he got up conspicuously and went out. This same Jacques Pichard had acquired a reputation as a hard case by calling a person who woke him when he dozed off during the sermon a baboon.[73] In September 1558 it became necessary to remind people again that all games should cease during preaching, in particular shooting practice with the arquebus or crossbow.[74] Children should also be prevented from playing in the street during preaching, thus interfering with the ability of the faithful to hear (November 27, 1559).[75] The question of skittles came up again in May 1561; it was recommended that steps be taken to prohibit it on days of the Lord's Supper because of "the scandal the papists could make of the fact that on such a day there is such general playing of skittles in all the streets and so many other places."[76]

Carters gained a notorious reputation, so much so that the expression "To swear like a carter" became proverbial. But the carters also sang, above all in taverns, where they also took their meals. Humbert Tardif, a carter by trade, was severely reprimanded for having carried his song a little too far:

> Mother, I want Robin.
> Robin has gone fully armed to hell
> To look for Calvin.
> Mother, I want Robin. (November 2, 1559)[77]

In March 1556 a thorny problem arose: the prison itself was filled with joyous feasters, come "to banquet and regale themselves." With the complicity of the guard and his wife, numerous inhabitants of the Saint-Gervais quarter had joined their friend Pontus, jailed "to receive punishment for his fornication." Draconian measures were taken: the guard and his wife were imprisoned for three days, thus finding themselves among the prisoners. As for Pontus, his punishment began over again, this time on bread and water.[78] Two years earlier Calvin had protested against the happy life one led in the prison of the Évêché. "When there is a whore in prison, pies have to be brought to feast her," he exclaimed in 1554 during a sermon.[79]

Sexuality was one of the main targets for the moral control of the people. Scandal was to be avoided by removing easy temptations. The struggle

---

73. *Annales Calviniani, OC* 21, col. 677.
74. *Annales Calviniani, OC* 21, col. 705, Registres du Conseil 54, fol. 295.
75. *Annales Calviniani, OC* 21, col. 724, Registres du Conseil 55, fol. 149v.
76. *Annales Calviniani, OC* 21, col. 749.
77. *Annales Calviniani, OC* 21, col. 725.
78. *Annales Calviniani, OC* 21, col. 632, Registres du Conseil 51, fol. 60v.
79. *OC* 34, col. 144, seventy-third sermon on Job.

against promiscuity was accompanied by a new arrangement of space. Encounters between men and women were increasingly proscribed. Public baths were the headquarters for lust. In December 1549 Calvin launched his campaign against these haunts of perdition, in which cleanliness served as a pretext for lewdness. He took up the same theme again in August 1555. Calvin was indignant at the "great confusion" and "scandal" that reigned in the public baths, where "men go in promiscuously with women." There was also talk of one of the employees "who went to bed with the women, etc." The greatest concern evidently resided in this enigmatic "etc.," which left room for the blackest suspicions.[80] A radical solution was therefore adopted: the mixing of sexes was prohibited in these establishments. Henceforward the baths of Saint-Gervais and those of Longemalle would be allotted to one or the other sex, with a rotation every two years.

In February 1555, similarly, there was concern that lust might conquer the sermons, which were conducive to wandering mind, salacious reveries, and furtive glances. "It has been brought to notice here that women mix among the men and men among the women at the sermon." Therefore the people should be told "not to mix with each other, or take the places of the women, or the women those of the men, and that each should take [a place] only for himself."[81] In March 1556, to strengthen the battle against the licentious, it was decided to expose offenders "in the collar" (a sort of pillory) in front of Saint-Pierre "on Wednesday after the sermon."[82]

Mobility posed thorny problems in its turn. The foreigners were a "grace," since they came to Geneva so they could fully receive the "Word of God." But certain abuses had to be severely denounced by Calvin before the Council. In particular they had to keep watch to prevent bigamy or the breaking of promises of engagement: "Great disorder arises from various foreigners who come here to marry lightly, although some are married and the others engaged, who then leave their wives. Which could be taken care of if the lord syndic who has charge of marriages would write on the banns the names of those who attest to those separated or married, since by this means those who attested falsely would be found out and the witnesses would be made afraid to do it."[83]

In December 1556 several people complained of the rigor of the measures taken against fornication "under the law of grace." These afflicted souls claimed picturesquely "that they no longer wanted to go to the Mollard to buy linen, because someone would think they were buying linen to make a sack in which to

80. *Annales Calviniani, OC* 21, cols. 612-13, Registres du Conseil 49, fol. 163v.
81. *Annales Calviniani, OC* 21, col. 595, Registres du Conseil 49, fol. 13v.
82. *Annales Calviniani, OC* 21, col. 639, Registres du Conseil 51, fol. 173v.
83. *Annales Calviniani, OC* 21, cols. 654-55, Registres du Conseil 52, fol. 98.

throw their wives into the Rhone."[84] A few days later, on December 31, 1556, Jacques Lempereur was imprisoned for having "made strong statements against the edicts last proposed on fornication, saying that we are under the law of grace and that it would be judaizing to condemn adulterers to death."[85]

Was sexuality forbidden in this Geneva? Certainly not. The Council merely sought to moralize relations that could not exist outside marriage. From this standpoint Protestantism actually reinforced marriage by rejecting the necessity of ecclesiastical celibacy. Procreation remained the purpose of relations between spouses.[86]

The control of matrimonial morality extended to the age of spouses. The age of marriage depended on ability to procreate. Intimate relations that had only enjoyment as their object were considered fornication. The union of the widow of Claude Richardot, said to be seventy years of age, with her servant Jean Achard, a "youngster of twenty-five to twenty-six," was forbidden. The Council gave the following decision (Tuesday, January 5, 1557): "Such a union would be against nature, and rather to support fornication than the marriage state, which should be kept holy. And indeed, in view of the circumstances of the present case, the servant wanted to take his mistress, not for the principal objects of marriage, to have descendants or for reproduction or other comforts, but for riches. So that it is not according to God."[87]

Neither lechery nor avarice could be acceptable motives. In this context the marriage of Guillaume Farel at sixty-nine raised some alarm. The happy woman was a "respectable girl" named Marie, originally from Rouen, whose father, Alexandre Turol, was a refugee in Neuchâtel.[88]

---

84. *Annales Calviniani, OC* 21, col. 656.

85. *Annales Calviniani, OC* 21, col. 657.

86. Here we have somewhat refined the analysis of André Biéler, *L'homme et la femme dans la morale calviniste* (Geneva, 1963), p. 110. "To the Catholic tradition that made reproduction the first and chief end of marriage, Calvinism opposed a new ethic that assured a preference for the couple as against procreation and saw the conjugal union as, in the first place, the site of fulfillment of human existence." This idea was taken up by A.-M. Piuz and L. Mottu-Weber, *L'économie genevoise de la Réforme à la fin de l'Ancien Régime, xvie-xviiie siècles* (Geneva: Georg, Société d'histoire et d'archéologie de Genève, 1990). In May 1561 there was also a desire to fight more effectively against infanticide (abortion). *Annales Calviniani, OC* 21, col. 747.

87. *Annales Calviniani, OC* 21, col. 658, Registres du Conseil 52, fol. 188.

88. *Annales Calviniani, OC* 21, col. 703: "This marriage was found very strange and unseasonable by most, and it seemed to them that since [Farel] had reached the age of sixty-nine without being bothered with marriage he could still have dispensed with it, being on the brink of the grave. Farel was also much annoyed by the censures of his friends and the various rumors of the mob, who were ignorant of the causes that moved him. But having taken as a shield against all remarks the divine vocation that obliged him to do this

Genevan Education

The determination to influence behavior derived from the Calvinist notion of *"institution."* This was both a pedagogy and a politics, and education was the central element in the system. The need for it was made more glaring by the difficulties of all sorts that assailed Calvin, who was a bourgeois of Geneva after October 30, 1559. Theological opposition threatened to reappear at any moment, as demonstrated by the case of the Italian community, influenced by Castellio's ideas. Moreover, the former Perrinists, or "libertines," found visible support among the Bernese, who were glad to weaken their Genevan rivals.

Sharp debates shook the Italian community at the end of the 1550s. There was regular worship in Italian in Geneva from 1542 on.[89] The Italians ended up meeting at the Church of La Madeleine. The death of their minister, Celso Martinengo, in July 1557 led to grave disagreements. Mateo Gribaldi, a jurisconsult and native of Piedmont, had criticized the Trinity.[90] Among his disciples was Giorgio Blandrate, an elder of the Italian community, who arrived in

---

now and the uprightness of his conscience, aiming at a good end and using legitimate means ordered by God, he made up his mind, considering these things and others, and all his friends later gave way to his arguments. And it has been the opinion of all ever since that in making such a marriage according as he was inspired by the Almighty (and it is very certain that people such as he have had extraordinary gifts and movements in their time) he proposed to himself to provide for his old age the proper and holy aid and solace, because of his weakness, by the means that God himself has ordered for man; and to make clear a formal disavowal of Roman celibacy, claimed to be necessary to salvation, since the grace of perpetual continence is not given to all or forever. And that not having a vocation to this or the requisite grace, [not to marry] is to oppose the ordinance of God and stubbornly displease and disobey him, and also to entrap one's soul in the toils of a perpetual torment and torture of the flesh, when this is not prevented by the power of a special grace."

89. Their first pastor was the famous Bernardino Ochino (1487-1564). Originally from Siena, this former Capuchin went to Basel, then to Strasbourg, and finally to England in 1547, before dying of plague in Moravia. Calvin and especially Beza accepted with suspicion this fiery southerner, who in his catechism thought it quite right for prayers to be addressed to saints, of all things. "Senza dubbio, non solo perche nella presente vita non è huomo che non habbia bisogno dell' aiuto de Santi il che se vedde in Paulo/Coloss. 4, Thess. 3/il quale piu volte pregò i Santi, che erano in terra, che facesseno oratione per lui, ma & anco per eccitargli a esercitarsi nelle Christiane virtù, si come spetialmente se fa nell' orare" [Without doubt, not only because in this present life there is no man who does not need the aid of the saints — as is seen in Paul (Col. 4, Thess. 3), who prayed many times to the saints who were on earth to offer prayers for him — but also to cause us to practice Christian virtue, as is done in prayer especially]. *Il catechismo, o vero institutione christiana* (Basel, 1551).

90. *OC* 17, col. 175, letter from Calvin to P. Martyr, May 22, 1558.

Geneva in 1557. Calvin drove him into flight. On May 16, 1558, Calvin and the pastor and elders of the said church went to the Council to denounce its contamination by the ideas of Servetus. The Italians of the Geneva community were forced to subscribe to the Confession of Faith, although each was permitted "to offer any objections he has, or state his scruples." The Piedmontese Giovanni Paulo did not wait to be told twice; he stated his reservations clearly and then fled, "having discharged his venom."[91] In July Valentin Gentilis (or Gentil) was arrested, along with Nicolas Gallo. The latter retracted and was freed. But Gentil was stubborn; to him the Trinity Calvin professed seemed to resemble a Quaternity. But, lacking courage, he went back on his statements at the beginning of August. His judges did not find him sincere: "His supposed penitence cannot free him from the deserved penalty, which should be exemplary, especially because this church, among others, has already been seen to be troubled repeatedly by such people and similar heresies and blasphemies, which should make one fear that there are many others of the same sect who might take advantage of the impunity of the said Valentin to press on to worse and worse things."[92]

He was finally granted mercy, after much hesitation. He was put to death in Bern in 1566, eight years later. In the meantime he had to make formal amends. This was the sentence:

> Although the malice you, Valentin Gentilis, showed well merited that you should be exterminated from among men as a seducer, heretic, and schismatic, nevertheless, considering the great repentance and conversion you have professed to us, and treating you with grace and mercy rather than severity, by this our final sentence which we issue here in writing, we condemn you, Valentin Gentilis, to be stripped to your shirt, and with bare feet and head uncovered, carrying a lighted torch in your hand, here before us on your knees to beg mercy of God and of our court, confessing having wickedly done wrong and held false and heretical doctrines and that your writings in their support were wicked, which with your own hands you must put in the fire that will be lit here to be burned and reduced to ashes as pernicious things. And as a further reparation to be led in this state through the crossroads of this city and around it to the sound of the trumpet, thus depriving yourself forever of all honors and declaring yourself forever infamous. And to be prohibited from leaving our city without permission, thus having it for a perpetual prison, on pain of our indignation, of being retaken and having

91. J. Calvin, *Lettres françaises*, 2:210-11, Calvin to Galeazzo Caracciolo, marquis of Vico, July 19, 1558.

92. Roget, *Histoire du peuple*, 5:159.

your head cut off in the customary way to give an example to others who might wish to commit such an act. And we command you, our lieutenant, to have this sentence of ours put into due execution.[93]

In August 1557 hostilities with Bern disturbed the Genevans, who were threatened with capture whenever they left the territory of their city. Bern had taken up the cause of Ami Perrin, who demanded reparation from his city for the wrong done him. In Geneva they responded with prayers and with pastoral exhortations to humble themselves before God.[94] In 1557 Nicod du Chesne, a printer of missals and other breviaries, was accused of wanting to deliver up the city to Bern for the benefit of the libertines. On August 13 his head was cut off, his body hung from the gibbet of Champel, and his head attached to a pillar of the Arve Bridge. Relations with Bern improved a little in the summer of 1558; the rival city forbade its pastors to speak of predestination from the pulpit.

On November 29, 1558, a city watchman, Claude Pellisson, was attacked in a baker's shop in Étrambières. His attacker was none other than Philibert Berthelier, who wanted to avenge the condemnation and execution of his younger brother, François-Daniel, three years earlier. During the squabble Berthelier announced indignantly that Calvin "was a wicked man, a traitor, and a bugger, and also all those who supported him."[95] On December 15 the same gang also shot dead a citizen of Geneva with a pistol.

In 1563 there was a new plot to deliver Geneva up to Savoy, organized by Balthasar Sept and André Philippe, son of the man decapitated in 1540, in company with Philibert Berthelier. Wednesday, December 22, a day of thanksgiving proclaimed by Calvin, marked the defeat of the attempt, which was repaid by the double execution of Pierre Panchaud and Jacques Papaz.

It is in this troubled context that we must place the foundation of the Academy of Geneva. In December 1558 the Reformed clergy of Lausanne, led by Viret, resisted the injunctions of Bern. The Bernese wanted to prevent pastors from pronouncing more excommunications. They also commanded them not to preach anymore on predestination. Excommunication and predestination in this period were two identifiable areas associated with Calvin's teaching or practice. Confronted by this manifest anti-Calvinism, the ministers suspended the celebration of the Lord's Supper on Christmas Day and put it off to January 1. Bern angrily deferred it to Easter, threatening to depose Viret and his colleagues; in February 1559 they were removed, except for several who submitted. In March Viret and several colleagues were very warmly welcomed in

93. Roget, *Histoire du peuple*, 5:164-65.
94. *Annales Calviniani*, *OC* 21, cols. 671-72.
95. Roget, *Histoire du peuple*, 5:198.

Geneva. Calvin, in difficulties at the time, found them a precious support; he also leaned on Theodore Beza.

At this juncture, in June 1559, the ordinances or statutes of the College of Geneva were published. This was not coincidental. The Ecclesiastical Ordinances of November 1541 had mentioned the fundamental purpose of teaching: "Since one cannot profit by such lessons [in theology] without first being taught languages and humane studies, and also because there is need to raise up seed for the times to come so as not to leave an empty church to our children, a college must be organized to teach children in order to prepare them both for the ministry and for the civil government."[96]

But things went slowly. In 1556 Calvin proposed to the Council to enlarge the school of Rive, using the grounds of the former Bolomier Hospital. The first practical decisions were put off until January 1558; the work was undertaken in the spring. At the same time Calvin wrote in vain to Jean Mercier, originally from Uzès, professor of Hebrew at the future Collège de France, to urge him to come to Geneva (March 16).[97] In August he wrote in the same terms to Tremelius, professor at Heidelberg, but had no success with him either. The plan was in fact for a double institution, both a college and an academy. Three professors were to teach Hebrew, Greek, and Latin. The college itself was divided into seven classes, "two for reading and writing, the third to begin declensions, the fourth where they will begin Latin syntax and the elements of the Greek language, the fifth where they will continue with Greek syntax and begin dialectic, the sixth and seventh always advancing farther."[98]

In October three chairs for lecturers (or professors) were established, along with seven regents (teachers). Theodore Beza took charge of Greek. Stipends were 280 florins for the professors and 240 for the regents. (Calvin's income, by comparison, was 500 florins.) The *Book of the College* underlined some points: "It is notorious that an infinity of errors customarily result from lack of knowledge, and . . . the chief strength of a republic consists in the virtue of its citizens."[99]

The new institution was hard to recruit for, until the opportune dismissal of the ministers of Lausanne.[100] On June 5, 1559, Calvin and Viret proposed

96. J. Calvin, *Calvin, homme d'Église* (Geneva: Labor et Fides, 1971), p. 34. See also R. Stauffer, "Calvinism and the Universities," in *University and Reformation: Lectures from the University of Copenhagen Symposium,* ed. L. Grane (Leyden: Brill, 1981), pp. 76-98.

97. *OC* 17, col. 94.

98. Roget, *Histoire du peuple,* 5:229.

99. Roget, *Histoire du peuple,* 5:230-31.

100. In May 1559 Calvin presented the Council with a complete list: Antoine Chevalier for Hebrew, François Béraud for Greek, Jean Tagaud for philosophy. The seven regents, or teachers, were Jean Randon, Jean Duperril, Claude Malbuet, Pierre Duc, Gervais Eynault, Jean Barbier, and Jean Lauréat.

the ordinances of the college to the Council. Their solemn promulgation took place in the Church of Saint-Pierre. "Let the regents, in reading, preserve a measured gravity in their faces, direct no invectives against the authors they are expounding, but take pains to explain their meaning faithfully. Let them keep the children silent, without making noise. Let them reprove rebels and sluggards, punishing them according to their faults. Above all let them teach them to love God and hate vice. Let them nourish mutual and truly Christian concord among themselves and not offend each other in their lessons."[101]

The principal, a man who must "fear God," was elected by the ministers and professors and confirmed by the syndics and Council. The life of the students was highly regulated: a sermon on Wednesday morning, two sermons on Sunday morning, and another on Sunday afternoon — without forgetting, one supposes, the catechism. In church they were under the vigilant observation of at least four teachers to enforce their assiduity and attention. Life followed an immutable rhythm: rise at six o'clock in summer, seven in winter, then prayers and teaching. Finally breakfast. Dinner at ten o'clock. Then the good children exercised their lungs by singing psalms for an hour before returning to their work. Any corporal punishment needed was administered at four o'clock, followed by the Lord's Prayer, the Confession of Faith, the Ten Commandments, and the principal's blessing. The discipline was rigorous: spanking, birching, and being given bread and water were part of a repressive arsenal employed against games, insolence, and absence from catechism. Nevertheless, in 1563 the teacher Claude Bardet was suspended for mistreatment of the children.

A Latin exercise completed the year in April, before a sort of distribution of prizes that took place in the Church of Saint-Pierre on May 1. This day of promotion was accompanied by gifts of money to the most meritorious. The academy numbered about 160 students in 1559, the college nearly 600 pupils.[102]

Strongly marked by Calvinist doctrine, the Academy of Geneva nevertheless was not an ecclesiastical institution. "We must be aware of the ambivalent position of the Academy of Geneva. It was primarily a governmental institution."[103] The inaugural address pronounced by Theodore Beza on June 5, 1559, in the Cathedral of Saint-Pierre hardly mentioned the church. It insisted, on the contrary, on the role and authority of the magistrates, called to protect the young institution. In his closing speech Calvin expressed the same opinion,

101. Roget, *Histoire du peuple*, 5:235.

102. Medicine was taught from 1559 on, thanks to Blaise Hollande, doctor of medicine.

103. W. F. Dankbaar, "L'office des docteurs chez Calvin," in *Regards contemporains sur Jean Calvin* (Paris: PUF, 1965), p. 122.

praising the "goodwill of the magnificent Council" and addressing his compliments to it in the name of the whole school.

This same secular evolution appeared again in the Ordinances of 1561, which completed the text promulgated twenty years before: "The church of Geneva is no longer only the church of the Genevan citizens."[104] The community of the faithful henceforth was not confounded with the "citizens" or "bourgeois" of the city.

Illness and Death, May 27, 1564

No man knoweth of his [Moses'] sepulchre unto this day.

DEUTERONOMY 34:6

Everyone admits that what moved Our Lord to hide the body of Moses was the fear that the people of Israel would err by worshipping it.

CALVIN, *TREATISE ON RELICS*, 1543[105]

In delicate health, Calvin suffered all his life from terrible migraines. In 1555 he began to have severe pains in his side; pleurisy was feared. Three years later at-

104. Otto Weber, "Compétence de l'Église et compétence de l'État d'après les Ordonnances ecclésiastiques de 1561," in *Regards contemporains sur Jean Calvin*, p. 77. "The Ordinances [of 1541] were published with the agreement of the 'people' of Geneva, who included, for legislative acts, all those who had the right to vote, that is the 'citizens' and 'bourgeois'; the mere inhabitants did not have the right to vote, enjoying neither the privileges of citizens nor the rights of bourgeois. By contrast with this, the edition of 1561 included an attachment, the fruit of a resolution adopted on February 9, 1560, that specified that not only the 'people' but the entire 'body of the church' had the right to participate in the election of ministers and elders. The text of the Ordinances [of 1561] reveals that henceforth there was no longer an identity between the personnel of the 'civil community' and the 'Christian community' (K. Barth). In the choosing of the elders the double formula, 'the people *and* the whole body of the church' was indeed completely *renounced;* one no longer spoke of 'all those of the church' who must be given the liberty of disputing the aptitude of a proposed elder who had previously been announced to the church. The attachment we have just been speaking of refers expressly to the text in force since 1541, which spoke of the 'company of the faithful.' One might observe that the ecclesiastical power was indeed in the hands of the magistrates of the city, but that the rights that were, so to speak, internal to the church were controlled by the ecclesiastical community, that is by all the inhabitants of the city as members of the church."

105. J. Calvin, *Traité des reliques* (1543), in *La vraie piété*, ed. I. Backus and C. Chimelli (Geneva: Labor et Fides, 1986), p. 164.

tacks of fever did not prevent him from working intermittently. He had to keep to his room for several months beginning in September 1558. He hardly ate or drank; his forty-eight-hour fasts were accompanied by a marvelous lucidity of mind. His illness paradoxically permitted him to work on the last revision of his *Institutes,* which appeared in 1559-60. He could hardly take his broth in the evening before being seized again by terrible headaches. Calvin was absent from all meetings of the consistory from October 20, 1558, to February 11, 1559, and wrote no letters between November 17 and January 15.[106] On December 24, 1559, he had to strain his voice to preach. The next day he spat blood. Consumption was diagnosed. Hemorrhoids also harassed him, and in 1561 gout made its appearance. Most fortunately, he could count on the friendship and devotion of his collaborators. Among them was Charles de Joinviller (ca. 1517-90), who often served as his secretary. He confided in 1563: "Seeing Calvin almost crushed by the continual labor of his correspondence and not employing the aid of a secretary, I finally begged him to spare himself, and added that his letters would not be less agreeable if written by another's hand, if only they were signed by his. He answered that he feared people would take the thing ill and believe themselves neglected if he did not write himself. I gave the arguments that appeared good to me. He finally let himself be conquered, and now he accepts the help of others."[107]

Like a number of his contemporaries — one thinks of Erasmus and Montaigne — Calvin had extremely severe kidney problems. "The pains, or rather the torments of a desperate colic[108] cannot let go of me. . . . The affliction of my body has almost stupefied my mind," he explained to a correspondent in the spring of 1563.[109] He added some days later, "I have been tormented for the space of two weeks by a colic so extreme that all my senses and my mind have been as it were made useless by its fierceness and pain."[110] These terrible attacks of kidney stones lasted until the end of June. Calvin courageously explained to Bullinger on July 2, 1563: "As the retention of urine was very painful to me, following the advice of the doctors I mounted on horseback so the jolting would help me pass the stone, large as a hazel-nut. On returning home, instead of urine, I passed murky blood. The next day the stone passed from the vesicle into the duct, with still crueler torments. For more than half an hour, by shaking my whole body, I strove to free myself. I accomplished nothing until I was helped by hot-water compresses. The duct

---

106. Roget, *Histoire du peuple,* 5:197.
107. *OC* 20, cols. 131-32, Joinviller to Bullinger, August 10, 1563.
108. [Translator: *Colique néphrétique,* attack of pain from kidney stones.]
109. *OC* 20, col. 30, letter of May 25, 1563, to Soubise.
110. *OC* 20, col. 34, letter of June 1, 1563, to the queen of Navarre.

was entirely ulcerated inside, and a strong flow of blood emerged. After two days it seemed to me that I was reborn."[111]

Headaches and gout poisoned the body that had hardly recovered from kidney stones; he was overcome by breathlessness. Almost a year to the day before his passing, Calvin wrote his last letter to his friend Farel. He gave a lucid account of his situation: "May you be well, very good and dear brother, and since it pleases God that you remain after me, live, remembering our union, the fruit of which awaits us in heaven, since it was profitable to the church of God. . . . I breathe with great difficulty and from hour to hour expect my breath to fail. It is enough that I live and die in Christ, who is gain for his followers in life and in death. I commend you to God with the brethren there" (May 2, 1563).[112]

Calvin died on May 27, 1564, at age fifty-four, one month and thirteen days from his fifty-fifth birthday. Here we follow the faithful account of Theodore Beza.[113] Feeling his time coming, Calvin symbolically shared a last meal with his friends:

[On] Friday, May 19, because according to the custom of this church all the ministers gather to judge each other's lives and doctrine and then in sign of friendship take a meal together, he agreed that the supper would be held in his house, where, having had himself brought in a chair, he said these words on entering, "My brothers, I have come to see you for the last time, since after this I will never come to the table."

This was a pitiable entrance for us, although he himself gave the prayer as he best could and forced himself to entertain us, although he could eat very little. Nevertheless before the end of the supper he took leave and had himself carried back to his room, which was nearby, saying these words with the happiest expression he could: "A wall between us will not prevent me from being joined in spirit with you."

Beza's account changes to direct quotation. Calvin's words evoke Christ's parting farewell at the Last Supper. Calvin's last supper takes on a testamentary character. Calvin passes away, having preserved to the end the greatest lucidity. "The day he died he seemed to speak more strongly and more at ease, but it was a last effort of nature. For in the evening about eight o'clock all of a sudden the signs of immediate death appeared, which being promptly told to me, because a

---

111. *OC* 20, cols. 53-54.

112. *OC* 20, cols. 302-3; French translation in *OC* 21, col. 44; life by Beza and Colladon.

113. See T. Beza, *L'histoire de la vie et mort de Calvin* (1565), *OC* 21, cols. 45-46, for the quotes that follow.

little earlier I had left; having hurried back with another of my brethren, I found he had already given up the spirit so peacefully that, never having given the death-rattle, having been able to speak intelligibly down to the moment of death, with good sense and judgment, without ever having moved hand or foot, he seemed rather asleep than dead."

Then, contrasting with this simplicity and unadorned style, Beza suddenly shifts to hyperbole. He lets his emotion break forth. "Behold how at the same instant on that day the sun went down and the greatest light there was in this world for the direction of the church of God was taken to heaven."

Not without modesty, Beza thus describes the effect of his passing on the city: "The following night, and during the day also, there was great weeping in the city. For its officials regretted the prophet of the Lord, the poor flock of the church wept at the departure of its faithful shepherd, the school lamented its true doctor and master, and all in general wept for their true father and consoler after God."

It was necessary, however, to control the spontaneous piety of the crowd and avoid the excesses of the multitude. Death must preserve its mystery.

Many desired to see his face again, as if not able to let him alone, either alive or dead. Many strangers had also come earlier from far away to see him, and not having been able to do so because it was still not thought he would die so soon, they greatly desired to see him, dead as he was, and applied to do so. But to prevent all calumnies he was shrouded about eight o'clock in the morning, and at two in the afternoon carried in the customary manner, as he also had ordered, to the common cemetery, called Plainpalais, without any pomp or show whatever, where he lies now, awaiting the resurrection he taught us about and so constantly hoped for. The body was followed by the greater part of the city and by people of all ranks, who would regret him all the longer because they had little expectation of recovering, at least for a long time, from such and so injurious a loss.

Calvin was not a saint. . . . Perhaps he was a prophet.

PART III

BELIEFS

CHAPTER 12

Calvin the Polemicist

Calvin, the advocate of God, made himself the accuser of men and censor of his contemporaries.

O. MILLET[1]

A reformer is a man involved in public affairs. Calvin had long experienced nostalgia for another destiny; he might have been a humanist, a man of letters, a writer, a professor, or a theologian. He had actually been all these, but he had exercised his calling among his fellow beings, in that century of rebirth when the status of intellectual was detached with difficulty, and sometimes with regret, from that of cleric. God had mysteriously decided this for him, by tearing him from his ivory tower to establish him in Geneva, after having led him to Basel and Strasbourg.

His literary production, however, was only part of his activity. And it still bore at times an offhanded, desultory character, dictated by the necessities of the moment. Calvin, author of the majestic *Institutes of the Christian Religion,* also excelled in the genre of the pamphlet. Indeed, he fought a war without quarter against the papists, the Anabaptists, and the "spiritual" libertines that amazes us a little with its combined verve, fire, and virulence. To adopt a recent formula, a true "logic of execration" on both sides consecrated the birth of doctrinal Calvinism.[2]

---

1. J. Calvin, *Oeuvres choisies,* ed. O. Millet (Paris: Gallimard, Folio classique, 1995), preface, p. 12.
2. A.-M. Brenot, "La peste soit des Huguenots. Étude d'une logique d'exécration au xvie siècle," *Histoire, Économie et Société,* no. 4 (1992): 553-70.

Was it fanaticism? No doubt, in part. Calvin was poorly adapted to pious idealization and bogus refinement. His intransigence was the reverse side of his convictions. But it would be wrong to fasten the role of narrow moralizer on someone who was above all a remarkable polemicist. His criticisms of papism hardly prevented him from raving against Geneva — far from it — or indeed from making it known to anyone who was listening that the Reformation was taking too long. Many examples of this impatience could be given. A long letter to Guillaume Farel in May 1544 reveals the Reformer's uneasiness when he cries, "I begin to learn again what it means to live in Geneva! I am in the midst of the thorns."[3]

Calvin was thus neither a saint nor a dictator, neither a Savonarola nor a Lenin. On the whole, he belonged to the prophetic tradition. He was one who proclaimed or was called. His writing derived from his speech; in polemics it preserved the spontaneity of invective. Often personal in the beginning, his attacks ended by defining a human type: the false "Nicodemites," ashamed of their faith; the "spiritual libertines," forgetful of the law; the astrologers and forgers, makers of horoscopes or of relics.

Confessional Construction

Calvin's activity can be understood only in relation to a process of "confessional construction" that affected both the Reformers and their Catholic adversaries. The denunciation of "Lutherans" was gaining ground in the kingdom of France after the Placards of 1534 (see app. 5). In August 1542 letters patent required the parlements to "search out and punish the Lutherans." "There is still some bad seed of errors and damnable doctrines that sprouts and grows from day to day to our very great regret and displeasure in many places and regions of our kingdom and country."[4]

This legislation culminated the following year in the statement of dogma ratified by the Sorbonne on March 10, 1543, and taken up by Francis I, "patron and protector of the Gallican church," on July 23. The elaboration of this text was a considerable departure; it is explained by the challenge of the "Lutheran" ideas that had already been strongly condemned by the faculty twenty years before. Until then the medieval church had been content with an extremely general declaration of faith, accompanied when necessary by the rejection of this or that error. But that had been a far cry from this single normative text, fixing

---

3. *Opera Calvini* (hereafter cited as *OC*) 11, cols. 719-22, May 31, 1544.
4. M. Isambert, ed., *Recueil des anciennes lois françaises* 12 (Paris: Belin-Leprieur, 1828), p. 786.

the contents of belief with precision.[5] This synthesis of Catholic faith on the eve of the Council of Trent has undeniable interest for the historian. Like any prescriptive text, it makes it possible to imagine in counterpoint the rule and its infringement. What should be believed? What were the points at issue between Catholics and "Lutherans"?

These French "Lutherans," it must be pointed out, were neither adherents of Luther's nor as yet sectaries of Calvin's. What can we know about what they believed, based on the denunciation of their errors? This vast panorama of the Catholic faith in the bosom of the French church contains twenty-five articles (see app. 6).

The intermediary role of the saints and the Virgin Mary was vigorously reasserted. The principal danger the French "Lutherans" presented was disciplinary and anthropological; they did not respect the ecclesiastical hierarchy and they infringed the norms of legitimate piety.

> It must not be doubted that both the saints who are in this mortal life and those who are in paradise work miracles.
>
> It is a thing holy and very agreeable to God to pray to the blessed mother of God, the Virgin Mary, and to the saints in heaven, so they may be advocates and intercessors for us with God.
>
> And therefore we should not only imitate and follow these saints reigning with Jesus Christ, but honor and pray to them.[6]

It is proper, under this head, to respect the forms of devotion. "It must not be doubted in the least that it is a good work to kneel down before the images of the crucifix, of the Virgin Mary, and of the other saints to pray to Our Lord Jesus Christ and to the saints."

However, this Gallican text grants the Holy See only limited power. While conceding to the pope a "divine right," it confers the supreme magistracy of the church in matters of faith and of morals on the general council, in conformity

---

5. Fidelity to Scripture, to the definitions of the councils, and to the decisions of the faculty were the three fundamental points in the oath taken before theological "disputations." J. K. Farge, *Orthodoxy and Reform in Early Reformation France: The Faculty of Theology of Paris, 1500-1543* (Leyden: Brill, 1985), pp. 160ff.

6. Isambert, pp. 822-23. The Eucharist was defined in fairly general terms, without referring explicitly to the scholastic distinction between substance and accidents (p. 822): "Every Christian is required to believe firmly that in the consecration performed in the true sacrament of the altar the bread and the wine are converted into the true body and blood of Jesus Christ, and after the said consecration there remain only the species of the said bread and wine, under which is really present the true body of Jesus Christ, who being born of the Virgin Mary suffered on the tree of the cross."

with the decrees of the Council of Constance (1414-18). Some concluding lines reaffirm the peril posed by the Lutherans. Those "running after new things and doctrines" abandon the "praiseworthy custom of imploring the grace of the gracious Holy Spirit through the intercession of the most blessed Virgin Mary," the Hail Mary. Moreover, the faithful are reminded of the devotion to the sweet name of Jesus. "There is no other name under heaven by virtue of which we could be saved." Finally, let them give up the irritating habit of saying Paul, James, Matthew, Peter, Augustine, or Jerome in place of Saint Paul, Saint James, Saint Matthew, Saint Peter, etc. The tract ends by enjoining prayers for the souls of the dead.

Obviously these French "Lutherans" were not Calvinists in a strict sense. The mention of infant baptism, indeed, indicates the likely presence of Anabaptists among them. Thus they did not have a unified confession of faith; the fear they inspired was much more anthropological than truly theological. They were characterized by their nonconformity and their rejection of certain acts — kneeling to statues, observance of Lent, Masses for the dead.

Calvin's response to these articles deprived the Mass of its propitiatory character, both for the living and the dead. "The instituting words of Jesus Christ say to take and eat, not to offer up."[7] The response was nourished, like Antoine Marcourt's Placards, on meditation on the Epistle to the Hebrews. It also introduced a radical attack on the social habits of a Christian people accustomed to see in the celebration of the Mass, and more generally in all liturgical rites, a reassuring system of symbolic exchanges.

Calvin hurled himself into all-out polemics against the Catholics. In 1544 the first *Index of Forbidden Books* appeared, about 230 titles cited by the faculty of theology of Paris. Calvin responded in his *Statement concerning the Censure Imposed by the Beasts of the Sorbonne on Books They Call Heretical.*[8] Do the "beasts" of the Sorbonne refer to the faculty of theology at that institution? Calvin used all the resources of the bestiaries and fables in this acrimonious denunciation; he compared the theologians to calves. It was George Orwell's *Animal Farm,* four centuries before its time. This gave way to a whole procession of metaphors based on the association of ideas or on substitution. "Following the proverb that says that an ox can be known by its horns, we cannot better discover what beasts these are than by their actions." Which leads us briefly to recall the proverb, "The habit does not make the monk." This little work of the

7. J. Calvin, *Les articles de la sacrée faculté de théologie de Paris . . . avec le remède contre le poison* (1544). Cited by F. Higman, *La diffusion de la Réforme en France* (Geneva: Labor et Fides, 1992), p. 143.

8. *Catalogue des livres censurés,* and *Avertissement sur la censure qu'ont fait les bêtes de Sorbonne, touchant les livres qu'ils appellent hérétiques.*

moment ends in a set piece in which the caricaturist moves gradually, if not from the cock to the ass, at least from the pig to the wolf, after having, in an extraordinary series of fade-outs, visibly gone through all the intermediate stages: dogs, calves, oxen, bulls, and wolves, eaters of sheep:

> In conclusion there remains what I asked in the beginning, that is, how one should name such beasts. One sees great drunkards, who overturn, like pigs with their snouts, all the holy doctrines of Our Lord. One sees, as it were, mastiffs who bay after the servants of God. One sees beasts foolish as calves and clumsy as oxen. One sees savage bulls who thrust furiously with their horns at both the Word of God and its ministers. One sees lions accustomed to devour whatever they meet. One sees wolves who ask only to invade the flocks and strangle and murder the poor sheep. One sees asses who have hidden only their ears. Thus one can know what they are.[9]

Then, maliciously: "But as for me, I cannot find any name for them accurate enough to express all their qualities."

False Devotees and True Hypocrites: the "Nicodemites"

Let us be secret disciples, like Nicodemus.

PIERRE VIRET, *LETTER SENT TO THE FAITHFUL*, 1543[10]

A faithful man associating with the papists cannot participate in their superstitions without offending God.

JOHN CALVIN, *APOLOGY TO THE NICODEMITES*, 1544[11]

The Gospel of John tells us the story of the Jewish dignitary who came to visit Jesus in secret. Nicodemus admitted the supernatural character of Jesus' acts, but he came by night, hidden from view. He later intervened to remind the other Pharisees who wanted to attack Jesus of what the law said. Finally he ac-

---

9. J. Calvin, *Advertissement sur la censure,* printed in full in Higman, *La diffusion de la Réforme en France,* pp. 158-66.

10. *Épître envoyée aux fidèles.* F. Higman, "Calvin polémiste," *Études Théologiques et Religieuses* 69 (1994): 355.

11. J. Calvin, *Excuse de Iehan Calvin à Messieurs les Nicodémites, sur la complaincte qu'ilz font de sa trop grand'rigueur* (1544), *OC* 6, col. 593.

companied Joseph of Arimathea in taking the crucified body to the tomb.[12] To underline better the character of this discreet and modest individual, at each of his brief appearances the Evangelist invariably recalls that he was the one who "came to Jesus by night."

It was tempting to be inspired by this example to preach a religion of the heart more than of observances, indifferent to external rites and received opinions. Was Nicodemus an authentic Christian or a dissimulator? Might one invoke his example in adversity? Was it permissible to reform oneself in one's heart to welcome Jesus Christ while externally sacrificing to the rites of popery?

This phenomenon was more complex than is generally believed. It is accompanied by a question of intellectual history, the possible difference between popular religion and that of the elite. To feign or dissimulate supposes a shrinking from received ideas and accepted practices; this ambivalence is impossible for the more humble. Calvin was all the more intolerant of the Nicodemites because he saw in them intellectuals betraying their vocation, or, to repeat the formula he adopted, "sensitive protonotaries."[13] Compromise quickly becomes compromise with conscience. In his always vivid fashion, Calvin scoffed at these people who wanted "to make Jesus Christ their cook, to prepare their dinner well."[14] Calvin likewise hardly spared those parlor evangelicals who, knowing the gospel, converted it to worldliness. "The sensitive protonotaries . . . are well content to have the Gospel and to talk happily about it with the ladies, provided this does not prevent them from living at their own pleasure. I would put the court favorites in the same rank, and the ladies who have never learned anything except to be fondled, and yet do not know what it is to have anyone speak at all rudely to their graces."[15]

Certain humanists also know the truth but do not try to spread it outside their own gatherings. "This group is almost entirely men of letters." These fine spirits "fall asleep in the belief that it is quite enough that they recognize God."[16]

In these disciplined pages Calvin strikes out at the French evangelism of his youth. Neither the entourage of Marguerite de Navarre nor the men of letters had finally embraced the Reform, from which they were turned aside by that singular egotism of salvation that lies in wait for the Christian conscience. The *Letter to Sadoleto* was already firmly decided on this point; the solitary

---

12. John 3:1ff.; 7:50ff.; 19:38ff.
13. Protonotaries are ecclesiastics who hold a high rank under bishops.
14. Calvin, *Excuse . . . à Messieurs les Nicodémites, OC* 6, col. 598.
15. Calvin, *Excuse . . . à Messieurs les Nicodémites, OC* 6, cols. 598-99.
16. Calvin, *Excuse . . . à Messieurs les Nicodémites, OC* 6, col. 600

quest for salvation and an excessive concern with the hereafter belong to the same clerical imposture. The future, like salvation, depends only on God; it is not achieved by the accumulation of merits. By wanting to save oneself alone, one can only lose oneself. "Whoever holds his soul for precious in this world will lose it."[17]

If the social and intellectual elites thus risk passing by the evangelical message, the common people turn away from it, preferring the tranquillity of their households. Finally Calvin brings up a last category, the atheists. He hardly uses this word, but refers to the "Lucianites or Epicureans," all "despisers of God," who think his Word is nothing but a "fable" and a lie.[18] The word "atheism" certainly requires some reservations; it brings up a debate that is already old, since Lucien Febvre refused to employ the word for the sixteenth century. Let us say that here atheism includes both those who denied God and the indifferent, who totally rejected the authority of the Bible.

The question of Nicodemism lends itself to divergent interpretations; does it mean deliberate dissimulation, a compromise unwillingly endured, or a nonconfessional form of Christianity?[19] The nickname "Nicodemism" can certainly be attributed to Calvin, but the phenomenon was far from new.[20] Bucer, for example, advised Christians to work for the reform of the church wherever they found themselves, including, for lack of anything better, in the bosom of Roman Catholicism.[21] Several publications already warned against the risks of dissimulation prior to Calvin's treatises. They were the work of Guillaume Farel and Pierre Viret, and they all appeared in Geneva from the presses of Jean Girard. Exhortation, consolation, remonstrance, and admonition were the master words of a literature of combat that preached exile or resistance.[22]

---

17. Calvin, *Excuse . . . à Messieurs les Nicodémites, OC* 6, col. 604.

18. Calvin, *Excuse . . . à Messieurs les Nicodémites, OC* 6, col. 602.

19. C. Ginzburg, *Il Nicodemismo. Simulazione e dissimulazione religiosa dell'Europa del'500* (Turin: Einaudi, 1970); F. Higman, "The Question of Nicodemism," in *Calvinus Ecclesiae Genevensis Custos*, ed. W. H. Neuser (Frankfurt: P. Lang, 1984); T. Wanegffelen, "Des Chrétiens entre Rome et Genève. Une histoire du choix religieux en France, vers 1520-vers 1610" (*thèse* at the University of Paris I [Panthéon-Sorbonne], November 12, 1994; typescript, 2 vols., 913 pp.). Wanegffelen describes with great skill Calvin's hesitations regarding the term "Nicodemism," which led him to speak in Latin of *"pseudo nicodemitae"* (1:111).

20. Higman, "Calvin polémiste," p. 349.

21. Bucer, *Consilium theologicum privatim conscriptum*, ed. P. Fraenkel (Leyden: Brill, 1988).

22. G. Farel, *Épître exhortatoire à tous ceux qui ont congnoissance de l'Évangile, les admonestant de cheminer purement et vivre selon iceluy, glorifiant Dieu et édifiant le prochain par parolles, et par oeuvres, et saincte conversation* (1544); P. Viret, *Épistre consolatoire, envoyée aux fidèles qui souffrent persécution pour le nom de Jésus et vérité évangélique*

Dated from Neuchâtel on August 11, 1542, but published two years later, Farel's *Letter of Exhortation* insisted on the need for the truly faithful to edify their neighbors. The glory of God and concern for others both require that one put one's life in accord with one's thinking, and one's acts in relation to one's faith. All double-dealing is thus proscribed; the service of God requires "faith in the heart and confession in the mouth."[23] The rejection of popery depends directly on faith in Christ, the only Savior; "the death and passion of Jesus" suffice, without all the encumbrances of the Mass and the cult of saints.

Issued in 1543, Viret's *Letter Sent to the Faithful* was contemporaneous with Calvin's *Short Treatise,* which also condemned dissimulation. But Viret shows himself more moderate than Calvin. He mentions the example of Nicodemus — "If Nicodemus went to Jesus Christ by night, nevertheless he did not blaspheme or deny him by day"[24] — and admits that everyone does not have a vocation to martyrdom; Nicodemism is legitimate in certain cases.

> If we cannot reach to this high degree and to this Christian perfection [of the martyrs], and we do not dare to confess Jesus Christ openly without danger to our lives, and we do not feel in ourselves the constancy to endure death for his name, let us at least come to the next stage. Let us be secret disciples, like Nicodemus. And if we do not manifest ourselves clearly, at least we do no dishonor to Jesus Christ and do not collaborate with his adversaries by participating at the devils' table.
>
> And if we find ourselves still more infirm than Nicodemus, and from fear of losing our goods, our honor, and our lives we are forced to dissimulate too much and to communicate with the idolaters, at least let us not justify ourselves, but condemn ourselves. Let us recognize our excessive weakness and the excessively burning love we still have for ourselves and the goods and

---

(1541); Viret, *Épistre envoyée aux fidèles conversans entre les Chrestiens Papistiques, pour leur remonstrer comment ilz se doyvent garder d'être souillez et polluez par leurs superstitions et idolâtries, et de déshonnorer Jésus Christ par icelles* (1543); Viret, *De la communication des fidèles qui congnoissent la vérité de l'Évangile, aux cérémonies des papistes, et principalement à leurs Baptesmes, Mariages, Messes, Funérailles, et Obsèques pour les trespassez* (1547); Viret, *Remonstrance aux fidèles, qui conversent entre les Papistes, et principalement à ceux qui sont en Court et qui ont offices publiques, touchant le moyen qu'ilz doivent tenir en leur vocation, à l'exemple des anciens serviteurs de Dieu, sans contrevenir à leur devoir, ny envers Dieu, ny envers leur prochain, et sans se mettre témérairement en danger, et donner par leur témérité et par leur coulpe juste occasion à leurs adversaires de les mal traitter* (1547); Viret, *Admonition et consolation aux fidèles qui délibèrent de sortir d'entre les Papistes, pour éviter idolâtrie, contre les tentations qui leur peuvent advenir, et les dangiers auxquelz ilz peuvent tomber en leur yssue* (1547).

23. Higman, "Calvin polémiste," p. 351.
24. Higman, "Calvin polémiste," p. 355.

honors of this world rather than for Jesus Christ and his Word. Let us recognize the misfortune and captivity we are in.[25]

There only remained for Viret to implore "the Lord to have pity and mercy on the poor weaklings and unfaithful."[26] Calvin was much more radical in his *Short Treatise Showing What a Faithful Man Who Knows the Truth of the Gospel Should Do when He Is among the Papists* (1543). This was a rewriting of the Latin *epistola* he sent to Duchemin in 1536. Calvin already implicitly identified the category of Nicodemism, but unlike Viret, he still did not use the word. "Our Lord is not content if we recognize him in secret and in our hearts, but he strictly requires us to declare before men by an external profession that we are his."[27]

Many things had changed since 1536, however. Calvin had been established in Geneva, where he carried on pastoral duties, and the existence of this asylum on the edge of the kingdom made it possible to go into exile and reach Geneva. Compromise was no longer excusable; one must choose. The solution proposed by Calvin took account of geopolitical evolution; besides Strasbourg, Neuchâtel and above all Geneva offered the persecuted believer temporary asylum. "The solution of exile was henceforth presented as desirable, if not essential; the struggle against 'Nicodemism,' which would take a decisive turn with the *Apology* of 1544, would serve to reinforce with an inflow of refugees the Reformed citadel the Reformer wished to build in the city on the Léman."[28]

The *Apology to the Nicodemites* of 1544 provided a conclusive statement of the Reformer's thought. The thesis of the work is simple: it is wrong to avail oneself of the example of Nicodemus, "who came to see Our Lord by night, and did not declare himself to be one of his disciples."[29] Calvin explains: "This doctrine is clear. I have proved it by testimony from Scripture and reasons so certain that it is impossible to contradict it. What is more, there is a peremptory reason, which settles things in a word. For since God created our bodies and our souls and supports and nourishes them, this is a good reason why he should be served and honored. Besides, we know that the Lord does us the honor to call not only our souls his temples, but also our bodies. Now I ask you, is it lawful to profane the temple of God?"[30]

The worthiness of the body was accompanied by an obsession with physi-

25. Higman, "Calvin polémiste," p. 355.

26. Higman, "Calvin polémiste," p. 356.

27. J. Calvin, *Petit traicté monstrant que c'est que doit faire un homme fidèle congnoissant la vérité de l'Évangile, quand il est entre les papistes* (1543), OC 6, col. 544.

28. O. Millet, *Calvin et la dynamique de la Parole. Essai de rhétorique réformée* (Paris: H. Champion, 1992), col. 810.

29. J. Calvin, *Excuse . . . à Messieurs les Nicodémites,* OC 6, cols. 589-614.

30. Calvin, *Excuse . . . à Messieurs les Nicodémites,* OC 6, col. 608.

cal purity: "Since the body of a faithful man is destined to the glory of God and should someday participate in the immortality of his kingdom and be made to conform to that of Our Lord Jesus, it is too absurd a thing for it to be abandoned to any pollution, such as to prostitute it before an idol."[31]

Even while recalling the fundamental dualism between the soul and the body, Calvin went beyond it. The body of the believer is destined for resurrection; it therefore cannot be "prostituted," or put into slavery. Prostitution and sexual permissiveness from this standpoint furnish the most perfect examples of sin. Metaphorically, idolatry itself is a form of prostitution — as prostitution depends on idolatry.

Calvin therefore challenged the accusations of rigor and inhumanity that were applied to him. He opposed Nicodemism because he would not accept a "mixture"; one could not be Reformed in heart and papist in practice. The repulsion Calvin felt for Roman Catholicism was like the nausea produced by excrement; "cleaners of privies," Calvin notes, are "by habit hardened to remain in their filth" and think "they are among roses." Similarly, people get used to everything, even the rites of Roman Catholicism.[32] A shocking proposition this, insulting, infamous in its Rabelaisian crudity, but it would be one of the mainstays of Huguenot sarcasm: Catholicism, in its taste for forms and celebrations, is attached to things that rot. Scatology here joins with theology in denouncing idolatry. From the lower depths to the lower parts, Calvin displays unawares the rules of modern modesty: repulsion from and fascination with the body, rejection of the mixing of substances, separation of spaces. The clean and the dirty, along with the high and the low, are the cardinal points of a psychology attentive to order and propriety, which has been considered, not without reason, one characteristic of Puritan societies.

The Babylonian captivity of the church (the formula was already used by Luther) brought certain elite souls to an unacceptable compromise. Falsely inspired by the example of Nicodemus, they hid their real sentiments and followed the practices of their neighbors, conforming through lip service, if not from the bottom of their hearts, to the reigning idolatry. "They borrow the name of Nicodemus to use as a shield, as if they were his imitators. I will call them this for the moment, until I have shown how they do great wrong to that great man in putting him on their own level, and what is more, glorifying themselves by his example."[33]

---

31. Calvin, *Excuse . . . à Messieurs les Nicodémites, OC* 6, col. 593.
32. Calvin, *Excuse . . . à Messieurs les Nicodémites, OC* 6, col. 595.
33. Calvin, *Excuse . . . à Messieurs les Nicodémites, OC* 6, col. 496.

Anabaptists and Libertines

A dog barks if he sees someone attacking his master; I would indeed be cowardly if, seeing the truth of God thus attacked, I played the mute, without saying a word.

CALVIN TO MARGUERITE DE NAVARRE, APRIL 1545[34]

It is not easy to define with precision the Anabaptism of the sixteenth century. The rejection of infant baptism (or pedobaptism) gave rise to this ambiguous label,[35] but this minimal definition does not prove very useful for delimiting that nebulous group of reformers who remained outside the system of the established churches. It is better, following recent usage, to speak of the Radical Reformation. Far from being a single, unified phenomenon, these were indeed several Radical Reformations distinct from the magisterial reformations associated with the names of Luther, Bucer, Zwingli, and Calvin.[36]

Calvin himself had great difficulty in defining these radicals and ecstatics. He employed for them the generic term "Anabaptists," then reconsidered and tried to distinguish another group, the "spiritual libertines." He perceived in the end that there were infinite variations within these heterogeneous gatherings, ranging from aristocratic worldliness to the most unbridled populism. It was no easy task to set limits to Anabaptism: "These vermin differ from all other sects of heretics in that they are not in error on certain points only, but have engendered as it were an ocean of foolish dreams. So that one can hardly find a single Anabaptist head that does not contain some fantasy of its own. Thus to want to examine, or even recount, all the wicked doctrines that have existed in this sect, this will never be done."[37]

Calvin, however, distinguished two main tendencies: one that still recognized the Holy Scriptures, and another that he called "spiritual libertines." The latter lost themselves in "an unparalleled labyrinth of fantasies so absurd that it is a marvel." Calvin barely granted them a trace of humanity, since in

34. J. Calvin, *Lettres françaises*, ed. J. Bonnet, 2 vols. (Paris: Meyrueis, 1854), 1:114, April 28, 1545.

35. On this subject see the article by A. Gounelle, "Pédobaptisme: le débat au xvie siècle," *Études Théologiques et Religieuses* 70 (1995): 191-206.

36. G. H. Williams, *The Radical Reformation* (Kirksville, Mo., 1992), p. xxix: "This Radical Reformation was a loosely interrelated congeries of reformations and restitutions which, besides the Anabaptists of various types, included Spiritualists and spiritualizers of varying tendencies, and the Evangelical Rationalists, largely Italian in origin."

37. J. Calvin, *Brière instruction pour armer tous bons fidèles contre les erreurs de la secte commune des anabaptistes* (Geneva: Jean Girard, 1544), *OC* 7, col. 53.

their "venomous malice" these wretched monsters "want to make men similar to brute beasts."[38] These poor eccentrics claimed to be inspired.[39] Like the
papists, they were not content with the Holy Scriptures but added their own
imaginings to them. The spiritual libertines, Calvin concluded, deserved a
separate treatise.[40]

Several works followed, from the presses of Jean Girard in Geneva. These
were the *Brief Instruction to Arm All Good Believers against the Errors of the
Common Sect of the Anabaptists* (1544), the treatise *Against the Fantastic and
Furious Sect of the Libertines Who Call Themselves Spiritual* (1545), and the *Let-
ter against a Certain Cordelier, an Associate of the Sect of the Libertines, Who Is a
Prisoner in Rouen* (1547).[41]

The *Brief Instruction* begins with a preface dated June 1, 1544, addressed
to the ministers of Neuchâtel. Calvin, wanting to find a particularly absurd example of Anabaptist pretensions, launched a campaign "against prophesying
women." Anabaptism was decidedly a world turned upside down.[42]

Calvin's refutation rested on several points: he defended infant baptism
and the taking of oaths, rejected "mortalism" and absolute nonviolence. "To
condemn the public sword, which God has ordained for our protection, is to
blaspheme against God himself."[43] The Reformer likewise supported the social
and political establishment; there must be temporal lords and magistrates. He
justified, in the name of his concept of "vocation," the diversity of conditions.
"One's calling is the principal part of human life." Or again, "All shepherds and
field laborers, all mechanics and other similar people should regard their state
as holy, and feel that it does not obstruct them at all with respect to Christian
perfection."[44] In the same way Calvin spoke in favor of private property against
those who claimed that "it is therefore wrong for a Christian to possess either a
house, a garden, or any inherited property."[45] And, carried away by anger, he

---

38. Calvin, *Brière instruction, OC* 7, col. 54.

39. Calvin, *Brière instruction, OC* 7, col. 56.

40. Calvin, *Brière instruction, OC* 7, col. 139.

41. Calvin, *Brière instruction, OC* 7, cols. 45-142; J. Calvin, *Contre la secte phan-
tastique et furieuse des libertins qui se nomment spirituels, OC* 7, cols. 145-248; Calvin,
*Épistre contre un certain cordelier suppost de la secte des libertins lequel est prisonnier à Roan,
OC* 7, cols. 341-64. This last text was printed in the same volume with the preceding in the
new edition of 1547.

42. N. Z. Davis, *Society and Culture in Early Modern France* (Stanford, Calif.: Stanford University Press, 1975), chap. 5, "Women on Top," pp. 124ff. French translation, *Les
cultures du peuple* (Paris: Aubier, 1979).

43. Calvin, *Brière instruction, OC* 7, col. 77.

44. Calvin, *Brière instruction, OC* 7, cols. 81 and 83.

45. Calvin, *Brière instruction, OC* 7, col. 90.

ended by using the most trivial terms to describe those communists who rejected all social hierarchies: "In the end, as a drunkard, after having belched, vomits up the villainous mixture that fills his stomach, so these wretches, after having slandered this holy state that Our Lord honored so much, finally vomit out of their open mouths much more reckless blasphemies. The government of magistrates, they say, is according to the flesh, and that of Christians according to the spirit."[46]

Calvin had pledged himself to treat separately the question of the "spiritual libertines." He attacked them directly the following year by writing *Against the Fantastic and Furious Sect of the Libertines Who Call Themselves Spiritual.* Why display such ill temper against this tiny group, who influenced at most modern Belgium and northern France? Why did they deserve their reputation as "the most pernicious and execrable sect there ever was in the world"?[47]

On May 26, 1544, Valérand Poullain warned Calvin from Strasbourg of a group of "Quintinists," bluntly described as "pests."[48] These Anabaptists apparently infested Valenciennes, where there was a risk of their turning aside weak spirits by preaching a false Reformation to them. Poullain, a priest from Lille, adhered to the Reformation about 1543 and settled in Strasbourg. He was connected with Pierre Brully, a former Dominican who directed the French church there and corresponded with Calvin. Confronted by Bucer's complaisance and moderation with regard to the Anabaptists, he turned to Calvin and sent him a sampling of libertine writings.[49] He begged Calvin to intervene, and a delegation from Tournai and Valenciennes also went to Geneva to carry their point. On September 5, 1544, Pierre Viret spoke of a "new sort of Anabaptists called libertines," known especially in Liège, Tournai, and Valenciennes.[50] Calvin made up his mind to act, and wrote his treatise on the spiritual libertines. Brully at this time was in Tournai, where he preached Calvinist doctrine, while conventicles gathered around Antoine Pocquet. But Brully was arrested and ultimately sentenced to the stake. Calvin then decided to publish his indictment of the libertines.[51]

The word "libertines" did not yet possess its later sexual connotations, and Calvin used it to designate that sect of ecstatics who claimed for themselves

---

46. Calvin, *Brière instruction, OC* 7, cols. 90-91.

47. Calvin, *Lettres françaises,* 1:216, to Marguerite de Navarre, April 28, 1545.

48. *OC* 11, col. 712.

49. Gérard Moreau, *Histoire du protestantisme à Tournai* (Paris: Belles Lettres, Bibliothèque de la Faculté de Philosophie et lettres de l'Université de Liège n° 167, 1962), p. 91.

50. J.-F. Gilmont, *Bibliotheca calviniana,* 2 vols. to date (Geneva: Droz, 1991-94), 1:182.

51. Calvin, *Contre la secte, OC* 7, col. 115.

the simple name of "spirituals." It was apparently Calvin who gave them the name "spiritual libertines."

Who were these "spirituals"? Calvin feared their spread; they were numerous in Holland, Brabant, and "other countries in lower Germany."[52] They included Coppin, a native of Lille; Quintin du Hainault; Bertrand des Moulins; Bertrand Perceval; and the "little priest" Antoine Pocquet. Quintin Thierry was born at Ath about 1480; a tailor by profession and a mystic by inclination, he died at the stake on December 24, 1546. Pocquet (†1559) was Jeanne d'Albret's almoner and one of her familiars in Nérac. From 1542 to 1544 he stayed intermittently with Bucer in Strasbourg and was particularly active in Tournai. Quintin and Pocquet both received the protection of Marguerite de Navarre, who was disturbed by Calvin's violence.

The Reformer behaved in many respects like a party activist confronted with the risk of disorder. He painted his adversaries as literally diabolical. "For twenty years the devil, in order to extinguish or suffocate the holy doctrine of the Gospel, which he sees overcoming him again, or to defame it and render it odious to the world, has encouraged many different heresies and wicked opinions."[53] What weapon should be used against heretics? Calvin insisted on his own vocation: "When some wicked and pernicious sect begins to be active, and especially when it spreads, the duty of those whom Our Lord has provided for the building of his church is to go forward and repel it actively before it can fortify itself for further destruction and corruption. And in fact, since they are pastors of the church, it is not enough for them to offer and administer good pasture to the flock of Jesus Christ if they are not also on guard against the wolves and thieves, so as to cry out against them and drive them back from the flock if they want to approach it."[54]

Calvin spins out the metaphor lyrically. It belongs to him as a pastor to repel the heretics who attack the flocks. "Although properly speaking heretics are not merely like thieves or wolves but much worse, since in corrupting the holy Word of God they are like poisoners, murdering poor souls under the pretense of feeding them and offering them good food. Moreover, since Satan does not cease to strive by every means to dissipate this holy unity we have in Our Lord Jesus through his Word, it is more than necessary for the preservation of the church that that same Word serve and be applied as a sword and shield to resist such machinations."[55]

Calvin specifies his role. The Lord has very particularly charged him to

---

52. Calvin, *Contre la secte*, *OC* 7, col. 159.
53. Calvin, *Contre la secte*, *OC* 7, col. 149.
54. Calvin, *Contre la secte*, *OC* 7, col. 150.
55. Calvin, *Contre la secte*, *OC* 7, cols. 150-51.

preach and to defend the truth. "Since it has pleased Our Lord, in his infinite bounty, without considering who I am, to add me to the number of those whom he has assigned not only to publish his truth to the world but also to maintain it against all adversaries, I must employ myself in this task according to the abilities he has given me."[56]

The libertine heresy is as old as Christianity. Calvin refers to the Second Epistle of Peter in denouncing the antinomians, who believe themselves freed from the constraints of all moral and physical laws. "Since those times there has been a sect of wicked people who under the name of Christianity lead simple people into a dissolute life, removing the distinction between good and evil and putting consciences to sleep with flatteries, so that without scruple everyone lives according to his appetites, abusing Christian liberty to give free rein to complete carnal license, taking pleasure in bringing confusion to the world by overthrowing all discipline, order, and human honesty."[57]

Just as when he attacked the "beasts of the Sorbonne," Calvin had recourse to the animal kingdom, or rather he accused the spiritual libertines of actually confounding men and beasts — which permitted him a second time to deny them all human characteristics. "Their object is to mix the heavens and the earth, nullify all religion, erase all knowledge from the understanding of men, deaden consciences, and leave no difference between men and beasts."[58] Further on he speaks of a "bestial" sect[59] and compares his adversaries to "pigs" who want to overturn everything with their "snouts."[60] This disorder extends to language: "The Quintinists have a wild language, in which they babble so that one can hardly understand them any more than the singing of birds. Not that they do not use ordinary words like others, but they disguise their meaning so much that one never knows the subject they are talking about or what they want to affirm or deny."[61]

These reflections on language continue. "Language was created by God to express thought so we could communicate with each other." And the author explains that "it is perverting the order of God to beat the air with a confused noise that is not understood."[62]

In the tradition of Greek philosophy, Calvin thus tends to identify reason with speech. Anabaptists are senseless because their use of language makes a confused noise. The word "babblers," common in his writings, describes the

56. Calvin, *Contre la secte, OC* 7, cols. 151-52.
57. Calvin, *Contre la secte, OC* 7, cols. 154-55.
58. Calvin, *Contre la secte, OC* 7, col. 162.
59. Calvin, *Contre la secte, OC* 7, col. 164.
60. Calvin, *Contre la secte, OC* 7, col. 224. The image is repeated in col. 229.
61. Calvin, *Contre la secte, OC* 7, col. 168.
62. Calvin, *Contre la secte, OC* 7, col. 169.

baseless chatter of the Anabaptists, compared in this passage, in another animal metaphor, to birds. Is this to say that the Bible is presented in entirely rational discourse? Not at all, because it takes account of the weakness of men: "In dealing with the mysteries of God, the Scriptures are a rule for us. Therefore we follow the language they show us without diverging. For the Lord, knowing well that if he spoke to us as was proper to his majesty our intelligence would not be capable of reaching so high, accommodates himself to our littleness. And as a nurse lisps to a child, so he uses with us a common manner of speaking so as to be understood."[63]

We do not know much about the circumstances of the *Letter against a Certain Gray Friar, an Associate of the Sect of the Libertines, Who Is a Prisoner in Rouen.* Dated August 20, 1547, and published the same year, this text apparently reproduces an authentic letter whose original manuscript had been lost. Nor has any trace been found of the writings of the Cordelier mentioned by Calvin.[64]

Fortunately, rejoices Calvin, Quintin Thierry died at the stake. It is now necessary to denounce this villainous friar, described in an admirable formula as a "false heretic." Informing is lawful when the object is to prevent the propagation of a pernicious doctrine: "A year ago I read a dialogue composed by him full of horrible blasphemies. . . . He knows only one song to which he always returns; it is, 'Since God is the author of all things there is no need any more to distinguish between good and evil, but everything we do is right, provided we make no scruples about anything.'"[65]

In reality, explains Calvin, the friar makes God the author of evil, contrary to what he claims. He thus distorts the doctrine of predestination — which he, Calvin, had elucidated.[66] In fact, under his apparent strictness, the good father hides the most complete laxity; if everything depends on the will of God, if one can change nothing, everything is permitted. "Provided a man says, 'I can do nothing,' he has leave to do anything that seems good to him."[67] Calvin thus sums up his grievances against the friar: "When this muddler has babbled at length to make an appearance of wanting to glorify God, it all comes down to our recognizing that everything is well done, since it is God who does everything, and that under this cloak all abominations are covered and all sorts of filth is found to be of good odor. In short, that God is the pimp for fornica-

63. Calvin, *Contre la secte, OC* 7, col. 179.
64. Gilmont, 1:250.
65. Calvin, *Épistre contre un certain cordelier, OC* 7, col. 345.
66. Calvin, *Épistre contre un certain cordelier, OC* 7, col. 347: "Under cover of predestination, he tries to make men so helpless that reprobates do nothing toward their perdition, which is to obscure this doctrine of predestination, as the sophists did."
67. Calvin, *Épistre contre un certain cordelier, OC* 7, col. 356.

tors, the receiver for thieves and murderers, which are such hideous blasphemies that all creatures should tremble at them."[68]

Idolatry and Rationalism

If the Calvinist resistance to astrology already involved, in the Reformer's works, rationalist elements, it rested above all on scriptural and theological foundations.

ÉLISABETH LABROUSSE[69]

Intransigent toward ecstatics, sarcastic toward Catholics, intractable toward heretics, Calvinism participated unwittingly in the disenchantment of the world.[70] Despite his obsession with Satan, despite his attachment to an obsolete biblical cosmology, many of Calvin's works, and not the least important, are permeated with rationalism. The author of the *Treatise on Relics* and the *Warning against Judicial Astrology* permanently dissociated the "true" religion from superstition and idolatry. Religion and magic were openly opposed at the transition from the Renaissance to the modern age.[71]

In many respects Calvin was already a modern. But rationalism was not his avowed end. "In the minds of the Reformers the criticism of 'superstitions' for reasons of verisimilitude and good sense was only a secondary argument. For Luther, Calvin, and their disciples rejected 'idolatry' primarily in the name of worship in spirit and in truth."[72]

To understand the satirical vein of the Reformers one should come to terms with the meaning of their criticism. It was from piety, and not from worldly derision, that they rejected as dangerous what appeared to them a travesty of Christian truth.

Calvin broke with the past, or rather he was a man of transition — so does Calvin appear to us in his time, as the author, in 1543, of a *Very Useful Proposal Concerning the Great Profit that Would Accrue to Christianity if There Were an Inventory of all the Bodies of Saints and Relics in Italy, France, Germany, Spain, and Other Kingdoms and Countries.*[73] To be convinced one need only read the fine

---

68. Calvin, *Épistre contre un certain cordelier, OC* 7, col. 361.

69. É. Labrousse, *L'entrée de Saturne au Lion* (La Haye: Nijhof, 1974), p. 82.

70. This formula of Max Weber's has recently been revived by M. Gauchet, *Le désenchantement du monde* (Paris: NRF, 1985).

71. K. Thomas, *Religion and the Decline of Magic* (Harmondsworth: Penguin, 1973).

72. J. Delumeau, "Les Réformateurs et la superstition," in *Un chemin d'histoire. Chrétienté et christianisation* (Paris: Fayard, 1981), p. 58.

73. *Avertissement très utile du grand profit qui reviendrait à la chrétienté, s'il se faisait*

pages recently devoted to the "flamboyant religion" of the fourteenth and fifteenth centuries: "God both close and distant. All the manifestations of flamboyant religion, even the most learned, the most sophisticated, the most refined, oscillate . . . without ceasing between the recognition of the unworthiness of man, the fear of divine omnipotence, and the need to approach God by every means, without as a rule arriving at any comfortable equilibrium."[74]

"God both close and distant." One could not better define Calvin's piety, made up of familiarity with the Father and fear of God. He distinguished himself from flamboyant piety, however, in one essential point: the omnipotence of God no longer gave way for him to that proliferation of intermediaries with the sacred, from relics to the worship of saints, that characterized the Catholicism of his time. Indeed, the "multiplication of devotions" was in this period the tangible sign of a "profound fear of being separated from God." There was insistence on the "tortures and wounds of Christ," on the "blood shed," and on his "sufferings." Numerous obsessions were expressed openly; the "corruption of the body" and the "fires of hell" were only the reverse side of a religion of accumulated merits that found in indulgences or the intercession of the "glorious Virgin Mary" and of all the saints a passport to the hereafter. Calvin felt only contempt and repugnance for this incandescent piety, whose carnal and worldly character he found indecent.

For Calvin the rejection of popery was not only theological. It was marked by physical repugnance toward a religion of ostentation that gave great emphasis to the body. Here also one senses Calvin in reaction against the declining Middle Ages, which unceasingly inventoried the wounds and injuries through which the saving blood of the Redeemer poured out.[75] Calvin's God was a tidy God. For him, cleanliness was next to godliness. The repugnance the Reformer admitted regarding the viscosity of the holy oil the Roman Church used periodically, what was it in the end but a gigantic disdain for the physical forms of a carnal religion, accused of giving way to the giddiness produced by morbidity and self-indulgence?

Calvin's comical vein, far from being the fruit of incredulity, was nourished on the most authentic piety. Worship can be given only to God. "The first vice and as it were the root of the evil has been that in place of searching for Jesus Christ in his Word, in his sacraments, and in his spiritual graces, the world, according to its custom, has amused itself with his robes, shirts, and linen, and in

inventaire de tous les corps saints, et reliques, qui sont tant en Italie, qu'en France, Allemagne, Espagne et autres royaumes et pays.

74. J. Chiffoleau, *Histoire de la France religieuse, xive-xviiie siècles*, ed. J. Le Goff and R. Rémond (Paris: Le Seuil, 1988), pp. 171-72.

75. G. Deregnaucourt and D. Poton, *La vie religieuse en France aux xvie-xviie-xviiie siècles* (Gap, Hautes-Alpes: Ophrys, 1994), pp. 28-29.

doing this has abandoned the principal to follow the accessory. It has done similarly with the apostles, martyrs, and other saints, since in place of meditating on their lives to follow their example it has given all its energy to contemplating and holding as treasures their bones, shirts, girdles, caps, and such trash."[76]

The criticism of astrology derived from the same concern not to give worship to any but the Lord. It is necessary to remove one's attention from the objects of the world to raise it to the Creator. The stars themselves testify to the glory of God; but one must be careful not to give them a magical power. The *Warning Against the Astrology Called Judicial* appeared in 1549.[77]

Whether it concerned participation in the mysteries of the Roman Church or giving way to superstition, the question of purity returned insistently. "Those who pollute their consciences by abandoning themselves to evil are not worthy to be maintained in the pure knowledge of God."[78]

As for astrology, it was "foolish curiosity to judge by the stars everything that will come to men and to inquire there and take counsel about one's affairs." It was "diabolical superstition."[79] Calvin distinguished this false science from "true astrology" — which we now call astronomy — which is the study of "the natural order and disposition" of the stars and planets.[80] Thus a good astrology and a superstitious and impious astrology oppose each other. Good astrology has many virtues: "Natural astrology shows that bodies here below indeed receive some influence from the moon, for oysters fill and empty themselves in conformity with it; also bones are full of marrow or less so as it grows or diminishes. It is also from the true science of astrology that doctors obtain the knowledge for ordering bleedings and drinks, pills, and other things at an opportune time. Thus we must indeed confess that there is some agreement between the stars and planets and the disposition of human bodies."[81]

Judicial astrology, on the contrary, "reposes on two principal articles: to know not only the nature and complexion of men, but also all their experiences . . . and all they will either do or suffer in their lives." In conclusion, it reflects "a curiosity, not only superfluous and useless, but also evil." In fact, judicial astrology "turns us aside from the confidence we should have in God, from the re-

---

76. J. Calvin, *Traité des reliques,* in *La vraie piété,* ed. I. Backus and C. Chimelli (Geneva: Labor et Fides, 1986), p. 163. Concerning relics see the recent book by P. Geary, *Le vol des reliques au Moyen Âge* (Paris: Aubier, 1992).

77. J. Calvin, *Advertissement contre l'astrologie qu'on appelle judiciaire: et autres curiosités qui règnent aujourd'hui au monde, OC* 7, cols. 509-42.

78. Calvin, *Advertissement contre l'astrologie,* p. 513.

79. Calvin, *Advertissement contre l'astrologie,* pp. 515-16.

80. Calvin, *Advertissement contre l'astrologie,* p. 516.

81. Calvin, *Advertissement contre l'astrologie,* p. 518, for this quotation and that following.

gard he wants us to have for his justice, mercy, and judgment, and from the duty we have toward our neighbors."[82]

In the sixteenth century astrology had considerable success, which remains connected even in our days with the name of Nostradamus.[83] Besides almanacs, all sorts of prognostications were published, which generally concerned the coming year. Bonaventure des Périers mocked this popular genre in 1537 by publishing a small octavo, *The Prognostication of Prognostications, not only for this present year 1537, but also for those to come, and indeed for all those that are past; composed by Master Sarcomoros, native of Tartary, and secretary to the Most Illustrious and Most Puissant King of Cathay, servants of the virtues.*[84]

On August 8, 1544, one of these works was intercepted in Geneva, taking Calvin by name for a target: *A Prognostication against the Preachers of Geneva, in which M. Calvin Is Named.*[85] In September 1548 Calvin opened a campaign against the almanacs printed in Geneva itself. This superstitious practice was also tied to belief in the magical virtue of this or that spring, another prohibited view (March 1557).[86] In April 1557 people were again warned against the "fountain of idolatry."[87]

Calvin's treatise was a direct response to the *Statement on the Judgments of Astrology to a Studious Young Lady*, published in Lyon in 1546. Born in Angoulême, Mellin de Saint-Gelais (1491-1558) was the ideal type of the court ecclesiastic, a player of the lute on occasion and a lover of pleasure. The poet demonstrated in his *Statement* that all branches of human knowledge (including theology) are marked by the mutability of the sublunary world. Astrology, however, escapes this law; it belongs to the domain of fixity and of classical assurance as against the play (which can be called "baroque") of opinion.

---

82. Calvin, *Advertissement contre l'astrologie*, p. 542.

83. Nostradamus, *Lettres inédites*, ed. J. Dupèbe (Geneva: Droz, 1983), pp. 20-21: "Without belonging to the Reformed churches, [Nostradamus] clearly inclined to the Reformation; he showed more understanding of the cause of the Protestants, whom he often called 'Christians,' than of that of the Catholics, the 'papists,' whose fanatical violence he detested." Nostradamus's religion was "A more or less Lutheranizing evangelism with which he bizarrely mingled a whole Neoplatonist hodgepodge."

84. *La Pronostication des Pronostications, non seulement de cette présente année MDXXXVII, mais aussi des autres à venir, voire de toutes celles qui sont passées; composée par maître Sarcomoros, natif de Tartarie, et secrétaire du très illustre et très puissant roi du Cathay, serfs des vertus.*

85. *Pronostication contre les prédicants de Genève, dans laquelle est nommé M. Calvin.* A. Cartier, ed., *Arrêts du conseil de Genève sur le fait de l'imprimerie et de la librairie de 1541 à 1550* (Geneva: Georg, 1893), p. 67.

86. *Annales Calviniani, OC* 21, col. 662, Registres du Conseil de Genève 53, fol. 38v.

87. *Annales Calviniani, OC* 21, col. 665, Registres du Conseil 53, fol. 108.

From this variety of opinions come the controversies there are now and always have been in all the professions of the world. For in religion how many divisions and sects are there? How many contentions in political life, governed by the laws? How many altercations in medicine, still not well resolved, of the quality of vinegar? And nevertheless on these three disciplines depends all the repose of our consciences, of our goods, and of our persons. I leave aside the innumerable other vocations to which men are drawn by their individual opinions, choosing, some the sea and navigation, others agriculture; some peace, others war; some contact with and government of the people, others solitude. . . .

If then in all things there are such different opinions, even in those that are touched and seen with the eye, it is no marvel if the science that teaches people to judge by the influence of celestial bodies about things to come encounters diverse judgments about itself; diverse, I say, not so much among those who practice it as among those who are not acquainted with it. For since astrology is based on demonstrations so evident that they cannot be denied and on movements so certain that they cannot fail, so the teachings that come from it are more settled and less variable than those of any other discipline.[88]

Nothing more was needed to inflame Calvin. Calvin, the enemy of the astrologers, nevertheless was not moved by scientific considerations. "While condemning judicial astrology with an energy not seen since Saint Augustine, Calvin granted much more to astrology than one would have supposed from the radical character of his positions."[89] Thus he did not renounce "the prodigious nature of certain comets, or in fact of magical practices."[90] He did not establish "a clear distinction between astronomy and astrology."[91] He remained, in fact, profoundly conservative in his vision of the universe. Attached to biblical cosmology, the author of the *Warning against Judicial Astrology* condemned the Copernican revolution. For Calvin it was impious to claim that the earth revolves around the sun.

We see some so frantic (not only in religion, but to show that they are of a monstrous nature throughout) that they say the sun does not move, and that

---

88. Mellin de Saint-Gelais, *Advertissement sur les jugements d'astrologie, à une studieuse damoiselle* (Lyon, 1546), in *Oeuvres complètes,* ed. Prosper Blanchemain, 3 vols. (Paris: P. Daffis, 1873), 3:248-49.

89. J. Calvin, *Advertissement contre l'astrologie judiciaire,* ed. O. Millet (Geneva: Droz, 1985), p. 36.

90. Calvin, *Advertissement contre l'astrologie judiciaire,* p. 37.

91. Calvin, *Advertissement contre l'astrologie judiciaire,* p. 9.

it is the earth that moves and that it turns around. When we see such spirits we must indeed say that the devil has possessed them and that God shows them to us as mirrors to make us remain in fear of him. Thus it is of all those who argue out of guile, and who do not mind being brazen. When you say, "This is hot," "Oh no," they say, "anyone can see it is cold." When you show them something black they say it is white, or the other way around, like the man who said snow was black. While its whiteness was evident, which is well known to everyone, he still wanted to contradict it openly. But behold how there are frantic people who would like to change the order of nature, indeed dazzle the eyes of men and brutalize all their senses.[92]

Toward Puritanism?

The criticisms of Nicodemism, relics, and astrology have one point in common: they derive from the quest for spiritual purity and the rejection of pollution. Calvin's correspondence testifies to this same concern. The Reformer untiringly advised his friends to abandon Egypt and Babylon, not to sacrifice to idols, and finally to flee to Reformed territory to adore God there according to God's precepts. His letter of June 13, 1548, "to a new convert" sets forth some clear principles; the Catholic Eucharist is sacrilege. "As for the question you ask me, that is whether it is not lawful for a Christian man to communicate in the Lord's Supper of Jesus Christ which is held in the place where you are, it would be easy to answer yes, provided there was a Lord's Supper of Jesus Christ. But when you have examined everything carefully there is no conformity or similitude between the Lord's Supper and the papal Mass, any more than between fire and water."[93]

How does Calvin describe the true believer in Jesus Christ, pure and fearing God, who flees from Roman rites? He is a "Christian," pure and simple. Similarly, his adversary is not defined as "Catholic"; Calvin is content with the adjective "papal." The formulation "Protestants" as opposed to "Catholics" would be in certain respects anachronistic; nevertheless we occasionally have recourse to it to make our point of view more understandable. The "papal" Mass is radically opposed to the Lord's Supper: "I deny to you that Jesus Christ instituted the Mass, but rather, despite him, it was forged by Satan in order to destroy the Lord's Supper, for it is something entirely contrary to it, since they make it a sacrifice, attributing to a foolishly invented act the virtue of the death

92. OC 49, col. 677, eighth sermon on 1 Cor. 10 and 11. It was Richard Stauffer who drew attention to this text in his article "Calvin et Copernic," *Revue d'Histoire des Religions* 179 (1971): 31-40.

93. Calvin, *Lettres françaises*, 1:253, for this citation and that following.

and passion of Jesus Christ. There are also manifest idolatries, not only because the bread is adored in it, but because they pray for the dead, they take refuge in the merits and intercession of the saints, and do many similar things that God rejects."

The very idea of concession or give-and-take is inadmissible. To preserve oneself from idolatry is to avoid scandalizing one's brethren. The Calvinist notion of scandal found in these years its most rigorous codification. Another letter in the fall of the same year warned against the risks of dissimulation: "When we are told that the whole earth is holy, this admonishes us that we should not pollute it in the least by living badly. Now we must only consider whether in simulating, as you do, you are not participating in the pollutions you rightly condemn in the infidels. I understand well that your heart is far from consenting to them, but by making an appearance of communicating there is no doubt that you make a profession of consenting. And like God we should detest idolatry, and also before men it is proper for us to abstain from anything that may make it thought that we approve of it."[94]

Neither simulation nor dissimulation; care for oneself joins with respect for others. The service of the Lord hardly allows concession. The faithful Christian should follow Abraham's example and leave his "country, his kindred, and all the rest."[95] In 1549 this overpowering sense of exile took on a symbolic meaning. The love of God and respect for his name transform all existence into an infinite pilgrimage that ends only with death: "We do not find it strange if we must be driven from a place for his name and must abandon the place of our birth to transport ourselves to an unknown place; since we must also be ready to leave this world whenever he summons us."[96]

In the eyes of the true faith, what are the "delights," "delicacies," and "pleasures of Egypt"? They are nothing but "bird droppings," Calvin wrote acidly.[97]

94. Calvin, *Lettres françaises*, 1:257, October 18, 1548.
95. Calvin, *Lettres françaises*, 1:259.
96. Calvin, *Lettres françaises*, 1:303, June 10, 1549.
97. Calvin, *Lettres françaises*, 1:304-5.

CHAPTER 13

Calvin the Preacher

Prophets are organs of the Holy Spirit.

CALVIN, SIXTEENTH SERMON ON JOB[1]

A history of preaching equals a history of reception; a history of reception equals a history of active appropriation; a history of appropriation equals a history of deformation or of infidelity. A preacher is someone who hears and transmits, who teaches and exhorts, who thunders and fulminates. Preaching was at the center of the Reformer's activity; in his last years it utterly exhausted him and wore him down. His frail appearance, his short breath, his voice as if from beyond the tomb, and his back bowed by illness regained a sudden energy and a last grandeur under the impulse of the Spirit that animated and subdued them. Calvin was a man who spoke.[2]

Theodore Beza has left us a faithful image of these twenty-five years of arduous labor: "Besides preaching every day from week to week, usually and as often as he could he preached twice every Sunday; he lectured three times a week on theology; he gave remonstrances in the consistory, and delivered as it were an entire lesson every Friday in the conference on Scripture that we call a

---

1. *Opera Calvini* (hereafter cited as *OC*) 33, col. 198.
2. R. Peter, "Genève dans la prédication de Calvin," in *Calvinus Ecclesiae Genevensis Custos,* ed. W. H. Neuser (Frankfurt: P. Lang, 1984), p. 23 n. 1; for an exhaustive bibliography, T. H. L. Parker, *Calvin's Preaching* (Edinburgh: T. & T. Clark, 1992); R. Stauffer, *Dieu, la création et la Providence dans la prédication de Calvin* (Bern: P. Lang, 1978).

congregation; and he so closely followed this program without interruption until his death that he never failed once except during extreme illness."[3]

In a more subtle fashion Florimond de Raemond also recognized the scale of his task: "Calvin hardly had an equal, for during twenty-three years that he maintained possession of the bishopric of Geneva he preached every day, and very often twice on Sunday, lectured on theology three times a week, and every Friday in the conference he called the congregation. His other hours were used for writing and answering the letters that came to him from all of heretical Christendom, as if to the sovereign Pontiff."[4]

Usually Calvin delivered two sermons on Sundays and preached daily every second week. Sunday was reserved for the Psalms and the New Testament, weekdays for the Old. Calvin's sermons were taken down in shorthand by one of his audience, Denis Raguenier, from September 29, 1549, on. Two thousand three hundred sermons were thus preserved until the nineteenth century. They filled some forty-four volumes, carefully bound. But through the criminal ignorance of librarians, they were sold for the weight of the paper. Most fortunately, it was possible to salvage some. At the present time we possess about fifteen hundred of them.[5]

Except in unusual cases, the text has reached us through the listener's transcription. It is therefore a record of what was heard, and not a text revised by Calvin. The author commented on Scripture according to the principle of running linear commentary, or *lectio continua*.

These sermons were works of the moment. The historian, with his sense of detail, has much to learn from this sort of testimony. But so do the theologian and the exegete, who can grasp the living thought of the Reformer. Did Calvin the preacher transmit exactly the same message as Calvin the writer and scholar? Did Calvin, confronted with a crowd of listeners, stick to edifying discourse? Did he try to influence attitudes? Did he modify views of the world? Did he alter behavior? Undoubtedly Calvin was never so much a man in his time and of his time as in his sermons. In them he spoke of men, of women, of animals, of the sea, of the mountains — and of God, of course; of a conservative God, the enemy of change and social subversion. In short, Calvin the preacher in many ways contradicted the "progressive" view of Protestantism. He was a man of order in a world swept along by change.

3. T. Beza, *L'histoire de la vie et mort de Calvin* (1565), OC 21, col. 33.

4. F. de Raemond, *L'histoire de la naissance de l'hérésie* (1605; Rouen: P. de La Motte, 1629), bk. 7, chap. 10, p. 886.

5. The *Opera Calvini* includes 872 sermons; 680 sermons still in manuscript have been published or are in process of publication elsewhere, in particular in the *Supplementa Calviniana*. They are divided among the Bibliothèque Publique et Universitaire in Geneva, the Bodleian Library in Oxford, and Lambeth Palace in London.

Contingent Texts

Preaching, like university teaching, is characterized by its ephemeral nature. These are words sown on the wind. The fleetingness of these casual expressions seized from the sands of time makes particularly precious the restoration of the sermons of the Reformer. As a general rule Calvin hardly wished in the beginning to publish these results of a pedagogical activity he no doubt found redundant with reference to his other writings, theological (the *Institutes*), exegetical (his *Commentaries*), and persuasive (his various treatises). His sermons were spread over the Reformer's whole life (see app. 7).

When exceptionally in 1552 he published his *Four Sermons . . . Dealing with Matters that Are Very Useful for Our Times,* the author took great care to specify the exceptional character of the undertaking: "Although I have already written two sufficiently ample treatises to show that it is not lawful for a Christian who knows the pure doctrine of the Gospel, when he lives in the papacy, to appear in any way to consent or adhere to the abuses, superstitions, and idolatries that reign there, nevertheless every day there are people who ask me again for advice about this, as if I had never spoken about it."[6]

The irascible Calvin almost regretted having to publish his sermons. Had he not already warned his contemporaries in two works in particular, his *Short Treatise Showing What a Faithful Man Should Do when He Is among the Papists* (1543) and his *Apology to the Nicodemites* (1544)? Revised and corrected by the author, the *Four Sermons* were an exception. Other sermons were published during Calvin's lifetime, but were based on notes taken by listeners. They responded to a demand that was difficult to satisfy otherwise. Commenting in 1554 on the printing of *Twenty-two Sermons,* Calvin wrote: "I did not write the twenty-two sermons on the Eighth Psalm in my room, but they were printed exactly as someone had been able to collect them from my mouth in the church. There you see our style in the ordinary way of teaching."[7]

A book written in the solitude of the study and a sermon taken from life are two dissimilar products. Calvin repeated this to saturation point, as if he wanted to apologize in advance to the reader. When the *Twenty-two Sermons* came from the presses of Jean Girard in 1554,[8] the printer's preface explained:

I prayed him [Master John Calvin], being also urged by many good Christians, that he would allow his sermons as they were collected from his mouth

6. *Quatre sermons . . . traitant des matières fort utiles pour notre temps, OC* 8, cols. 373-74.

7. *OC* 15, col. 446, letter to the church of Poitiers, February 20, 1555.

8. *OC* 32, cols. 481-752, *Vingt-deux sermons auxquels est exposé le psaume 119.* These were sermons preached in Geneva from January to July 1553.

to be published, so that their benefit could spread farther. Now although he made difficulties, liking better to have printed (when the opportunity served) some brief commentary than to fill paper with such long discourses that people delighted in from the pulpit; nevertheless not hoping that this could be done for a long time in view of the slight leisure he has, and because meanwhile the world would be deprived of the great utility that the reading of the said sermons as they are presented might be, I thought it would be better to publish them. If it should please God to give the author the grace of producing a more polished and perfect work there will be nothing lost if the children of God have been edified by the holy doctrine they will find here. I do not doubt that you, the readers, will feel goodwill to me for the pains I have taken, receiving their fruits as I desire, and this by the grace of the Holy Spirit, without which one labors in vain. For although men may plant and irrigate, growth must come from the source of all light.[9]

Jean Girard was the more in haste because plagiarists were at work, and a clandestine edition emerged, without a publisher's name, from the firm of Zacharie Durand. The two publishers were already disputing their literary property in the martyrology of Jean Crespin. It is likely that an agreement was finally reached between Girard and the pirate. This sort of publication developed during the last ten years of Calvin's life. One may cite for example *Two Sermons Taken from the Second Chapter of the First Epistle to Timothy* (Geneva: Jean Girard, 1555).[10] The publishing was handled by Denis Raguenier. The book contained two sermons given in November 1554. The printer explained in the preface, "After having heard these two sermons and considered the doctrine that is contained in them, it seemed good to me to bring them to light, to the end that such a treasure might not remain hidden but be able to benefit the whole church, not only the papists but also those who profess the Gospel."[11] In 1557 it was the turn of the *Sermons on the Ten Commandments,* delivered during the two previous years. The editor, Conrad Badius, explained the enterprise as follows:

> Because all poor believers who are scattered through the countries of the world and the places where the Pope still rules cannot enjoy this precious gift every day, I thought I would give them great consolation if, using the power of my art, I let them see with what fodder we are nourished and with what simplicity, purity, truth, reverence, and zeal the Word of God is announced to

9. J.-F. Gilmont, *Bibliotheca calviniana,* 2 vols. to date (Geneva: Droz, 1991-94), 1:540.

10. *Deux sermons pris de la première épître à Timothée au second chapitre,* OC 53, cols. 159-84.

11. Gilmont, 2:585.

us by those whom the Lord Jesus has designated as pastors for his poor flock in this country. . . . For which purpose I have chosen among others the sermons of our faithful pastor, John Calvin, on the Ten Commandments of God, which have been gathered from him (like all the others he gives) by the ordinary writer, without his having put his hand to them afterwards or revised them in any way. Which I say, because it might be thought that he filed and polished them at home at his leisure to be presented; but I can assure you that they are as God gave them to him to deliver publicly, without a word being added or taken away.[12]

While avowing his admiration for the orator, the editor was forced to admit Calvin's reservations when faced with this demand for sermons, which was difficult to satisfy. The reticent Calvin only agreed to have his sermons published when forced by the publishers, who were constantly pestered by a public eager to read his words. Badius gives the rules Calvin followed in his preaching to the humble:

This was more by a constrained and forced permission, or rather through importunity, than from free will and consent. . . . Not that he is so irritable and difficult by nature; but since his whole intention is that the works he brings to light should come out with all their adornments, it bothers him that what he preached simply and nakedly to accommodate the coarseness of the people, without elaborate apparatus or arrangement, should be suddenly exposed to view, as if he thought everything he said would immediately be disseminated everywhere and the world would be filled with his writings. This is why he has always refused to have either his lessons or his sermons printed. However, he is so good-natured that he cannot so well defend himself against the importunities of those around him that he does not sometimes give way, although he nevertheless always makes it understood that he would rather it were otherwise.[13]

The same Badius said in his edition of *Several Sermons Concerning the Divinity, Humanity, and Nativity of Our Lord Jesus Christ* in 1558, "[Calvin] would rather have his sermons heard no farther than his own sheepfold."[14] Other sermons were published on the First Epistle to the Corinthians in 1558, on Melchizedek in 1560, on predestination and on the two epistles to Timothy in 1561,

12. Gilmont, 2:650.

13. Gilmont, 2:650.

14. *Plusieurs sermons touchant la divinité, humanité et nativité de notre Seigneur Jésus-Christ.* Gilmont, 2:678.

and on the Epistle to the Ephesians in 1562. These culminated in the *Sixty-five Sermons* of 1562, presented thus by Badius: "Many are now astonished that sermons are presented that have not been polished or arranged, just as they came from the forge, that is without having been revised by their author."[15]

There was considerable commercial pressure. The remarkable sermons on Job came out only in 1563 but went back to 1554-55. Calvin deplored this haste; he had a humanist's feeling for a well-turned page of writing, and regretted not being able to polish his sermons with the same care as the *Institutes*. What interest do they have for us now, these works that are not really works, these words saved from oblivion and published at the time, not to mention the remaining sermons that wait wisely in some university library for their ultimate exhumation?

The Preacher's Art

I am not here to forge a new law, or articles of faith.

CALVIN[16]

Calvin was undoubtedly a talented preacher. If he had written out the whole of his sermons, would he have so easily accepted their transcription by another pen? Badius's testimony confirms that Calvin's tone from the pulpit was inimitable. Besides this we get a glimpse from our reading. His incisive style followed the reactions of his audience. He could be familiar, urgent, or with a turn of the hand evoke the beauty of creation. "Calvin united gestures and speech. Along with changes of voice, dramatizations, and shifts to the first person singular, these gestures showed the animation of Calvin's preaching."[17] Certainly one cannot conclude from this that Calvin did not prepare his effects. "It is as though I mounted to the pulpit and did not deign to look at the book, but invented some frivolous fantasy and said, 'Ah well, when I come there, God will give me enough to talk about.' And as though I did not deign to read or think about what I would put forward and came here without having carefully considered how the holy Scriptures should be applied to the edification of the people; and I would be presumptuous, and God also would confound me in my audacity."[18]

15. Gilmont, 2:956.
16. *OC* 27, col. 538.
17. M. Engammare, "Le paradis à Genève. Comment Calvin prêchait-il la chute aux Genevois?" *Études Théologiques et Religieuses* 69 (1994): 344.
18. *OC* 26, cols. 473-74, forty-ninth sermon on Deuteronomy.

Sacred eloquence, however, is distinguished from the common art of oratory by the dignity of its subject. "When the Gospel is preached in the name of God, it is as though He himself spoke in person."[19] Whence comes a proposition that borders on solipsism: "I speak, but I must also listen to myself, being taught by the spirit of God; since otherwise the words that proceed from my mouth would not profit me any more than all the others, unless they were given to me from on high and not from my own head. Therefore it is only a sound that vanishes in the air, the voice of a man, and nevertheless it is the power of God for salvation to all believers."

Calvin speaks and Calvin listens; the two operations are the same in the case of the Word of God. Or again, the Word immediately stimulates its sharing. "I am not here for myself alone. It is true that we should all profit in common, for when I mount to the pulpit it is not to teach others only. I do not withdraw myself apart, since I should be a student, and the Word that proceeds from my mouth should serve me as well as you, or it is the worse for me."[20]

To teach is also to learn. Pastors and congregation both hear a message that surpasses them. A preacher should utterly efface himself behind the revelation he brings: "If I am here in the pulpit, and I claim to be heard in the name of God, and nevertheless I come to seduce the people, this is an arrogance that surpasses all others."[21]

This has fundamental consequences for the method of interpreting the text. "For my part, in conforming to the method that God established here, I would force myself to follow briefly the true thread of the text, and without declaiming long exhortations I would take pains merely to chew, so to speak, the words of David so that they can be digested."[22]

He did not advocate a purely speculative attitude, however. "What good would it do if we had been here half a day, and I had expounded half a book and, without regard for you or for your benefit, I had speculated in the air, treating many things in a confused way? Everyone would return to his house just as he came to church, and this would be to profane the Word of God so much that it would have no use among us."[23]

Calvin had an acute awareness of his audience. "Therefore when I expound the holy Scriptures I must always regulate myself so that those who hear me receive profit from the doctrine I advance, so that they are edified for their salvation. If I do not have this desire and do not achieve the edification of those who

19. *OC* 58, col. 54, for this citation and that following, from the third sermon on the election of Jacob and the rejection of Esau.
20. *OC* 34, col. 424, ninety-fifth sermon on Job.
21. *OC* 27, col. 537, 111th sermon on Deuteronomy.
22. *OC* 37, col. 483, first sermon on Psalm 119 (1553).
23. *OC* 34, col. 423, ninety-fifth sermon on Job.

hear me, I am a sacrilege profaning the Word of God."[24] These recommendations take their full meaning if one keeps in mind the disillusioned description of medieval sermons that Calvin provided in his *Letter to Sadoleto* (1539-41):

> What sermons there were then throughout Europe, representing the simplicity in which Saint Paul wished Christian people to spend their whole lives! Indeed where was that sermon from which foolish old women would not learn more nonsense than they could repeat in a whole month over their hearths? For their sermons were so constructed that one part was made up of obscure and difficult questions from the schools to raise the admiration of poor and simple people; the rest passed in happy tales and entertaining speculations to excite and move their hearts to joy. A few words of the Word of God were included so that by their majesty they might give color to these dreams and fantasies. But as soon as our leaders raised their banner, in a moment all these shadows were cleared up among us. Now your preachers, in part taught by the books of those aforesaid, and in part constrained by shame and the murmuring of the people to conform to their example, still cannot contrive not to smack plainly of this old stupid asininity. So that if someone compares our fashion of preaching and theirs, even with the method most esteemed among them, it will be easily recognized that you have done us great injury.[25]

For Calvin, therefore, preaching was not just one literary genre among others; it was the very essence of the Reformation. The first requirement of a preacher was humility. Not only should he avoid intruding his own personality into the sermon, he also must keep within the comprehension of ordinary humanity. Ethical requirements are combined with evangelical purposes. "I who speak now, I should not bring in anything of my own, and also should not raise myself above others. For I say this to the whole company, that this doctrine must be addressed to me in the first place, but must govern all without any exception whatever."[26]

Using the metaphor of a trumpet, Calvin compares the function of the preacher to that of a resonant instrument that echoes the Word of God. The pastor in fact perceives that in reality he belongs with the flock. Jesus Christ is the only pastor, caring for his sheep: "[Our Lord] wanted me to be like a trumpet in order to gather to himself in obedience the people that is his, and that I

---

24. *OC* 54, col. 287, twenty-fourth sermon on 2 Timothy.

25. I. Backus and C. Chimelli, eds., *La vraie piété* (Geneva: Labor et Fides, 1986), p. 94.

26. *OC* 50, col. 327, fifth sermon on Galatians.

should be of the flock like the others. Therefore when my voice is heard it is so that you and I may all be assembled to be the flock both of God and of Our Lord Jesus Christ."[27]

The Congregations

Paralleling the sermons, another exercise allowed for more informal exchanges. These "congregations," to use the term adopted for them, were weekly conferences, probably in imitation of the "prophecies" of Zürich. This institution undoubtedly dated back to 1536; it was codified by the Ordinances of 1541 and retained in 1561. "All the ministers, to preserve purity and agreement of doctrine among them, should come together on a certain day of the week to confer about the Scriptures, and no one should be absent without a legitimate excuse. If anyone is negligent let him be admonished. As for those who preach in the villages depending on the Seigneurie, let them be exhorted to come as often as they can. Moreover, if they default for an entire month this should be held to be excessive negligence unless there is illness or some other legitimate obstacle."[28]

Some sixty persons met on Friday morning in the Church of the Auditoire, the majority of them informed laymen. The pastors explained the text in question, then discussion began; this resembled what occurred in a university seminar or a Bible-study class. At the close of the session the Company of Pastors met and exchanged fraternal admonitions and doctrinal corrections. Here follows the "Prayer that the ministers are accustomed to give at the beginning of the congregation": "We pray to our God and Father, asking that it may please him to pardon us for all our faults and offenses and illuminate us by his Holy Spirit to have true understanding of his holy Word, giving us the grace to be able to discuss it purely and faithfully for the glory of his holy name, for the edification of the church, and for our own salvation. Which we ask of him in the name of his only beloved son, Our Lord Jesus Christ."[29]

Circumstances lent themselves to the settling of accounts. In the spring of 1542 a Carmelite from Lyon arrived in Geneva, asking to be admitted immediately into the pastoral ministry. He was courteously answered that it was necessary to "be well and duly approved."[30] But our man learned nothing from this language of common sense; the next day he openly criticized the pastors in the

---

27. *OC* 53, cols. 219-20.

28. Cited by R. Peter, ed., *Jean Calvin, Deux congrégations et exposition du catéchisme* (Paris: PUF, 1964), introduction, p. ix.

29. *OC* 8, col. 93, *Congrégation faite en l'église de Genève* . . . (1562).

30. J. Calvin, *Lettres françaises*, ed. J. Bonnet, 2 vols. (Paris: Meyrueis, 1854), 1:59.

taverns. It was unlucky for him, for his virtues appeared very slight. "He knows a little less of the Latin language than a child of eight ought to. Of the Scriptures he is as ignorant as a hypocrite, and nevertheless he is so drunk with ambition that he cannot stand on his feet."[31] This gluttonous monk, "devoted to food," decidedly deserved a lesson; he was charitably permitted to participate in the Friday congregation in order to make himself ridiculous in public. "Our conscience did not permit us to receive him immediately, until his pride was a little reduced. . . . There was ignorance at which we were much astonished, for in our congregation, when someone read a text from Saint Paul that contained good and abundant matter that should be well known to all those who preach there, because it is the epistle for the first Sunday in Advent; when his turn came he not only spoke little, but he overturned everything Saint Paul said, not from malice, as we think, but from sheer stupidity."[32]

But things did not always turn out to Calvin's advantage. Castellio sharply rapped the knuckles of all the pastors in the congregation of Friday, May 30, 1544. As for Bolsec, he took advantage of the exercise to criticize the Reformer impudently in 1551 — before paying for his insolence with prison and banishment (see chap. 10). This risk of disturbance or of doctrinal subversion explains the vigilance that led Calvin's entourage in 1562 to publish a *Congregation Held in the Church of Geneva . . . , in which the Question of the Eternal Election of God was Briefly and Clearly Discussed by Him and Ratified by the Common Accord of his Brother Ministers.*[33] This manifesto of Calvinist orthodoxy was directed against Bolsec's partisans, who again called predestination into question. Calvin delivered some concluding words, repeated in full in these pages: "My brethren, we must thank God very affectionately for having chosen us before we could know it. For we would have been banished and rejected from our salvation, and of our own nature we could have done nothing but draw back from it, if it had not been that he had elected us from the creation of the world. And on the other hand, seeing the wicked reproved, who should be examples to us of the judgment of God, we know that we have merited just the same, because of our own nature we would not have been in a better condition than they."[34]

---

31. Calvin, *Lettres françaises,* 1:64.

32. Calvin, *Lettres françaises,* 1:66-67.

33. *Congrégation faite en l'église de Genève . . . en laquelle la matière de l'élection éternelle de Dieu fut sommairement et clairement par lui déduite et ratifiée d'un commun accord par ses frères ministres,* OC 8, cols. 85-140.

34. *OC* 8, cols. 136-37.

Beauty of the World, Grandeur of God

Why does God offer the earth to us as a mirror? It is so that we can contemplate in it his glory, his wisdom, his virtue, and his infinite power.

CALVIN, 148TH SERMON ON JOB[35]

"The order of nature is a spectacle."[36] We must "contemplate the works of God" and inquire about their maker, while being aware of the limits of human knowledge. "Could we do greater dishonor to God than to want to enclose his power within our minds? It is more than if a man wanted to clutch the sea and the earth in his fist, or hold them between two fingers. It is a still more excessive madness."[37]

Richard Stauffer, in his fine study of Calvin the preacher, analyzed skillfully the infinite distance that separates man from God. Only the mediation of Scripture permits an imperfect bridge over this chasm. "All comparison, all analogy between God and man being impossible, it is evident that our minds cannot conceive or 'enclose' him, as Calvin said."[38] But, Stauffer goes on, "the will of God to put himself at the level of man controls . . . the style of Scripture. It is because of divine condescension toward us that this contains a large number of figures and comparisons."[39] Calvinism is thus the opposite of fundamentalism. Calvin recognized in the text a linguistic datum susceptible of figurative interpretation, a thousand miles away from literalism.

The book of the world still enables us to judge of the majesty of the creator. Although his insistence on revelation kept him far from the Deism of the century of Enlightenment, Calvin lifted up his mind and heart to the great architect. The God of Calvin, like the later one of the *philosophes,* was equipped with a square and compass. "The divine architect has established such proportion and measure that the earth will always remain in its place."[40] Calvin expressed his admiration for the stars, those "celestial armies" or infinite *"gendarmerie."* He marveled at the regularity of their courses, which seemed traced with a compass. But he again expressed his distrust of judicial astrology. "It is wrong to fear things as those unbelievers do who think their lives depend on

---

35. *OC* 35, col. 368.

36. *OC* 35, col. 413, 151st sermon on Job.

37. *OC* 34, cols. 441-42, ninety-sixth sermon on Job.

38. R. Stauffer, *Creator et rector mundi. Dieu, la création et la providence dans l'oeuvre homilétique de Calvin,* 2 vols. in 1 (Lille: Atelier de reproduction des thèses, 1978), 1:11.

39. Stauffer, *Creator et rector mundi,* 1:35.

40. *OC* 35, col. 368.

the sun and the moon and the stars and that their encounters are good or bad for them; but let us know that everything is in the hands of God." He distinguished this imposture from "true astrology," which has no connection with the unhealthy activity of "diviners and sorcerers when they want to predict good luck and similar things." Good astrology (or astronomy) should be praised. It is the science that permits us to comprehend "the order of the heavens, and that beautiful array seen there."[41] The alternation of day and night likewise gives an idea of the grandeur of the Most High. "This beautiful order we see between day and night, the stars we see in the heavens, and all the rest, this is like a living picture for us of the majesty of God."[42]

His cosmology remained traditional. Calvin remained convinced that the earth occupies a central position between the waters above and those below. "The sea is above us," he cried. Besides, the Reformer continued, appealing to common sense, "When we are near the sea we recognize that it is higher than the land." He explained the deluge thus: "By this horrible judgment . . . God showed us as in a mirror what would be perpetually the case over all the earth if he did not miraculously restrain the waters." That the sea does not engulf the earth — this is a "fully manifest" miracle.[43]

Each time Calvin spoke of the sea, of the mountains, of mists, he acknowledged his emotion. But the perfection of the world should not lead to a naturalistic or pantheistic explanation of it; the universe had a creator. Calvin clearly described those "profane and unbelieving people" who always have this "word 'nature' in their mouths."[44]

God was detectable to the eye, and to the heart. The later arguments of Jean-Jacques Rousseau had here one of their points of origin. But Calvin was not content with directing toward divinity the reassuring mirror of the sky or the lakes; he also asked himself about the scandal of evil. The surface of the world is wrinkled all at once, and clouds appear. In the end God withdraws and hides himself. "God hides his face from us so he cannot be seen. This is when men are confused in this world, and we see neither reason nor purpose in what is done; as in the opposite case, if God gives us grace to see that he governs everything and we see things in good order and well disposed, then it is as if his face shone on us like a sun."[45]

God withdraws himself from the world, but he leaves men his Word. It is a food for souls, a complete diet, a remedy for all anguish and sleeplessness. It

41. Stauffer, *Creator et rector mundi*, 2:239-41, for all of these citations.
42. *OC* 35, col. 370, 148th sermon on Job.
43. *OC* 35, cols. 372-73, 148th sermon on Job.
44. *OC* 46, col. 243, twentieth sermon on the harmony of the three Gospels.
45. *OC* 35, col. 193, 134th sermon on Job.

satisfies, quenches the thirst of the believer, and benefits the humors. "The Word of God serves us now as a purge, now as a bleeding, now as a medicine, now as a diet. In short, everything the doctors can apply to human bodies to cure them of their illnesses is not the tenth part of what the Word of God does for the spiritual health of our souls."[46]

The Bible became the sole rule of faith. Calvin here criticized the papists, accused of not relying on Scripture alone. "The first point of Christianity is that the holy Scriptures are all our wisdom, and that we must listen to God who speaks in them, without adding anything to them."[47] Calvin compares the Catholics to Muslims, who admit the new revelation of Mohammed after that of Jesus Christ. "Just as Mohammed said that his Koran was the sovereign wisdom, so says the Pope, for these are the two horns of Antichrist."[48] Were the papists new Muslims or old Pharisees? Calvin amalgamated them:

> We know that the Scriptures were villainously corrupted, and the pharisees above all introduced the custom of glossing holy Scripture. . . . And it was a principle in that sect, as it is today in the papacy, that one must not simply stop at the holy Scriptures but also have the traditions of the Fathers, and that all that was required for salvation was not in the Law or in the Prophets. . . . In short, the corruption that existed in Judea and that reigned at the coming of Our Lord Jesus Christ was entirely similar to that which exists today in the papacy. For what do we principally debate about with the papists? If they would grant us this article, that all our wisdom is contained in the holy Scriptures and that God taught us enough about his will there, and that it is not lawful to add or remove anything whatever, it is certain that we would soon settle all the differences by which the world is now so much troubled.[49]

Or again, elsewhere: "It is true that the papists have the Scripture, but it is not known to them; they have as it were buried it."[50] The papists have a "bastard Gospel."[51] The criticism of the Pharisees does not imply the abolition of the law. Calvin took care to point out his total opposition to the libertines who claimed that "there is no more need for either Law or prophets."[52]

If God is hidden, one must be resigned to speaking of him through images. The high, the low, the earth, the heavens: one must be careful not to inter-

46. *OC* 53, col. 61, fifth sermon on 1 Timothy.
47. *OC* 26, col. 131, twenty-first sermon on Deuteronomy.
48. *OC* 27, col. 502, 108th sermon on Deuteronomy.
49. *OC* 46, cols. 471-72, thirty-eighth sermon on the harmony of the three Gospels.
50. *OC* 41, col. 534, twentieth sermon on Daniel.
51. *OC* 50, col. 329, fifth sermon on Galatians, and p. 399, tenth sermon on Galatians.
52. *OC* 54, col. 84, twenty-fourth sermon on 2 Timothy.

pret these many metaphors in a realistic fashion. The language that serves to designate God risks at every instant locking him up, enclosing him. How can one avoid idolatry? By recourse to grammar or to the analysis of texts.

> We do not find it strange if the holy Scriptures, when they want to bring us to honor God, tell us that he is above in the heavens. And in fact if anyone told us, "God is in this world," since we are carnal, and since our spirits always tend downward, we would attach him to a pillar, to a house, to a mountain, we would plunge him into a river. Such are the fantasies of men. Now so that we may learn by thinking of nothing to imagine nothing terrestrial, also so that we may learn to pass beyond this world and not be stopped by our senses and imaginations, it is said, "God lives in the heavens," so we may know that it is not for us to enclose him in this world to understand what he is . . . , but rather that we should learn to adore him in all humility.[53]

"Humility" is required of the theologian, the humility of a wise man before the grandeur of the universe. One cannot know everything, one cannot say everything about God. Part of the mystery remains forever impenetrable to man: "To consider rightly the power of God we must not search here and there to know whether God could make the sun black and yet shining, whether he could make the earth change to another nature, make wheat be produced in the air without any ears, or other such things. It is not a question of going astray this way in our own foolish curiosity."[54]

Certainly, men spontaneously reject this limit set to their curiosity. Tirelessly they inquire, they pose questions, they invent hypotheses — and, believing themselves serious, they show themselves to be frivolous. "Men never tire of inquiring about things that are too high for their understanding, indeed about things frivolous and useless, such as wanting to know what God did before he created the world."[55]

Calvin placed man in the center of creation, in a world that ignored the revolution in astronomical knowledge. But he assigned him a certain number of duties with respect to his environment. In particular, Calvin preached respect for the animal kingdom. All useless suffering must be avoided. "An ox cannot file a lawsuit when it is deprived of its food after being used for work; but God sees it with pity, since it is his creature."

If someone answers that it is an animal, Calvin answers: "Indeed, but it is a creature of God. When God subdued them to our use, it was on no other con-

---

53. *OC* 34, col. 295, fifty-third sermon on Job.
54. *OC* 46, col. 95, eighth sermon on the harmony of the three Gospels.
55. *OC* 28, cols. 682-83, 179th sermon on Deuteronomy.

dition except that in employing them in our labor we should also exercise humanity. We should treat them humanely, so that in exercising equity we may do our duty even to brute beasts, which have neither reason nor intelligence and cannot complain of the injuries someone does them."[56]

Man, Master and Possessor of Nature

Was Calvinism a social ethic oriented toward action, ambition, and success? The "bourgeois" component of Calvin's thought has long been overestimated. One could no longer pretend that Calvinism was addressed primarily "to the classes engaged in trade and industry, who formed the most modern and progressive elements in the life of the age."[57] From this viewpoint predestination mysteriously exalted saving and inventiveness, seeing them as marks of election by God. To succeed was to be chosen.[58]

The picture offered by Calvin's teaching is clearly bolder in tone. His *Four Sermons* of 1552 were presented as an open letter to "all true Christians who desire the advancement of the reign of Our Lord Jesus Christ." The Reformer begins by recalling "what baseness it is for those to whom God has given knowledge of the truth of his Gospel to pollute themselves with the abominations of the papists, which are entirely contrary to the Christian religion, since in doing this they disavow as far as they can the Son of God who redeemed them."[59]

The first solution suggested by Calvin is testimony, carried to the point of martyrdom, which he calls "the cross." This is one of the means of fulfilling the Christian life. "The doctrine of purely adoring God would be useless unless men were disposed to despise this fragile and precarious life and search for the kingdom of God, following Jesus Christ to the cross to achieve the glory of his

56. *OC* 28, cols. 220-22, 142nd sermon on Deuteronomy, February 12, 1556.

57. R. H. Tawney, *Religion and the Rise of Capitalism* (1926; Harmondsworth: Penguin, 1972), p. 113.

58. This thesis has been vigorously opposed on a theological level in É. Fuchs, *La morale selon Calvin* (Paris: Le Cerf, 1986), p. 35: "One cannot impute to Calvin the famous 'practical syllogism' that according to M. Weber was the driving force of Puritan morality. This syllogism is as follows: election has as its consequence the leading of a holy life, hence one who leads a holy life is elect; consequently to be sure one is elect one must lead a holy life. No one says that such a life can earn salvation, which depends only on the grace of God; but one can confirm that one is saved by the practice of good works. This reasoning Calvin did not maintain." But here we need to distinguish between Calvin and Calvinism. In its Puritan version in England and especially America, it is evident that Calvinism was accompanied by a contractual theory that linked man and God in a common enterprise of which material success was one aspect.

59. *OC* 8, cols. 373-76.

resurrection." But one may also think of exile "in strange and distant countries" in order to find "a well-regulated and disciplined church where the Word of God is preached and where the sacraments are administered properly."[60] Moreover, the author strongly affirms the collective character of authentic Christian faith: "These glorious villains who today do not take account of all these things show clearly by this that they do not have a single drop of Christianity. I speak of our parlor philosophers who are under the papacy. It is quite proper, they say, not to be a Christian, not to trot off to Geneva to have one's ears steeped in sermons and follow the ceremonies observed there! Can one not read and pray to God by oneself? Must one go to church to be taught when everyone has the Scriptures in his own house?"[61]

A feeling of martyrdom, separation, rejection of religious individualism — in no case does Calvin's thought appear to encourage any sort of bourgeois accumulation of capital. It is true, however, that Calvin showed himself favorable to urban civilization. Thus in expounding the prophet Isaiah he took care to explain that the prophetic comparison of Tyre to a prostitute is not a condemnation of cities:

> It is true that this similitude is hardly honorable to the profession of merchant, but it was not without cause that the prophet used such a style and language. It is true that marketing in itself is something useful for the life of men; and how could one do without commerce? It would be necessary to die of hunger, and go about naked. Men therefore have need of merchants, and that condition should be holy and respectable. But here the prophet did not consider what marketing and traffic was. He observed how men abused them, and that corruption that has been fashionable for everyone at all times.
>
> If therefore one argues about market dealing, one will say that it is a holy vocation approved by God and that it is useful, indeed necessary for the whole human race; and if a man engages in it he should apply himself to it as if he served God. For in fact no one will ever acquit himself well in his vocation, whatever way of life he follows, if he does not know and is not entirely persuaded that God finds his service agreeable. When men earn their living it is certain that it is first of all necessary that they act in such loyalty and uprightness that they do not serve themselves, but rather their neighbors and all those who are associated with them. If they have this view and this feeling God accepts such loyalty as a sacrifice of good odor. Thus merchants should serve God in their trade, knowing that he has called them and that he wants to guide them by his Word.

60. *OC* 8, cols. 373-76.
61. *OC* 8, col. 412.

But if, by contrast, we consider the common fashion of men and what they permit themselves, what is marketing, for the most part, but fornication? As if a woman abandoned herself to every evil, having neither honesty nor shame, and still less the fear of God. This is how people behave.

And in fact we see that today no traffic is carried on except with lies, indeed with perjuries; that the name of God is in the mouths of all those who wish to deceive; that it is not enough for them to lie and conceal, but that the name of God must be blasphemed into the bargain. Afterwards we see the falsehoods that each is on the watch to surprise his companions with; each asks only to pillage and to enrich himself at the expense of another. We see the fraud committed in everything, everywhere; one overcharges, the other will not give lawful merchandise.

Indeed all can say this, and not only will the merchants deceive each other, but all those in the trade will say that there is nothing left but corruption; that if one considers how business was carried on forty years ago, there was greater loyalty than there is today, for everything is disguised, there is nothing but deception and fraud, things are so disordered. This is what is said and what experience shows.

Calvin brought his remarks up to date: "Tyre was much more than either Venice or Antwerp is today, and nevertheless we know what hell-holes these cities are. For although to sell merchandise cheaply everywhere there should be some equity and reasonable proportion, it seems the large cities were made only for monopolies, so that the rest of the world might be oppressed, and it seems that those great merchants who have great influence want to cut the throats of all the rest of the world. The city of Tyre was in such a position."[62]

Did Calvinism preach a morality of individual effort? There is no clear-cut answer to this question. Salvation through faith exalted the grandeur of God, but by minimizing the role of merit. "We must have this general rule, that riches do not come to men through their virtue, or wisdom, or labor, but solely by the blessing of God."[63] A rich man should not falsely attribute to himself the merit of his success. It is his duty to praise the Lord in these specified terms: "God shows me that it is he who labors and who here gives me a sign; I must therefore apply this to my instruction, and not say, 'This came to me by accident, I had good luck,' but, 'I know that my God aided me, that I prosper by his bounty.'"[64]

---

62. *Supplementa Calviniana* (Neukirchen-Vluyn: Neukirchener Verlag, 1961), 2:317ff., sermon of May 20, 1557, on Isa. 23. Cited by Henri Meylan, "Calvin et les hommes d'affaires," in *Regards contemporains sur Jean Calvin* (Paris: PUF, 1965), pp. 161-63.

63. *OC* 26, col. 627, sixty-first sermon on Deuteronomy.

64. *OC* 28, col. 257, 145th sermon on Deuteronomy.

It was certainly on the subject of women that Calvin showed himself most conservative. If the Reformer rejected in advance the equality of all men, he was even more worried by the pretensions of wives to raise themselves to the same level as their husbands. Women should learn to be content with their situation: "If women want to plead their cause here, and complain, as if God had abased them without reason, let them consider what is shown to us in the holy Scriptures. Who was first, Adam or Eve? Since the man preceded and the woman came from him, is this not a reason why she should be like a part or an accessory, and not usurp the principal honor? Will a branch wish to have more regard than the root or the trunk of the tree? Here is a branch that is separated from the trunk; will it glorify itself in opposition to it? And what does this lead to? Now woman is like a branch that came from man, for she was taken from his substance, as we know."[65]

The equality of men and women would destroy "all order and discipline." The daughters of Eve should know that their mother misled Adam. There remains for women only to abase themselves justly and to "bear patiently the subjection God put them under, which is only a declaration of humility and modesty."[66] "God requires of women such modesty that they know what is proper to their sex, and that there not be any women similar to mercenary soldiers." Certain women of Geneva, apparently, actually shot "arquebuses as boldly as men." Such women were "villainous monsters" who perverted "the order of nature."[67]

This distrust of women no doubt derived from the unease the preacher felt in dealing with the "facts of life." Sexuality and procreation elicited in Calvin contradictory reactions of mingled disgust and admiration. Conception and fetal development appeared shameful to him; the words "corruption," "stench," even "excrement" crop up in his preaching when speaking of gestation. Composed of "filth and corruption" in the beginning, the human body is startling in its perfection, willed by God.[68]

Calvin, although he distrusted the body, let his admiration for the work of the creator seep through. Man is striking in his completeness; he is the masterwork of the greatest of artists, God. "When someone makes a fine tapestry only the front will appear beautiful, and what is hidden will be entirely shapeless. But with man we see that he is finished from the top of his head to the soles of his feet . . . , and one can find nothing to find fault with, down to the end of a fingernail."[69]

65. *OC* 49, cols. 728-29, twelfth sermon on 1 Cor. 10 and 11.
66. *OC* 31, col. 739, thirty-ninth sermon on Ephesians.
67. *OC* 28, col. 234, 143rd sermon on Deuteronomy.
68. Stauffer, *Creator et rector mundi*, 2:311.
69. *OC* 33, col. 481, thirty-ninth sermon on Job.

The smallest detail has its meaning when one examines the creation. God watches over the finishing of every part. Is there anything more perfect than the human fingernail? Calvin shows how a principle of utility reigns in biology; nothing is superfluous: "Behold our nails, which are as it were a superfluity of the body, and nevertheless if we observe the nails we see marvelous artifice in them. For they serve in putting the hands to work, to strengthen them and enable us to bend the fingers. It is therefore certain that the nail of a man, which is only a superfluity, is for us a mirror of the providence of God, so that from this we may know that he has so worked in us that it is impossible for us to know the hundredth part of the skill he has used."[70]

Certainly one can rightly go into ecstasies over the marvels of the creation. But how does one accept the gratuitousness of evil, which lies in wait at every moment for humanity? The various evils that afflict the universe also have a providential function. "It is necessary for God to inform us that it is he who sends all the punishments we see in the world; if there is any war, any disturbance, he declares to us that he is punishing the sins of men."[71]

It sometimes happens that sickness is obviously a punishment for sin. Calvin showed himself convinced of it in the case of syphilis. The pox was a consequence of the collapse of morals.

> I ask you, after fifty years is it not seen that God has raised up new illnesses against fornication? Whence came this pox, all these foulnesses which there is no need to list? Whence do all these things come, unless God has deployed vengeances that were unknown previously? The world was amazed, and for a time it is true that people were terrified; but even today they have not observed the hand of God. And today we are accustomed to know that the despisers of God, those who are dissolute in their lives, the fornicators, when they abandon themselves to every villainy, only thumb their noses. If God strikes them with some sort of leprosy [syphilis], as this truly is, so that they are eaten by cancer or other foulness, they do not leave off following their course, and do nothing but jeer.[72]

Is illness the effect of sin and health a consequence of virtue? Under no circumstances. One must avoid extreme simplification of Calvin's views. On this question the preacher maintained an ambivalent position. Like the majority of his contemporaries, he saw plague, suffering, martyrdom, and war as appeals to conversion. But on the other hand, this did not imply that the just prosper and

---

70. *OC* 33, col. 488, thirty-ninth sermon on Job.
71. *Supplementa Calviniana*, 2:94.
72. *OC* 28, col. 404, 157th sermon on Deuteronomy.

that the reprobates fail in this world. The God of justice does not necessarily intervene in the course of events. The righteous man does not always have good fortune or success, Calvin concluded when speaking of Job. "These two things can very well go together, that is that the good may be, as here, as though accursed, so that their lives are subject to many evils, and that the wicked may make merry, be prosperous, triumph, and have everything they want."[73]

The scandal of evil emerges particularly in the sermons on Job. God is not the author of evil or of sin, but he mysteriously decides to test his servant. The righteous man, in an inexplicable fashion, also suffers. "Let us take . . . the example of Job, for there as in a mirror we can contemplate how God acts, and the devil on the other side. For all the afflictions that came to Job were not simply by the leave of God, but he willed them thus to test the patience of his servant. It is therefore God who afflicted Job. Now by whose hand? We see that the devil was the agent in all this, and that still he can do nothing except insofar as God commands him. And Job, when he was thus beaten down, knew well that it was with God that he had a dispute."[74]

Calvin was determined to maintain his certainty and confidence in God. "It is impossible for the elect (as Our Lord Jesus Christ says) ever to be turned aside from the road to salvation."[75]

Reprobation or election proceeds from the mysterious decision of God, who has chosen or condemned certain men without apparent reason from the beginning of time. Though its ends and purposes remain obscure to us, can one nevertheless identify the divine strategy? Later Calvinism tempered predestination by insisting on its hereditary character. The great dogmatic text of the beginning of the seventeenth century, the Canons of Dordrecht of 1618-19, stated, "The children of the faithful are holy, not, certainly, by nature, but by benefit of the covenant of grace in which they are included with their fathers and mothers."[76] This familial trend was already begun by the Reformer. Calvin's God "visits the sins of the fathers on the children."[77] The preacher explains: "God not only punishes the wicked and the despisers of his majesty in their own persons, but this vengeance extends to their children. It is true that we find this strange to our minds, but it has already been declared above that God can punish the children of the wicked without doing them wrong. And why? We are all accursed in Adam, and carry only condemnation with us from the mother's womb."[78]

73. *OC* 34, col. 218, seventy-ninth sermon on Job.
74. *Supplementa Calviniana*, 1:726.
75. *OC* 33, col. 592, forty-seventh sermon on Job.
76. *Le solide fondement. Canons de Dordrecht* (Fondation d'Entraide chrétienne réformée, 1988), p. 39.
77. *OC* 28, col. 161, 140th sermon on Deuteronomy.
78. *OC* 34, col. 484, 100th sermon on Job.

Calvin's attachment to the idea of original sin stands out clearly in a recent study. In October 1559 Calvin delivered eight sermons on the episode of the Fall in Genesis. There he developed the theme of original sin. In his methods Calvin was a conscientious exegete who used the Hebrew version of the text. He often gave at first only an approximate translation, which he completed on a later day or week.[79] This did not prevent him from grafting a Christian theme onto the biblical statement, as he did for original sin, and even Communion. It was thus that he interpreted the tree of life. "In short, this tree of life . . . was a sacrament, as today baptism and Communion are to us."[80] The Fall was therefore a form of excommunication.

However, despite these interpolations, Calvin generally tended to reject the received interpretations. In contrast to the theologian, the exegete expressed his "distrust of the arbitrary character of all allegories." He wanted to explain "each biblical text as a function of its narrative coherence and individual rhetoric." Finally, in the Old Testament he did not see only "figures announcing the Christian faith and the New Testament."[81] This reservation is particularly clear in the case of the Trinity, Father, Son, and Holy Spirit. If Calvin the theologian manifested his attachment to this dogma, Calvin the preacher expressed himself less clearly on the subject.[82] Did this entail a desire to return to the letter of the text? A limitation of allegorical interpretation? Calvin was still far from the historico-critical methods of the seventeenth century. But the burning of the heretic Servetus was also without doubt a demonstration of the uncertainty of the exegete, overcome by the vertigo induced by the text.

79. Engammare, p. 333.
80. Bodleian Library, cod. 740, sermon 20, fol. 109v. Cited by Engammare, p. 338.
81. O. Millet, "Exégèse évangélique et culture littéraire humaniste: entre Luther et Bèze, l'Abraham sacrifiant selon Calvin," Études Théologiques et Religieuses 69 (1994): 369.
82. Stauffer, Creator et rector mundi, 1:117.

CHAPTER 14

The Institutes
of the Christian Religion

Can I know myself, can I know thee?

SAINT AUGUSTINE[1]

*The whole sum of our wisdom . . . is as it were contained in two things,
that is the knowledge of God and of ourselves.*

JOHN CALVIN, 1536[2]

One enters into the *Institutes* as though into a cathedral, a sort of gigantic edifice where the succession of words, paragraphs, and chapters testifies to the glory of God and the enterprise of man. This airy and diaphanous text in fact depends on a wise use of shadow and light, sin and hope, damnation and salvation. The predestination of the elect and the reprobates, the terrible divine decree that consigns some to eternal torment and others to infinite bliss, must be looked upon as chiaroscuro, the work of a painter or an architect, sensed more in the mass than in detail, as that careful life of forms which, even in their unwieldiness, generate grace and movement.

1. *"Noverim me, noverim te,"* *Soliloquia* (V.386-87). Fine analysis by J. J. O'Donnell, *Augustine* (Boston: Twayne, 1985), p. 80: "The irrefutable solipsism of self confronted with the absolute reality of God . . . ; all of Augustine's thought moves between these two poles."
2. J. Calvin, *Institution de la religion chrestienne,* (Paris: Belles Lettres, 1961), I, chap. 1, "De la connaissance de Dieu," p. 40.

The *Institutes* is a stone structure, built to last. It is sometimes condemned for its aridity, for its austere God — too austere, so austere that one asks if he is not human, too human, on the level of human ambition. Calvin speaks of God with the passion of a lawyer or a geometer. He chills us a little. But how to say the unutterable, how to define the ineffable while at the same time rejecting effusion and being restrained by modesty? In his very circumspection Calvin lets an acknowledgment seep through, of God's love for his elect and of the love of the elect for God. The sovereign decree, the terrible decree of election that saves or condemns without appeal, is here the mark of a passion that is exclusive, jealous, at its limit insane. God damns because he loves. Could he love so much if he did not damn?

The *Institutes* is built over time, a cathedral in which every pillar, every pilaster is endowed with a history. A primitive core goes back to 1536; it has the charm, the sturdiness of the Romanesque churches. It comprises six chapters, six sober and fluent arguments in the Latin of Renaissance humanism. Calvin clearly borrows from Judaism in the first chapter, "On the Law" ("De lege"). This is the Torah of the Jews; the commentary centers on the Decalogue, minutely analyzed point by point. This version "follows the classical plan of Luther's catechisms: Law, Creed, Lord's Prayer, sacraments of baptism and Communion, false sacraments, Christian liberty, all preceded by the famous 'Letter to the King.'"[3]

The edition of 1539-41[4] adds to this structure a patristic, or more precisely Augustinian, porch. The knowledge of God precedes self-knowledge; original sin is clearly affirmed. Justification by faith, criticism of the merit of works, Christian liberty, and predestination receive substantial development. This second version clearly represents a constitution for a Reformed or Calvinist church, distinct from other currents of reform.

The third great version was completed in 1559, after several intermediate stages.[5] The text is now four and a half times longer than the original. While preserving the grand architectural principles of 1539, this internal remodeling establishes books, distinguished according to their content. This increasing complexity already takes on a baroque character, expansion conflicting with strict order. Old chapters disappear, transmuted by majestic concords: the knowledge of God the creator, the knowledge of God the redeemer, the perception of the grace of Christ, the means of salvation. Christ is henceforth at the heart of the system.

One text comes to us in three versions, but three distinct versions, equally

---

3. P. Gisel, *Le Christ de Calvin* (Paris: Desclée, 1990), p. 23.

4. Latin version in 1539, French version in 1541.

5. Two dates for each edition: 1543 for the Latin version, 1545 for the translation; and 1550 and 1551, respectively. The 1550-51 version introduced the subdivision of the chapters into paragraphs.

estimable, carried forward by an increasing dramatization in a vast circular movement that goes from the Torah to salvation in Christ. This trilogy poses an evident methodological problem: Which version should one select or prefer? Must one indeed choose? G. Lanson maintains the superiority of the French version of 1541 to that of 1560.[6] Also from a literary perspective, O. Millet has recently vigorously identified the stylistic characteristics of this last version: "more concrete and more dramatic spiritual language," "a feeling for cosmic and terrestrial realities," "omnipresence of diatribe," "a simplification of figures, and persistent development."[7] It seems to us, however, that our more historical than theological interest should naturally lead us to prefer the *Institutes* of 1541, the most significant version during the Reformer's lifetime.

The Latin version of 1559, written during an attack of quartan fever, displays an impassioned temperament, and one may note "the increasing presence of controversies which year after year had often taken a personal turn in the battles the Reformer had waged against his adversaries." A preacher as well as a writer, Calvin "addresses his readers as though they were present as listeners. The words 'I ask you' abound."[8]

Self-Knowledge

"Know thyself." Carved before the gates of the temple of Delphi, this injunction still fascinated Erasmus in his *Adages*, which he revised many times during his life.[9] The device was one of the imperatives, incessantly frustrated, of Western consciousness. Like its older relative, Judaism, Christianity undoubtedly participated strongly in establishing this identity. Self-knowledge, that antique ideal, here was joined to the knowledge of God. Introspection is one of the virtues of prayer, and of that examination of conscience which accompanies the recognition of sin. "This book [of Psalms] brings us a good which is desirable above all others; it is that we not only have familiar access to God, but we are also permitted freely to reveal our infirmities to God, which we are ashamed to declare before men."[10] Moving through that indecisive space that separates duplicity

6. G. Lanson, "L'Institution chrétienne de Calvin: examen de l'authenticité de la traduction française," *Revue Historique* 54 (1894): 60-76.

7. O. Millet, *Calvin et la dynamique de la Parole. Essai de rhétorique réformée* (Paris: H. Champion, 1992), pp. 862-70.

8. Millet, p. 861.

9. D. Erasmus, *Adages* (1500-1536), in *Oeuvres choisies*, ed. J. Chomarat (Paris: Librairie Générale Française, Le Livre de Poche Classique, 1991), pp. 365ff.

10. J. Calvin, preface to *Commentaire des psaumes* (1557), *Opera Calvini* (hereafter cited as *OC*) 31, col. 18.

from ingenuousness, Protestantism still overestimates the role of conscience. It insists on a direct conversation between the believer and his God, without the mediation of the priest, leading to the most sublime autonomy or the most extreme neurosis, sometimes both.

What does one discover in oneself? The outlines of the image of God, partially erased by sin. "There is in the human spirit, by a natural inclination, some feeling of divinity."[11] The observation of the world, similarly, leads one to ask oneself about the great artisan: "Since by nature he is incomprehensible and hidden from human intelligence, he has engraved in each of his works certain signs of his majesty by which he makes himself known to us according to our small capacity."[12]

Calvin possessed the indisputable gift of evoking "divine wisdom," or "admiration for the artisan" responsible for the "variety of stars."[13] The beauty of the world as described by Calvin remains directly connected with biblical cosmology; thus the waters literally surround the whole visible universe. It is God's work "to so support the sea in the air that it cannot damage the earth."[14] God speaks through nature; he also speaks through history by showing his providence for his faithful.[15]

The author then contrasts the "miserable condition of men," marked by "hereditary corruption, which the ancients called original sin."[16] He follows Luther in his denial of free will, and refers to Saint Augustine. He denounces the illusion of the person who believes himself to will, when God is willing through him.[17] But despite this warning, Calvin completely accepts direct contact with divinity. The knowledge of God takes on for him an experiential character. "We are invited to a knowledge of God that does not rest only on vain speculation, but which is useful and fruitful, if it is once understood by us. For God is manifest to us in his works, and when we feel their power in us and receive its benefit we must be more sharply touched by such a knowledge than if we imagined God nebulously without having a feeling of him in ourselves by experience."[18]

In a Pauline vein, recalling the apostle's stay in Greece, Calvin imagines the possibility of wisdom outside of the Judeo-Christian revelation. What was the position of the philosophers of antiquity? Calvin recognizes, in part, the

11. Calvin, *Institution*, I, p. 43.
12. Calvin, *Institution*, I, p. 51.
13. Calvin, *Institution*, I, p. 53.
14. Calvin, *Institution*, I, p. 54.
15. Calvin, *Institution*, I, p. 76.
16. Calvin, *Institution*, I, chap. 2, "De la connaissance de l'homme," pp. 84 and 87.
17. Calvin, *Institution*, I, p. 166.
18. Calvin, *Institution*, I, p. 56.

virtues of the pagans: "God gave them some small taste of his divinity."[19] But he immediately corrects himself by pointing out the impotence of natural religion, quickly infected by idolatry: "For as soon as we have conceived some small taste for divinity from the contemplation of the world, then, departing from the true God, in place of him we put the dreams and imaginations of our minds, transferring to them the praise of justice, wisdom, generosity, and power."[20]

The revelation was addressed to Adam, Noah, Abraham, "and the other patriarchs."[21] Calvin's God was actually the God of Abraham, Isaac, and Jacob, who speaks in the Bible. But it is remarkable to observe, despite all his precautionary remarks about corrupted nature, the authentic love, sometimes bordering on lyricism, that he demonstrates for the creation. Unwittingly, and without its affecting the explicit character of his theology, it is possible that Calvin was already preparing the way for Deism. This comes through even more clearly in his preaching, where the humble are spontaneously told to rely on the testimony of their senses to judge the grandeur of God. A Calvin who was a romantic at times — why not?

The Law

> Think not that I am come to destroy the law, or the prophets: I am not come to destroy, but to fulfil.
>
> MATTHEW 5:17

> Because the eye of our understanding sees so poorly that it cannot be moved by the mere beauty and honesty of virtue, the Lord in his benignity has desired to bring us to love and desire it by the sweetness of the reward he offers us.
>
> JOHN CALVIN[22]

The question of the law, in Christian civilization, implicitly harks back to another debate, that about the links between Judaism and Christianity. Certain snap judgments that have obscured these relations are well known. In particular, certain Christians have a tiresome propensity to reproach their Jewish "friends" — as they call them, mixing gall with honey — for their legalism, without always perceiving in return the stifling conformity that reigns in their own churches.

19. Calvin, *Institution,* I, p. 121.
20. Calvin, *Institution,* I, p. 61.
21. Calvin, *Institution,* I, p. 62.
22. Calvin, *Institution,* I, chap. 3, "De la loi," p. 200.

Calvin appeared more perceptive. He sharply criticized the "ignorant people" who "rashly" reject Moses and abandon respect for the law "because they do not think it would be proper for Christians to pause to consider a doctrine which includes the administration of death."[23] This wish to defend the Old Testament was usual with Calvin; he had the magistrates seize an Anabaptist who professed the "abominable maxim that the Old Testament has been abolished."

Here Calvin refers explicitly to Saint Paul's Epistle to the Romans, more often cited than read, more often read than understood. "When we were in the flesh, the motions of sin, which were by the law, did work in our members to bring forth fruit unto death."[24]

A text, any text, should be read with reference to its background. The way certain Christians read their Bibles and Saint Paul in particular resembles those interviews edited for television in which sentences are isolated from their context. The Bible is neither a collection of oracles nor a florilegium of pious citations, still less a cookbook from which one can extract at need some miraculous recipe.

At the very center of Romans is the opposition and the complementarity of the faith and the law, in which are manifested the tensions of the first century between the partisans of Jesus and the opponents of his messiahship. This debate, André Chouraqui points out, preceded the destruction of the temple of Jerusalem in 70; it testified to the "spiritual pluralism"[25] of the Jewish world. There is great risk of an anachronistic reading of this text that would improperly oppose the Christians, holders of grace, to the Jews, bogged down in sterile legalism. It is only necessary to read further in Paul's text: "The law is holy, and the commandment holy, and just, and good."[26]

Calvin here warns his readers against one whole side of Christian anti-Semitism that is rooted in a reading that he contends is erroneous to Romans. There is no need here to sum up all the quarrels that have arisen from this key text, one of the foundations of the Protestant Reformation from Luther's time on because of its affirmation of justification by faith. We shall content ourselves with a few remarks.

23. Calvin, *Institution*, I, p. 295.

24. Rom. 7:5.

25. A. Chouraqui, *Jésus et Paul, fils d'Israël* (Aubonne, Vaud: Éditions du Moulin, 1988), p. 66.

26. Rom. 7:12. Of course, in the heart of the apostle Paul's text comes the statement, "The motions of sins, which were by the law, did . . . bring forth fruit unto death" (Rom. 7:5). But Calvin explains this statement by referring to Moses' last discourse, Deut. 32:47, to argue that the law is the principle of life for the faithful, while producing death for the sinner (*Institution*, I, p. 295).

Calvin, and more generally Reformed Protestants, reacted against Christian anti-Semitism, whose intellectual emptiness they demonstrated. This ethical tendency accompanied a rereading of the Bible, Old and New Testaments, that recognized the complexity and argumentative depth of the text. The misunderstanding of the Pauline corpus derived from two sources, the truncated reading of the text and cultural incomprehension. As for the former, law and grace have a dialectical relationship. "So then with the mind I myself serve the law of God; but with the flesh the law of sin."[27] It is wrong to plaster over this fundamentally dynamic thought with a dualist opposition between law and grace, and still more to read into it a contradictory relationship of Judaism and Christianity. Without pretending to exhaust the subject, we may propose finally, following Calvin's brilliant analyses, an explanation of the misunderstanding: the word "law," the Jewish "Torah," was misunderstood when translated into Greek and into Western languages. The Hebrew word *Torah* is distinguished from the Greek *nomos* in more than one respect. André Chouraqui explains clearly that *Torah* meant "teachings of God himself," which was equivalent to his "word," before it came to designate the first five books of the Bible, otherwise known under the name of Pentateuch.[28] The law therefore does not have a solely prescriptive, legislative, or judicial content. Neither was it out of juridicism that Calvin reevaluated the law; no, Calvin had recognized the admirable beauty of the Old Testament, and he refused to oppose the teachings of Jesus to those of Moses. "Those who did not understand this imagined that Christ was a second Moses, who brought in the evangelical law to correct the defects of the Mosaic law. Whence came the commonplace statement that the perfection of the evangelical law is much greater than it was under the old law. Which is a very perverse error."[29]

Calvin thus defines a common error among Christians, which he also calls "perverse": the fallacious idea that a law of Jesus, an "evangelical" law, had completed the Jewish Torah. This is not the case, according to the author of the *Institutes*: "When we sum up below the precepts of Moses it will appear by his very words how one does great injury to the law of God by saying this. . . . The error is easy to refute, because this sort of people thought that Christ added to the law, whereas he simply restored it in its entirety, that is, by purging it of the lies and the leaven of the pharisees, by which it had been obscured and polluted."[30]

Calvin's Christ was a reformer of Judaism. Now a reformer, in the sixteenth-century sense, was not exactly an innovator or a revolutionary; on the contrary, he fought against novelties. Similarly, the Jesus Calvin presented en-

27. Rom. 7:25.
28. A. Chouraqui, *L'Univers de la Bible,* 10 vols. (Paris: Lidis, 1985), 10:271-73.
29. Calvin, *Institution,* I, p. 206.
30. Calvin, *Institution,* I, pp. 206-7.

tered into conflict with the Pharisees in the name of the original authenticity of the Jewish law. He wanted to restore it in its purity.[31] From this viewpoint, therefore, Jesus was not a second Moses to Calvin; he did not promote a new law, nor did he abolish the old one.

Is this to say that Christianity prolongs the Jewish law without discontinuity? By no means. Calvin was as much aware of the specific qualities of each religion as he was an opponent of anti-Semitism. The Christianity of the first age was distinct from Judaism, and Calvin took note of this difference. It had two aspects, the messiahship of Jesus, rejected by the Jews, and the ritual observances, called by the author "ceremonial."

What should be understood by this distinction? Calvin applied it primarily to the Pauline epistles, showing that the extension of the Jewish revelation to the pagans did not embrace circumcision or the stricter prescriptions, in particular the dietary laws (the *kashruth*), to which the children of Israel were subjected. This argument appears justified by later research; in the first century of our era, alongside full and complete conversions to Judaism, there existed was a sizeable group of "semiproselytes," or those "fearing God." How does one define these men? The specialists in the ancient world have fully restored to us the reasoning behind their behavior: "[The semiproselytes] renounced idolatry, acknowledged the one God, and complied with the fundamental rules of the moral law and with a minimum of ritual observances, all codified in the commandments called Noachian, so called because God had dictated them to Noah to be the religious charter for the whole of humanity."[32]

Although not a historian himself, Calvin seems to have understood very well the situation of early Christianity. His humanist culture alone, his intelligent reading of the texts, especially the biblical ones, already enabled him to raise the question of Jesus' messianic consciousness. He did not fail to recall Jesus' injunction to his apostles: "Go not into the way of the Gentiles, and into any city of the Samaritans enter ye not. But go rather to the lost sheep of the house of Israel."[33] From this he deduced, "Even Jesus Christ, at the beginning of his preaching, did not want to make overtures to the Gentiles."[34]

Thus the non-Jews, the Gentiles, were not the first targets of the evangeli-

---

31. The Jewish theology of the "restoration" is the subject of a correction by P. Fredriksen. "The 'theology of the restoration' is the anticipation of the redemption of Israel and the world upon the establishing of the Kingdom of God." *De Jésus aux Christs* (Paris: Le Cerf, Jésus depuis Jésus, 1992), p. 43.

32. M. Simon and A. Benoit, *Le judaïsme et le christianisme antique* (Paris: PUF, Nouvelle Clio, 1968), p. 76.

33. Matt. 10:5-6.

34. Calvin, *Institution*, III, chap. 7, "De la similitude et différence du vieil et nouveau testament," p. 54.

cal message. The Christians, sprung from the pagan world, for Calvin were adoptive children "of the family of Abraham," "raised to the same degree of honor as the Jews."[35] From this he drew ethical consequences, desiring "to remove from the Christians that vain confidence of thinking that they are more excellent than the Jews because of their baptism."[36]

A Jew is not a Christian, a Christian is not a Jew. At no time did Calvin deny this obvious fact. His message was addressed to Christians; he did not try to "salvage" the Jews. His benevolence began from the established fact of differences fully acknowledged. It was as a Christian thinker and not as an onlooker or a philanthropist that he sharply criticized the anti-Semites, who, he wrote, "have no more respect for the people of Israel than for a herd of pigs."[37] No, Christianity has no intrinsic superiority to Judaism. According to Calvin, "Abraham, Isaac, Noah, Abel, Adam, and the other patriarchs" obviously have a right to salvation, and precede the Christians with God.[38]

It would be fallacious, however, not also to mention the difficulties Calvin encountered in the elaboration of his theory. Despite his attachment to Saint Paul, he lets his impatience show regarding chapter 2 of Romans. He presses the potential contradiction on his readers when he cries, "One might allege what [Saint Paul] says to the Romans about circumcision, where it seems that he makes it far inferior to baptism, which is not true."[39] After having affirmed that circumcision is not inferior to Christian baptism, Calvin was seized by doubts: Could the testimony of Saint Paul not be used against him? Did not the apostle oppose the "circumcision of the heart" to that of the "flesh"?[40] Calvin answers, exasperated, with a laconic "which is not true" whose meaning remains implicit. Does Calvin contradict Saint Paul? Or rather, in a more admissible fashion, does he warn against the usual interpretation of his writings? He continues that the same reasoning applies to Christian baptism; does not a baptism of the heart surpass in intensity a baptism of the flesh? He also interrupts himself to caution against Augustine — whom he likes so much otherwise. Did not Saint Augustine claim, falsely according to Calvin, that the old covenant merely promised a salvation that only Christianity granted?

The salvation of the Jews therefore appeared certain to Calvin. But for all that, he did not renounce the prospect of their conversion. In language inspired by the Gospel of John, he compares their "blindness" to the "light" of the gos-

35. Calvin, *Institution*, III, p. 55.
36. Calvin, *Institution*, III, p. 12.
37. Calvin, *Institution*, III, p. 8.
38. Calvin, *Institution*, III, p. 15.
39. Calvin, *Institution*, III, chap. 10, "Des sacrements," p. 221.
40. Rom. 2:28-29.

pel.[41] Or again, he wishes them to recognize Jesus as the Messiah. "Who then will dare to deprive the Jews of Christ?"[42] For Calvin, however, the messianic kingship of Jesus belongs to the end of time; the recognition of the Savior by the whole of humanity takes on a cosmic aspect. In the course of his discussion, he describes this "fullness of time" when "there will be no more consideration of Jew or of Greek, of circumcision or of foreskin." Jesus Christ will then "be all in all, to whom all peoples of the earth were given in inheritance, and the ends of the earth to rule, so that without distinction he will govern from one sea to the other, from the east even to the west."[43] The conversion of the Jews is presented by Calvin as a sign of the parousia; it will indicate the glorious coming of the Messiah of the last days. One does not have the feeling in reading him that this is a missionary field. Will it involve human activity? This is unlikely; it is for God alone to fix the dates of events. The Jews, who were at the beginning of revelation, are naturally concerned in its final end.

As for his historical perspective, Calvin was uneasy with apocalyptics. His exegesis remained more learned than inspired. One remark is nevertheless necessary: these last times are described, not in the future, but in the present. The gathering around Jesus Christ is more spiritual and internal than historical. The end of time is confounded with the kingdom announced in the Gospels; it has the ambivalence of a hereafter that is conjugated in the present.

As a legal historian, Dean J. Carbonnier has written admirably about Calvin's attitude to the law.[44] Humanist philology, he tells us in substance, restored the Hebrew character of the first five books of the Bible. Could this law be applied to the societies of the Christian West, and under what conditions? The movement began in the fifteenth century with the reemphasis on the Ten Commandments at the expense of the seven deadly sins.[45] Moreover, the popular movements that developed also did not fail to refer to the Bible in their egalitarian claims: the English peasants' revolt of 1381, the German peasants' war condemned by Luther in 1524. Jean Carbonnier describes Calvin's attitude in the following terms: "Calvin tackled the question in his own way, which was that of a jurist, with a *distinguo* that had already been taught by the scholastics. All the laws in the Law are not of an identical nature, and they do not emerge from the

41. Calvin, *Institution*, III, p. 36.
42. Calvin, *Institution*, III, p. 11.
43. Calvin, *Institution*, III, p. 53. This discussion may be a reminiscence of Isaiah; see Isa. 11.
44. J. Carbonnier, "Le calvinisme entre la fascination et la nostalgie de la loi," *Études Théologiques et Religieuses* 64 (1990): 507-17.
45. J. Bossy, "Moral Arithmetic: Seven Sins into Ten Commandments," in *Conscience and Casuistry in Early Modern Europe*, ed. E. Leites (Cambridge: Cambridge University Press, 1988), pp. 214-34.

sieve of the Good News with the same connotations. The ceremonial laws were abrogated without recourse, while the moral laws preserved their entire force. Between these two categories, the judicial laws — meaning the laws that were juridical in a strict sense, regulating social conduct under the sanction of an organized authority — the judicial laws occupied a distinct position."[46]

Faith, Belief, and Fidelity

The law surreptitiously fills a pedagogical role; its function is not so much to prescribe or proscribe, but to lead the believer to recognize his own limits in his individual existence. By establishing an impossible ideal of love for God and one's neighbors, the law shows the vanity of works and of human actions; it leads to discouragement, weariness, and self-disgust. The law is an experiencing of finitude; for Calvin, the reader of Saint Paul, it assumes a sublime, revealed, divine character. Like God, it remains inaccessible to fallen man. From this viewpoint the law is in part synonymous with the Word. "The Word, from whatever direction it comes to us, is like a mirror in which faith should observe and contemplate God."[47] Through the law man discovers that he is a sinner; through faith he experiences salvation. In the dialectical progression of the work, the discussion of faith follows that of the law. This is not an accident. The knowledge of God is nourished on human misery, from which the pain of sin is born. The experience of the law is equivalent to repentance: "Not only is it difficult for men to carry out the law, but . . . it is a thing entirely beyond their power. From which we see that, considering what we deserve, there does not remain to us a single bit of hope, but rather a certain reduction to death, since we are entirely separated from God. Then afterwards it was shown that there is only one way to avoid this calamity, that is the mercy of God, provided we receive it in firm faith and repose certain hope in it."[48]

Faith is born of despair. Just as men no longer understand the meaning of the word "law," they misunderstand the term "faith." Faith, Calvin says, is distinguished from "vulgar credulity" and "opinion." Its object is not of an historical or narrative character, as when one judges "what one reads in history or sees with the eye to be true."[49] In short, authentic faith does not accept any argument from authority.[50] It is not "content with a simple knowledge of the [bibli-

46. Carbonnier, p. 510.
47. Calvin, *Institution*, II, p. 11.
48. Calvin, *Institution*, II, p. 7.
49. Calvin, *Institution*, II, pp. 8-9.
50. Calvin returned to this point in his preaching when he opposed faith (Protestant) to belief (Catholic). "The papists cannot say that they are assured of their religion;

cal] history, and takes its seat in the heart of man."[51] Does the history therefore disappear? Calvin maintained an equilibrium between the religion of the heart and the evangelical narrative, individual effusions and the testimony of Scripture. From this standpoint he rejected any divinization whatever of the narrative: "The object of our faith and the thing considered by it is the history; its end and purpose is the contemplation of things invisible and incomprehensible, which is taken from the history."[52]

For Calvin, therefore, faith is not reducible to belief. Or rather, it is necessary to add "trust" and "hope" to belief.[53] Calvin, moreover, here standardized the meaning of the word *fides,* "faith," in medieval Latin: "confidence placed in someone"; "a conviction that commitments made will be accomplished."[54] A simple remark about grammar illustrates the distinction between faith and belief: to believe *in* God, as the Apostles' Creed says, does not mean merely "to believe that God exists."[55] To believe *in* God is to testify to your attachment, your adherence to him, as Calvin explains, referring to the Hebrew.[56] In French, on the other hand, one does not believe "in" the universal church *(croire en l'Église universelle),* but "believes" the church *(croire l'Église).* This grammarian's distinction speaks strongly of the dissociation Calvin established between faith, reserved for God, and belief, applicable to the church.[57] One can believe (or not believe) the church; one can have faith only in God.

---

the whole is based on a supposition, a belief. . . . They say, Our fathers taught us this way; it is the custom of our holy mother church; this has been accepted from ancient times." 168th sermon on Deuteronomy, *OC* 28, col. 540.

51. Calvin, *Institution,* II, p. 10.

52. Calvin, *Institution,* II, p. 47.

53. Calvin, *Institution,* II, p. 46.

54. J. Wirth, "La naissance du concept de croyance (xiie-xviie siècles)," *Bibliothèque d'Humanisme et Renaissance* 45 (1983): 13.

55. Here also the Calvinist distinction recalls the medieval teachings of Peter Lombard, who in the twelfth century in his *Sentences* distinguished three stages in the act of faith: *credere Deo,* to believe what God says; *credere Deum,* to believe he is God; *credere in Deum,* to give oneself to God. Wirth, p. 19.

56. Calvin, *Institution,* II, p. 76. One may also recall, in the same way, the translation of the concept called "faith" by "adherence" by A. Chouraqui in his translation of the Bible into French.

57. Calvin, *Institution,* II, p. 120. Certainly, Calvin admits, one currently says incorrectly "I believe *in* the church" ("Je crois en l'église"), but this is a usage he considers erroneous.

To Have Too Much and to Know Too Much: Predestination

All errors in religion come either from wanting to know too much or from wanting to have too much, that is from either curiosity, avarice, or ambition. The last of these evils corrupted the Roman church; but Satan is trying to corrupt ours through the first.

PIERRE DU MOULIN, 1615[58]

What is this singular mystery of predestination? The God who saves is also the one who condemns. Doctrinal Calvinism is often, perhaps too often, identified with this proposition that shocks the sensibility of many. God the creator chose certain people and damned others without appeal. Calvin produced the most radical version of this doctrine by insisting on "double predestination," to damnation and to salvation. "Some are predestined to salvation, others to damnation."[59]

"Qualms," "obsession," "terrible fear of never being sufficiently justified"[60] — thus is characterized the anthropology of the end of the Middle Ages. This anthropology sometimes found its natural result in Calvinism and was transcended by it. It found its result in Calvinism if we have taken into account the unfathomable anguish, the frantic distress, the terror that seized the believer who meditated on the grandeur of the most high God, but it was also transcended by it if it is pointed out that predestination, paradoxically, was reassuring in the calm it conferred on the elect to whom God had shown his face. "The elect should no longer worry about a salvation that has already been granted them," Jean Delumeau remarks. "It is God who gives faith, but this itself is a sign of election."[61]

For Calvin predestination was indeed a limiting case; it stood at the frontier of theology. Beyond this, God is entirely incomprehensible. "When they inquire about predestination, [men] enter the sanctuary of divine wisdom, into which if anyone thrusts himself and intrudes with too much confidence and

58. P. du Moulin, "Écrit pour travailler à l'union des Églises chrétiennes" (May 1615), in *Actes authentiques des Églises réformées,* ed. D. Blondel (Amsterdam: Jan Blaeu, 1655), pp. 72-73. This work was sent from London to the provincial synod of the Île-de-France. See Bossuet's commentary, *Histoire des variations des Églises protestantes,* 2 vols. (1688; Paris: Garnier, n.d.), 2:223.

59. Calvin, *Institution,* III, chap. 8, "De la prédestination et providence de Dieu," p. 57. Calvin had also criticized the moderation of Saint Augustine; see *Institution,* I, p. 162.

60. J. Chiffoleau, *Histoire de la France religieuse, xive-xviiie siècles,* ed. J. Le Goff and R. Rémond (Paris: Le Seuil, 1988), p. 171.

61. J. Delumeau, *Le péché et la peur* (Paris: Fayard, 1983), p. 603.

boldness he will never be able to satisfy his curiosity and will enter a labyrinth he will never find a way out of."[62]

The terrifying aspect of this sovereign decree is emphasized with malign pleasure by the Reformer: "Since the disposition of all things is in the hands of God and he can give life or death at his pleasure, he dispenses and ordains by his judgment that some, from their mothers' wombs, are destined irrevocably to eternal death in order to glorify his name in their perdition."[63]

It is a system of death, implacable logic, and necessity. This iron law brings out the inexplicable mystery of election by God. To be chosen, to be called — this is the individual experience of each believer. Calvin's God is all the more reassuring because he can show himself terrifying. What is believing but being chosen? What is being chosen but being saved? Potentially the Calvinist doctrine, in its implacable character, promises salvation without conditions; it does not depend on any works, on any will, on any contrition, on any repentance. It is purely, totally existential, a free act, as unjustified as it is unjustifiable in the eyes of men.[64] Finally, "election," "faith," "vocation," and "conversion" are practically equivalent. All these terms are the expressions of a single mystery, the gift of salvation.

Predestination should be a limit set to human curiosity.[65] The treatise *On Scandals* advanced a "rule of wisdom" that Calvin might well have been inspired to follow himself: "As for predestination being as it were a sea of scandals, whence does this arise, if not from the foolish curiosity of men or their overweening presumption? It is a question of the secret judgments of God, whose brightness not only dazzles the minds of men when they presume to approach them too closely, but destroys and consumes them utterly."[66]

Calvin was not wise. Carried away by polemics and his authorial vanity, over the years he gave an increasing emphasis to predestination in his work. Caroli and Servetus forced him to specify his support of the trinitarian dogma. Similarly Bolsec's reservations and those of numerous contemporaries, known and anonymous, led Calvin to sharpen the edges of his doctrine rather than smoothing them down, to such a point that it is right to ask whether Calvinism is not simply predestination.[67] This is a reductionist statement, certainly, but it

62. Calvin, *Institution*, III, p. 58.

63. Calvin, *Institution*, III, pp. 78-79.

64. Calvin, *Institution*, III, pp. 86-87, "election," "vocation," "free vocation from God."

65. E. P. Mejring, *Calvin wider die Neugierde* (Nieuwkoop, S. Holland: B. de Graaf, 1980).

66. J. Calvin, *Des scandales*, ed. O. Fatio (Geneva: Droz, 1984), p. 123.

67. As an example of the identification of Calvinism with predestination, we cite the major work by N. Tyacke, *Anti-Calvinists: The Rise of English Arminianism, c. 1590-1640* (Oxford: Clarendon Press, 1987).

is explained by the drift of Reformed doctrine in Calvin's own time. Fifty years later adherence to predestination became an absolute criterion of orthodoxy when a more liberal form of Protestantism, nourished on the teachings of Arminius, arose in Holland.

Calvin, therefore, was partially responsible for this identification of Calvinism with predestination. Certainly his thought was of great subtlety. Thus he carefully distinguished predestination from the ancient *fatum* and from destiny: "It will not take me long to show the wrong our adversaries do us in saying we are like the Stoic philosophers in ancient times, who subjected the lives of men to the stars or who imagined I do not know what labyrinths of fatal causes, as they called them. We leave such fantasies to the pagans, and the predestination of God has nothing in common with them."[68]

It didn't matter. The doctrine of predestination was the subject of scandal. Calvin was stubborn, dug in his heels, stormed, and became exasperated. In the last edition of the *Institutes* (1559-60), he devoted substantially more space to this doctrine, misunderstood because it was incomprehensible.[69] A recent theologian sums up the situation:

> The place of the doctrine of predestination in the work of Calvin is the subject of lively debate among specialists. Some think that this doctrine was at the center of Calvin's theology; others, on the contrary, hold that predestination was neither central to the theological views nor important in the pastoral practice of Calvin. We agree with the latter; in fact it was only under the influence of the more and more active polemics unleashed by this doctrine that Calvin finally gave it an important place in the *Institutes*. . . . It was only in the last edition of his *magnum opus*, that of 1559, that Calvin placed his treatment of predestination at the end of the third book, after having dealt with justification and sanctification. In the edition of 1539, as in that of 1554, predestination was instead linked with the doctrine of providence. These hesitations at least signify that Calvin did not at first give this doctrine a major and central role, even if he always considered it important.[70]

Poor Calvin, a victim of his system. Predestination became the werewolf of Reformed theology, which could not be approached without terror. However, this doctrine, regarded as disturbing, at first had the opposite purpose: it

68. Calvin, *Des scandales,* p. 124.

69. The doctrine of predestination took up chapter 8 of the edition of 1541, "On Predestination and the Providence of God." In 1559 it was moved back to chapter 21 of book 3, "On Eternal Election, by which God has Predestined Some to Salvation and Others to Damnation." *OC* 4, cols. 454ff.

70. É. Fuchs, *La morale selon Calvin* (Paris: Le Cerf, 1986), pp. 33-34.

was intended to reassure believers and guarantee their autonomy by showing that their salvation depended only on God, and not on the priests. "Calvin's chief intention was always to preach the positive election of believers and to show the reassuring and edifying character of this doctrine. If he unfortunately also believed he had to speak of the negative election of reprobates, it was to keep intact at any cost the power of God. . . . It would not be just to take this ultimate consequence of his system for the central element of his teaching."[71]

As Karl Barth has demonstrated, "the fateful parallelism of the concepts of election and rejection" governed Calvinist predestination.[72] In other words, there are elect only because there are reprobates. This exchange doubtless entailed sterile consequences; for decades it obscured more than it clarified the mystery of election and of salvation taken from Saint Paul: "Whom he did foreknow, he also did predestinate to be conformed to the image of his Son, that he might be the firstborn among many brethren."[73]

Calvin, Man of the Church

Did a religion of the elect equal a religion of the elite? Often intractable, indeed dogmatic when he chose to be, Calvin always rejected the temptation of the sect, the small group of the elect, isolated from social life. The "visible church" is by definition imperfect, composed of a mixture of "the good and the bad."[74] The "universal" church itself is composed of the sum of the local churches. Calvin therefore did not at all renounce "catholicity," in its Greek sense of universality, but he rejected the submission of all the churches to a single magistracy, comparable to that which Rome exercised in the West. Also, every church that respects "the ministry of the Word of God and of the sacraments" is legitimate.[75] From this standpoint even the corrupted churches, such as the Roman Catholic Church, despite their "idolatry," "superstitions," and "false doctrines," still belong to the "covenant of God" and provide baptism.[76]

It is also necessary to avoid giving the *Institutes* too radical a character. On social questions the text remains perfectly conservative; the author explains carefully, for example, that the community of saints is not at all a community of

71. Fuchs, p. 37.

72. K. Barth, *Dogmatique* II/2 (Geneva: Labor et Fides, 1958), p. 16.

73. Rom. 8:29.

74. Calvin, *Institution*, II, chap. 4, "De la foi," p. 134.

75. Calvin, *Institution*, II, p. 142. Moreover, Calvin employed the terms "sacrament" and "church" in referring to Judaism, as K. Blaser recently emphasized. "Calvin's Vision of the Church," *Ecumenical Review* 45 (1993): 316-27.

76. Calvin, *Institution*, II, p. 145.

goods.[77] It would also be anachronistic to give him too individualistic an interpretation.[78] The "argument" placed at the beginning of the book gives definite pledges of moderation. The later evolution of Protestantism and its indubitable attachment to the autonomy of the subject and to individual tolerance lent themselves to benevolent simplifications which one would search in vain for the least indication of in the *Institutes*. There is no endorsement of any sort of free inquiry in these pages. Quite to the contrary, according to Calvin, laymen risk "losing their way" in their personal reading of the Bible. They need the counsel of the educated, who are charged with guiding them: "The duty of those who have received more ample light from God than others is to assist simple people at this point and as it were offer them a hand to conduct them and help them to find the whole of what God wanted to teach us in his Word."[79]

In its methodical arrangement, in the clarity of its propositions, and indeed in the generosity of certain of its intuitions — as in the dialogue with the Jewish world — did the *Institutes* provide a final model for Reformed Protestantism? It would be absurd to claim this. The dynamics of faith, defended by Calvin, contradicted the spirit of system, or at least relativized it. Certainly Calvin himself, and especially later Calvinism, sometimes gave way to the very faults they denounced; the giddy debates about predestination demonstrate this sufficiently. But it is appropriate here to recall with Richard Stauffer that Calvin the man of knowledge was also Calvin "the theologian of mystery."[80] His only assurance was that of salvation.

---

77. Calvin, *Institution*, II, p. 125.

78. J. Baubérot has clearly traced the fortunes of the individualist and universalist principles in later Protestantism. *Le retour des huguenots* (Paris: Le Cerf; Geneva: Labor et Fides, 1985), pp. 29ff.

79. Calvin, *Institution*, Argument, I, p. 3.

80. R. Stauffer, "Un Calvin méconnu: le prédicateur de Genève," *Bulletin de la Société de l'Histoire du Protestantisme Français* 123 (1977): 202.

CHAPTER 15

Calvin, French Writer

*We are all fragments, and of a composition so irregular and so diverse
that each piece and each moment plays its part. And there is as much
difference between us and ourselves as between us and others. . . .*
MONTAIGNE, 1580[1]

Calvin and Montaigne — they are so close, and yet so different. What do the
Reformer from Picardy and the gentleman from Périgord have in common?
Temporal proximity, for one thing, despite the generation gap. Calvin was in his
twenties when Montaigne was born in 1533; when Montaigne passed on in
1592, Calvin had already been dead for more than a quarter-century.

Being contemporaries, however, is an ambiguous concern; it is only partly
a matter of strict chronology. The contradictory parallelism of Calvin and
Montaigne reflects above all the national choices of founding fathers that presided at the establishment of French national identity. Either the *Institutes* or
the *Essays* could serve as an inaugural document; the historians have revealed in
these two monuments, dissimilar though they are, the firstfruits of a literature
of ideas, divided between Gallic clarity and conjecture. Dependent on an evolu-
tionist philosophy, Albert Thibaudet noted at the beginning of this century
with secret pride, "The task of French literature after the generation of Ronsard
was to become a literature of ideas." More precisely, "Calvin has been correctly
seen as an author who already made the French language capable of expressing
ideas." But he added:

1. Montaigne, *Essais*, II, 1, "De l'inconstance de nos actions," *Oeuvres* (Paris: Le
Seuil, 1967), p. 145.

It was with Montaigne's *Essays* that French literature became aware and assumed the role of a literature of ideas. French literature was a literature in which the *Institutes* did not find a free road, and in which the *Essays* not only found it, but in which a favoring current, a conspiracy of all the intellectual and literary powers predestined it for the function and effectiveness of a key book.

Ideas enter into literary reality less through their logical force than through their humanity, through the vitamins they gain from the warmth and internal sunshine of an individual. To give the literature of ideas its initial impetus we did not need the book of an ideologue, of a thinker, but the book of a man who had no other end than to speak of himself, to depict himself.[2]

Calvin and Montaigne

Was Calvin an "ideologue," as Thibaudet wrote? Was he the man of a system? In these pages we shall adopt a more complex point of view. Certainly Calvin was the author of a summa theologica, the *Institutes of the Christian Religion,* incessantly rewritten from 1536 to 1560. But the work of one of the major writers of this century of rebirth cannot be reduced to this fundamental theological treatise alone. Let us read together the fine page he devoted in his *Institutes* to man and the terrors that assail him:

Human life is surrounded and as it were besieged by infinite miseries. To go no further, since our bodies are receptacles of a thousand maladies and nourish their causes in themselves, wherever a man goes he carries many sorts of death with him, so that his life is as it were enveloped in death. For what else can we say, when one cannot get cold or sweat without danger? Moreover, in whatever direction we turn everything around us is not only suspect but almost openly threatens us, as if it wanted to bring death to you. If we enter a boat there is only a foot between death and us. If we are on a horse it has only to stumble with one foot to make us break our necks. We walk through the streets; there are as many dangers for us as there are tiles on the roofs. If we carry a sword, or if anyone near us carries one, nothing at all is needed to wound us. Whenever we see animals, either wild or rebellious or difficult to manage, they are all armed against us. We shut ourselves into a beautiful garden, where there is nothing but pleasure; a serpent will sometimes be hidden

2. A. Thibaudet (1874-1936), "Place des Essais," in Montaigne, *Essais*, 3 vols. (Paris: Le Livre de Poche, 1965), 1:5-6.

there. The houses we live in, since they are often subject to fire, by day threaten to impoverish us, by night to crush us. Whatever lands we have, inasmuch as they are subject to frost, hail, drought, and other bad weather, threaten us with sterility, and consequently famine. I leave aside the poisonings, entrapments, and violence by which a man's life is attempted, partly at home, partly abroad. Among such perplexities, must a man not be more than miserable? That is, since in living he is only half alive, maintaining himself with difficulty in weakness and distress, as if he saw himself with a knife at his throat every minute.[3]

Are we so far from Montaigne here? Is it not clear that "philosophy, for Calvin as for Montaigne, is learning how to die"? Calvin and Montaigne were men with the same anguish, the same nostalgia, the same melancholy. Calvin could have written, like Montaigne, on the subject of man: "A breath of contrary wind, the croaking of a thieving raven, the false step of a horse, the accidental passage of an eagle, a dream, a voice, a sign, a morning mist suffices to overthrow him and bring him to the ground."[4]

Comparison is not argument. It would be wrong to infer from this formal coincidence an identical point of view. Ideologically everything separated Calvin and Montaigne — including what the Augustinian Reformer and the Catholic fideist believed and did not believe. But they were both witnesses of the same transition that led stoically from the certainties of Renaissance humanism to the torments of the baroque.

Montaigne, as his distant successor in the mayoralty of Bordeaux confided, taught his readers "the humble heroism of daily life."[5] Among the unconscious collectivity of the French, periodically weary of their wars of religion, the common image of Montaigne expressed the general view; in the author of the *Essays* they sought the supreme enemy of the spirit of system. Calvin suffered from the opposite reputation, that of a doctrinaire divider, attached to his own ideas to the point of fanaticism — a popular image, in great part unjustified. Doubt and method, the essay and the synthesis: Calvin and Montaigne in fact expressed two complementary facets of French culture.

The religion of Montaigne is the subject of constant revision. In the late eighteenth century the discovery of his *Journal of a Journey in Italy*, which had long remained unpublished, disturbed his admirers. Montaigne was thought to be a freethinker, until the story of his pilgrimage to Notre-Dame-de-Lorette in

3. J. Calvin, *Institution de la religion chrestienne* (Paris: Belles Lettres, 1961), III, chap. 8, "De la prédestination et de la providence de Dieu," p. 124.

4. Montaigne, *Oeuvres*, p. 197.

5. J. Chaban-Delmas, *Montaigne* (Paris: Laffont, 1992), p. 7.

April 1581 was discovered.[6] Despite his hostility to the Protestant Reformation in general and to Calvinism in particular, "in the language itself there is an astonishing similarity between certain statements of Montaigne's and the *Institutes of the Christian Religion*."[7] In fact, "in reading Calvin's *Institutes* Montaigne could not have helped recognizing some of the fundamental aspirations of his whole generation, the great need for a renovated faith." Certainly Montaigne was "hostile to the Reformation from the triple viewpoint of theology, morals, and politics." He "condemned all theological pretensions; rightly or wrongly, Calvinist morality did not appear to him to have improved behavior; finally, in the establishment of a rival church to that of Rome he saw only the source of bloody conflicts."[8] More recently Marc Fumaroli has insisted on the "liberal spirituality" of the layman Montaigne, in reaction to the Protestant Reformation and to that "old disease of Christianity, the infeudation of laymen and clerics."[9]

Calvin was not, as the late Richard Stauffer pointed out acutely, "the author of only one book."[10] He was also not a writer only. Writing for him was inseparable from speaking, from preaching, from the Word, from the living text that is addressed to an audience from the height of the pulpit — not to mention an active correspondence that made him one of the great letter writers of this Renaissance century.

Calvin was a writer; he was a French writer. Certainly a number of his works had first versions in Latin, but his feeling for language and his passion for communicating ideas naturally led him to express himself in the language of his compatriot. The Gallican jurist Étienne Pasquier praised his gifts as a stylist. In his *Studies of France*, which appeared beginning in 1560, he devoted several pages to the Picard. Calvin, he said, was "a man who wrote well, both in Latin

6. Montaigne, *Journal de voyage en Italie*, ed. P. Michel (Paris: Librairie générale française, 1974), pp. 324ff.

7. G. Nakam, *Les Essais de Montaigne, miroir et procès de leur temps* (Paris: Nizet, 1984), p. 108.

8. Nakam, p. 107.

9. M. Screech, *Montaigne et la mélancolie. La sagesse des Essais* (Paris: PUF, 1992). Preface by M. Fumaroli, p. ix. Fumaroli explains: "Until now, and in great part due to the secretly determining influence of Pascal, I would say that Montaigne's religious attitude has been studied in the negative. The subject has been relegated to the margins of the best studies devoted to the *Essays*. While Montaigne has been judged an agnostic, a pre-libertine, or a good Catholic for political reasons, he has passed as the ideal type of the humanist layman who is a stranger to religious experience, and especially to that methodical and *reflexive* refinement of it that is called spirituality" (p. viii).

10. R. Stauffer, *Creator et rector mundi. Dieu, la création et la providence dans l'oeuvre homilétique de Calvin*, 2 vols. in 1 (Lille: Atelier de reproduction des thèses, 1978), p. 1.

and in French, and to whom our French language is indebted for having been enriched with an infinity of beautiful turns of speech."[11]

Calvin's monodic prose always strikes us by the modernity of its tone; all allowances being made, even when they express the apparently most complicated ideas, his sentences preserve an immediacy and a feeling of concreteness that make them curiously accessible. Of all our sixteenth-century authors, from Rabelais to Montaigne, Calvin is, strangely, one of the easiest to read even today. A number of his lexicological inventions have passed into the standard language: *tergiverser, hyperbolique,* even *manigance* and *antiquailles.*[12]

The comparison with Montaigne is illuminating; without doubt both men expressed themselves as easily in Latin as in French. But the coexistence of the two languages took a different form in the two of them. While Calvin often wrote in Latin, the French versions of his writings are monolingual. Montaigne, on the other hand, wrote in French, interspersed with Latin citations. Calvin's bilingualism was *consecutive,* while Montaigne's was *simultaneous.* Should we deduce from this a different fundamental attitude to truth? This is likely, if we admit that, following a recent author, "Bilingualism for Montaigne was a universal metaphor for the Essays; he oscillated between two languages as he hesitated among various truths. His mind, constantly in movement, may have seen this alternation as an occasion to show in a tangible fashion . . . his constant dualism."[13]

And yet, despite all these tokens of familiarity, Calvin does not occupy a central position in our national culture, even though he was as French as Luther was German.

Calvin the Humanist?

There is such corruption in our nature that we bring from our mothers' wombs nothing but malice and perversity.

J. CALVIN[14]

11. É. Pasquier (1529-1615), *Recherches de la France* (Paris: G. de Luyne, 1660), p. 783.

12. [Translator: Meaning "to equivocate," "hyperbolical," "finagling," and "bric-a-brac."] F. Higman, ed., *Jean Calvin: Three French Treatises* (London: Athlone Press, 1970), introduction, p. 28.

13. F. Gray, *Montaigne bilingue: le latin des Essais* (Paris: H. Champion, 1991), p. 1. In some cases the French version of the *Institutes* keeps patristic citations in Latin, but this is exceptional for Calvin, and connected here with the difficulties of a translation that was not by his hand.

14. J. Calvin, *Des scandales,* ed. O. Fatio (Geneva: Droz, 1984), p. 119.

If by humanism one means a concern for fine literature and the restoration of texts, Calvin was unquestionably a Renaissance humanist. At least he belonged to the second generation of French humanism, forced to choose sides after the Affair of the Placards in 1534. If, on the other hand, one means by humanism faith in man, in his rights and his virtues, or confidence in the indefinite progress of the human spirit, Calvin was the absolute opposite of a humanist. We must renounce the necessary association of these two complementary meanings of the word "humanism." Renaissance humanism was not always "progressive," and it did not necessarily prepare "the triumph of Luther's ideas over those of Rome."[15]

Calvin, the reader of Saint Paul, distrusted the people, as he also distrusted women, the lower classes, and the illiterate. Calvin associated two problems: social insubordination and the theological arrogance of the faithful won over to the Reformation.

> It is not that many now take occasion to lift up their horns under cover of the Gospel. Not without cause the apostles often admonished people to practice Christian liberty soberly and in all modesty, from fear that it might be turned into license for the flesh. For the flesh does not need any special opportunity to rejoice. And because servitude is something distressing and contrary to the human spirit, most people think that felicity for us is to reject the yoke in any way possible. We see that in the time of the apostles the slaves, with this excuse, became proud and rebellious, thinking their masters did them wrong to keep them in subjection. Others wanted to exempt themselves from obedience to princes and superiors. Similarly, today we see many of low condition who by having tasted the Gospel a little become insolent and haughty. Servants want to become companions for their masters, and without shame or modesty presume more than the greatest. But still the worst is that many emancipate themselves from the service of God and give themselves leave not to be obedient to him at all, as if in adopting us for his children he had given up all paternal rights and authority over us.[16]

It was not enough to invoke "Christian liberty," according to the formula popularized by Luther;[17] it was still necessary to respect proper behavior. Calvin evidently was anxious about the storms raised by the Reformation. He feared its theological consequences. Although in theory a partisan of universal

---

15. J.-P. Massaut, *Josse Clichtove. L'humanisme et la réforme du clergé,* 2 vols. (Paris: Belles Lettres, 1968), 1:24.

16. Calvin, *Des scandales,* pp. 152-53.

17. See especially M. Luther, *Werke,* Weimarer Ausgabe, vol. 7, pp. 20ff.

priesthood, in practice he feared the anarchical development of contradictory interpretations of Scripture. Favoring the maintenance of social hierarchies, he dreaded that the spiritual equality of Christians might lead to political claims impossible to satisfy. Masters and servants should remain distinct, like pastors and laymen, the educated and the ignorant. Is this to say that Calvin's views were totally conservative and obsolete? Not at all, and for two reasons. Calvin did not renounce the internal hierarchy of society or of the church, but he wanted to give it a rational basis by recalling the duties that belonged to each condition. Moreover, he insisted on the role of knowledge, or more generally of competence and of talent, which should be fully recognized. Was he not himself a man of knowledge? Did not his gifts as a writer and preacher and his knowledge of texts justify his being listened to and given a place in society? The fears expressed by Calvin betrayed real discomfort, but they nevertheless did not lead him to renounce his principles. By exalting the condition of laymen, the Protestant Reformation reinforced the autonomy of the faithful. Calvin perceived very well that his authority itself depended primarily on knowledge and not on power, and he had to give a demonstration of it every day. Nothing guaranteed Calvin any monopoly of interpretation. A pastor is a man who speaks, who pleads, and who convinces. Calvin dreaded argument. His mixture of pride and timidity, of assurance and suspicion, permitted him to diagnose serenely the grandeurs and the limits of Christian liberty. "Augustine said very truly that arrogance is the mother of all heresies."[18]

In many respects Calvin behaved as a bourgeois, an adherent of a formal liberty whose effects he feared. One may give as an example his commentary on 1 Corinthians 7:22: "For he that is called in the Lord, being a servant, is the Lord's freeman: likewise also he that is called, being free, is Christ's servant." For Calvin, this became:

> For since the liberty of the spirit should be greatly preferred to the liberty of the flesh, [Paul] admonishes the slaves that the harshness of their servitude should be tolerable when they consider the inestimable gift they have received; and those who are at liberty should not be proud, since in what is most important they have no advantage over the slaves. Nevertheless we must not gather from this that those at liberty must be less esteemed than slaves or that the political order should be disturbed. . . . Now these things tend rather to the confirmation of the political order when he points out that the injury that is according to the flesh is recompensed by a spiritual good.[19]

18. Calvin, *Des scandales,* p. 148.
19. J. Calvin, *Commentaires sur le Nouveau Testament,* 4 vols. (Paris: C. Meyrueis, 1855), 3:304.

In the treatise *On Scandals,* Calvin similarly gave a social interpretation of the celebrated hymn to Christ as a slave in the Epistle to the Philippians: "But [he] made himself of no reputation, and took upon him the form of a servant" (Phil. 2:7). This important text on the incarnation was reduced under Calvin's pen to a discouraging banality:

> Those who excel according to the world, as much in riches as in dignity, to conform to the example of the master, must forget their grandeur and make themselves similar to the lowly. It would therefore be greatly excessive arrogance for those who are lowly to inflate themselves and want to magnify themselves under cover of the Gospel. For God does not command the great to descend from their heights so that those who were of base condition may occupy their places, usurping another's rights. This doctrine should serve us, not only to show each one what is the duty of his estate, but also as a correction, to humble the pride of those who elevate themselves too much.[20]

In fact, while preaching moderation to the powerful, who should not abuse their position, Calvin especially condemned the social elevation of upstarts. Moreover, mused Calvin, searching for consolation, these disorders existed as much among the papists as among Protestants. The Reformation alone was not responsible for a disorder that lay in wait for all human societies. Insubordination was everywhere. "The papists agree all too well on one point; this is to bark enviously at the truth of God and to maintain in all obstinacy their superstitions and impieties. But when they are among themselves they cry out against each other so that everything is in confusion, as in a marsh full of frogs."[21]

Obsessed with the quarrels of Geneva, the scalded Calvin mentions "those who make war against us every day" because they are upset that anyone might take away their liberty to live at their own will. He concludes that these people, described in the passage as "fornicators, debauched and dissolute," are in the pay of the pope.[22] But there were those who were worse than the papists and the Protestants taken together — the "Epicureans." Calvin waxed indignant in his *Commentary on the Epistle to the Galatians* (1548): "And there is no sort of persecution more mortal than when someone attacks the salvation of the soul. The swords of the wicked do not reach us who are delivered from the tyranny of the Pope. But how witless we are if we are not moved by this spiritual persecution, when they try in every way they can to extinguish this doctrine

20. Calvin, *Des scandales,* p. 154.
21. Calvin, *Des scandales,* p. 169.
22. Calvin, *Des scandales,* pp. 193-94.

from which we take and hold our lives, when by their blasphemies they assail our faith, and even shake the faith of some who are infirm. As for me, truly the rage of the Epicureans causes me greater distress than that of the papists."[23]

A God by Divine Right

A man who listens is also a man who sees.

JÉRÔME COTTIN, 1994[24]

Calvin's God was an absolute sovereign, in great part unknowable, apart from the narrow road of a revelation limited by the understanding of men. "Could we do greater dishonor to God than to want to enclose his power within our minds? It is more than if a man wanted to clutch the sea and the earth in his fist, or hold them between two fingers. It is a still more excessive madness."[25] His decisions indeed escape our judgment; they appear arbitrary to us. "What about, I ask you, the austere and hidden counsels of God, when he ordains and determines in heaven what pleases him? And if we do not see the reason for it, what shall we say? Must we be so presumptuous as to want to judge it by our fancy, when it surpasses our understanding?"[26]

One may also note the numerous occurrences of the formula of God's "good pleasure": "You have already meditated for a long time on the last battle you will have to endure, if it is his good pleasure to lead you to it."[27] Or again, "And where should we search for God's good pleasure, if not in the holy Scriptures?"[28] Likewise, in the *Institutes*: "Now, that the covenant of life is not equally preached to everyone, and that even where it is preached it is not equally received by all; in this diversity appears an admirable secret of the judgment of God. For there is no doubt that this variation serves his good pleasure."[29] The formula is repeated a few pages later: "The salvation of the faithful

---

23. *Commentaire sur l'épître aux Galates.* Calvin, *Commentaires sur le Nouveau Testament,* 3:726.

24. J. Cottin, *Le regard et la parole. Une théologie protestante de l'image* (Geneva: Labor et Fides, 1994), p. 302. For Catholic aspects see M. Fumaroli, *L'école du silence. Le sentiment des images au xviie siècle* (Paris: Flammarion, Idées et Recherches, 1994).

25. *Opera Calvini* (hereafter cited as *OC*) 34, col. 442, ninety-sixth sermon on Job.

26. *OC* 35, col. 364, 148th sermon on Job.

27. J. Calvin, *Lettres françaises,* ed. J. Bonnet, 2 vols. (Paris: Meyrueis, 1854), 1:372, March 7, 1553, to five prisoners in Lyon.

28. Calvin, *Lettres françaises,* 1:388, letter in May 1553 to M. D'Aubeterre.

29. Calvin, *Institution,* III, p. 57.

is based on the good pleasure of the election of God, and . . . this grace is not acquired by them through any works, but comes to them of his free bounty."[30]

With its arbitrariness of grace, its free gift of salvation, its mystery of election, the Calvinist system found in the society of the old regime one of its obvious political expressions. Tired of war, the Huguenots accomplished "the extension of predestination to the domain of the state."[31] If one whole side of Protestant experience was, potentially at least, republican, Calvin's theology anticipated his followers' adherence to absolute monarchy.

There resulted a contradictory treatment of images. How to speak of God without having recourse to the creation? How can one avoid the constantly lurking snare of idolatry? The Calvinist suspicion of images, in particular in their liturgical use, is well known. It is all the more striking when compared with Catholic exuberance, and even with Lutheran (or Anglican) moderation. A recent author could thus contrast Calvin and his "esthetics without images" to Luther's "images without esthetics."[32] A recent work reaches complex conclusions:

> God in himself is unknowable and invisible, but at the same time he gives us analogues of his presence; there is an element of beauty in the divine essence. . . . This is why in his sermons Calvin invites us to contemplate the beauty of God, referring to the glory of the Lord. . . . This divine splendor is often associated with images of light; God resides in an inaccessible light that irradiates the universe with its rays. In this connection Calvin also talks of a "visibility of God." . . . One cannot then separate the beauty of God from the spectacle of the world. The universe is beautiful because it is the theater of the glory of God.[33]

The same author explains, "Esthetics points toward ethics, and Calvin sometimes appeals to the invisibility of truth as against the visibility of appearances."[34] What is the theological origin of these reservations? They are not without an echo of Plato, but they find their principal source in the interpretation Calvin proposes of the Ten Commandments. Representations must be distrusted, above all when they take God as their subject. Calvin had a tendency to confound idols and images. "Calvin rejected only images of God, not images in general, which remained a fundamental anthropological reality; it is sufficient to read a few pages of the *Institutes* to recognize that the sense of sight was

30. Calvin, *Institution,* III, p. 67.

31. D. Richet, *La France moderne: l'esprit des institutions* (Paris: Flammarion, 1973), p. 56.

32. Cottin, pp. 259 and 285. See also L. Wencelius, *L'esthétique de Calvin* (Paris: Belles Lettres, 1937).

33. Cottin, pp. 303-4.

34. Cottin, p. 307.

highly developed and recurred constantly in the writings of the Reformer."[35]
The preacher, in particular, constantly emphasized the beauty and harmony of
the world. This also stands out in the *Commentaries*. "Even if God is invisible,
his glory is still visible. When it is a question of his essence, certainly he resides
in an inaccessible light; but as long as he shines through the entire world, this
glory is the vestment in which he who in himself was hidden appears to us all
the same in a certain visible fashion."[36]

Calvin's distrust of visual images nevertheless reinforces the interest of
figures of speech. Calvin the writer is deeply aware of the attraction of images.
We will cite but one example, the metaphor of a mirror, which returns frequently in his writings.

The theme of the mirror was not new. Its roots lie in Scripture itself. The
Second Epistle to the Corinthians says, "But we all, with open face beholding as
in a glass [a mirror] the glory of the Lord, are changed into the same image
from glory to glory, even as by the Spirit of the Lord" (3:18). Calvin did not fail
to draw inspiration from this in numerous passages, as when he described Peter's fall as "a very clear mirror of our infirmities."[37] The mirror, of course, plays
a negative role here. It recalls our common humanity, represented by Peter, to
recognition of its faults. But, depending on what it reflects, a mirror can also
have a positive content. This applies to the church, when it is a mirror of Christ.
"It is very reasonable that the living image of Jesus Christ should appear in the
state of the church as in a mirror."[38] Calvin also mentioned "the regard God has
for his church when he puts it before our eyes as in a mirror."[39] A mirror can
also represent a bad example. "We must think that God points out all such people [the incredulous] to us as mirrors, to warn us to follow his call with fear and
solicitude, from fear that the same thing will happen to us."[40] The Scriptures
themselves are a sort of mirror of humanity:

> I have been accustomed to call this book an anatomy of all the parts of the
> soul, because there is no emotion in man which is not represented here as in a
> mirror. Indeed, in better words, the Holy Spirit has here depicted from life all
> the pains, sadnesses, fears, doubts, hopes, worries, perplexities, and confused
> emotions by which the spirits of men are accustomed to be agitated. The rest
> of Scripture contains the lessons that God has commanded his servants to
> announce to us; but here the prophets, because in speaking to God they re-

35. Cottin, p. 302.
36. *OC* 32, col. 85, *Commentaire du Psaume 104*.
37. Calvin, *Commentaires sur le Nouveau Testament*, 1:683.
38. Calvin, *Des scandales*, p. 86.
39. Calvin, *Des scandales*, p. 105.
40. Calvin, *Des scandales*, p. 140.

veal all their internal emotions, call or rather require each of us to examine himself, so that nothing of all the infirmities we are subject to and all the vices with which we are filled remains hidden.[41]

But the ideal mirror is Christ. Is he not at the same time the double reflection of man and of God? "Christ . . . is like a mirror in which we should contemplate our election, and in which we shall contemplate it without deceit."[42] Calvin's Christ is "at the same time the God who elected and the man who was elected."[43] Recalling the teaching of the Gospel of John, one finds in Calvin an entrance into the abyss of the Father through the view of the Son. "These holy men never knew God except by regarding him in his son, as in a mirror."[44] Calvin the preacher, moreover, used the same image as Calvin the writer. "God, therefore, being himself invisible, shows himself in the mirror that is proper for us, that is in his Word."[45]

This obsession with mirrors is at the center of both the biblical revelation and the Christian mystery. If man was created in the image of God as Genesis proclaims, Calvin's Christ is found in a series of mirrors that reflect on man the awareness of his sonship.

These mirror games had particular significance during the Renaissance. The meaning of the metaphor was reversed as one progressed toward the seventeenth century and the baroque age. "Mirrors had a singular destiny in the sixteenth century, and this metaphor experienced one of the most interesting changes of meaning in the history of language."[46] "In the time of Rabelais a mirror represented a person. Likewise history was held to be an exact reflection of the truth." But soon after, "the reflection was deceitful" and "truth was no longer one." In Montaigne the result was an invasion by mirrors. "For him everything in everyday life was a mirror. All his books were mirrors. And in his own book his heroes, positive and negative, were mirrors."[47] One might continue, with the help of a recent work, "In a society of reflections in which personal expression is suspect the ego, to exist, needs to be supported by echoes."[48]

To what extent, then, is the work here a reflection of the author? Unlike Montaigne, Calvin did not have as his principal object the depiction of himself.

41. J. Calvin, preface to *Commentaire des psaumes* (1557), *OC* 31, col. 16.

42. Calvin, *Institution*, III, p. 91.

43. K. Barth, *Dogmatique*, II/2 (Geneva: Labor et Fides, 1958), p. 1.

44. Calvin, *Institution*, IV, p. 154.

45. *OC* 35, col. 247, 138th sermon on Job.

46. Nakam, pp. 18-19.

47. Nakam, p. 19.

48. S. Melchior Bonnet, *Histoire du miroir* (Paris: Imago, 1994). Preface by J. Delumeau, p. 154.

His discreet personality emerges, however, on a number of occasions, although interpretations vary. When Calvin says "I," what does this actually mean? A few years ago the late Richard Stauffer drew several indisputable conclusions. "When Calvin speaks in the first person in his preaching, the 'I' he employs has a quadruple significance, prophetic, polemical, autobiographical, and mystical."[49] The "I" of the orator, or more exactly here of the preacher, is only rarely the isolated individual. Similarly, the saint, the great man, or the Reformer equally insists on his sense of a mission that goes beyond himself. This applies to Calvin: "Calvin was by nature not very prodigal of confidences about his own person; a certain timidity, an aristocratic taste for hiding himself from the public, and finally his conviction that the individual is nothing in himself, but only to the extent that he is an instrument of the divine will, led him to pass by in silence many of the events that would be of interest for biography."[50]

It is no less true that it is all a question of proportions. The roles of the single ego and of the collective body are at the present time the objects of constant readjustments. According to some interpretations, Calvin's legendary discretion about his personality was "real only in part." Calvin, "by choice or by necessity . . . spoke more than once of himself. By choice in certain sermons and, certainly, in his *Correspondence*. By necessity when he had to respond to the attacks of his adversaries."[51] Other studies have minimized the personal aspect for the sake of "an epic dramatization in which the biographical and individual traits of the Reformer were toned down in favor of the anonymous heroism of an exemplary attitude."[52]

The Grammar of Revelation

What good would it do us to eat a small morsel of bread and drink three drops of wine if that voice did not resound from on high that the flesh of Jesus Christ is the true food of our souls, his blood is truly the spiritual drink?

CALVIN, *BRIEF RESOLUTION*, 1555[53]

49. R. Stauffer, "Les discours à la première personne dans les sermons de Calvin," in *Regards contemporains sur Jean Calvin* (Paris: PUF, 1965), pp. 237-38.

50. F. Wendel, *Calvin, sources et évolution de sa pensée religieuse* (1950; Geneva: Labor et Fides, 1985), p. 3.

51. D. Ménager, "Théodore de Bèze, biographe de Calvin," *Bibliothèque d'Humanisme et Renaissance* 45 (1983): 239-40.

52. O. Millet, *Calvin et la dynamique de la Parole. Essai de rhétorique réformée* (Paris: H. Champion, 1992), p. 510.

53. J. Calvin, *Calvin, homme d'Église* (Geneva: Labor et Fides, 1971), p. 165.

Calvin's true aesthetic approach deals more with language than the visual arts. It is that of a grammarian, haunted by sacred rhetoric. His conception of the Lord's Supper particularly illuminates the Reformer's attitude. Two chief texts illustrate this question: the *Agreement Proposed and Concluded Concerning the Matter of the Sacraments between the Ministers of the Church of Zürich and Master Calvin* in 1549-51 and the *Brief Resolution* of 1555.[54] The latter work mentions "the disputes there have been in our time about the sacraments." There were in fact many debates about the Eucharist. The Reformers could hardly reach agreement. In 1529 the Marburg Colloquy ended in bitter failure; the Zürichers, partisans of Zwingli, and the Lutherans met without finding the least possibility of compromise. The great stars appeared. Luther and Zwingli were of course on hand, but they were surrounded by a symposium of famous intellectuals: Oecolampadius, Bucer, Jacob Sturm, Melanchthon. Zwingli held that the Lord's Supper is a mere memorial whose meaning is symbolic. Luther readily admitted that the sharing of bread and wine had a commemorative value as a remembrance of the Last Supper of Christ before the crucifixion. But he insisted on the real presence of the body and the blood of the Crucified within the elements.

These points of view were in many respects irreconcilable. Calvin tried to achieve a synthesis: he admitted a real presence, but specified that this could only be spiritual. The term "spiritual," however, did not have a purely psychological meaning for him. The presence of Christ in the elements was perceptible only to the eyes of faith. In May 1549 an agreement was reached between Calvin and Bullinger, Zwingli's successor. It is generally known by the Latin name of *Consensus Tigurinus.*[55] Calvin and the Lutherans continued to be opposed in later controversies.[56]

Calvin's basic originality was his recourse to grammar to elucidate the meaning of the institution of the Eucharist. What in fact did the words spoken by Christ during the Last Supper, "This is my body, this is my blood," mean? Calvin had recourse to a figure of speech, metonymy: "We therefore reject as bad expositors those who insist on the exact literal sense of the words, This is my body, this is my blood. For we hold it to be notorious that these words should be interpreted judiciously and with discretion, that is as meaning that the names of what the bread and wine signify are attributed to them. And it

54. *Accord passé et conclu touchant la matière des sacrements, entre les ministres de l'Église de Zurich et Maître Calvin* and *Brève résolution.*

55. P. Sanders, "Henri Bullinger et l'invention (1546-1551) avec Jean Calvin d'une théologie réformée de la cène: la gestion de l'héritage zwinglien lors du 'Consensus Tigurinus' (1549) et de la rédaction des 'Décades' (1551)" (*thèse* at Paris IV, 1989).

56. It was on this occasion that the Hamburg pastor J. Westphal published his *Farrago* (1552).

should not be found new or strange that through a figure called metonymy the sign borrows the name of the reality it stands for, since such a manner of speaking is more than frequent in Scripture."[57]

The *Brief Resolution* explained, "The name of the thing signified is given to the symbol, through a figure called metonymy, which means transfer of name." And Calvin concluded, "If they prefer another figure, this argument should be referred to the schools of grammar, so far is it from deserving to trouble the whole of Christianity."[58]

The disagreement was linguistic before it was theological. Metonymy was radically distinct from metaphor, according to the rhetorical treatises of the period. In Pierre Le Fèvre's *Great and True Art of Ample Rhetoric* (1521), the following explanation is found: metaphor implies similarity, metonymy assumes proximity. Thus, Le Fèvre continues, it is by metaphor that a simple man is called a lamb, but by metonymy that one names the contained when meaning the container.[59]

When he said "This is my body, this is my blood," Christ did not identify himself with the bread and the wine. But the bread and the wine have a memorial value. This is a relationship between words more than a representation. The bread and the wine signify the body and the blood of Christ. They are not identified with him. Might Calvin have used very modern thinking that anticipates the development of linguistics? The truth is more complex; here Calvin once more showed himself the heir of the declining Middle Ages. The nominalist movement had already brought about a dissociation of words and things.[60] The Protestant Reformation, in its plurality, could not be separated from this new feeling of contingency that restored God to his otherness.[61]

Thus words and things were not identical, according to Calvin. There was no similarity between them. Michel Foucault was only a century or two off when, thirty years ago, he tried to determine "the moment in time when resem-

57. Calvin, *Calvin, homme d'Église,* pp. 140-41.

58. Calvin, *Calvin, homme d'Église,* p. 190.

59. *Grand et vrai art de pleine rhétorique.* On this subject see B. Cottret, "Pour une sémiotique de la Réforme. Le Consensus Tigurinus de Calvin," *Annales ESC* 39 (1984): 265-85. On the Calvinist Lord's Supper see B. Roussel, "'Faire la cène' dans les Églises réformées du royaume de France au seizième siècle (ca. 1555–ca. 1575)," *Archives de Sciences Sociales des Religions* 1994 (85), pp. 99-119.

60. P. Vignaux, *Le Nominalisme au xive siècle* (Paris: Vrin, 1948); P. Hochart, "Guillaume d'Occam: le signe et sa duplicité," in *Histoire de la philosophie,* ed. F. Chatelet, 7 vols. (Paris: Hachette, 1972-73), 2:183-203. According to the hypothesis of R. Stauffer, however, Calvin departed from the nominalist position on God to avoid the risk of making God's power absolute and arbitrary. *Creator et rector mundi,* 1:83.

61. H. A. Oberman, *The Dawn of the Reformation: Essays in Late Medieval–Early Reformation Thought* (Edinburgh: T. & T. Clark, 1986), p. 27.

blance gave up its connection with knowledge and disappeared, at least in part, from the horizon of understanding."[62] In concentrating on the seventeenth century, poor Foucault simply left out the Middle Ages and the Reformation.[63] If he had taken them into account, how could he have written that "until the end of the sixteenth century resemblance played a fundamental role in the scholarship of Western culture"?[64]

The nominalist crisis of the fourteenth century, like the religious reformations of the sixteenth, anticipated precisely this dissociation of existence and appearance. Calvin already opposed magic to learning, particularly in his criticism of relics and of judicial astrology. One could also apply to him the concept of symbiotics that, according to Foucault, characterized the following century.[65] In a word, all Calvin's thought consisted of a rejection of analogy. While his theology insisted on the otherness of God the creator, his conceptions of Christ the redeemer and of the sacraments rejected all mixing of substances. Jesus is true God and true man, but the characteristics of his divinity do not concern his humanity. In the same way the bread and the wine of the Lord's Supper do not possess in themselves any sacred character, once they have been shared among the participants. The bread and the wine are of value simply as signs.

Eucharistic doctrine joins up with the analysis of the two natures of the Savior. There is no mixing of the bread and the body, of the blood and the wine of the Lord's Supper, just as the humanity of Christ does not contain his divinity. The term "mixing," moreover, was strictly negative for Calvin. In his preaching he used it to describe the tradition of the papists that had obscured the meaning of Scripture. "In the papacy everyone has tried to add his own bit. . . . It seemed it was not enough to go strictly according to the Word of God and that it would be good to add some mixture to it." Or again, "It is not that the papists flatly renounce God, but that they want to make a mixed and confused doctrine from all the religions of the world."[66]

62. M. Foucault, *Les mots et les choses. Une archéologie des sciences humaines* (Paris: NRF, 1966), p. 32.

63. On this point read the fine clarification by O. Boulnois in his introduction to Duns Scotus, *Sur la connaissance de Dieu et l'univocité de l'étant* (Paris: PUF, 1988), pp. 11ff., "La destruction de l'analogie et l'instauration de la métaphysique."

64. Foucault, p. 47.

65. Foucault, p. 59: "The system of symbols became binary and . . . the symbolism was reflected in the form of the representation; literature was now indeed formed of signs and things signified and deserved to be analyzed as such."

66. *OC* 26, cols. 412-13, forty-fourth sermon on Deuteronomy, and *OC* 26, col. 464, forty-eighth sermon. Pierre Gisel shows a Monophysite tendency in Luther, "primacy, in fact, of the divine nature over the human nature," and on the contrary a Nestorian one in Calvin, "rejection of all *mixing* of the two natures." P. Gisel, *Le Christ de Calvin* (Paris: Desclée, 1990), p. 15.

Calvin, in his conception of knowledge, showed himself in his own fashion an iconoclast. He rejected the argument from authority in both the religious and the secular domains. There was something of Descartes in the Reformer, in the insolence he displayed toward established values, whether of church or state. The Reformation was in its way also a first experiment, a falling back on obvious fundamentals. But there the resemblance between the two men, the bourgeois from Picardy and the gentleman from Touraine, stops. Calvin did not share Descartes's aristocratic contempt for books; he was rather a devotee of a special book, the Bible, that he decoded as a grammarian and a rhetorician. One can indeed say, from this standpoint, that he was a "modern." In fact, "He participated in advance in the great housecleaning of the seventeenth century, the great disencumbering, the clearing out of rubbish. He was sober and lucid. He thought one could bring order into tradition by reconstructing it from the necessary and sufficient warehouse that is Scripture."[67]

Was Calvin a "pre-Cartesian," as Alain Besançon wrote? No doubt. The fortunes of the Reformation were also those of the French language. The *Institutes* shared that illusion of clarity and transparency that gave mystery its fixed place in the baroque world of appearances, symbolized by the mirror. From this standpoint Calvin was already opening the way to classicism. Not that it is necessary here to take up again an outdated apologetics that by a dialectic reversal tried to establish a (minority) Protestantism at the center of the (majority) experience of Frenchmen. But Calvin, even in the reaction of rejection that he aroused in Bossuet, for example, participated in the fortunes of the French language and in the double wager on coherence and clarity that would find its outcome in Rousseau.[68] But this is simply to admit that transparency was deceiving in its turn and to recognize that Calvin himself hardly escaped the problem of an unquiet conscience.

67. A. Besançon, *L'image interdite. Une histoire intellectuelle de l'iconoclasme* (Paris: Fayard, 1994), pp. 253-55 for this and the following development.

68. Read here M. Fumaroli's remarks on Rousseau, "L'apologétique de la langue française classique, ou l'enthousiasme de la transparence," *Commentaire* 27 (fall 1984): 433-43.

Saint Luther, Saint Calvin, Saint Jansenius

Which saint should one honor? Where should one place "Saint Luther," "Saint Calvin," "Saint Jansenius"? This was the humorous question of Lord Bolingbroke in the very middle of the eighteenth century.[1] The English lord, plagiarized by Voltaire (one of many), understood in his unbelieving fashion that sainthood is an ambiguous notion. We shall not dedicate altars to Calvin; he would not have wanted it, and also did not deserve it. But visiting him remains an enriching experience in the literary field, as well as the spiritual and historical. He was one of the basic figures of a Western awareness that extends far beyond France alone. "Calvinism," in all the imprecision of the term, has permanently influenced the ethical and political views of modern thinkers, from Hobbes to Locke or Rousseau. He also began, as is less well known, an analysis of language that led to contemporary semiotics. Finally, he fashioned an exacting spirituality that reconciled faith and the secular world.[2]

Should one like Calvin? "The Geneva Reformer," one of the greatest specialists wrote, "has not found a better welcome among many Protestants than

---

1. B. Cottret, *Bolingbroke. Exil et écriture au siècle des Lumières* (Paris: Klincksieck, 1992), p. 626.

2. J. Baubérot, *Le retour des huguenots* (Paris: Le Cerf; Geneva: Labor et Fides, 1985); Baubérot, *Le protestantisme doit-il mourir?* (Paris: Le Seuil, 1988); Baubérot, *La laïcité, quel héritage?: de 1789 à nos jours* (Geneva: Labor et Fides, 1990); B. Cottret, "Du bon usage de l'anticléricalisme. Jacques Fontaine, réfugié en Angleterre et en Irlande (1658-1728)," *Bulletin de la Société de l'Histoire du Protestantisme Français* 140 (1994): 515-40.

among his Catholic adversaries."[3] Who will complain? It is undoubtedly in the domain of religious history that the need for impartiality is greatest. Can one attempt a balanced portrait of Calvin that avoids the two usual ruts of monotonous piety or systematic denigration?

Calvin the Reformer

Everything is so obscured that there is not even a hope of returning the world to the true Christianity of the past.

ERASMUS, "LETTER TO MARTIN DORP," 1554[4]

To change nothing, and not to innovate.

CALVIN[5]

A persistent illusion dogs us; it is the fruit of the ideology of progress that has developed since the eighteenth century. Innovation for us has become a cardinal value that extends over the sphere of consumption as well as the more abstract one of ideas. The situation was entirely different during the Renaissance. Whether the subject was literature or the Christian faith, the past was the surest criterion of authenticity. This did not mean the whole past indiscriminately, but rather certain illuminating episodes: Greco-Latin antiquity, prodigal of its wisdom; and the primitive church of apostolic times, the guarantor of sanctity. Of course, these two models, the sacred and the profane, were not interchangeable. Nature, fortune, and virtue were so many ambiguous concepts that threatened to dethrone the creating God of the Christians. In many respects Renaissance naturalism was opposed to Christianity.[6]

The love of literature and the search for the biblical heritage, however different in their objectives, took the same path. "Humanity recovered the Gospel as it recovered the Iliad."[7] The restoration of the texts and the reformation of the church both depended on the idealization of a glorious past, whether it was that of the poets, the philosophers, or the apostles, of Homer, Plato, or Jesus Christ.

3. R. Stauffer, *L'humanité de Calvin* (Neuchâtel: Delachaux & Niestlé, 1964), p. 17.

4. Erasmus, *Lettre à Martin Dorp* (1515), *Oeuvres choisies*, ed. J. Chomarat (Paris: Librairie Générale Française, Le Livre de Poche Classique, 1991), p. 300.

5. *Opera Calvini* (hereafter cited as *OC*) 9, cols. 893-94.

6. R. Lenoble, *Mersenne ou la naissance du mécanisme* (1943; Paris: Vrin, 1971).

7. F. Buisson, *Sébastien Castellion. Sa vie et son oeuvre (1515-1563)* (Paris: Hachette, 1892), 1:53.

A Reformer, from this standpoint, could not be an innovator, nor did he claim to be a revolutionary either. A Reformer, *above all,* it may be said, was not an innovator or a revolutionary. On the contrary, he rose up against the "novelties" that had corrupted the sense of Scripture and altered the evangelical message. Calvin's English biographer has said this very well: "[He was] a man of order and of peace who was born into a world of conflict. A conservative by nature, by upbringing, by conviction, his ideas became among the most revolutionary in Europe. The order, aristocratic in tendency, which he prized and which he devoted his life to establishing, became one of the platforms for democracy in succeeding centuries."[8]

This concise and provocative summary contains a great deal of truth. Calvin, like his contemporaries, detested the very idea of innovation. The synthesis he produced of Christian truth was in many respects unprecedented. But to see Protestantism as a "new" faith, in opposition to the ancient faith, Catholic and Roman, aroused denial and disavowal in a conservative century. Étienne Pasquier noted correctly that, while the French Protestants presented themselves as "reformers" insisting on a return to the primitive church, their adversaries described their faith as a "new opinion."[9] The "dread" or "awe" *(crainte)* of God manifest in Calvin was radically distinguished from the "fear" *(peur)* of God.[10] Calvin's God is indeed a God of love, and also a familiar God who actually lowers himself to his creatures. Thus the preacher, in one of his sermons, uses an astonishing image in comparing God to a hen: "Let us not be deterred from coming to him by any dread or doubt; for what more could he do than when he stooped down as if he were a hen, so that his majesty would no longer be terrible to us and would not appall us?"[11]

This "hen God" certainly does not correspond to the commonly accepted clichés that see in the Reformer's teaching a dark and pessimistic doctrine of corrupted human nature, forgetting, it seems, the whole positive aspect of his program. The multiplying diversity of the flamboyant religion of the end of the Middle Ages was succeeded by a principle of unity. Christ, as already for Luther, was the sole intercessor; the seven sacraments were reduced to two, baptism and the Lord's Supper; faith alone, grace alone, Scripture alone supplanted the traditional forms of piety and tradition itself. Calvin, moreover, here was content with systematizing the common basis of the Protestant Reformation.

Calvin was also a man of melancholy. He had one foot in the fifteenth

---

8. T. H. L. Parker, *John Calvin: A Biography* (London: J. M. Dent & Sons, 1975), p. xi.

9. É. Pasquier, *Recherches de la France* (Paris: G. de Luyne, 1660), p. 737.

10. J. Delumeau, *Leçon terminale . . . 9 février 1994* (Paris: Collège de France, 1994), p. 9.

11. *OC* 28, col. 697, 181st sermon on Deuteronomy. Christ, it is true, used the metaphor to describe himself: Matt. 23:37 and Luke 13:34.

century, the other in the seventeenth. His form of speech, already classical, and his desire to separate existence from appearances are pre-Cartesian. All in all, the gentleman from the north of France, crossed with a Genevan, deliberately ignored the Mediterranean tradition of pagan hedonism. His antique model was Seneca, not Epicurus. But it would be wrong all the same to relegate to complete austerity this admirer of the stars: "We would indeed have to be senseless beasts for the sight of the heavens not to move us, and all the order that is seen in the stars, and such a fine and exquisite arrangement, which gives us sufficient testimony that there is an admirable majesty of God."[12]

A History of Faith

All things both in heaven and on earth are mutable, but God does not vary.

J. CALVIN[13]

Thus one finds in Calvin the heavens, the sea, the planets, and the stars. In this restless man the interior view never eclipsed the spectacle of the world; the variation of the seasons, the alternation of day and night, the "fish of the waters" and the "birds of the air" persistently appeared in sermons accessible to the humble. Certainly the world of John Calvin was still the world of the Bible stories and the Hebrew cosmology. But one cannot deny that this excitable man seized, better than any other, the "fluctuating and various" — to cite Montaigne — character of the creation. God, on the other hand, is characterized by permanence.

This dialogue between the human and the divine, what is it but the very content of faith? More than any other thinker in our language, Calvin reflected on the definition of faith. It is a personal relationship with God, which he distinguished from simple "belief."[14] To describe my undertaking, I coined some years ago the term "history of faith."[15] This work is a history of faith, a history of the faith of a man, the history of the individual. In the case of Calvin, the undertaking takes on a wider significance; in one of his key passages the author of

12. *OC* 34, col. 297, eighty-fifth sermon on Job.

13. J. Calvin, *Supplementa Calviniana* (Neukirchen-Vluyn: Neukirchener Verlag, 1936), 1:564.

14. In this domain, little explored until recently, we nevertheless cite the illuminating article by J. Wirth, "La naissance du concept de croyance (xiie-xviie siècles)," *Bibliothèque d'Humanisme et Renaissance* 45 (1983): 7-58.

15. B. Cottret, *Le Christ des Lumières* (Paris: Le Cerf, 1990), p. 9 and introduction, and "La religion de Cromwell. Pour une histoire de la foi," *Historiens et géographes, Histoire religieuse I,* reprint no. 341, October 1993, pp. 157-64.

the *Institutes* took care to distinguish faith from belief. How can one write a life of Calvin without taking account of this distinction?[16] Religious history, in fact, cannot be limited to the ecclesiastical domain[17] or to the abstract study of religion. All history is singular; the biography of Calvin is the story of a life and not a mere dogmatic pronouncement.

The history of a particular man is also the history of the hope he entertained as much as the history of what actually happened. Faith is a point fleeing over the edge of the horizon. Fictional or actual, real or invented, the relationship with God occupied the central place in the life of Calvin. For this anxious man, the advocate of the predestination of both the elect and reprobates, everything became in its way a symbol, a sacrament, or a testimony, including his disappointed ambitions. A history of faith also becomes virtual history, a history of contingency and transience. It is necessary to end with the retrospective illusion of historical necessity. Or, as T. S. Eliot remarked: "What might have been and what has been/Point to one end, which is always present."[18]

16. Ferdinand Buisson, as a lay thinker in the nineteenth century, was inspired, he explained, by the formula "faith is not belief." Buisson, 1:xiii.

17. L. Febvre, *Au coeur religieux du xvie siècle* (Paris: SEVPEN, 1968), p. 8.

18. T. S. Eliot, *Four Quartets* (London: Faber & Faber, 1970), p. 13.

The Youth of Calvin

Standard version:
Born July 10, 1509
1523-27/28: Paris
1528-29: Orléans
1529-31: Bourges
1531-33: Paris and Orléans
1533-34: Paris, Angoulême, Noyon
1534: Basel

Alternative version:
ca. 1520-21: La Marche
ca. 1521-22: Faculty of Arts
ca. 1525-26: M.A.
ca. 1525-26: Orléans
1529-30: Bourges
Oct. 1530–March 1531: Orléans
Beginning of 1531: *licence* (in law)
(following T. H. L. Parker)

The University System in France

Dates of foundation of provincial universities: Montpellier 1220, Toulouse 1229, Caen 1452, Bourges 1464, Bordeaux 1473. The University of Paris included four faculties: three higher faculties (theology, law, medicine) and the faculty of arts for beginners. The faculty of arts (or faculty of letters) granted only the degree of master of arts, a prerequisite to later obtaining the title of bachelor in one of the other three faculties (theology, law, medicine), followed by the *licence* and the *thèse*. The arts degree corresponded to a first course at the university, required for pursuing studies in the three higher faculties. The students were divided into four "nations": France, Picardy, Normandy, and Germany. Instruction in arts comprised the trivium (grammar, rhetoric, and dialectic) and the quadrivium (arithmetic, geometry, music, astronomy). Philosophy was added to this. The rector, the head of the university, had an appointment renewed every three months.

Young men ordinarily began their studies about the age of thirteen with grammar. About age fifteen they enrolled, in Paris, in one of the four "nations," to pursue courses in one of about forty existing colleges. The first examination, the *determinatio*, permitted them to obtain the title of bachelor, followed by three and a half years of study for the *licence*. It was generally necessary to complete five years of study, the *quinquennium*, to obtain the license, *licentia docendi*, and the title of master of arts about the age of twenty-one. This in turn permitted them to become "regents" and to teach, while following courses in the higher faculties of theology, law, and medicine. See in particular J. K. Farge, *Orthodoxy and Reform in Early Reformation France: The Faculty of Theology of Paris, 1500-1543* (Leyden: E. J. Brill, 1985), pp. 11ff.

APPENDIX 3

The Small Council

From 1544 on the Small Council had twenty-five members. It met in the City Hall and played an executive role, also assuming part of the legislative power. The Council generally sat three times a week, on Monday, Tuesday, and Friday. The first syndic presided. From 1557 on, fraternal admonitions took place among the councillors on the Wednesday before the celebration of the Lord's Supper.[1] This council predominated because of its oligarchical tone and its stability; fourteen of its members sat without interruption from 1541 to 1555.

1. R. Guerdan, *Genève au temps de Calvin* (Geneva: Éditions du Mont Blanc, 1977), p. 197.

Chronology of the Establishment of Calvinism in France

1555   Establishment of the Reformed church of Paris

1557   Edict of Compiègne, increasing the repression of Protestants (July)

Disaster of Saint-Quentin (August): defeat of the French by the Spaniards

Affair of the Rue Saint-Jacques: arrest of Calvinists assembled for worship (September)

1558   Calvinist gathering and singing of psalms in the Pré-aux-Clercs in Paris in the presence of Antoine de Bourbon, king of Navarre

1559   Treaty of Cateau-Cambrésis (April)

First national synod of French Reformed churches (May)

Letters Patent of Écouen against Protestants (June). Arrest of Anne du Bourg

Death of Henry II (July)

1560   Tumult of Amboise: Huguenots attempt to kidnap Francis II (February-March)

Projected national council (March)

Appeasing speech by Michel de l'Hospital (July)

Death of Francis II (December)

1561   Failure of Colloquy of Poissy between Reformers and Catholics (September-October)

1562   Edict recognizing Reformed churches (January)

Massacre of Wassy in Champagne (March): beginning of Wars of Religion

1563   Peace of Amboise (March)

End of the Council of Trent, begun in 1545 (December)

1564   Death of Calvin (May 27)

Chronology of Royal Repression

1525	Order of the Parlement of Paris prohibiting the diffusion of the ideas of Luther (February)
1534	Affair of the Placards (October)
1535	Edict calling for the extirpation of the Lutheran "sect" (January)
	Edict of Coucy halting prosecutions (July)
1539	Edict aimed at purging the kingdom of the "diabolical" errors of the Lutherans (June)
1540	Edict of Fontainebleau, entrusting the repression of heresy to the parlements instead of the ecclesiastical officialities (June)
1543	Articles of faith enacted by the faculty of theology of Paris
1544	Publication of *Index of Forbidden Books* (August)
1547	Edict of Blois, creating the *"Chambre ardente"* to deal with heretics as a section of the Parlement of Paris (October)
1551	Edict of Châteaubriant strengthening repression and increasing the regulation of books (June)
1555	Reformed church of Paris organized
1557	Edict of Compiègne, punishing the profession of heresy with death
1559	First synod of the Reformed churches of France
	Edict of Écouen, ordering the extirpation of heresy in all provinces of the kingdom (June)
1560	Edict of Romorantin, transferring the repression of heretics to ecclesiastical tribunals (May)

APPENDIX 6

Decrees of the Sorbonne, 1543

Article 1	Necessity of infant baptism
Article 2	Free will
Article 3	Auricular confession
Article 4	Justification by faith and works
Article 5	Eucharistic definition
Article 6	Value of sacrifice of the Mass for the living and the dead
Article 7	Uselessness of Communion in both kinds
Article 8	Necessity of ordination to consecrate the Eucharist or confess sins
Article 9	Validity of sacraments administered by an unworthy priest, *ex operato operando*
Article 10	Institution of confirmation and extreme unction by Jesus Christ
Articles 11, 12, 13, 14, 15, 16	Need to pray to and imitate interceding saints and the Virgin Mary
Article 17	Existence of purgatory
Articles 18, 19, 20, 21, 22	Existence of one universal church having as its supreme authority a general council which is infallible for faith and morals
Article 23	Divine right of the pope and existence of indulgences
Articles 24, 25	Validity of fasts and religious vows

APPENDIX 7

List of Sermons

(following R. Stauffer's Ph.D. dissertation)

1549:	25 sermons on Jeremiah
1550-51:	28 sermons on Micah
1552:	47 sermons on Daniel
1553:	22 sermons on Psalm 119
1554-55:	159 sermons on Job
1554-55:	54 sermons on 1 Timothy
1555:	30 sermons on 2 Timothy
1555:	17 sermons on Titus
1555-56:	200 sermons on Deuteronomy
1556:	19 sermons on 1 Corinthians
1557:	66 sermons on Isaiah
1557:	4 sermons on the Canticle to Hezekiah
1557-58:	43 sermons on Galatians
1558:	7 sermons on Isaiah
1558-59:	48 sermons on Ephesians
1559-60:	65 sermons on the harmony of the Gospels
1559-60:	97 sermons on Genesis
1560:	3 sermons on Melchizedek
1560:	4 sermons on justification
1560:	3 sermons on the sacrifice of Abraham
1560:	13 sermons on God's free election of Jacob and rejection of Esau
1561-63:	194 sermons on 1 and 2 Samuel

Other sermons are hard to locate chronologically: on the passion (according to Matthew), the nativity (according to Luke), the divinity of Jesus Christ (according to John), the ascension and Pentecost (according to Acts), and the last days (according to 2 Thessalonians).

Select Bibliography

Calvin's Works

Complete Works

Ioannis Calvini Opera quae supersunt omnia. 59 books in 58 volumes. Edited by G. Baum, E. Cunitz, and E. Reuss. Brunswick and Berlin: Braunschweig, 1863-1900.

Selected Works

J. Calvin, *Oeuvres choisies.* Edited by O. Millet. Paris: Gallimard, Folio classique, 1995.

Advertissement contre l'astrologie judiciaire. Edited by O. Millet. Geneva: Droz, 1985.

Calvin, homme d'Église. Geneva: Labor et fides, 1971.

Calvin's Commentary on Seneca's De Clementia. Edited by F. L. Battles and A. M. Hugo. Leiden: Brill, 1969.

Commentaires sur le nouveau testament. 4 volumes. Paris: C. Meyrueis, 1855.

Correspondance française avec Louis du Tillet. Edited by A. Crottet. Geneva: Cherruliez, 1850.

Des scandales. Edited by O. Fatio. Geneva: Droz, 1984.

Institution de la religion chrestienne. 4 volumes. Edited by J. Pannier. Paris: Belles Lettres, 1961.

Jean Calvin, Deux congrégations et exposition du catéchisme. Edited by R. Peter. Paris: PUF, 1964.

La vraie piété. Edited by I. Backus and C. Chimelli. Geneva: Labor et Fides, 1986.

Lettres à Monsieur et Madame de Falais. Edited by F. Bonali-Fiquet. Geneva: Droz, 1991.

Lettres françaises. 2 volumes. Edited by J. Bonnet. Paris: C. Meyrueis, 1854.

Œuvres françaises. Edited by P.-L. Jacob. Paris: G. Gosselin, 1842.

Opera Selecta. 5 volumes. Edited by P. Barth. Münster: C. Kaiser, 1926-1936.

Supplementa Calviniana. 6 volumes. Neukirchen-Vluyn: Neukirchener Verlag, 1936-1971.

Attributed Works

Défense de Guillaume Farel et de ses collègues contre les calomnies du théologastre Pierre Caroli par Nicolas Des Gallars. Edited by F. Gounelle. Paris: PUF, Études d'histoire et de philosophie religieuses, 1994.

Studies

Armogathe, Jean-Robert. "Les vies de Calvin aux xvie et xviie siècles." In *Historiographie de la Réforme*, pp. 45-59. Edited by Philippe Joutard. Neuchâtel: Delachaux et Niestlé, 1977.

Armstrong, Brian G., and Wilhelm Neuser, eds. *Calvinus Sicerioris Religionis Vindex*. Sixteenth-Century Essays and Studies, vol. 36 (1997).

Alves, Abel Athouguia. "The Christian Social Organism and Social Welfare: The Case of Vives, Calvin, and Loyola." *Sixteenth Century Journal* 20 (1989): 3-21.

Aux origines du catéchisme en France. Paris: Desclée, 1988.

Babelotzky, Gerd. *Platonischer Bilder und Gedankengänge in Calvins Lehre vom Menschen*. Wiesbaden: Franz Steiner Verlag, 1977.

Backus, Irena. "Calvin's Judgment of Eusebius of Caesarea: An Analysis." *Sixteenth Century Journal* 22 (1991): 419-37.

Bainton, Ronald H. *Michel Servet, hérétique et martyr*. Geneva: Droz, 1953.

Bedouelle, Guy, and Bernard Roussel, eds. *Le temps des Réformes et la Bible*. Paris: Beauchesne, Bible de tous les temps, 1989.

Bergvall, Åke. "Reason in Luther, Calvin, and Sidney." *Sixteenth Century Journal* 23 (1992): 115-27.

Berriot, François. "Un procès d'athéisme à Genève: l'affaire Gruet (1547-1550)." *Bulletin de la Société de l'Histoire du Protestantisme Français* 125 (1979): 577-92.

Biéler, André. *L'homme et la femme dans la morale calviniste.* Geneva: Labor et Fides, 1963.

Blaser, Klauspeter. "Calvin's Vision of the Church." *Ecumenical Review* 45 (1993): 316-27.

Boegner, Alfred. *Étude sur la jeunesse et la conversion de Calvin.* Montauban: Imprimerie coopérative, 1873.

Bohatec, Josef. *Budé und Calvin. Studien zur Gedankenwelt des französischen Frühhumanismus.* Graz: H. Böhlaus, 1950.

Boisset, Jean. *Calvin et la souveraineté de Dieu.* Paris: Seghers, 1964.

———. "La Réforme et les Pères de l'Église: les références patristiques dans l'*Institution de la religion chétienne* de J. Calvin." *Migne et le renouveau des études patristiques. Actes du colloque de Saint-Flour (juillet 1975).* Edited by A. Mandouze and J. Fouilheron. Paris: Beauchesne, 1985.

Bost, Hubert. "Protestantisme: une naissance sans faire-part." *Études Théologiques et Religieuses* 67 (1992): 359-73.

Bouwsma, William J. *John Calvin: A Sixteenth-Century Portrait.* New York: Oxford University Press, 1988.

Buisson, Ferdinand. *Sébastien Castellion. Sa vie et son œuvre (1515-1563).* 2 volumes. Paris: Hachette, 1892.

Cadier, Jean. *Calvin. L'homme que Dieu a dompté.* Geneva: Labor et Fides, 1958.

———. *Calvin, sa vie, son œuvre, avec un exposé de sa philosophie.* Paris: PUF, 1967.

Carbonnier, Jean. "Le calvinisme entre la fascination et la nostalgie de la loi." *Études Théologiques et Religieuses* 64 (1990): 507-17.

Chambers, Bettye Thomas. *Bibliography of French Bibles: Fifteenth and Sixteenth-Century French Language Editions of the Scriptures.* Geneva: Droz, 1983.

Chaunu, Pierre. *Le temps des Réformes.* Paris: Fayard, 1975.

———. *Église, culture et société. Essais sur Réforme et Contre-Réforme (1517-1620).* 2nd edition. Paris: SEDES, 1981.

———. *La mort à Paris: xvie, xviie et xviiie siècles.* New edition. Paris: Fayard, 1984.

———, ed. *L'aventure de la Réforme. Le monde de Jean Calvin.* Paris: Hermé, 1992.

Chenevière, Marc-Édouard. *La pensée politique de Calvin.* Geneva: Slatkine, 1970.

Christin, Olivier. *Une révolution symbolique. L'iconoclasme huguenot et la reconstruction catholique.* Paris: Minuit, 1991.

Cottin, Jérôme. *Le regard et la parole. Une théologie protestante de l'image.* Geneva: Labor et Fides, 1994.

Cottret, Bernard. "Pour une sémiotique de la Réforme. Le *Consensus Tigurinus* de Calvin." *Annales ESC* 39 (1984): 265-85.

————. "Max Weber Revisited. Le puritanisme anglais: de la réussite économique au salut." *Americana* 4 (1989): 75-96.

Crouzet, Denis. *Les guerriers de Dieu. La violence au temps des troubles de religion, vers 1525–vers 1610.* 2 volumes. Seyssel: Champ Vallon, 1990.

————. *La nuit de la Saint-Barthélemy. Un rêve perdu de la Renaissance.* Paris: Fayard, 1994.

Delumeau, Jean. *Naissance et affirmation de la Réforme.* Paris: PUF, 1965, new edition, 1973.

————. *La Peur en Occident.* Paris: Fayard, 1978.

————. *Rassurer et protéger.* Paris: Fayard, 1989.

Deregnaucourt, Gilles, and Didier Poton. *La vie religieuse en France aux xvie-xviie-xviiie siècles.* Gap: Ophrys, 1994.

Dompnier, Bernard. *Le venin de l'hérésie.* Paris: Le Centurion, 1985.

Doumergue, Émile. *Jean Calvin. Les hommes et les choses de son temps.* 7 volumes. Lausanne: G. Bridel, 1899-1917.

Douglass, Jane Dempsey. *Women, Freedom and Calvin.* Philadelphia: Westminster, 1985.

Eire, Carlos M. N. *War against the Idols: The Reformation of Worship from Erasmus to Calvin.* Cambridge: Cambridge University Press, 1986.

El Kenz, David. "Le roi de justice et le martyr réformé: État sacré et désacralisé, jusqu'à la veille de la première guerre de religion." *Bulletin de la Société de l'Histoire du Protestantisme Français* 140 (1995): 27-69.

Engammare, Max. "Le paradis à Genève. Comment Calvin prêchait-il la chute aux Genevois?" *Études Théologiques et Religieuses* 69 (1994): 329-47.

Farge, James K. *Orthodoxy and Reform in Early Reformation France.* Leiden: E. J. Brill, 1985.

————. *Le parti conservateur au xve siècle. Université et Parlement de Paris à l'époque de la Renaissance et de la Réforme.* Paris: Collège de France, 1992.

Fatio, Olivier, et al., eds. *Confessions et catéchismes de la foi réformée.* Geneva: Labor et fides, 1986.

Febvre, Lucien. *Au cœur religieux du xve siècle.* Paris: SEVPEN, 1968.

————. *Michelet et la Renaissance.* Paris: Flammarion, 1992.

Fischer, Danièle. "Nouvelles réflexions sur la conversion de Calvin." *Études Théologiques et Religieuses* 58 (1983): 203.

Forstman, H. Jackson. *Word and Spirit: Calvin's Doctrine of Biblical Authority.* Stanford: Stanford University Press, 1962.

Friedman, Jerome. *Michael Servetus: A Case Study in Total Heresy.* Geneva: Droz, 1978.

————. *The Most Ancient Testimony: Sixteenth-Century Christian Hebraica in the Age of Renaissance Nostalgia*. Athens, Ohio: Ohio University Press, 1983.

Fuchs, Éric. *La morale selon Calvin*. Paris: Le Cerf, 1986.

Ganoczy, Alexandre. *Le jeune Calvin. Genèse et évolution de sa vocation réformatrice*. Wiesbaden: F. Steiner, 1966.

———. *Amt und Apostolozität*. Wiesbaden: F. Steiner, 1975.

Garrisson, Janine. *Royaume, Renaissance et Réforme (1483-1559)*. Paris: Le Seuil, 1991.

———. *Guerre civile et compromis (1559-1598)*. Paris: Le Seuil, 1991.

Garside, Charles. *The Origins of Calvin's Theology of Music*. Philadelphia: American Philosophical Society, 1979.

Gilmont, Jean-François. *Bibliotheca calviniana*. 2 volumes to date. Geneva: Droz, 1991-1994.

Ginzburg, Carlo. *Il Nicodemismo. Simulazione e dissimulazione religiosa dell'-Europa del'500*. Turin: Einaudi, 1970.

Girardin, Benoit. *Rhétorique et théologique. Calvin, le Commentaire de l'épître aux Romains*. Paris: Beauchesne, 1979.

Gisel, Pierre. *Le Christ de Calvin*. Paris: Desclée, 1990.

Guichonnet, Paul, ed. *Histoire de Geneva*. Toulouse: Privat, and Lausanne: Payot, 1974.

Hamman, Gottfried. *Entre la secte et la cité. Le projet d'Église du Réformateur Martin Bucer (1491-1551)*. Geneva: Labor et Fides, 1984.

Higman, Francis. *The Style of John Calvin in His French Polemical Treatises*. Oxford: Oxford University Press, 1967.

———. "Calvin and the Art of Translation." *Western Canadian Studies in Modern Language and Literature* 11 (1970): 5-27.

———. *Censorship and the Sorbonne. A Bibliographical Study of Books in French Censured by the Faculty of Theology of the University of Paris, 1520-1551*. Geneva: Droz, 1979.

———. "The Question of Nicodemism." In *Calvinus Ecclesiae Genevensis Custos*. Edited by W. H. Neuser. Frankfurt: P. Lang, 1984.

———. *La diffusion de la Réforme en France*. Geneva: Labor et Fides, 1992.

———. "Calvin polémiste." *Études Théologiques et Religieuses* 69 (1994): 349-65.

———. *Piety and the People: Religious Printing in French, 1511-1551*. St. Andrews Studies in Reformation History. Aldershot: Scolar Press, 1996.

Huseman, William H. "A Lexicological Study of the Expression of Toleration in French at the Time of the Colloque of Poissy (1559-1565)." *Cahiers de lexicologie* 48 (1986): 89-109.

Junod, Éric, ed. *La dispute de Lausanne, 1536. La théologie réformée après*

Zwingli et avant Calvin. Lausanne: Bibliothèque historique vaudoise, 1988.

Kingdon, R. M. *Geneva and the Coming of the Wars of Religion in France, 1555-1563*. Geneva: Droz, 1956.

Krusche, Werner. *Das Wirken des Heiligen Geistes nach Calvin*. Göttingen, Vandenhoeck & Ruprecht, 1957.

Lane, A. L. S. "Calvin's Sources of St Bernard." *Archiv für Reformationsgeschichte* 67 (1976): 253-83.

Lecoq, Anne-Marie. *François Ier imaginaire. Symbolique et politique à l'aube de la Renaissance française*. Paris: Macula, "Art et histoire," 1987.

Lefranc, Abel. *La jeunesse de Calvin*. Paris: Fischbacher, 1888.

Le Gal, Patrick. *Le droit canonique dans la pensée dialectique de Jean Calvin*. Fribourg: Éditions Interuniversitaires, 1984.

Le Goff, Jacques, and René Rémond, eds. *Histoire de la France religieuse, xive-xviiie siècles*. Paris: Le Seuil, 1988.

Leites, Edmund, ed. *Conscience and Casuistry in Early Modern Europe*. Cambridge: Cambridge University Press, 1988.

Léonard, Émile G. *Histoire générale du protestantisme*. 3 volumes. Paris: PUF, 1961-1964.

Le Roy Ladurie, Emmanuel. *Le siècle des Platter, 1499-1628*. 3 volumes. Volume 1: *Le mendiant et le professeur*. Paris: Fayard, 1995.

Lestringant, Franck. "Tristes tropistes: du Brésil à la France, une controverse à l'aube des guerres de religion." *Revue de l'Histoire des Religions* 202 (1985): 270-71.

———. *Le huguenot et le sauvage*. Paris: Aux amateurs de livres, 1990.

———. *La cause des martyrs*. Mont-de-Marsan: l'Éditions InterUniversitaires, 1991.

———. "Genève et l'Amerique: le rêve du Refuge huguenot au temps des guerres de Religion (1555-1600)." *Revue de l'Histoire des Religions* 210 (1993): 331-47.

———. *Le cannibale. Grandeur et décadence*. Paris: Perrin, 1994.

Longeon, Claude, ed. *Premiers combats pour la langue française*. Paris: Le livre de Poche, 1989.

McGrath, Alister E. *A Life of John Calvin*. Oxford: Blackwell, 1990.

Malet, Nicole. *Dieu selon Calvin*. Lausanne: L'Âge d'homme, 1977.

Mandrou, Robert. *Des humanistes aux hommes de science, xvie-xviie siècles*. Paris: Le Seuil, 1973.

Massaut, Jean-Pierre. *Josse Clichtove. L'humanisme et la reforme du clergé*. 2 volumes. Paris: Belles Lettres, 1968.

Mejring, E. P. *Calvin wider die Neugierde*. Nieuwkoop: B. de Graaf, 1980.

Ménager, Daniel. "Théodore de Bèze, biographe de Calvin." *Bibliothèque d'Humanisme et Renaissance* 45 (1983): 231-55.

Millet, Olivier. "Le thème de la conscience libre chez Calvin." In *La liberté conscience (xvie-xviie siècles)*, pp. 21-37. Geneva: Droz, 1991.

―――. *Calvin et la dynamique de la Parole. Essai de rhétorique réformée.* Paris: H. Champion, 1992.

―――. "Exégèse évangélique et culture littéraire humaniste: entre Luther et Bèze, l'Abraham sacrifiant selon Calvin." *Études Théologiques et Religieuses* 69 (1994): 367-80.

―――. "Calvin et les 'libertins': le libertin comme clandestin, ou de la sphère clandestino-libertine." *La Lettre clandestine* 5 (1996): 225-39.

―――. *Calvin et ses contemporains: acts du colloque de Paris 1995.* Geneva: Droz, 1998.

Monheit, Michael L. "The Ambition of an Illustrious Name: Humanism, Patronage, and Calvin's Doctrine of the Calling." *Sixteenth Century Journal* 23 (1992): 267-87.

Mottu, Henry. "Le Témoignage intérieur du Saint-Esprit selon Calvin." *Actualité de la Réforme.* Geneva: Labor et Fides, 1984.

Naphy, W. N. *Calvin and the Consolidation of the Genevan Reformation.* Manchester: Manchester University Press, 1994.

Neuser, Wilhelm, ed. *Calvinus Sacrae Scripturae Professor: Calvin as Confessor of Holy Scripture.* Grand Rapids: Eerdmans, 1994.

Nugent, Donald. *Ecumenism in the Age of the Reformation: The Colloquy of Poissy.* Cambridge, Mass.: Harvard University Press, 1974.

Oberman, Heiko Augustinus. *The Dawn of the Reformation: Essays in Late Medieval–Early Reformation Thought.* Edinburgh: T. & T. Clark, 1986.

―――. *Initia Calvini: The Matrix of Calvin's Reformation.* Amsterdam: Koninklijke Nederlandse Akademie van Wetenschappen, 1991.

Parker, T. H. L. *John Calvin: A Biography.* London: J. M. Dent & Sons Ltd., 1975.

―――. *Calvin's Preaching.* Edinburgh: T. & T. Clark, 1992.

Perrot, A. *Le visage humain de Calvin.* Geneva: Labor et Fides, 1986.

Pfeilschifter, Frank. *Das Calvinbild bei Bolsec.* Augsbourg: FDL, 1983.

Piaget, Arthur, ed. *Les actes de la dispute de Lausanne, 1536.* Neuchâtel: Secrétariat de l'Université, Mémoires de l'Université de Lausanne, VI, 1928.

Pitkin, Barbara. "Imitation of David: David as a Paradigm for Faith in Calvin's Exegesis of the Psalms." *Sixteenth Century Journal* 25 (1994): 3-27.

Regards contemporains sur Jean Calvin. Actes du colloque Calvin. Strasbourg, 1964; Paris: PUF, 1965.

Renaudet, Augustin. *Humanisme et renaissance.* Geneva: Droz, 1958.

Rillet, Jean. *Le vrai visage de Calvin.* Toulouse: Privat, 1982.

Roget, Amédée, *L'Église et l'État à Genève du temps de Calvin. Étude d'histoire politico-ecclésiastique.* Geneva: J. Jullien, 1867.

———. *Histoire du peuple de Genève depuis la Réforme jusqu'à l'escalade.* 7 volumes. Geneva: John Jullien, 1870.

Schmidt, Albert-Marie. *Jean Calvin et la tradition calvinienne.* Paris: Le Cerf, 1984.

Schummer, Leopold. *Le ministère pastoral dans l'*Institution chrétienne *de Calvin à la lumière du troisième sacrement.* Wiesbaden: F. Steiner, 1965.

———. *L'Ecclésiologie de Calvin à la lumière de l'Ecclesia Mater.* Berne: P. Lang, 1981.

Selinger, Suzanne. *Calvin against Himself: An Inquiry in Intellectual History.* Hamden, Conn.: Archon Books, 1984.

Stauffer, Richard. *L'humanité de Calvin.* Neuchâtel: Delachaux et Niestlé, 1964.

———. *Dieu, la création et la Providence dans la prédication de Calvin.* Berne: P. Lang, 1978.

———. *Creator et rector mundi. Dieu, la création et la providence dans l'œuvre homilétique de Calvin.* Lille: Atelier de reproduction des thèses, 1978.

———. "Calvin et la catholicité évangélique." *Revue de Théologie et de Philosophie* 115 (1993): 135-56.

Steinmetz, David C. *Calvin in Context.* New York: Oxford University Press, 1995.

Teisser du Cros, Rémi. *Jean Calvin. De la Réforme à la Révolution.* Paris: L'Harmattan, 1999.

Thomas, Keith. *Religion and the Decline of Magic.* Harmondsworth: Penguin, 1973.

Thompson, John L. "The Immoralities of the Patriarchs in the History of Exegesis: A Reappraisal of Calvin's Position." *Calvin Theological Journal* 26 (1991): 9-46.

———. *John Calvin and the Daughters of Sarah: Women in Regular and Exceptional Roles in the Exegesis of Calvin, His Predecessors, and His Contemporaries.* Geneva: Droz, 1992.

———. "Patriarchs, Polygamy, and Private Resistance: John Calvin and Others on Breaking God's Rules." *Sixteenth Century Journal* 24 (1993): 843-60.

Turchetti, Mario. *Concordia o tolleranza? F. Bauduin e i "Moyenneurs."* Milan: F. Angeli, 1984.

Venard, Marc, ed. *Le temps des confessions (1530-1620/30),* volume 8 in *Histoire du christianisme des origines à nos jours.* 14 volumes. Edited by Jean-Marie Mayeur, Charles Piétri, André Vauchez, and Marc Venard. Paris: Desclée, 1992.

———. *Réforme protestante, Réforme catholique dans la province d'Avignon — xvie siècle.* Paris: Le Cerf, 1993.

Vincent, Gilbert. *Exigence éthique et interprétation dans l'œuvre de Calvin.* Geneva: Labor et Fides, 1984.

Voss, Jürgen. *Das Mittelalter im Historischen Denken Frankreichs.* Munich: Wilhelm Fink, 1972.

Walch, R. *Untersuchungen über die lexikalischen und morphologischen Varianten in den vier französischen Ausgaben der* Institution de la religion chrestienne von Jean Calvin. Dombirn: H. Mayer, 1960.

Wanegffelen, Thierry. "Les chrétiens face aux Églises dans l'Europe moderne." *Nouvelle Revue du Seizième Siècle* 11 (1993): 37-53.

———. "La reconnaissance mutuelle du baptême entre confessions catholique et réformée au xvie siècle." *Études Théologiques et Religieuses* 69 (1994): 185-201.

———. "Des Chrétiens entre Rome et Genève. Une histoire du choix religieux en France, vers 1520–vers 1610." *Thèse* at the University of Paris I (Panthéon-Sorbonne), November 12, 1994; typescript, 2 volumes.

———. *La France et les Français. xvie–milieu xviie siècles. La vie religieuse.* Gap: Ophrys, 1994.

Warfield, B. B. *Calvin and Calvinism.* New York: Oxford University Press, 1931.

Wencelius, Léon. *L'esthétique de Calvin.* Paris: Belles Lettres, 1937.

Wendel, François. *Calvin, Sources et evolution de sa pensée religieuse* (1950). Geneva: Labor et Fides, 1985.

William, George Huntston. *The Radical Reformation.* Kirksville, Miss., 1992.

Wirth, Jean. "La naissance du concept de croyance (xiie-xvii siècles)." *Bibliothèque d'Humanisme et Renaissance* 45 (1983): 7-58.

Zuber, Valentine. "Pour en finir avec Michel Servet. Les Protestants du début du xxe siècle entre mémoire et histoire." *Bulletin de la Société de l'Histoire du Protestantisme Français 140* (1995): 97-120.

Index